PQ 6056 SCR

Also by Ilan Stavans

Fiction
The One-Handed Pianist and Other Stories

Nonfiction
The Inveterate Dreamer
On Borrowed Words
Octavio Paz: A Meditation
The Hispanic Condition
Art and Anger

Anthologies
Wachale!
The Oxford Book of Jewish Stories
Mutual Impressions
The Oxford Book of Latin American Essays
Tropical Synagogues
Growing Up Latino (with Harold Augenbraum)

Cartoons
Latino USA
(with Lalo López Alcaráz)

Translations
Sentimental Songs, by Felipe Alfau

General
The Essential Ilan Stavans

THE SCROLL
and CROSS
the

1,000 YEARS OF JEWISH-HISPANIC LITERATURE

EDITED BY
ILAN STAVANS

ROUTLEDGE
New York and London

Published in 2003 by
Routledge
29 West 35th Street
New York, NY 10001
www.routledge-ny.com

Published in Great Britain by
Routledge
11 New Fetter Lane
London EC4P 4EE
www.routledge.co.uk

10 9 8 7 6 5 4 3 2 1

Cataloging-in-Publication Data is available from the Library of Congress

ISBN 0-415-92930-X (hb)
ISBN 0-415-92931-8 (pb)

For Alison,
with unending love

This volume is made possible thanks to a generous grant from
the Lucius N. Littauer Foundation

CONTENTS

CONTENTS

CRITERIA

The forty-one entries in this anthology—nineteen from Spain, twenty-two from Hispanic America—range from the tenth to the twentieth century. They were selected for their representative nature. In putting together the book, my objective was to highlight the tensions in each period, from the age of cohabitation in the Iberian Peninsula to the modern-day *Nuevo Mundo*. I have collected correspondence, stories, poems, segments of novels, testaments, theological disputations, mystical treatises, and historical documents, such as the Edict of 1492 which forced the Jews out of Spain. The authors included were influential figures in their time, and the texts chosen attempt to highlight their respective oeuvres as well as the context in which those oeuvres emerged. I am, by principle, allergic to fragments, but in this case—given the limitation of space and the costs of permissions to reprint material—I've given in to the temptation so as to broaden the intellectual spectrum.

The rowdy original manuscript had over a hundred entries that ranged from a segment of the *Poem of El Cid*, the work of Arcipreste de Hita, and *Don Quixote of La Mancha*, part II, chapter 54, as well as a portion of *The Swindler* by Quevedo, to parts of *La Celestina* by Fernando de Rojas, a chapter of *Dialogue of Love* by Leon Ebreo and one from *The Kuzari* by Yehuda Halevi, and a repatriation essay by the Spanish senator Angel Pulido, plays by the Argentine authors Germán Rozenmacher and Jorge Goldemberg, and poetry by the Cuban José Kozer and the Mexican Myriam Moscona. Some authors at that stage were represented by between two and four pieces. I also intended to include material by Hasdai ben Shaprut, Todros Halevi Abulafia, Abraham Abulafia, Isaac de Carrión, Solomón ben Verga, and a generous piece from the popular *Me'am Lo'ez*, by Yaakov Culi (1689-1732). To me Jewish-Hispanic letters are an extraordinarily rich and diverse kaleidoscope of explorations, overt and subliminal. But I was faced with the need to make choices: I eliminated more than half the authors; I also reduced entries per author to a single one (with the exception of Maimonides, whose chapter XV of the *Guide of the Perplexed* is reproduced; its line "we do not ascribe to God the power of doing what is impossible" has been with me, awake and in dreams, ever since I came across it in 1985). The Roman, Visigothic, Moorish, and Frankish periods, say up to 900 C.E., are not contemplated. It goes without saying, of course, that in the roster at hand, *ni son todos lo que están, ni están todos los que son*—only a minuscule fraction of that kaleidoscope is in view for the reader to appreciate.

I know of no volume similar to this one in scope. In the section of "Further Readings" I list compendiums that offer a smorgasbord of Jewish literary possibilities in either Iberian or Latin American letters. The rationale behind *The Scroll and the Cross* is to map the thorny relations between Jews and Hispanics centuries after the first settlements in the period of the Roman Empire. The category "Jewish" in this case means the religious and ethnic transient diaspora unified by the Mosaic faith; "Hispanic," instead, I take it to understand as a more geographical term: the landscape in which Iberian civilization has flourished, from the population that gave place to the images in the Caves of Altamira to the colonies that the Spanish empire established across the Atlantic Ocean. Jews have been *visitors* in these lands. My quest has been to understand the outcome of those visitations.

This, then, is *not* an anthology of the Sephardic tradition. It focuses on *Sepharad*—the Hebrew word for Spain, a synonym of *Ispamia*—from Samuel Hanagid up to the expulsion. From that point on, the route it follows is not to Turkey, the Netherlands, North Africa, and the Middle East, where a substantial number of the Jews expelled from the Iberian Peninsula went; instead, it travels westward to the so-called New World. It seeks a representation of the crypto-Jewish and New Christian behavior in these territories, and then it focuses on the arrival of Yiddish-language Ashkenazic Jews from Eastern Europe and, later on, the culture of the Jews from the former Ottoman Empire, all this without forgetting that in Spain *per se*, even while Jews were an absence, their ghostlike nature kept on inspiring debate among the literati.

Of the entries included, originally written in seven different languages (Hebrew, Arabic, Latin, Spanish, Ladino, Yiddish, and English), only about half are by Jews. This explains the appearance in the Contents of figures such as Gonzalo de Berceo, Francisco de Quevedo y Villegas, Miguel de Unamuno, Federico García Lorca, Jorge Luis Borges, Julio Cortázar, and Mario Vargas Llosa. I have organized *The Scroll and the Cross* as a double-faceted mirror: What have been the dreams by Jews in Hispanic lands? What has been their reaction to the native civilization? And, conversely, how do non-Jews approach their presence? I have refrained from mentioning in every headnote if the author is or isn't Jewish, simply because this isn't an exercise in exclusion.

My research into the Jewish-Hispanic tradition, still in a state of growth, began with *Tropical Synagogues* (1994). It continued with the series *Jewish Latin America* from the University of New Mexico Press, launched in 1998 with a revamped version of Prudencio de Pereda's translation of *The Jewish Gauchos of the Pampas* by Gerchunoff. It then found a partial critical expression in various sections of *The Inveterate Dreamer: Essays and Conversations on Jewish Culture* (2001). I've structured the material in this anthology in chronological order by each author's date of birth. The headnotes showcase the most significant works by each contributor. The dates given are of original publication and not of translation. If a title is given in English, it is because that work is available in translation; otherwise, the title appears in the original, with the English in brackets. Also, the headnotes include, when available, the date in which the entry was either drafted or made public.

A word of gratitude. This book started over a placid lunch conversation with my friend and editor Gayatri Patnaik, formerly at Routledge, whose vision, ambition, and perseverance I've learned to admire over the years. Many friends offered suggestions and encouragement. To list them all is impossible. A few also shaped, inadvertently at times, the content of the volume and of my own knowledge: Dana Asbury, Harold Augenbraum, David Holtby, Blake Eskin, Isaac Goldemberg, Hillel Halkin, Robert Mandel, Daniel Asa Rose, and Jonathan Rosen. Bobbie Helinski helped with the permission maze. Jennifer M. Acker and the staff of *Hopscotch* were invaluable in the preparation of various parts of the manuscript. Neal Sokol, in a series of conversations, has pushed my thought into previously unexplored terrain. Damon Zucca kept me on target, even when I was obnoxiously off schedule. Finally, *The Scroll and the Cross*, it strikes me, is the result of years of study, embarked upon with teachers, colleagues, and students. I want to invoke the names of my teachers, Dwayne E. Carpenter, Gerson D. Cohen, Moshe Idel, Seymour Feldman, Neal Gilman, David G. Roskies, Reymond P. Scheindlin, Gonzalo Sobejano, and Chava Turniansky; of colleagues such as Jules Chametzky, Morris Dickstein, Lawrence R. Douglas, John Felstiner, Sander L. Gilman, David M. Gitlitz, Steven T. Katz, Steven G. Kellman, Stanley J. Rabinowitz, Stephen A. Sadow, Gershom Shaked, Leo Spitzer, and James E. Young; and of my beloved students at Amherst College in the "Jewish-Hispanic Relations" course, where these entries were hotly scrutinized time and again, with enlightenment and joy.

INTRODUCTION: IN THE CHAMELEON'S PATH

Judío. *Voz de desprecio y injuria, que se usa en casos de enojo o ira.*
[**Jew.** Voice used to denote contempt and insult, used in cases of anger and ire.]
—*Diccionario de Autoridades* (1732)

Buenos Aires, shtot mein liebe, Ich bin farlibt in dein tsebliter yugnt.
[Buenos Aires, beloved city, I'm in love with your flowering youth.]
—Carlos Gardel (in Yiddish)

I. The Semantic Quagmire

As of late in the United States, the term *marrano*, a pejorative Hispanic noun, has curiously undergone a swift and surprising revitalization. In its 1992 edition, the *Diccionario de la Lengua Española de la Real Academia*, the official Spanish legislative source of everything verbal, traces the word to the Arabic *mahran*, a forbidden item. It then announces, somewhat pompously, that the word is applied to "*conversos* that Judaize beyond the public eye." It adds: "Used as an adjective, it means accused or excommunicated. In this sense it is not much used. Latin: *marranus*.... In the Spanish language, *marrano* Jew is the same as excommunicated Jew." And, "from the time the Jews were in Spain, a pig was called *marrano*." A decidedly less objective, more emphatic view was offered in 1611 by Sebastián de Covarrubias Orozco in his *Tesoro de la Lengua Castellana o Española*, the source of sources of Spanish lexicography, on which the *Diccionario de la Lengua Española* is partially based. Covarrubias defines marrano thus:

The recent convert to Christianity, and we have a low opinion of him for having converted falsely. Diego Velázquez, in a little book he wrote entitled *Defensio statuti Toletani*, says as follows: "*Se eos hispani* marranos *vocare solemus, qui ex indaeis descendentes et baptizati ficti christiani sunt.*" When the Jews who were left in Castile converted, one of the conditions that they sought was that they should not therefore be forced to eat pig meat, which they protested was not in order to keep the law of Moses, but only because they were not used to it and it gave them nausea and disgust. Moors call a one-year-old pig *marrano*, and it could be that the newly converted, for this reason and for not eating pig meat, was called marrano.

This is not to mean, of course, that what dictionaries say goes without hesitation. People often move at one pace, and dictionaries at another. Today the average Spanish-language speaker, if aware of the religious connotation of the term, is likely to mean by it exactly what the dictionary of the Royal Academy currently does: *swine*, and perhaps *ignominious* too. In Spain during the Middle Ages, the concept of *pureza de sangre*, purity of blood, was regarded among Christians as a ticket of authenticity. The *marranos* were crypto-Jews, hidden believers in the Torah who agreed to convert to Christianity—but only publicly. In the privacy of their homes they remained loyal to the Jewish faith. If caught by the Holy Office of the Inquisition, these crypto-Jews faced incarceration, torture, and death.

In English, the *Oxford English Dictionary* echoes the Spanish dictionary definition, but the meaning of the word nowadays, in North America and England, particularly in intellectual circles, is altogether different. In the parlance of such circles, *marrano* is taken to signify a secretive, concealed, closeted person. These surely are not derogatory adjectives. On the contrary, they imply a sense of infatuation. To have a secret and keep it for centuries is to be the owner of an ancestral treasure. In a society such as ours, easily prone to superficialities, such ownership makes for astonishing riches. The looseness and equivocality of this definition, it strikes me, makes room for all sorts of interpretations. In the library only a few weeks before this writing, I stumbled upon a literary study released in 1996 by Elaine Marks entitled *Marrano as Metaphor: The Jewish Presence in French Writing*. Its main assertion, expounded from the first page to the last, is that a *marrano* is an assimilated modern Jew, especially a member of the literati, whose cultural identity remains shallow in the context of gentile society. This allows him or her to write either openly Jewish works for a non-Jewish readership or works without a single iota of Jewish consciousness in them. Thus the Greek-French novelist Albert Cohen, who wrote *Belle du Seigneur*, is a *marrano*, in spite of the fact that he never doubted his Jewishness, was a fervent Zionist, and worked for it throughout his life. Conversely, in Marks's eyes, Marcel Proust is also a *marrano*, because of his repressed homosexuality and his dual identity: he is and he isn't French; by extension he must be crypto-Jewish.

This elasticity is infuriating. Isn't modernity as a whole a state of mind ruled by inner doubt? And isn't Jewishness an essential feature of European modernity? The looseness of the term reminds me of the way the concept of *la frontera* began to be abused a decade ago: from its literal meaning of "the U.S.-Mexican border," it was abruptly modified to signify any hyphenated cultural manifestation. And to this day that is what *la frontera* is taken to mean: a no-man's-land. Even if you've never traveled to Tijuana or Corpus Christi, by the sheer act of listening to a song by the *Tejana* singer Selena you carry *la frontera* with you. The shifts of the word *marrano* are the tip of an iceberg: the obsession with "the hidden Jewish self." From the late nineteenth century to the dusk of the twentieth century, the interest in the lost tribes of Israel has been ubiquitous. From Arthur Koestler's reflections on the Khazar Empire in *The Thirteenth Tribe* to the ethnographic studies suggesting that the American Indians have Jewish blood, from Freud's interpretation of Moses of Egypt to the most recent travelogues of attempts to reach the Jews of India and Peru, the boutique of exotic explanations is without apparent end. In fact, it often seems that every couple of years, in some language or culture, someone is ready to propose yet another revisionist theory on the demographic and sociological birth of the Jewish people. Exotic is a key word: the more outrageous and unsettling, the wider the appeal these theories seem to have.

Why this obsession with roots? The explanation might be traceable to the emergence of the European Jews from the ghetto, a traumatic event that symbolizes our birth to modernity. The thirst for individual and family origins, which the Holocaust, by its destruction, took to an unforeseeable height, is a way to return, to look back at a utopian time. ("Utopia" comes from the Greek word for "there is no such place.") But uprootedness among Jews is older than modernity. It dates back at least to the destruction of the First Temple in the year 179 B.C.E., if not earlier. And uprootedness is the mother of ambiguity. Jewish literature and thought are inundated with works that allow themselves to be understood differently by various audiences. Think of Maimonides, for instance: he is the author of the *Mishneh Torah*, a rabbinical exegesis with the Torah as its supreme center of gravity, but also of the *Guide of the Perplexed*, a philosophical treatise that embraces Aristotle rather than the Bible as the main source on the laws of nature. Might this bifurcated talent be described as an aspect of the *marrano* self?

Surely not. Strictly speaking, Maimonides wasn't a *marrano*, and neither was Proust. There is nothing tight-lipped about them, at least not as far as their Jewish identity is concerned. As for the actual *marranos* and their descendants, they are intriguing because of their stubbornness, but beyond that, what precious secret do they hide? I, for one, am struck less by why they have survived through the ages than by what they eclipse—what we refuse to see in our own milieu—when they capture our attention. Why is it, for example, that *marranos* have become the subject of numerous studies but Sephardic civilization as a whole remains unappealing? A trip to the local Jewish library evidences the unavoidable: compared with the overwhelming number of books on the Holocaust, the Middle East, and Eastern Europe—from novels to memoirs, from nonfiction to poetry and scholarly works—the number of items on Sephardic topics, and on Jewish-Hispanic relations, is minimal. One is more likely to find a book on the Jews in German sports than one on the life and rituals of the Jewish community in the Ottoman Empire. If and when such books exist, they limit themselves to the fringe identity of marranos in places such as New Mexico and Arizona, as if they were the sole creatures Sephardic civilization produced. What is it that makes secret-bearers so appetizing?

Exoticism is again the answer: the *marrano* is exotic—an enigma, a testament against uprootedness—whereas the average Sephardic person is a plain sinner just like us. The *marrano* has the potential of "coming out," and that potential is fascinating only because our own Jewish identity is too flat, too normal, without any secrets left. I'm often asked to talk about Jewish Latin America to English-language audiences. My initial tactic is invariably the same: to use words as a mirror to unravel stereotypes. The accidents of history have forced me to learn well the tortured patterns of the region that extends from *la frontera* to Tierra del Fuego. Strange as it may seem, North Americans often assume that Jews in these republics are *mestizos*—persons of mixed blood. Actually, most are white, with ancestry from Poland, Russia and Ukraine. In successive waves of immigration from 1890 to 1910, thousands of them, arriving from the *shtetl*, settled in the Argentine and Brazilian pampas, Cuba, and Mexico. Their connection with the *marranos* past and present is at best tenuous. In spite of the colonial-era *converso* and crypto-Jewish past of Latin America, few Jews there speak Ladino or have even a basic knowledge of medieval Hebrew culture. It wasn't until the 1960s that a Sephardic immigration—*los nuevos sefardíes*—arrived to the Spanish- and Portuguese-speaking Americas, mainly from Syria, Lebanon, Turkey, and Iraq. Their community flourished, often surpassing its Ashkenazic counterpart in achievement. But they too have little interest in colonial Jewish roots.

The term *mestizo* has its own connotations. Again, herein the definition offered by the *Diccionario de la Lengua Española*: *mestizo*, from the Latin *mixticius*, a person born of parents of different race, especially of a white father and Indian mother or Indian father and white mother. The word originated in New Spain—today's Mexico—during the seventeenth century to refer to a caste crossbred from Spanish and Indian blood, and the verb *mestizaje* is understood to mean the process of social formation. Like *marrano*, it was, even after independence in the 1820s, a derogatory word to denote members of the lower strata without social endowments. Above them in the hierarchy were the Spaniards and Creoles (Spaniards born in the New World); below them, the Indians, mulattos, and blacks.

Each of the nations that Latin America comprises has a different social and racial texture. For instance, Argentina, which has the largest Jewish community (approximately 200,000 strong) in the Americas after the United States, is almost entirely white. Unlike in Mexico, this whiteness has precluded the emergence of a mixed race, what in Spanish-American jargon is described as *ni de aquí, ni de allá*, from neither here nor there. Some Argentine Jewish intellectuals, among them the novelist Ricardo Feierstein, have infused a spirit of symbolism into the word *mestizo*. For them the word clearly refers to a cross-fertilization that is cultural and not hereditary. A *mestizo*, they argue, is a person with Jewish ancestry born to Jewish immigrants in Argentina and almost paralyzed by the duality: duality of selves, duality of loyalties. In Feierstein's novel *Mestizo* (1994), released in an English translation by Stephen A. Sadow under the aegis of the University of New Mexico in 2000, a crime occurs: a Lebanese woman is assassinated in Buenos Aires. The only witness is the protagonist, David Schnaiderman, an unemployed, forty-year-old, married Argentine Jew who has children and a bachelor's degree in sociology, but instead of speaking out, he abruptly enters a state of temporary amnesia. His recovery, of course, happens only after he reappropriates his past, but this act of reappropriation is slow, fastidious, peripatetic, and painful. Multiple voices impregnate his convalescence, from the many Eastern European newcomers to the New World at the turn of the nineteenth century to what Feierstein calls, fittingly, "the generation of the wilderness," the offspring of those immigrants (Schnaiderman included) whose identity is, as the title claims, *mestizo*.

Perhaps the figure of the *mestizo* is not exotic enough. The infatuation with the term *marrano* is nothing but a smoke screen. Behind it a whole civilization, shaped as a hall of mirrors, complete with its mysteries and platitudes, awaits being deciphered: the Hispanic world. In it the Jew, real and imaginary, a chameleon—a creature capable of adapting to the environment by changing its appearance (in the Middle Ages it was thought that the chameleon lived on air alone)—has found both solace and fear. Our uprootedness might find itself more at ease when we dare to look honestly, without masks. In the age of multi-culturalism, not only in the United States but in the world at large, the uneasy partnership between Jews and Latinos often comes as a surprise. What do these two minorities have in common? Aren't their differences far more striking than their similarities?

II. Alongside Muslims and Christians

The ruminations in the section above should serve to paint the backdrop against which to reevaluate a literary tradition at the dawn of its second millennium, a tradition infused by Jewish and Hispanic ingredients that begins in Al-Andalus (a.k.a. Andalusía) in the year 900 C.E. and continues to this day under endless transformations in places like Havana and Lima. Demographically, the cross-fertilization that gave birth to this tradition started approximately in the year 200 B.C.E., when the first Jewish settlers found their route to the Iberian Peninsula. But the intellectual outpouring, in cohesive, convincing form, didn't take place until several hundred years later, in and around Córdoba, built under the Caliphate of leader 'Abd ar-Rahman I (756–1788), 'Abd ar-Rahman II (822–852), and especially in the tenth century with 'Abd ar-Rahman III (912–961) and al-Hakam II (961–976), which turned that city-state of the Islamic empire into an environment of religious tolerance and coexistence.

This environment became the stage for development in the fields of philosophy, medicine, and poetry. Jewish military and political figures such as Hasdai ben Shaprut and Samuel Hanagid became prominent. The latter came of age when the Caliphate had already dissolved and was eventually named the vizier of Córdoba while the city-state was under Berber rule. Hanagid was a philosopher, poet, and biblical commentator, but his place in history is also due to his role as a military man for the Muslim army. Progressively, a lineage of Hebrew poets, Talmudists, translators, and moralists came to the fore. A crucial figure in it was

Yehudah Halevi, a poet, bon vivant, and philosopher. His odyssey serves as a paradigm to understand the enlightenment but also the ambivalence that colored Jewish life: in 1140, Halevi decided to give up his life in Spain to travel to Palestine, the Promised Land. On the way, he disappeared, probably at sea. Less than a decade later, the Almohades, a zealous tribe from Northern Africa, invaded Andalusía and abruptly ended any remnants of goodwill and benevolence.

The Spain of Hanagid and Halevi was intensely literary. This was the age of the *jarchas*, folk songs inspired by Muslim and Jewish culture, in which might be traced the roots of Ladino—*Spanioli* or Judeo-Spanish—a hybrid blend of Castilian, Hebrew, Turkish, Arabic, and other verbal elements. An example:

Vayse mio corayon de mib;	My heart leaves me;
ya Rab, ¿si se me tornarad?	Oh, wise man, will it return?
tan mal mio doler li-l-habid:	My lover has caused me such pain:
Enfermo yed: ¿cuand sanarad?	(My heart) is ill; when will it be well?
Des cuando mio Cidiello vienid	When my master comes,
tan buona alixara:	what spendid news:
como rayo de sol exid	He comes like a ray of sunlight
En Wadalachyara.	To Guadalajara.

And this is also the age of the *juderías*, the Jewish ghettos (Arabic equivalent: *aljamia*), and the age of the *Siete partidas*, the code of law established by the scholarly Alfonso X, also known as "The Wise." The so-called Spanish Golden Age of politics took place some two hundred and fifty years later, between 1479 and 1516, and the *Siglo de Oro Español*, the one in literature that includes Lope de Vega, Quevedo, Góngora, Calderón, and Cervantes, occurred somewhat later. The Jewish growth, therefore, is earlier. It occurred due to the atmosphere of tolerance, which gave room to what has come to be known as the "era of cohabitation" of the three largest Western religions: Muslim, Christian, and Jewish. Such a peaceful epoch has been difficult to replicate elsewhere in time and space. By the time of the quest for *la reconquista* at the hands of the Christian soldiers, which started in the first and second crusades (1096–1147) and culminated in 1492 with the incorporation of Granada, the cohabitation was in shambles.

Jews were at once actors and witnesses in the transition from a Spain that was under Muslim rule to one that was recovered by Christians. This transformation was dramatic: it involved another set of values, and more important, a nationlistic viewpoint that was instrumental in the development of Spain in the road to its troubled modernity. The perception of Jews—Who are they? What do they believe in? Are they part of us?—in Christian Spain was an explosive minefield. By the dawn of the seventeenth century, Covarrubias defined the word *judío* [Jew] as follows:

> In the Hebrew word we say the fashion in which that people, that God chose for himself, was called Hebrews and then Israelites, and finally Jews. Today they are those that didn't believe in the coming of the Redeemer Messiah, Jesus Christ, our Lord, and continue to profess the Law of Moses, which is a shadow of this truth.

More than a hundred years later, the *Diccionario de Autoridades*, as it appears in one of the epigraphs that opens this essay, aggravated the definition even more: a Jew, it stated, is taken to be the "Voice used to denote contempt and insult, used in cases of anger and ire." Even in the twenty-first edition of the *Diccionario de la Lengua Española*, released in 1992, the year of the Columbian Quincentennial, an expression ("*cegar como la judía de Zaragoza, llorando dulos ajenos*") was included as meaning, literally, "to censor a person who, without obligation or justified reason, is overly interested in the affairs of others." Again, it was the concept of "purity of blood" (*pureza de sangre*) and the establishment of the Holy Office of the Inquisition that inaugurated the emphasis on the twists and turns of identity—religious, ethnic, national—the one that shaped, just as Modernism was setting in, the nature of Jewish-Hispanic relations for the next one thousand years.

In the English-language world, particularly in the United States, the age of cohabitation in the Iberian Peninsula, although heavily scrutinized by scholars in important volumes—such as those by Cecil Roth and Yitzhak Baer—hardly holds a place in the popular imagination. Jewish history is seen in progress from Biblical and Talmudic times to the nineteenth-century ideological movements such as Zionism, Socialism, Marxism, Communism, Bundism, and onward from there to World War I. It is as if the Spanish experiment was of little consequence and cannot offer a clue to what makes a Jew today. But the "purity of blood" and the presence of *conversos* and crypto-Jews is at its core, whether we acknowledge it or not. The year of 1492 marks the dividing line: Spain not only expelled *los indeseables*, the undesirable from its midst (first the Jews, eventually also the

Muslims), thus cleansing itself internally; externally, it also pushed the Spanish Christian empire beyond its border in search of mercantile routes to India and, by accident, originated a colonial expansion across the Atlantic.

III. Across the Atlantic

I'm especially interested in the views of Jews in the Americas. To what extent have these changed since 1492? Until the last quarter of the twentieth century, scholarly attention to the Jewish communities of the Spanish- and Portuguese-language Americas was scarce. This is surprising given the size of the population in the region: a total of around half a million Jews, the largest concentrations being found in Argentina. The literature generated by this population is substantial. To understand the change from eclipse to full academic recognition, it is crucial to see in context the three major waves of immigration across the Atlantic Ocean: the crypto-Jewish in the colonial period; the Ashkenazic between 1880 and 1930, with additions at the time of World War II; and the Sephardic from parts of the former Ottoman Empire which started around 1880 and extended into the 1970s.

Jews arrived in the Americas with Christopher Columbus and played an important role in the three-hundred-year colonial period that spans 1525 to 1825. Discussions of Columbus's own Hebraic ancestry has been the subject of muddy debate, which I will pass by in this essay. Far more important is the role played by Jews during the period of Spanish colonization. At first the main cultural centers were Mexico, Colombia, the Philippines, and Peru, where crypto-Jews as well as New Christians from the Iberian Peninsula sought refuge from the Inquisition, but the Caribbean Basin and the region of the River Plate were also magnets. Of course, to describe this as a wave of Jewish immigration is deceiving, because those who arrived in the New World didn't identify themselves as Jews, instead hiding their identity. And how many of them were? The demographic estimates vary. The Jews expelled from the Iberian peninsula were probably no more than 20,000, and it is unlikely that the number of these who crossed the ocean, either as overt or as secret Jews, was ever higher than 2,000. In his encyclopedic volume *Secrecy and Deceit: The Religion of the Crypto-Jews* (2002), David M. Gitlitz, mainly through secondary sources, explored the path through which the *conversos* and the so-called *marranos*—in Hebrew, *anusim*—

manifested their tradition not only in Spain but in the Americas, Turkey, and the Mediterranean area. This is an important scholarly contribution to the field whose central handicap is that it is almost solely based on secondary sources.

The scholarly examination of the colonial period in the Americas didn't begin in earnest until the late nineteenth century, in large part because the fever for independence that swept the continent from approximately 1810 to 1865 focused on breaking away from Spain not only politically but also culturally, and the interest in aspects of intellectual and artistic life in the centuries of colonialism was minuscule. By the time books began to be published, they related primarily to history. These included José Toribio Medina's examination of the Inquisition in Peru, the Philippines, Colombia, Chile, Mexico, and Argentina, released between 1887 and 1905. In the United States and Europe, similar academic studies were implemented by the American Jewish Historical Society. But they amounted to a partial, half-baked picture. References to the literature of the era were largely restricted to encyclopedias. Martin A. Cohen, Professor of Jewish History at Hebrew Union College–Jewish Institute of Religion, one of the leading figures in such intellectual forays, described Jewish-Latin American studies as marked by "imbalance." He expressed his dismay thus:

> The Jewish experience in Latin America is known only fragmentarily. A number of books and a host of articles deal with various aspects of this experience, but together they tell only a fraction of the story. The rest remains imbedded in rich stores of manuscripts and printed materials. Many of these are readily available, while others are difficult to reach. Some day patient scholars will distill this material into reliable monographs.

Perhaps the most significant historical figure in the Americas in colonial times among these was Luis de Carvajal the Younger, also known as *El Iluminado*. He left behind in the hands of his inquisitors an array of autobiographical papers that have literary value. The best scholarship on him and his legacy is by Seymour B. Liebman and by Cohen himself. A crypto-Jew from a prominent family in Benavente, Spain, that resettled in Nueva España, as Mexico was known in colonial times, Carvajal was arrested in 1589 by the Inquisition under suspicion of being a Judaizer, that is, a proselytizer. Such an accusation, even if untrue, usually meant a life of misery that went from bankruptcy and social ridicule to imprisonment of some length and torture. He was put on trial but somehow managed to persuade his victimizers of his innocence. But six years later he was arrested again, this time under charges of impenitent heresy, and was burnt at the stake in 1596, at the age of thirty, in the most notorious of all autos-da-fé ever seen in the region. From his birthplace in the Iberian peninsula to the site of his death in the Plaza del Quemadero in the Mexican capital, his odyssey is emblematic of the quest for religous freedom in colonial times.

Carvajal was the nephew of Don Luis de Carvajal the Older, a formidable *conquistador*, a pacifier of the Indies, and by most accounts a true humanitarian whose reputation brought him an appointment by the kings as governor of the New Kingdom of León in northern Mexico. The younger Carvajal, his sisters, and mother were brought to Mexico by their famous relative. It was precisely that atmosphere that propelled *El Iluminado* to explore his Jewish roots, acknowledged by various members of the family but kept quiet for fear of the Inquisition. The Inquisition began to function in Mexico in 1570. Some eighty years previously, Columbus had sailed across the Atlantic in search of a new way to the Indies. He surely served as a bridge between the Old World and the New at a time of distress to the Jewish people, when the Catholic kings, in an edict of expulsion in 1492, exiled a large and mature community from the Iberian peninsula. The Holy Office had been active in Spain, and in a far more vicious manner than anything ever seen in the Americas, for at least a hundred years. The colonies were perceived by some as a place of religious tolerance, as is evident in, among other places, the literature of the time, including a handful of *comedias* by Lope de Vega and an emblematic chapter in the second volume of *Don Quixote*.

A handful of intellectuals and historians have devoted their energy to studying the impact of the Inquisition on the literature of Spain, the Netherlands, Turkey, and northern Africa, among them Américo Castro, Cecil Roth, Amador de los Ríos, Haim Beinart, Miguel de la Pinta Llorente, and Benzion Netanyahu. But the influence of the institution on the literature of the Americas, from Peru to Mexico and the Caribbean Basin, remains a research field tested shyly today. A handful of provocative book-long studies, articles, and biographies have appeared on the subject, most prominently by Alfonso Toro but they lack scientific rigor as a result of the academic and technological tools used at the time, are filled with errors, and often fall prey to anti-Jewish sentiments. Liebman's work is far more consistent: *The Jews of New Spain: Faith, Flame, and the Inquisition* is a historical survey that also offers invaluable insights into Carvajal's literature; prior to it, *The Enlightened: The Writings of Luis de*

Carvajal, el Mozo (1967) allowed readers to read for the first time in English translation the words of *El Iluminado*. Even sharper and ambitious in his quest, is the oeuvre of Martin A. Cohen. A few years later, Cohen released his magnum opus, *The Martyr: Luis de Carvajal, a Secret Jew in Sixteenth-Century Mexico*.

A native of Philadelphia, Cohen is an ordained rabbi of Ashkenazic descent and a former president of the American Society of Sephardic Studies. For years he was devoted to early rabbinical Judaism and Christianity but felt attracted to the topic of *marranos* and the Inquisition after reading the oeuvre of Cecil Roth. In the early seventies he edited a couple of volumes on the Jewish experience in Latin America, especially the colonial period, and he contributed entries to the *Encyclopedia Judaica* on such themes as crypto-Judaism. Most notably, Cohen, long before *The Martyr* was ready for the press, wrote essays on various members of the Carvajal family and translated the lengthy autobiography that *El Iluminado* wrote between 1591 and 1592. (His translations, published by the American Jewish Historical Society, appeared a year before those of Liebman.) This autobiography, in fact, is one of three writtin by Carvajal and by far the most important pillar on which Cohen based his research for the book. The second is a series of epistles to his mother and sisters that Carvajal wrote during his second imprisonment. The uniqueness of these letters is a result of the oppressive atmosphere of the jail. Prisoners were permitted to communicate neither with the outside world nor with other prisoners. His mother and sisters were in a cell next to him. In order to reach them, Carvajal inscribed a message on the core of an alligator pear, hid it in melon and asked the jailer to bring the fruit to his relatives. Of course, his victimizers suspected the strategy but didn't discourage it. *El Iluminado* continued to be provided alligator pears and other fruit. And the third pillar is a Last Will and Testament that Carvajal composed in the last months of the second trial. As Cohen suggests, this was more than a will, but an expression of painstaking commitment to the Jewish religion of his forebears.

The enduring power of *The Martyr* is to be found in the way Cohen makes Carvajal's journey pertinent to present-day readers. When it was published, English-language Jewish audiences had little interest in topics that did not relate to Zionism and the Holocaust. Things have changed substantially since then. The Jewish population in the United States has grown more complex. It is less provincial, more cosmopolitan; it is also less sure of itself, exploring unexplored routes to define its role locally and internationally. Cohen's book was reissued in 2001 as part of the *Jewish Latin America* series of the University of New Mexico Press. It has found a new public that is intrigued by its own lost ethnicity, by the identity that Jews elsewhere managed to keep secretly alive for generations as a mechanism of endurance. Among other symptoms of maturity of American and British Jewry is the need to look for roots at other regions of the globe beyond Central and Eastern Europe and the Middle East as a fountain of cohesion. It is symptomatic, though, that *The Martyr* remains unavailable in a Spanish version. This might be proof that the Americas are still incurious about the Jewish presence in the colonial period.

IV. *Shtetl* in the Pampa

The second wave of Jewish immigration to the Spanish- and Portuguese-language Americas took place at the end of the nineteenth century until World War II. The newcomers were Yiddish-speaking *shtetl* and ghetto dwellers. Their oscillation to the Argentine and Brazilian Pampas was, to a large extent, the result of efforts by philanthropists such as Baron Maurice Hirsch and the *Alliance Israélite Universelle*.

Argentina is the country with the richest Jewish letters. In connection with the Ashkenazic influx, these started with folkloric manifestations in agricultural communes such as Rajil and Moisésville. The anthology *Los mejores relatos con gauchos judíos*, edited by Ricardo Feierstein, offers a sampler of memoirs and stories by *colonos*, as the Jewish immigrants were called. Their foundational literary figure is Alberto Gerchunoff, responsible for the early classic *The Jewish Gauchos of the Pampas*, published in Spanish in 1910 as a token of appreciation to Argentina at its first centennial of independent life. In Spanish academica, ruminations on Gerchunoff abound, written by Argentine scholars such as Saúl Sosnowski. An English translation of Gerchunoff's book was released in English in 1955 and was reissued in 1997 with a kaleidoscopic introduction that places him in the context of the Yiddish, Jewish, Spanish, and Latin American intellectual traditions. Beyond Gerchunoff's work, the transgenerational development in literature is the subject of a study published in 1989 by Naomi Lindstrom, a professor at the University of Texas at Austin. (For this and other points of arrival and departure, I refer the interested reader to the section of Further Readings.) Lindstrom's volume is concerned with issues of identity, political and religious fragile life, and responses to anti-Semitism. Unfortunately, it suffers from challenges that also color the work of Leonardo Senkman and Sosnowski: its pages feel parochial and hypernationalistic, failing to place the fiction produced by Argentine Jews within the scope of modern Jewish literature world-wide. Several anthologies follow a similar path, including *The Silver Candelabra and Other Stories: A Century of Jewish Argentine Literature* (1997), edited by Rita Gardiol.

More than half a century after his death, Gerchunoff remains the paradigmatic figure. Up until very recently, the Spanish language resisted embracing the Jewish sensibility. This becomes clear in a sentence found in the 1974 edition of the *Encyclopædia Judaica*, in which *The Jewish Gauchos of the Pampas* is described as "the first work of literary value to be written in Spanish by a Jew in modern times." The astonishing implication is that roughly between 1492 and 1910, when Gerchunoff compiled his twenty-six interrelated fictional vignettes on life in the agricultural communities in South America in the late nineteenth century into a hymn to transculturation, not a single literary item of merit appeared in the language. Prior to the expulsion from the Iberian Peninsula, Jews prayed in Hebrew and wrote in Aramaic and Latin, but communicated mostly in Ladino. This means that the only literature by Jews in Spanish before *The Jewish Gauchos* is a product of *marranos*, crypto-Jews and New Christians.

No wonder Gerchunoff is such a quixotic figure in the eyes of intellectuals and scholars: his lifelong project—to turn Spanish into a home for the Jews, to acclimate the language not only to Hebraisms and Yiddishisms but to a Weltanshauung totally alien to it—went against the currents of history. In fact, he was not only a modern litterateur, as the *Encyclopædia Judaica* describes him, but more importantly, part of the *modernista* generation that renewed Hispanic American letters between 1885 and 1915. It did it by drawing heavily upon Parnassianism and Symbolism and by establishing a new, crystalline, and harmonious Spanish syntax based on restraint and precision, a new language musically elegant and spiritedly metaphorical. Gerchunoff befriended Rubén Darío, Leopoldo Lugones, and Delmira Agustini—a Nicaraguan, an Argentine, and an Uruguayan respectively, pillars of the *modernista* revolution. But his struggle went beyond: born into the Yiddish culture, he appropriated Quevedo's tongue, making it his own, and dreamed of inserting Spanish-speaking Jews into the twentieth century by building a three-way bridge between Renaissance Spain, nineteenth-century Russia and Eastern Europe, and modern Hispanic America. An authentic polyglot (aside from Yiddish and Spanish, he was fluent in Italian, French, English, Portuguese, and Russian), his heroes were Spinoza and Heinrich Heine, both uprooted speakers and "alien guests," as well as Sholem

Aleichem and Cervantes, whose verbal talent and florid imagination explain the two facades of Gerchunoff: his Jewish side and his Hispanic side. Not surprisingly, Miguel de Unamuno once described him as "the cosmopolitan man of letters *sine qua* non."

His enterprise wasn't easy, though; it often clashed against insurmountable obstacles within and outside his milieu: scattered outbursts of anti-Semitism and an occasional pogrom in Argentina, and the extermination of his direct ancestry in Europe. His views on socialism and democracy, on freedom and Jewish morality often pushed him against his people, turning him into an outcast. Partial studies on some aspects of Gerchunoff have been published, but these are limited in scope. A full-fledged biography is sorely needed, and it is hoped that the next generation of Jewish–Latin American scholars will attempt to understand the contribution of this major Jewish literary figure. In his twenties, for instance, he portrayed Argentina as a *país de advenimiento*, a Promised Land, the real Palestine where Jews could thrive in total harmony with gentiles. But his hope quickly tuned sour in 1919 with the *semana trágica*, an explosion of xenophobia that amounted to a full-blown pogrom in Buenos Aires.

By then he had already been a member of the Partido Socialista and had switched to the Partido Demócrata Progresista, had been incarcerated for a brief period for siding with Cuba during the Spanish-American War, had fought against the right-wing "radicalism" of President Hipólito Irigoyen, and, after a visit to Germany, had actively campaigned against its anti-Jewish sentiments. All this pushed Gerchunoff inward: he became more introspective and mystical, less hopeful for earthly utopias. He was often accused of being too slow to recognize and publicly denounce the existence of anti-Semitism. His strategy was to put the best face on Jewish-Gentile relations, and this relentlessly positive outlook cut down on his ability to criticize evil tendencies in society. Still, he never lost his militant edge: later on, in an unpopular stand at home, he was active in gathering support against Hitler and became the most prominent Hispanic-American intellectual to tackle "the Jewish problem"; and then, between 1945 and his death, already suffering from a heart condition, he traveled within Argentina and beyond—to Chile and Peru—to harvest political support for Zionism. Eliezer ben Yehudah had metamorphosed Hebrew into *the* Promised Land, but Gerchunoff was already too old to master the language. The Zeitgeist of history had taken him to the wrong Palestine, and he was forced to recognize Spanish as another diasporic home for the Jewish people, not the center stage he had believed it to be.

V. A Fragmented Life

By virtue of their number, Argentine Jewish authors have inspired a solid scholarship. Various motifs in the oeuvres of César Tiempo, Marcos Agunis, Marío Goloboff, Alicia Steinberg, Ricardo Feierstein, and Ana María Shúa have become the topic of articles in scholarly journals. In comparison, other countries of Latin America have generated far fewer academic commentaries. This doesn't translate into a lack of intellectual interest. On the contrary, whereas the Jewish role in the colonial period remains an eclipsed terrain, the literature by Ashkenazis, from the immigrant generation onwards, has been plentiful, and, in the last twenty-five years, so has the scholarship that reflects upon it. Authors from Peru, Mexico, Chile, Uruguay, Guatemala, and Venezuela, including Isaac Goldemberg, Ariel Dorfman, and Marjorie Agosín, Mauricio Rosencoff and Teresa Porzecanski, Alcina Lubitch Domecq, and Alicia Freilich, respectively, have also elicited erudite considerations. Their work has been translated into several languages. Individual studies on them are available in Spanish, English, and Hebrew.

The case of Goldemberg—novelist, poet, editor—should serve as an example. He is best known for his novel *The Fragmented Life of Don Jacobo Lerner*. Its plot is Biblical—or perhaps Joycean: a son's pursuit of his shadowy father, whose severe profile is so complex that an omniscient narrator is not capable of encapsulating it all, a chronological story frequently interrupted by the "obnoxious" news of the day. It is dedicated in part to José Kozer, an émigré Jew from Cuba, stationed in Queens, responsible for a syncretic poetry—Jewish, Catholic, Buddhist. Emigration, apparent from the volume's dedications onward, is the main theme: Don Jacobo Lerner, a memorable creation, a diasporic creature, a displaced soul, a wanderer in a strange land, is made to symbolize the fracture of modernity. A *plazos* means in Spanish "in installments," but Roberto S. Picciotto's English translation happily finds a better substitute: fragmentation, that quintessential feeling of our most tumultuous century. The novel, in short, is about ambivalence: about disloyalty, an immigrant's double home, the old and the new. It is a sharp critique of the unwillingness of Jewish immigrants to adapt, to become part of the milieu opening its arms to them. Not surprisingly, when first published in 1978, while praised by non-Jewish critics (José Miguel Oviedo, in Octavio Paz's monthly *Vuelta*, applauded the fashion in which Goldemberg did not succumbed to *idées fixes*, shaping characters, he claimed, "possessed by a magisterial blindness" found only in people defeated by fate), it was attacked by some in Peru's Jewish community as anti-Semitic. Bizarrely, the accusation is a form of endorsement, for Goldemberg's is a intrepid depiction of interfaith relations, a nasty topic in a milieu known for its ancestral xenophobia.

The element I personally find striking about Goldenberg's book is the parallel it establishes between man and society, between Don Jacobo and Peru as a whole. At the beginning the protagonist is on his deathbed, trying desperately to find some coherence in his fragmented life. His odyssey is recounted, *á la* Rashomon, by personal reminiscences, crónicas of the Jewish community, and announcements posted between 1925 and 1935 in the local newspaper, *Alma Hebrea*. These clippings insist on the philanthropic nature of Jews. Immigrants are exhorted to adopt Peru's citizenship and to sing, at the Unión Israelita community center, the nation's anthem. On the surface everything is benign, but in reality the country is falling apart: the Leguía government is overthrown in a coup led by Luis Sánchez Cerro, while the populist leader Victor Raúl Haya de la Torre instigates the masses to rebellion. But the Jews are untouched. They dance and frolic and do business as usual. When they react, it is only to European affairs, and at a retarded pace. They are guests at the Hotel Peru, just another lodging they have found in their diasporic pilgrimage. While they might not say it aloud, they neither love it nor are they intricately related to it. It is but a temporary stop.

This restlessness is obviously at the heart of Goldemberg's literary enterprise, both as a Peruvian and as a writer. "Nobody in Peru who takes literature seriously will ever feel at ease," novelist Mario Vargas Llosa once said. Society forces writers to live in a state of anxiety. Still, they remain relentless, proud in their "uneasiness." They will struggle to portray what their eyes see, even if their work creates a commotion. That, I trust, explains why I immediately identified with Goldemberg's novel, finding it so amorphous, so magnetic, so enclosed in modern readers. He was an authentic writer—a voice crying in the wilderness. His novel's protagonist, and the character's mistress, his in-laws, his bastard child Efraín are not characters invented out of the blue. The apathy felt by the characters toward Peru mirrors perfectly that of Mexican Jews, for instance. Is his view too despairing, too cynical? Is there room for coexistence of Jews and Gentiles? Might the Hispanic Americas have been turned into a Promised Land? And what, if any, is the role of literature in the quest for understanding? Therein, it seems to me, is Goldemberg's lesson: by their sheer inquisitiveness, his characters justify me, that is, they prove that my existential dilemma, my duality— Jewish *and* Hispanic—is not, as I often feared, a mere oxymoron but a legitimate conflict out of which art, germane, pure, and memorable, could emerge. If, indeed, Peru is a land of errors and misunderstandings, as poet César Moro once stated, then *The Fragmented Life of Don Jacobo Lerner* turns that quality into a fountain of metaphors.

VI. *Ma, ¿qué escrivites?*

The third wave of Jewish immigration to the Americas is defined by a constituency that originated in parts of the former Ottoman Empire. It began to arrive on the shores of the Americas in 1880, approximately when the Ashkenazic newcomers were also disembarking, and extended into the 1970s. Until recently the literary outpourings of this community have been comparatively small, yet its sheer existence allows one to reflect on a major component of the Jewish–Latin American tradition that forms a bridge to the colonial past: the modern Sephardic voices. Arguably the most important figure in this component is the Mexican academic, poet, and novelist Angelina Muníz-Huberman. She is prolific, with dozens of titles to her credit and several doctoral dissertations and academic articles written about the overall contribution of her works. Muníz-Huberman's oeuvre juxtaposes Spanish mysticism and Kabbalah with contemporary motifs. It is important in this essay to highlight a couple of her academic volumes: *La lengua florida: Antología sefardí* (1989), which includes poems by Samuel Hanagid and Yehuda Halevi, among scores of other medieval Ibero-Jewish authors; and *Las raíces y las ramas: Fuentes y derivaciones de la Cábala hispanohebrea* (1993), a somewhat derivative examination of Kabbalah based on the work of Gershom Scholem.

An author whose oeuvre is popular and whose themes are contemporary Sephardic is Rosa Nissán, responsible for the autobiographical novel *Like a Bride* and its sequel *Like a Mother*. These, to my knowledge, are the only fictional narratives, at least since World War II, to include a portion in Ladino. (Around 98 percent of the text is in Spanish; a Ladino glossary for the remaining 10 percent appears at the back of the original editions.) This might not explain their overall historical importance, but it surely is a hint. Furthermore, some scholarly commentary on Nissán and her novels has also been in Latino. For instance, *"Ma, ¿qué escrivites?"* wondered the poet Myriam Moscona when *Novia que te vea*, the first of the two, was released in Mexico in 1992. And Moscona, singing further praise to a storyteller of her same ethnic background, added: *"¿Ande tupates tanta historia, tanta memoria, tanta palavrica de las muestras? ¿Dí que queres arrevivir ista lingua casi muerta que conocites por la banda de tus padres y abuelos? ¿Quén te ambezó a dezir las cosas como las dices? ¿Escrivana salites?"* In translation, these queries seem mundane: "But what have you written? Where have you, Rosa, found so much history, so much memory, so many of these words that are close to our heart? Do you want to revive this almost defunct tongue that you got acquainted with through your parents and grandparents? What urged you to say things the way you do? Have you turned out to be a writer?" Yet in the original, the utterance, of course, has magic; or better, it has zest. It is a modified form of Ladino; Moscona and Nissán, as Sephardic Jews from Mexico, came of age listening to it. Curiously, it is not heard from the mouth of Nissán's protagonist, Oshinica, but from those in her entourage, most of them immigrants from Turkey and Persia.

¿Escrivana salites? is the correct question to ask of Nissán. Although she is unquestionably a novelist—aside from *Like a Bride*, she is the author of its sequel, *Hisho que te nazca*, translated into English as *Like a Mother*; a travelogue about Israel entitled *Las tierras prometidas* that is also an exploration of her inner conflicts as a Mexican and a Jew; and a collection of stories, *No sólo para domir es la noche*—her quest for space and a voice came rather circuitously. That journey, in fact, is narrated in her books about Oshinica. With a plethora of tales inside but no way to articulate them, Nissán, enrolled in a creative writing course—*un taller literario*—with Elena Poniatowska, one of Mexico's most prominent women authors. This delayed encounter with her artistic self, it ought to be added, is not atypical in her ethnic group, where, as she herself explains lucidly in her fiction, the education of women until recently was, if not forbidden, at least delegated to the status of nonessential. Indeed, it was Poniatowska herself, a non-Jew, who first recognized Nissán's energy and encouraged her to pursue her literary exercises. Soon those exercises turned into full-fledged narratives about the Sephardic idiosyncrasy, filled with humorous and linguistic puns. As in the case of many artists, her imaginative formulations might have represented an attempt by Nissán to distance herself from her community. But it is clear that, not only in the plot of her novels but in life, too, as her people put it, *"la engrandecimos"*—her pilgrimage enriched her. The result

held by the reader, is, in my mind, unique in Mexican letters and equally in the tradition of Jewish fiction in Spanish.

A capacious study of Nissán's characters is available in Yael Halevi-Wise's article *"Puente entre naciones,"* in the journal *Hispania* (1998); this, as far as I know, is the most comprehensive analysis by an academic of her work. Her uniqueness is twofold: first, I know of no other *Bildungsroman* where the main character is a Sephardic woman, whose odyssey is contemplated from adolescence to maturity; and second, the inclusion of Ladino, not inconsequential, makes this a rarity. To understand these reasons I've just stated requires that I offer some context. To begin, it is illustrative to consider the question of why Eastern Europe, in its rise to modernity, became the cradle for the novel in the Jewish literary tradition. With the French Revolution came the emergence of the bourgeoisie as a major class, and the novel, as an artistic artifact, served as a thermometer of its angst. Ironically, *Don Quixote*, published in two parts in 1605 and 1615, is perhaps the first novel to implement a reflection on actual change—internal and external—in human nature. Its protagonist, Alonso Quijano, transforms himself from a loquacious *hidalgo* to a fool and back to a down-to-earth old man. But Cervantes's masterpiece stands alone as a door opener in Spain. The majority of groundbreaking novels, such as those written from Defoe to Diderot, were produced elsewhere in Europe. By the dawn of the seventeenth century, the Jews and also the Muslim populations of the peninsula had already been expelled. For this and other reasons, for years Sephardic literature focused on the liturgical and philosophical: the poetry of Samuel Hanagid, Solomon ben Gabirol, and Yehuda Halevi are highlights, as are the treatises by Halevi himself, Maimonides, and Hasdi Crescas.

Fiction as such was not, in any significant way, an ingredient. Paloma Díaz-Mas, in the authoritative *Los Sefaradíes: Historia, lengua y cultura* (1986), embarks on an inventory of literature by Judeo-Hispanic authors that ranges from *coplas* to proverbs and ballads (e.g., *canticas* and *romansas*). About a fourth of her catalog is devoted to "adopted genres": journalism, narrative, theater, and "autograph" poetry. It is intriguing, though, that among the *romansos* (novels) she lists, almost all are described as *aranjados*: imitations. The earliest of these, published in places such as Cairo, Smyrna, Constantinople, and Salonika, are traceable to the period of 1900 to 1933 but never earlier. In other words, while a distinct Judeo-Hispanic ethos was apparent in the Middle Ages—Abraham Joshua Heschel discusses it thought-provokingly in essays and, in passing, in his biography of Maimonides—its role in modernity is that of an addition, not a source.

Nissán's *Like a Bride* and *Like a Mother* are not included in Díaz-Mas's register, probably because Hispanic America never became a centrifugal center of Sephardic culture. In fact, to my knowledge, the number of published Sephardic narratives in the region is minuscule; Angelina Muníz-Huberman, in her 1989 anthology of a Ladino literature, corroborates this statement: her list of suggested further readings might best be described as sparse. Hence Nissán, at sixty-one years of age, is a *rara avis*, to employ an oxymoron, she is an *aranjado* novelist with an original voice, one that is modern, Jewish, and *muy mexicana*. And, another asset of hers ought to be contemplated: in 1993, *Like a Bride* was successfully adapted for film by Guita Schyfter, her husband Hugo Hiriart, and Nissán herself, in a production by the Instituto Mexicano de Cinematográfia. This allowed Oshinica, and the immigration she has come to be an emblem of, to be better known in Mexico and beyond. A succinct evaluation of the film is included in my book *The Riddle of Cantinflas* (1998).

VII. *Ni de aquí, ni de allá*

The Holocaust has become a fixture in American-Jewish life. It often seems as if every aspect of the catastrophe has been explored in historical and eyewitness films, TV documentaries, poetry, and fiction. But the examination has been limited mostly to the Europe-U.S. and Europe-Israel equation. The links and echoes in the so-called Third World of the Nazi annihilation of six million Jews between 1939 and 1945 have hardly received the attention they deserve. Latin America, for instance, remains an area not contemplated in so-called genocide studies. The Holocaust played an important role in the history of these communities, particularly among Ashkenazic Jews, although also among those from Greece and Turkey, not only by bringing refugees and survivors before, during, and after World War II but also by making them live face-to-face with Nazi fugitives and asking them to interact with the Spanish-speaking natives in ways many of them were unprepared for. (Famous cases of Nazi fugitives are Adolf Eichmann, Josef Menguele, and Klaus Barbie.)

Yet the literature remains limited and peripheral, not only in general but among Jews too. It has long been a puzzle to me, for instance, that Octavio Paz, a Renaissance man whom I admire wholeheartedly and whose work fills my library shelves, reflected on just about anything, from Buddhism and T. S. Eliot to Sor Juana Inés de la Cruz and Surrealism—but not on the Jewish presence in his homeland and especially not on the Holocaust. The more than a dozen hefty tomes of his *Obras Completas* are a veritable map that links Mexico to the rest of the globe. But absent in those reflections is any serious consideration of Jewishness. So ubiquitous in Western civilization, Jews seem to have been non-existent in Paz's eyes.

The disinterest is not always as blunt. Mario Vargas Llosa's *The Storyteller* is about a Jew in Lima who is described as "strange," and the writer's essays tackle controversial issues, including the entangled Middle East conflict. The novels of Carlos Fuentes, from *A Change of Skin* to *Terra Nostra*, analyze Jewish-Hispanic relations since the Middle Ages. But even in the oeuvres of those authors, Jews, although mentioned, are usually dealt with superficially, not as a significant part of Hispanic culture. (Various individual academic articles in scholarly journals analyze the Jewish topics in Fuentes and Vargas Llosa.) The opposite should be said about Jorge Luis Borges. Albeit non-Jewish, he is unquestionably a crucial figure in the development of Jewish-Argentine letters, one especially interested in the Nazi atrocities. A substantial amount of scholarly ink has also been spilled over his oeuvre; indeed, there is a phenomenon called "the Borges industry": scores of reference volumes and theoretical, philosophical, and critical examinations on this or that aspect of his work, including the Jewish elements, which are substantial and have become a touchstone to various generations.

The scholarship on Jewish literature in the Americas since 1492 still lacks a period of splendor. The groundwork began over a century ago, but intense intellectual explorations have taken place only from 1975 to the present. Structurally and financially, the Spanish- and Portuguese-language worlds this side of the Atlantic Ocean have limited academic resources, technological tools, and attention, even though the largest primary sources are still to be found here. Many of these sources are unavailable for readers of Spanish, and those that are come in mediocre editions. In spite of the contributions by Liebman and Cohen, little that is pathbreaking has taken place in the scholarship on this period. Indeed, no major study has appeared that is exclusively devoted to the literature of the crypto-Jews and *conversos*. (Gitlitz's *Secrecy and Deceit*, to a large extent, focuses on customs as reflected in historical documents.) Meanwhile, novelists have been busy exploring the religious and social dilemmas. Proof is an array of insightful narratives, such as Angelina Muníz-Huberman's *El mercader de Tudela* and Mexican poet and eco-activist Homero Aridjis's *1492: Life and Times of Juan Cabezón de Castilla*. These works have generated limited critical commentary. Driven by multiculturalism on campus, Jewish-American academic interest in the colonial period has reoriented its attention to the Southwestern region of the United States, where a resurgence of conversions to Judaism by people self-defined as descendants of *conversos* has become a trend. An example is *Hidden Heritage: The Legacy of the Crypto-Jews* (2002) by Janet Jacobs. Literature as a form of imaginative expression is only a passing concern in these types of research. Clearly, the field of colonial studies remains a fertile, unexplored one—"imbalance" in Martin A. Cohen's depiction—as it was thirty years ago and more. Scores of documents are unscrutinized, and translations into English, Hebrew, and other languages still remain to be done.

In the literature of the twentieth century the situation is equally problematic. To begin with, this literature—novels, memoirs, poems, stories, folklore—has a limited continental circulation: a reader in Lima, for instance, has no access to Gerchunoff's *The Jewish Guachos of the Pampas*, and a reader in Buenos Aires is equally incapable of putting his hands on Goldemberg's *The Fragmented Life of Don Jacobo Lerner*. This is because book distribution is precarious and inconsistent beyond national borders. In terms of translations, an effort has been made since the mid-nineties. Borges is widely available, followed by only a handful of Jewish authors. Translation has been a tool to fight silence and obscurity. Ironically, a reader in English today has far more Jewish–Latin American literary works at his disposal than does his or her counterpart south of the Rio Grande. Only a small fraction of the literature from the colonial period onward has been rendered into Shakespeare's tongue, and almost none is available in other languages. The largest challenge for scholars today is the articulation of a sensible, panoramic context though which to help non-Hispanics understand the dilemmas faced by Jews in the Americas. These challenges only partially parallel those of Jews in the United States. Colonialism and racial miscegenation are also important factors. What impact do these institutions play in the landscape of the imagination? How have they evolved over time? To what extent are Jews witnesses and participants in them?

The latter question is, arguably, at the core of the Jewish-Hispanic literary tradition. *Ni de aquí, ni de allá* . . . Jews have been guests, *huéspedes*, in the Hispanic world for over a thousand years. Their journey has been one marked by twists and turns: at times they have been able to flourish intellectually, in others they have been forced to hide their identity in order to survive. This doesn't mean their worldview is that of a *marrano*. In fact, it is closer to the *mestizo*: a mixture of ancestries, a plentiful ground for cross-fertilization. They are Jews in their tradition, in their culture, in their religion; but they struggle to fit into the environment, and in so doing, they incorporate elements from it into their identity. Their prose and poetry is an invaluable testimony of their chameleon-like qualities.

FURTHER READINGS

A complete bibliography of Jewish-Hispanic books is beyond my scope. This list is designed as a road map for the interested audience. Included are only volumes of general appeal (anthologies, nonfiction, and scholarly) in history, religion, and literature. Other sources and writers are mentioned in the introduction. Individual authors included in this compendium have important works cited in their respective headnotes.

Agosín, Marjorie, ed. *Passion, Memory and Identity: Twentieth-Century Latin American Jewish Women Writers*. Albuquerque, NM: University of New Mexico Press, 1999.

Aizenberg, Edna. *The Aleph Weaver: Biblical, Kabbalistic, and Judaic Elements in Borges*. Potomac, MD: Scripta Humanistica, 1985.

Baer, Yitzhak. *A History of the Jews in Christian Spain*. Translated by Louis Schoffman. Introduction by Benjamin R. Gampel. Philadelphia: Jewish Publication Society, 1992.

Barr, Lois B. with David Sheinin, eds. *The Jewish Diaspora in Latin America: New Studies on History and Literature*. New York: Garland, 1996.

Beinart, Haim. *The Expulsion of the Jews from Spain*. Translated by Jeffrey M. Green. Portland, OR: Littman Library of Jewish Civilization, 2002.

Benbassa, Esther, with Aron Rodrigue. *Sephardi Jewry: A History of the Judeo-Spanish Community, 14th to 29th Centuries*. Berkeley and London: University of California Press, 2000.

Carmi, T., ed. *The Penguin Book of Hebrew Verse*. Harmondsworth, Middlesex, UK: Penguin Books, 1981.

Carpenter, Dwayne E. *Alfonso X and the Jews: An Edition of and Commentary on* Siete partidas 7.24: *"De los judíos."* Berkeley: University of California Press, 1986.

Cohen, Martin A. *The Martyr: Luis de Carvajal, a Secret Few in Seventeenth-Century Mexico*. Albuquerque, NM: University of New Mexico Press, 2001.

————, ed. *The Jewish Experience in Latin America: A Survey Study for the American Jewish Congress*. Waltham, MA: American Jewish Publication Society/KTAV, 1971.

de la Pinta Llorente, Miguel. *Aspectos históricos del sentimiento religioso en España: Ortodoxia y heterodoxia*. Madrid: Consejo Superior de Investigaciones Científicas, Escuela de Historia Moderna, 1961.

Díaz-Mas, Paloma. *Sephardim: The Jews from Spain*. Translated by George K. Zuker. Chicago and London: University of Chicago Press, 1992.

Elkin, Judith. *The Jews of Latin America*. New York: Holmes and Meier, 1998.

————, with Gilbert W. Merkx, eds. *The Jewish Presence in Latin America*. Boston: Allen & Unwin, 1987.

Feierstein, Ricardo, ed. *Cien años de narrativa judeoargentina: 1889–1989*. Buenos Aires: Milá, 1989.

Gardiol, Rita, ed. *The Silver Candelabra and Other Stories: A Century of Jewish Argentine Literature*. Pittsburgh, PA: Latin American Literary Review Press, 1997.

Gerber, Jane S. *The Jews of Spain: A History of the Sephardic Experience*. New York: The Free Press, 1992.

Gerchunoff, Alberto. *The Jewish Gauchos of the Pampas*. Translated by Prudencio de Pereda. Albuquerque, NM: University of New Mexico Press, 1998.

Gitlitz, David M. *Secrecy and Deceit. The Religion of the Crypto-Jews*. Albuquerque, NM: University of New Mexico Press, 2002.

Glatzer, Nahum N. *The Judaic Tradition*: Vol. 1: *The Rest is Commentary: A Source Book of Judaic Antiquity*; Vol. 2: *Faith and Knowledge, The Jew in the Medieval World*; and Vol. 3: *The Dynamics of Emancipation, The Jew in the Modern Age*. Boston: Beacon Press, 1969.

Glickman, Nora, and Robert DiAntonio, eds. *Tradition and Innovation: Reflections on Latin American Jewish Writing*. Albany, NY: State University of New York Press, 1993.

Goldemberg, Isaac, ed. *El gran libro de la América judía*. San Juan, Puerto Rico: Editorial de la Universidad de Puerto Rico, 2000.

————. *The Fragmented Life of Don Jacobó Lerner*. Translated by Robert S. Picciotto. Albuqurque, NM: University of New Mexico Press, 1999.

Jacobs, Jane. *Hidden Heritage: The Legacy of the Crypto-Jews*. Berkeley and London: University of California Press, 2002.

Liebman, Saymour B. *The Jews of New Spain: Faith, Flame, and the Inquisition*. Coral Gables, FL: University of Miami Press, 1970.

———. ed. and trans. *The Enlightened: The Writings of Cuis de Carvajal, el Mozo*. Coral Gables, FL: University of Miami Press, 1967.

Lindstrom, Naomi. *Jewish Issues in Argentine Literature: From Gerchunoff to Szichman*. Columbia, MO: University of Missouri Press, 1989.

Lockhart, Darrell B., ed. *Jewish Writers in Latin America: A Dictionary*. New York and London: Garland, 1997.

Menocal, María Rosa, with Raymond P. Schendlin and Michael Sells, eds. *The Literature of Al-Andalus*. New York: Cambridge University Press, 2000.

Muníz-Huberman, Angelina, ed. *La lengua florida: Antología sefardí*. Mexico: Fondo de Cultura Económica, 1989.

Netanyahu, Benzion. *The Marranos of Spain: From the late 14th to the early 16th Century, According to Contemporary Hebrew Sources*. Ithaca, NY: Cornell University Press, 1999.

———. *The Origins of the Inquisition in Fifteenth-Century Spain*. New York: Random House, 1995.

Roth, Cecil. *A History of the Marranos*. 4th ed. With an introduction by Herman S. Salomon. New York: Schocken Books, 1974.

Sachar, Howard M. *Farewell España: The World of the Sephardim Remembered*. New York: Knopf, 1994.

Sadow, Stephen A., ed. *King David's Harp: Autobiographical Essays by Jewish Latin American Writers*. Albuquerque, NM: University of New Mexico Press, 1999.

Schendlin, Raymond P. *Wine, Women, and Death: Medieval Hebrew Poems on the Good Life*. Philadelphia: Jewish Publication Society, 1986.

Scholem, Gershom G. *Major Trends in Jewish Mysticism*. New York: Schocken Books, 1941.

Sosnowski, Saúl. *La orilla inminente. Escritores judíos argentinos*. Buenos Aires: Legasa, 1987.

Stavans, Ilan, ed. *The Oxford Book of Jewish Stories*. New York and London: Oxford University Press, 1998.

————, ed. *Tropical Synagogues: Short Stories by Jewish–Latin American Writers.* New York and London: Holmes and Meier, 1994.

Swietlicki, Catherine. *Spanish Christian Cabala: The Works of Luis de León, Santa Teresa de Jesús, and San Juan de la Cruz.* Columbia, MO: University of Missouri Press, 1986.

CHRONOLOGY

200 B.C.E.–200 C.E.	Migration of Jews throughout the Roman diaspora, including Spain (a.k.a. Ispamia and Sepharad).
Circa 900	Apex of Andalusian civilization, with Córdoba as its capital. The so-called Jewish Golden Age (philosophy, poetry, science) covers the tenth and eleventh centuries.
Circa 940	Hasdai ben Shaprut becomes a prominent figure in public life.
1013	The Caliphate of Córdoba is dissolved. Samuel Hanagid (aka Samuel ben Nagrela) is twelve years of age. He will become *vizir* of Granada, the highest diplomatic position ever for a Jew.
1085	Toledo falls into Christian hands.
1090	Granada is conquered by the Almoravids.
1096–1147	First and Second Crusades.
1135–1204	Life of Maimonides (a.k.a. Moisés ben Maimón), doctor and the leading thinker of Sephardic Jewry. He will write the *Mishna Torah*, the *Commentary on the Misha*, and the *Guide of the Perplexed*.
1140	Yehuda Halevi renounces the "good life" in Spain and leaves for Palestine. Halevi will write *bon vivant* as well as philosophical poetry, and the *Kuzari*.

1238	The Papal Inquisition is established in Aragón.
1248	Capitulation of Seville by Ferdinand III.
1263	Disputation of Barcelona between Nahmanides and Pablo Christiani.
1378–1389	Jews protest anti-Semitic preachings by Catholic leaders.
1391	The Jews of Seville are attacked. In the Iberian Peninsula, the proliferation of pogroms—a Russian term that means "anti-Jewish outbursts"—initiates a period of conversion of Jews to Christianity.
1449	Riots in Toledo, Ciudad Real, and elswhere destroy Jewish districts.
1462–1467	Riots against *conversos* in Seville and Toledo.
1478	The Catholic Monarchs, Ferdinand and Isabella, establish the Holy Office of the Inquisition.
1481	First auto-da-fé in Seville.
1482	Tomás de Torquemada is named Chief Inquisitor in Castile.
1492	January: Granada, the last Muslim bastion in the peninsula, surrenders to a military effort known as the Reconquista. March: Edict of expulsion of the Jews from Spain, ordering some 300,000 to leave in a span of four months. August: deadline for the departure of Jews. Christopher Columbus sets out across the Atlantic Ocean. He will arrive in the Bahamas. Jewish emigration to Portugal, the Netherlands, the Middle East, and northern Africa. In successive years groups of New

Christians (*cristianos nuevos*) and crypto-Jews move to the so-called New World.

1497	Jews who settled in Portugal after the Spanish expulsion are forced to convert.
1570	The Inquisition is established in Peru.
1596	Luis de Carvajal the Younger and his family are burnt at the stake by the Holy Office of the Inquisition in Mexico.
1623	Arrival of the first Jewish settlers from Holland and the Iberian Peninsula to Brazil.
1665	Miguel Leví de Barrios, also known as Daniel Leví de Barrios, leads a double identity: Christian in Brussels, Jewish in Amsterdam. He publishes the collection of poetry, *Flor de Apolo*.
1722–1725	The last wave of Inquisition cases takes place in Spain.
1810–1823	The age of independence sweeps the Americas. The Inquisition is slowly abolished.
1834	The Inquisition is abolished as an institution in Spain.
1830–1889	Emigration of individual Jews from France, Germany, and northern Africa to Argentina. The period of agricultural colonization begins, sponsored by the Alliance Israelite Universelle and philanthropists such as Baron Moisés de Hirsch. In 1889 the SS *Weser* brings around 825 Russian-Jewish immigrants to Argentina.
1842	Moroccan Jews establish the congregation Porta de Ceu in Belem, Brazil.

1860   The Alliance Israélite Universelle is founded in France.

1889–1914   Jewish immigration from Eastern Europe to other sec-
                      tions of the Americas. From 1900 onward a substantial
                      wave of immigrants is of Sephardic descent.

1898   The Spanish-American War takes place.

1900   From Dutch-owned Curaçao, Jews move to Venezuela.

1903   Angel Pulido, Spanish physician and senator, calls for
                      the repatriation of Spanish Jews expelled in 1492 to
                      their ancient homeland. Pulido is the author of *Los
                      israelitas españoles y el idioma castellano* (*Spanish Jews
                      and the Spanish Language*) and *Españoles sin patria y la
                      raza sefardí* (*Spaniards without a Homeland and the
                      Sephardic race*).

1908   Jews from the Ottoman Empire immigrate to the
                      Americas.

1910   *The Jewish Gauchos of the Pampas*, by Alberto
                      Gerchunoff, is published in Argentina, as a token of
                      gratitude in the celebration of the nation's centennial of
                      independence. Gerchunoff will become a leading intel-
                      lectual in his adopted country.

1914–1918   World War I takes place. In 1917 the Jews in Santiago,
                      Chile, celebrate the Balfour Declaration.

1918–1956   Completion of the foundations of the Jewish communi-
                      ties in Latin America.

1919   The only pogrom ever of the Americas, known as
                      Semana trágica, takes place in Argentina and Uruguay.

1927	Rabbis in the Americas forbid conversion to Judaism by non-Jews.
1930	Jewish immigrants from Germany arrive in Brazil.
1932	Some 20,000 Jewish-German refugees arrive in Bolivia.
1938	World War II begins. Refugees arrived to the Americas in small numbers. Sometime later the SS *St. Louis*, filled with refugees from World War II, arrives in Havana Harbor, but is denied entry. The boat is known as *The Ship of Fools*. Around 476 Jews become farmers in a colony in Sosua, Dominican Republic.
1940	The Instituto Arias Montano for Sephardic Research is established in Madrid.
1948	The State of Israel is established.
1956–1963	Egyptian Jews arrive in Brazil.
1958–1959	Fidel Castro orchestrates a revolution in Cuba. Jewish emigration from the island will takes place during the sixties, mainly to Florida.
1960	Israeli commandos kidnap the high-ranking Nazi Adolf Eichmann in Buenos Aires. They fly him overnight to Israel, where he will stand trial.
1966	Spanish law guarantees religious freedom.
1967	The Six Day War is fought in the Middle East.
1968	The edict of expulsion of 1492 is revoked.
1973	The Yom Kippur War takes place in Israel.

1975	Anti-Semitic outbreak in the Argentine stock exchange. It is televised on the government-funded TV channel.
1976–1983	A disproportionate number of Jews participate in the so-called Dirty War in Argentina. Scores become *desaparecidos*. The record of this period appears in *Prisoner without a Name, Cell without a Number*, by Jacobo Timerman. A number of Jews from Latin America resettle in the United States.
1982	The Israeli army invades Lebanon. Protests, along with scattered anti-Semitic outbursts, take place throughout the Americas.
1990	A total of 430,400 Jews live throughout Latin America, 208,000 of them in Argentina, 100,000 in Brazil, 40,800 in Mexico, and 23,600 in Uruguay.
1992	The quincentennial of Columbus's first voyage across the Atlantic Ocean takes place worldwide. The expulsion of 1492 and the "birth" of the Sephardic Diaspora are also memorialized in symposia and art festivals.
1993	A bomb explodes in the Israeli Embassy in Buenos Aires. Thirty people are killed.
1994	The A.M.I.A., the Jewish community Center in Buenos Aires, is the target of a pro-Iranian Hezbullah terrorist attack. Eighty-six people die and hundreds are injured.
2002	The Israeli army enters the Occupied Territories in the West Bank and Gaza in an effort to confront Palestinian suicide bombers. Repercussions are felt throughout the world, including anti-Semitic acts in Latin America.

THE
SCROLL
and the CROSS

Samuel Hanagid
(Spain, 993–1056)
"Short Prayer in Time of Battle"
Translated from the Hebrew by T. Carmi

A major figure in the so-called Golden Age of Hebrew poetry in Spain, Samuel
Hanagid was also a Talmudist and a statesman, and was the first to be given the
title of Nagid ("Prince"). Thus he renovated the Biblical tradition of artists *qua*
political figures. Hanagid was born in Córdova, but when the Berbers invaded it,
he left the city. He was appointed vizier under Badis, the Berber ruler of
Granada, and triumphantly led the armies of Granada against Seville under the
forces of Isma'il ibn Abbad. He wrote and sent poems to his son during his days
on the battlefield, and he is remembered for the quality and scope of these.
Hanagid composed the following verses the battle near the Sangil River, in
1039. According to one of his translators, the Israeli poet T. Carmi, Hanagid
recited them instead of the afternoon service on that day. Carmi also suggests
that in his childhood, Hanagid had a vision in which the archangels Michael and
Gabriel brought him God's promise of protection. It is that vision to which he
refers in the fourth line of the poem as "Your promise." The son referred to at
the end of the poem is Hanagid's own son, Yehosef, who succeeded his father as
army commander and vizier. Yehosef, according to Carmi, began to copy and
arrange his father's poetry when he was eight and a half years of age.

See my distress today;
listen to my prayer,
and answer it.
Remember Your promise to Your servant;
do not disappoint my hope.
Can any hand do me violence,
when You are my hand and my shelter?
You once made me a pledge and sent me good tidings with Your angels.
Now I am passing through deep waters—lift me out of my terrors.

I am walking through searing fire—snatch me from the flames.
If I have sinned—what am I, what are my sins?
I am in danger, and cannot pray at length.
Give me my heart's desire; oh, hasten to my aid.
If I am not deserving in Your eyes—
do it for the sake of my son and my sacred learning.

Solomon ben Gabirol
(Spain, 1021/22–c. 1055)
Fragments of "Night Storm"
Translated from the Hebrew by T. Carmi

Solomon ben Gabirol was born in Malaga, lived in Saragossa, and died in Valencia. He was also a major philosopher, responsible for *Keter Malkhut* (*The Kingly Crown*) and *Mekor Hayim* (*The Source of Life*), the later a work preserved only in Latin (*Fons Vitae*) and for centuries known as the legacy of a Muslim or Christian scholar, Avicebron. But it is as a poet, whose support depended on the mercy of the wealthy, that he reached astonishing heights. He introduced the poetic form *piyut*. His work addresses his internal conflicts with Destiny, which he described as "Time." He also wrote riddles, panegyrics, and laments. T. Carmi, his translator, described him as "a cantankerous soul."

> I am the man who braced himself
> and will not desist until he fulfills his vow—
> whose heart recoiled from his heart,
> whose spirit scorned to dwell in his flesh,
> who chose wisdom even as a youth—
> though he be tested seven times in the crucible of Time,
> though it pull down whatever he has built,
> though it uproot whatever he has planted and breach all his barriers.
>
> As I slept—and the skies were spotless—
> the radiant, pure-hearted moon led me over the paths of wisdom
> and, as he led me, instructed me in his light.
> And I, fearing some misfortune, was filled with pity for his light,
> as a father for his first-born son.
>
> Then the wind assailed the moon with sailing clouds,
> and they covered his face with a mask.

It was as if the wind craved for streams of rain
and pressed upon the clouds to make them flow.
The skies robed themselves in darkness.
It seemed as if the moon had died,
and the cloud had buried him.
And all the other clouds of heaven wept for him,
as the people of Aram wept for the son of Beor.

Then the night put on an armor—
plate of darkness;
thunder, with a spear of lightning, pierced it;
and the lightning pierced it;
and the lightning flew about the skies,
as if it were jousting with the night,
spreading its wings like a bat;
the ravens of the dark fled when they saw it.
And God closed in my thoughts.
He barred my heart's desire from all sides.
He bound my heart with ropes of darkness.
Yet it arose like a warrior breaking out of a siege.

But I dare not hope, my friends,
for the light of the moon,
which has turned into pitch-black darkness,
as though the clouds were jealous of my soul and therefore deprived
    me of his light.
And when I chance to see his face revealed,
I rejoice like a slave who sees that his master remembers him.
When a mortal wages war,
his spear is beaten down;
and when he tries to run, his steps falter.
And even the man whose spirit dwells in the shining heavens—
misfortune overtakes him.

Moisés ben Ezra
(Spain, c.1055–c.1135)
"The Two Sons"
Translated from the Hebrew by T. Carmi

A portion of Moisés ben Ezra's supplications (*selihot*) has entered Jewish liturgy. He was born in Granada, a city eventually destroyed by the Almoravids, but ben Ezra stayed behind alone. "Throughout my life," he wrote, "I have known success. . . . But now the tears flow from my eyes as I seek to overcome my grief at my loneliness in my native land, without a companion at my side . . . and I see no man about me of my family and kin." He added: "I remain in Granada, a city of declining bustle and splendor, like a stranger in the land. . . ." Around 1095, he finally fled the city, as T. Cami puts it, "after a romantic episode involving his elder brother's daughter," and moved to Christian Spain. For four decades he moved from one place to another, unsettled, always at the mercy of supporters. He is the author of *The Book of Conversations and Memories*. He was among the first to embark on secular poetry; his poems are about wine, friendship, and nature.

I shall always seek God's favor, His alone;
I shall never reveal the secret of my heart to any mortal.
Can any man help his fellow man?
What use are the words of a wretch to a pauper?
Scorn the World, who with her hands
debases her own glory and wears out her treasures.
She has given birth to two sons:
the one in her belly is dead, and the one on her back is dying.

Yehuda Halevi
(*Spain, before 1075–after 1141*)
"My Heart Is in the East"
Translated from the Hebrew by T. Carmi

Yehuda Halevi is a foundational figure in Hebrew literature. In the late nineteenth century the Zionists positioned him as an early inspiration, but his existential poetry also left a deep influence on diasporic Jewish literature (the biblical Edom), as the poem "My heart Is in the East" shows. He was born in Tudela and spent his youth in Andalusía. A friend of Moisés ben Ezra, he was a doctor and philosopher who lived also in Toledo and later on in Córdoba. He is the author of *The Kuzari*, a philosophical and theological volume made of a trialogue between Muslim, Christian and Jewish leaders whose goal it is to convince the king of the Khazars that their religion is the right one to choose in a popular act of conversion. Toward the end of his life, Halevi abandoned the Diaspora to travel to Zion and thus cure the injury that divided his heart. He stopped in Alexandria, where he was received with acclaim. But he died on the voyage and never made it to the Promised Land. Halevi's work is an enlightened display of the tensions between Muslims, Christians, and Jews at the time of *La reconquista*, as the period of fruitful interreligious cohabitation came to an end. The poem included in this anthology evidences the pledge by Halevi to leave Spain for Zion. The reference to "the domains of Edom," as T. Carmi, Halevi's translator, puts it, refers to the conquest of Jerusalem by the Crusaders in 1099.

My heart is in the East
and I am at the edge of the West.
Then how can I taste what I eat, how can I enjoy it?
How can I fulfill my vows and pledges
while Zion is in the domain of Edom,
and I am in the bonds of Arabia?
It would be easy for me to leave behind all the good things of Spain;
it would be glorious to see the dust of the ruined Shrine.

Benjamin of Tudela
(Spain, twelfth century)
"Jerusalem"
Translated from the Hebrew by Nahum N. Glatzer

Travel, for obvious reasons, is at the core of the Jewish experience in the Diaspora, but the records of so-called "proficient" travelers of the sort who make it their business, to borrow a line from the black poet Langston Hughes, to "wander as I wonder," are sparse. Thanks to Benjamin of Tudela, historians today have firsthand knowledge of Jewish communities around the globe in the twelfth century. His traveled extensively for years, up to 1173, visiting Rome, Greece, Constantinople, Palestine, Damascus, Baghdad, and Persia. His chronicles have the taste of anthropology: he reflects on costumes, politics, and communal life. He wrote his *Masaot Benjamin* in Hebrew (in English, *The Travels of Benjamin of Tudela*) based on notes taken on the spot. The book was first published in 1543. This segment about Jerusalem is revealing in that it ponders the sorrowful status of the capital after the First Crusade of 1099. As Nahum N. Glatzer puts it, "Benjamin came . . . not only to study the sorry present; mainly, he wanted to relive the glories of Israel's past and to behold its remains." The *Masaot Benjamin* has been incredibly influential in Jewish letters. S. J. Abramovitsh (1835–1917), known as the cornerstone of Yiddish literature, published a parody of it (*The Travels of Benjamin III* [1878]), and in this anthology, the Mexican author Angelina Muníz-Huberman is represented with a fragment of an appropriation of the journey, delivered in modern Spanish.

Jerusalem . . . is a small city, fortified by three walls. It is full of people whom the Muslims call Jacobites, Syrians, Greeks, Georgians and Franks, and of people of all tongues. It contains a dyeing-house, for which the Jews pay a small rent annually to the king, on condition that besides the Jews no other dyers be allowed in Jerusalem. There are about two hundred Jews who dwell under the Tower of David in one corner of the city. The lower portion of the wall of the Tower of David, to the extent of about ten cubits, is part of the ancient foundation set up by our ancestors, the remaining portion having been built by the Muslims. There is no structure in the whole city stronger than the Tower of David.

The city also contains two buildings, from one of which—the hospital—there issue forth four hundred knights; and therein all the sick who come thither are lodged and cared for in life and in death. The other building is called the Temple of Solomon; it is the palace built by Solomon, the king of Israel. Three hundred knights are quartered there, and issue therefrom every day for military exercise, besides those who come from the land of the Franks and the other parts of Christendom, having taken upon themselves to serve there a year or two until their vow is fulfilled. In Jerusalem is the great church called the Sepulchre, and here is the burial-place of Jesus, unto which the Christians make pilgrimages.

Jerusalem has four gates—the gate of Abraham, the gate of David, the gate of Zion, and the gate of Gushpat, which is the gate of Jehoshaphat, facing our ancient temple, now called Templum Domini. Upon the site of the sanctuary Omar ben al Khataab erected an edifice with a very large and magnificent cupola, into which the Gentiles do not bring any image or effigy, but they merely come there to pray. In front of this place is the Western Wall, which is one of the walls of the Holy of Holies. This is called the Gate of Mercy, and thither come all the Jews to pray before the wall of the court of the temple. In Jerusalem, attached to the palace which belonged to Solomon, are the stables built by him, forming a very substantial structure composed of large stones, and the like of it is not to be seen anywhere in the world. There is also visible up to this day the pool used by the priests before offering their sacrifices, and the Jews coming thither write their names upon the wall. The gate of Jehoshaphat leads to the valley of Jehoshaphat, which is the gathering-place of nations. Here is the pillar called Absalom's Hand and the sepulchre of King Uzziah.

In the neighborhood is also a great spring, called the Waters of Siloam, connected with the brook of Kidron. Over the spring is a large structure dating from the time of our ancestors, but little water is found, and the people of Jerusalem for the most part drink the rainwater, which they collect in cisterns in their houses. From the valley of Jehoshaphat one ascends the Mount of Olives; it is only the valley which separates Jerusalem from the Mount of Olives. From the Mount of Olives one sees the Sea of Sodom, and at a distance of two parasangs from the Sea of Sodom is the Pillar of Salt into which Lot's wife was turned; the sheep lick it continually, but afterwards it regains its original shape. The whole land of the plain and the Valley of Shittim as far as Mount Nebo are visible from here.

In front of Jerusalem is Mount Zion, on which there is no building, except a place of worship belonging to the Christians. Facing Jerusalem for a distance of three miles are the cemeteries belonging to the Israelites, who in the days of old buried their dead in caves, and upon each sepulchre is a dated inscription, but the Christians destroy the sepulchres, employing the stones thereof in building their houses. These sepulchres reach as far as Zelzah in the territory of Benjamin. Around Jerusalem are high mountains.

On Mount Zion are the sepulchres of the House of David and the sepulchres of the kings that ruled after him. The exact place cannot be identified, inasmuch as fifteen years ago a wall of the church of Mount Zion fell in. The Patriarch commanded the overseer to take the stones of the old walls and restore therewith the church. He did so, and hired workmen at fixed wages; and there were twenty men who brought the stones from the base of the wall of Zion. Among these men there were two who were sworn friends. On a certain day the one entertained the other; after their meal they returned to their work, when the overseer said to them: "Why have you tarried today?" They answered: "Why need you complain? When our fellow workmen go to their meal we will do our work." When dinnertime arrived and the other workmen had gone to their meal, they examined the stones and raised a certain stone which formed the entrance to a cave. Thereupon one said to the other: "Let us go in and see if any money is to be found there." They entered the cave and reached a large chamber resting upon pillars of marble overlaid with silver and gold. In front was a table of gold and a scepter and crown. This was the sepulchre of King David. On the left thereof in like fashion was the sepulchre of King Solomon; then followed the sepulchres of all the kings of Judah that were buried there. Closed coffers were also there, the contents of which no man knows. The two men essayed to enter the chamber, when a fierce wind came forth from the entrance of the cave and smote them, and they fell to the ground like dead men, and there they lay until evening. And there came forth a wind like a man's voice, crying out: "Arise and go forth from this place!" So the men rushed forth in terror, and they came unto the Patriarch, and related these things to him. Thereupon the Patriarch sent for Rabbi Abraham el Constantin, the pious recluse, who was one of "the mourners for Jerusalem," and to him he related all these things according to the report of the two men who had come forth. Then Rabbi Abraham replied: "These are the sepulchres of the House of David; they belong to the kings of Judah, and on the morrow let us enter, I and you and these men, and find out what is there." And on the morrow they sent for the two men, and found each of them lying on his bed in terror, and the men said: "We will not enter there, for the Lord doth not desire to show it to any man." Then the Patriarch gave orders that the place should be closed up and hidden from the sight of man unto this day. These things were told me by the said Rabbi Abraham.

Yehuda ben Tibbon
(Spain, 1120–1190)
"On Books and on Writing"
Translated from the Hebrew by Nahum N. Glatzer

Yehuda ben Tibbon comes from arguably the most important Jewish family of translators. Born in Granada, he delivered canonical works from Arabic into Hebrew, including the *Guide to the Duties of the Heart* by Bahya ben Pakuda and *The Kuzari* by Yehuda Halevi. His reflections on translation, some of which appeared as introductions (as in the case of ben Tibbon's preface to the book by ben Pakuda), are as insightful as those by Dante and Walter Benjamin, among others. The following text was addressed to Samuel ben Tibbon, a physicist and philosopher, who rendered the *Guide of the Perplexed* by Maimonides from Arabic into Hebrew. This is one of the most inspired confessions by a bibliophile I know of.

I have honored you by providing an extensive library for your use, and have thus relieved you of the necessity of borrowing books. Most students must bustle about to seek books, often without finding them. But you, thanks be to God, lend and borrow not. Of many books, indeed, you own two or three copies. I have besides made for you books on all sciences, hoping that your hand may "find all as a nest."

My son! Make your books your companions, let your cases and shelves be your pleasure grounds and gardens. Bask in their paradise, gather their fruit, pluck their roses, take their spices and their myrrh. If your soul be satiate and weary, change from garden to garden, from furrow to furrow, from prospect to prospect. Then will your desire renew itself and your soul be filled with delight!

My son! Take it upon yourself to write one leaf daily and to mediate for an hour. Read every week the Pentateuchal section in Arabic. This will improve your Arabic vocabulary and will be of advantage in translating, if you should feel inclined to translate.

My son! If you write, read it through a second time, for no man can avoid slips. Let not any consideration of hurry prevent you from revising a short epistle. Be punctilious as to grammatical accuracy, in conjugation and genders, for the constant use of the vernacular sometimes leads to error in this regard. A man's mistakes in writing bring him into disrepute; they are remembered against him all his days. As our sages say: "Who is it that uncovers his nakedness here, and it is exposed everywhere? It is he who writes a document and makes mistakes therein." Be careful in the use of conjunctions and adverbs, and how you apply them and how they harmonize with the verbs. I have already begun to compose for you a book on this subject, to be called *Principles of Style*, may God permit me to complete it! And whatever you are in doubt about and have no book to aid in, abstain from expressing it! Endeavor to cultivate conciseness and elegance, do not attempt to write verse unless you can do it perfectly. Avoid heaviness, which spoils a composition, making it disagreeable alike to reader and audience.

See to it that your handwriting is as beautiful as your style. Keep your pen in fine working order, use ink of good color. Make your script as perfect as possible, unless you are forced to write without proper materials or in a pressing emergency. The beauty of a composition depends on the writing, and the beauty of the writing on pen, paper, and ink; and all these excellences are an index of the author's worth.

Examine your Hebrew books at every new moon, the Arabic volumes once in two months, and the bound copies once every quarter. Arrange your library in fair order, so as to avoid wearying yourself in searching for the book you need. Always know the case and chest where the book should be. A good plan would be to place in each compartment a written list of the books therein contained. If, then, you are looking for a book, you can see from the list the exact shelf it occupies, without disarranging all the books in the search for one. Examine the loose leaves in the volumes and bundles, and preserve them. These sheets contain very important matters that I collected and copied out. Do not destroy any writing or letter of all that I have left. And cast your eye frequently over the catalog, in order to remember what books are in your library.

Never refuse to lend books to anyone who has not the means to purchase books for himself, but only lend to those who can be trusted to return the volumes. You know what our sages said in the Talmud on the text: "Wealth and riches are in his house; and his merit endureth for ever." But "withhold not good from him to whom it is due," and take particular care of your books. Cover the bookcases with rugs of fine quality; and preserve them from damp and mice, and from all manner of injury, for your books are your greatest treasure. If you lend a volume, make a memorandum before it leaves your house, and when it is returned, strike out the entry with your pen. At each Passover and Tabernacles, call in all books out on loan.

Make it a fixed rule in your home to read the Scriptures and to peruse grammatical works on Sabbaths and festivals, also to read Proverbs and the *Son of Proverbs*. Also, I beg you, look at the chapter concerning Jonadab, son of Rechab, every Sabbath, to instill in you diligence to fulfill my commands.

Maimonides

(Spain, 1135–1204)

Fragment of "Epistle to the Jews of Morocco"

Translated from the Hebrew by Avraham Yaakov Finkel

The preeminent Jewish thinker, Moises ben Maimon (in Latin, Maimonides) was born in Córdova. When he was thirteen years old, the city was conquered by the Almohads, a tribe that forced Jews to convert to Islam. Maimonides' family went into exile, first into Andalusía, then to Fez in northern Africa. Then they stayed in Jerusalem and finally settled in Fostat, in Cairo. Before their arrival in Egypt, the father died, and also Maimonides' brother David, whose occupation as a dealer of jewels supported the family. Maimonides fell into depression, but he took on medicine and excelled as a physician. He was appointed physician to the court of Sultan Saladin. His Biblical and Talmudic knowledge was such that the Jewish community in Cairo named him chief rabbi. He used his influence to improve the situation of the Jews in Egypt and in Palestine, the latter in distress after the First Crusade. The work of Maimonides is rich and diverse. He is remembered for his *Commentary on the Mishnah* (1168), written in Arabic, which attempted to make the dense Mishnah, compiled by Yehuda Hanassi, accessible to readers; for his *magnum opus, Mishneh Torah* (1180), written in precise Hebrew, the first comprehensive codification of all the Laws of the Torah; and for his philosophical treatise, *Guide of the Perplexed* (1190), written in Arabic, in which he attempted to reconcile the Bible and Aristotle. The first entry by Maimonides in this anthology comes from a letter of 1165, *"Ma'amar Kiddush Hashem,"* in English "Discourse on Martyrdom," also known as the "Epistle to the Jews of Morocco," in which Maimonides ponders the issue of a suicide performed in the name of God in troubled times. Needless to say, this is a timely topic today, and the reader should not be deceived by the abundance of Biblical and Talmudic quotes and references and by rabbinical terminology. It is possible to go beyond these apparent ornaments to seize the powerful argument Maimonides develops with clarity and conviction. The Jews of Morocco to whom he replies were forced to convert to Islam by the Almohads, the same tribe that forced Maimonides' family out of Córdova. He reacts to a previous correspondent, a Talmudic scholar whose view it was that any adherence to religion in a secret fashion by a Jew who has converted to another religion is a sinful act. The second entry by Maimonides in this volume is Chapter XV of the *More Nebuhim*, which is the Hebrew title of his influential philosophical book, the *Guide of the Perplexed*, shaped in response to a student whose queries on the conflict between reason and belief made Maimonides think that sophisticated intellects needed more than the Code of Law to navigate life. The book was written in Arabic, then translated into Hebrew by Samuel ben Tibbon. This chapter is part of a section that discusses the power of God. The life and times of Maimonides are indelibly printed in Jewish memory. He is the subject of endless study, riddles, folk tales, imagery, and even modern biographies, such as the accessible one by Abraham Joshua Heschel: *Maimonides* (1982), translated into English by Joachim Neugroschel.

A contemporary of mine inquired about how he should act during these times of persecution, in which he is forced to acknowledge "that man" [Muhammad] as God's messenger and a true prophet. He directed his question at someone whom he calls a sage and who [himself] was not affected by the persecutions that wreaked havoc on many of the Jewish communities, may Hashem end them soon. He asked whether he should make the confession in order to save his life; and that he be able to raise his children so that they will not be lost among the Gentiles. Or does the Torah of Moshe demand that he die and not accept their creed. We must also take into consideration that this confession may eventually cause him to abandon the observance of all the mitzvos.

The man whom he asked his question gave a weak and pointless answer, a reply that was repulsive both in meaning and language. He made statements that are utterly meaningless, as even unlearned women can realize.

Although his reply is long-winded, weak, and tedious, I thought I would respond to his every point. However, I took pity on the gift Hashem bestowed on us, by that I mean [the power of] speech, as it says in the Torah, "Who gives man speech?...Is it not I, Hashem?" One should use words more sparingly than money. Indeed, the Wise Man (Shlomoh) has denounced [people who] talk much and say things of little substance, stating, "Just as dreams come with much brooding, so does a fool's voice come with much speech" (Koheles 5:2). In the same way, you see what Iyov's friends said when he talked on and on: "Is a multitude of words unanswerable? Must a talkative person be right?" (Iyov

11:2): "Iyov does not speak with knowledge; his words lack understanding" (Iyov 34:35). Many other examples can be cited.

Since I am thoroughly familiar with this situation and I do not want to burden you with the ignorance of this man, I think it is worthwhile to mention the thrust of what he said and omit that which does not deserve an answer. Although, on reflection, nothing he said is worthy of a reply.

He states at the outset that whoever acknowledges that [Muhammad] is a [divine] messenger has thereby automatically renounced his belief in Hashem, the God of Yisrael. He proves his assertion by citing the saying of our Sages: "Whoever acknowledges idolatry is considered as if he denied the entire Torah" (Nedarim 28a). In making this analogy, he does not differentiate between a person who voluntarily accepts idolatry, like Yerovam and his clique, and one who says under duress that someone is a prophet, because he fears death by the sword.

When I read this first statement of his, I said to myself, "It is not right for me to attack him before reading all he has to say, in compliance with the words of Shlomoh, 'To answer a man before hearing him out is foolish and disgraceful'" (Koheles 18:13). . . .

I will now begin to outline the magnitude of the error that this poor creature committed and the [damage] he caused through his ignorance. He meant to do good, but instead he caused harm [by making statements] that are not substantiated. His long-drawn-out prose demonstrates self-love of his own style of writing.

It is well known from the commentaries of our Sages that in Moshe's time, before the Exodus, the people of Yisrael had gone astray and broken the covenant of *bris milah*. None except for the tribe of Levi, were circumcised (Shemos Rabbah 19:6). [This situation prevailed] until the *mitzvah* of Pesach was announced. Hashem said to Moseh "No uncircumcised may eat it" (Shemos 12:43). He then told them to perform the *milah*-circumcision. Our Rabbis give an account of the procedure: Moshe did the circumcision, Yehoshua performed the *periah*, and Aharon did the *metzitzah*. Then they piled the foreskins in heaps. The blood of *milah* became mixed with the blood of the *korban Pesach* (the paschal lamb), and this made them worthy to be redeemed. This is the meaning of Hashem's message to Yechezkel, "When I passed by you and saw you wallowing in your blood, I said to you, 'Live by your blood'; yea, I said to you, 'Live by your blood'" (Yechezkel 16:6). Our Sages remark that [the Jewish people] had become debased with incest, as it is described [in the chapter that begins with] "Once there were two women, daughters of one mother" (Yechezkel 23:2).

Although they were perverted to such an extent, when Moshe said, "But they will not believe me" (Shemos 4:1), Hashem admonishes him saying, "Moshe, they are believers, children of believers; believers, for it says, 'and the people believed' (Shemos 14:31); sons of believers, for it says, 'He [Avraham] believed in Hashem, and He counted it as righteousness' (Bereishis 15:6). But you [Moshe] will end up not believing, as it says, 'You did not have enough faith in Me to sanctify Me'" (Bamidbar 20:12). As a matter of fact, [Moshe] was punished immediately, as the Rabbis expounded: "He who suspects the innocent is punished physically. From where is this derived? From Moshe."

In the same vein, in Eliyahu's days, they all willfully worshipped idols, except for "the seven thousand—every knee that has not knelt to Baal and every mouth that has not kissed him" (Melachim I 19:18). Nevertheless, when [Eliyahu] accused Yisrael at Chorev, he was taken to task for it, as can be gathered from the verse, "[Hashem said to him], 'Why are you here Eliyahu?' He replied, 'I am moved by zeal for Hashem, the God of Hosts, for the Israelites have forsaken Your covenant, torn down Your altars, and put Your prophets to the sword. I alone am left, and they are out to take my life'" (Melachim I 19:9, 10).

[The Sages interpret this verse as a dialogue between Hashem and Eliyahu. Eliyahu: They have forsaken Your covenant.]

Hashem: Is it your covenant by any chance?
Eliyahu: They also tore down Your altars.
Hashem: Were they your altars perhaps?
Eliyahu: They put Your prophets to the sword.
Hashem: But you are still alive!
Eliyahu: I alone am left, and they are out to take my life.
Hashem: Instead of accusing Yisrael, shouldn't you rather denounce the Gentile nations? They maintain a house of debauchery, a house of idol worship, and you indict Yisrael! "Forsake the cities of Aroer" (Yeshayah 17:2). "Go back by the way you came, and on to the wilderness of Damascus" (Melachim I 19:15). This is all explained by the Rabbis in Midrash Chazisa (Shir Hashirim Rabbah 1:6).

Likewise, in Yeshayah's days, the Jewish people were deeply steeped in sin, as it says: "Ah, sinful nation! People laden with iniquity!" (Yeshayah 1:4). They worshipped idols, as it says: "Behind the door and doorpost you have directed your thoughts" (Yeshayah 57:8). There were also murderers among them, as it says: "Alas, she has become a harlot, the faithful city that was filled with justice, where righteousness dwelt—but now murderers" (Yeshayah 1:21). They also desecrated God's Name, saying: "Eat and drink, for tomorrow we shall die" (Yeshayah 22:13). They treated Hashem's *mitzvos* with contempt, saying: "Leave the way! Get off the path! Let us hear no more about the Holy One of Yisrael" (Yeshayah 30:11).

In spite of all this, when Yeshayah said "And I live among a people of unclean lips," he was punished immediately, as it says: "one of the seraphs flew over to me with a live coal. . . . He touched it to my lips and declared, 'Now that this has touched your lips, your guilt shall depart and your sin purged away'" (Yeshayah 6:5–7). According to the Sages, his sin was not forgiven until Menashe killed him (Sanhedrin 103b).

When the angel appeared and pleaded unfavorably against Yehoshua the son of Yehotzadak because his sons had married women who were unsuitable to be the wives of priests, Hashem distanced himself from the angel, as it is written: "Hashem rebuke you, O Satan, may Hashem Who has chosen Jerusalem rebuke you! For this is a brand plucked from the fire" (Zechariah 3:2).

This is the kind of punishment that has been meted out to the pillars of the world—Moshe, Eliyahu, Yeshayah, and the ministering angels—for speaking just a few disparaging words about the Jewish people. You can imagine [what will happen to] the least among the lowly if he unleashes his tongue and speaks out against Jewish communities, rabbis and their students, priests and Levites, calling them sinners, evildoers, disqualified to testify as witnesses, and heretics who deny Hashem the God of Yisrael. Remember, the writer recorded these [slanderous remarks] in his own handwriting! Just think what his punishment will be! [The forced converts] did not rebel against God to seek pleasure and enjoyment. They did not abandon the Jewish religion to attain status and mundane delights. "For they have fled before swords, before the whetted sword, before the bow that was drawn, before the stress of war" (Yeshayah 21:15). This man did not realize that these were not willful transgressors. Hashem will not abandon or forsake them, "for he did not scorn, He did not spurn the plea of the poor" (Tehillim 22:25). Concerning such people the Torah says: "[Yitzchak] smelled the fragrance of his (Yaakov's) clothes" (Bereishis 27:27). Said the Sages, "Instead of reading *begadav* (his clothes), read *bogdav* (those that deceive him)" [Bereishis Rabbah 65].

Whatever this man said are things he dreamed up. During one of the persecutions in which the great rabbis were killed, Rabbi Meir was arrested. People who knew him said, "You are Meir, aren't you?" and he replied, "No, I am not." Pointing at the meat of a pig, they ordered, "Eat this if you are not a Jew." He answered, "I'll be glad to eat it," and made believe he was eating but in fact did not (Avodah Zarah 16b–18). No doubt, in the view of this "humble" person who knows the true meaning of the Torah, Rabbi Meir, who worshipped Hashem secretly, is considered a Gentile, since in his *responsum* he writes that whoever acts publicly like a Gentile while secretly behaving like a Jew is a Gentile.

There is also the famous story of how Rabbi Eliezer was seized by heretics, whose offense is worse than idolatry. The heretics—may Hashem cut them down—ridicule all religion and say such things as: "Believers are fools!" "Students of religion are crazy!" They deny prophecy entirely. Rabbi Eliezer was a famous scholar in the sciences. They asked him: "How can you have reached such a high level of scholarship and still believe in religion?" He answered them, appearing to have adopted their creed, whereas he really had in mind the true faith and no other.

This story is told in the Midrash (Koheles Rabbah 1:8) as follows:

> It happened that Rabbi Eliezer was seized [by heretics] in order to convert him to heresy. The general brought him to the capital and said: "How is it that an old man like you spends his time on things like that?" He replied: "I accept the judge's words as the truth." The general thought that he meant him, whereas he was really referring to Hashem. The general then said: "Rabbi, I see you have faith in me...." [Turning to his men he said]: "I really was wondering, how could he have been led astray by such things?" Thereupon he said [to Rabbi Eliezer]: "I pardon you. You are free to go!"

You see that Rabbi Eliezer pretended to the general that he was a heretic, although in his heart he was devoted to Hashem. Heresy is much more serious than idolatry, as has been outlined throughout the Talmud. Yet according to the writings of this "devout" individual, Rabbi Eliezer should be disqualified. In this current persecution, [our transgression is far less serious,] we do not pretend that we are idol worshippers, we only declare that we believe their creed. They are well aware that we do not believe one word of it. We are saying so only to deceive the king, similar to what the prophet said, "Yet they deceived him with their speech, lied to him with their words" (Tehillim 78:36).

It is well known what happened to the Jewish people in the days of the evil Nebuchadnezzar. The entire population of Babylon, except Chanaiah, Mishael, and Azariah, bowed to the statue. Hashem testified about that generation, stating: "No more shall Yaakov be shamed, no longer his face grow pale" (Yeshayah

29:22). Even the great Torah scholars, if they were present at the time, perhaps bowed down [to the image] in Babylon. I have not come across anyone who called them wicked, Gentiles, or disqualified to testify as witnesses. Neither has Hashem counted their action as the sin of idolatry, because they were forced to do it. The Sages confirm this, with reference to the time of Haman, saying: "They performed [the act of prostrating themselves] outwardly, I will also deal with them only outwardly" (Megillah 12a).

The author of this response is no doubt a God-fearing man; [he should take a lesson from the Almighty how to treat his people]. "Shame on him who argues with his Maker, a potsherd with the potsherds of earth! Shall the clay say to the potter, 'What are you doing?'" (Yeshayah 45:9).

It is known what happened to the Jewish people under the wicked rule of the Greeks. Harsh and evil decrees were issued. There even was a rule that no one was allowed to close the door of his house, so that he would not be alone and be able to fulfill a *mitzvah*. In spite of this, the Sages did not consider them Gentiles or evildoers, but completely righteous. They pleaded for them to Hashem and added in the special prayer of thanksgiving, *Al Hanissim*—"For the Miracles"—the phrase: "and the wicked in the hands of the righteous."...

It is useful to divide my remarks on this subject into five parts: 1) The obligation to *mitzvos* during times of compulsion; 2) Parameters of *Chillul Hashem*—desecration of Hashem's Name—and its punishment; 3) The status of one who gives his life *al Kiddush Hashem*—for the sanctification of Hashem's name—and of one who transgresses under duress; 4) How the present persecution differs from previous ones, and how one should act during this situation; 5) How a person should perceive himself during this persecution, may Hashem end it soon. Amen.

The three prohibitions of idolatry, incest, and manslaughter have a particular stringency. Whenever a person is forced to violate any of these, he is at all times, everywhere, and under all circumstances commanded to give up his life rather than transgress. When I say "at all times," I mean in a time of persecution or otherwise; when I say "everywhere," I mean in private or in public; when I say "under all circumstances," I mean whether the oppressor intends to make him violate his religious beliefs or not. [In any of these situations], he must choose death.

If he is forced to transgress any other commandment, excluding the aforementioned three, he must evaluate the circumstances. If the oppressor does it for his own benefit, be it at a time of persecution or not, privately or publicly, he may violate the law and thereby save his life. This may be found in the Talmud (Sanhedrin 74b,): "But Esther was [forced to sin] in public? Abaye said, 'Esther was passive.' Rava said, 'If it is for his own enjoyment it makes a difference.'" We have a standing rule that the Halachah is decided according to Rava.

To summarize, if the oppressor is doing it for his personal benefit, one should transgress and avoid being killed, even if it is in public and during a time of persecution.

If the oppressor intends to make him [violate his beliefs] and commit a sin, he must evaluate [the times]. In a time of persecution he must give up his life and not transgress, whether in private or in public. If it is not a time of persecution, he should transgress and save his life, if it is in private, but he should choose death if it is in public.

This is the relevant text in the Talmud: "When Rav Dimi [Ravin] arrived, he said in the name of Rabbi Yochanan that even if it is not a time of persecution, he may transgress and not die, only in private; in public he may not violate even a minor *mitzvah*, even changing the way he ties his shoes." By "in public" is meant [in the presence of] ten Jewish males.

The parameters of *Chillul Hashem*—desecration of Hashem's Name—can be divided into two categories: one that applies to [the] general [populace] and one to specific [people].

That which applies to the general populace takes two forms. The first form: when a person commits a sin out of spite, not for the pleasure or enjoyment to be derived from that act, but because he treats it lightly and disdainfully, he is thereby desecrating Hashem's Name. Hashem says concerning one who swears falsely, which is an act that brings him no pleasure or enjoyment: "Do not swear falsely by My Name; [if you do so] you will be desecrating your God's Name" (Vayikra 19:12). If he does it in public, he is openly desecrating Hashem's Name. I explained above that "in public" means in the presence of ten Jews.

The second form: when someone consciously fails to correct his behavior to the point that people begin to talk disparagingly about him. He may not have committed a sin, but he has nonetheless desecrated Hashem's Name. When he is [being perceived as] sinning by his fellow man, a person should be as careful as he is of sinning to his Creator, for Hashem said: "You shall be innocent before Hashem and Yisrael" (Bamidbar 32:22).

The Talmud (Yoma 86a) asks regarding this subject, ["What is meant by *Chillul Hashem*?"] Rav Nachman bar Yitzchak replied: "For example, if people say about someone, May God forgive so-and-so." Another example cited is: "When friends are embarrassed by his reputation."

The parameters of *Chillul Hashem* that apply to specific people also take two forms:

The first form: when a learned person does something that a person of his stature should not do, even though others may do so without compunction. Because he has a reputation of being a man of virtue, people expect more of him. [By his action] he has desecrated Hashem's Name. Rav gave the following definition of *Chillul Hashem*: "For example, when I buy meat and do not pay right away" (*Yoma* 86a). In other words, a person of his eminence should not buy anything unless he pays immediately, at the time of purchase, although the practice [of buying on credit] is quite acceptable with the general public. Rabbi Yochanan said the following on the subject: "For example, if I walk four ells without wearing my *tefillin* and without being engrossed in Torah thoughts [it is considered a *Chillul Hashem*]." He is referring to a man of his stature. Very often we find that the Talmud draws a distinction when the person is an important personality.

The second form: when a learned man behaves in a lowly and loathsome way in his dealings with people. He receives people angrily and with contempt. He is not genial with people and does not treat them with decency and respect. Such a person has desecrated Hashem's Name. The Sages phrased it this way: "When a person is learned but is not honest in his dealings with people and does not speak gently to people, what do people say about him? Woe is to so-and-so who studied Torah!"

If I were not concerned about being long-winded and going off on a tangent, I would explain to you how a person should behave toward others, what his actions and words should be like, and how he should receive people. Thus anyone who spoke to him or had dealings with him would speak about him only in glowing terms. I would explain the meaning of the phrases "being honest in one's dealings with people" and "speaking gently to people." But this would require a full-length book. So I will pick up where I left off.

Kiddush Hashem—Sanctification of Hashem's Name—is the opposite of *Chillul Hashem*. When a person fulfills a *mitzvah* and is inspired by no other motive than his love of Hashem and the desire to serve Him, he has publicly sanctified Hashem's Name. So too, if good things are said about him, he has sanctified Hashem's Name. The Sages phrased it like this: "When a person has studied Torah and Mishnah, attended to Torah scholars and dealt gently with people, what do people say about him? 'See how pleasant is his conduct, how seemly are his deeds!'" Scripture says this about such a man: "And He said to me, 'You are My servant, Yisrael in whom I glory'" (Yeshayah 49:3). Regarding *Kiddush Hashem*, a great person is also special. If a great man avoids distasteful situations, he is sanctifying Hashem's Name. And so we read: "Put crooked speech away from you" (Mishlei 4:24).

Chillul Hashem is a grave sin. Both the deliberate sinner and the inadvertent sinner are punished. The Rabbis phrased it succinctly: "Both unintentional and intentional are liable regarding desecration of the Name" (Avos 4:5). A man is granted a delay in punishment for all sins, but not for the desecration of Hashem's Name. The Rabbis stated: "For the desecration of Hashem's Name no credit is extended. What do we mean that no credit is extended? He is not treated as he is by the storekeeper who extends credit" (Kiddushin 40a). In other words, he will be required to pay for his transgression immediately. The Sages also teach that: "Whoever desecrates Hashem's Name in secret, is punished in public" (Avos 4:5).

This sin is more serious than any other. Neither Yom Kippur, nor suffering, nor repentance can atone for *Chillul Hashem*. This is what the Rabbis say about it: "He who is guilty of *Chillul Hashem* cannot have his sin erased by either repentance, Yom Kippur, or through suffering; they all suspend punishment until death affords forgiveness, for so it says, 'Then the Lord of Hosts revealed Himself to my ears: This iniquity shall never be forgiven you until you die'" (Yeshayah 22:14). This entire discourse refers to the person who willingly desecrates the Name of Hashem, as I shall explain.

Just as *Chillul Hashem* is a grave sin, so is *Kiddush Hashem*—the Sanctification of Hashem's Name—a great *mitzvah* for which you are richly rewarded. Every Jew is required to sanctify Hashem's Name. It is written in Sifra: "I am Hashem your God, who brought you out of the land of Egypt to give you the land of Canaan, [and] to be a God for you" (Vayikra 25:38), on condition that you sanctify My Name publicly. We also find in the Talmud (Sanhedrin 74b) it says: "Rabbi Ami was asked, Is a Noachide commanded to sanctify Hashem's Name?" With regard to a Jew this question was not raised; obviously it may be inferred that a Jew is indeed commanded to sanctify His Name, as it is stated: "I must be sanctified among the Israelites" (Vayikra 22:32).

You must realize that wherever the Sages ruled that one must give up his life rather than transgress, and he does so, he has sanctified Hashem's Name. If ten Jews witnessed his death, he has sanctified the Name publicly. For example:

Chananiah, Mishael and Azariah, Daniel, the Ten Martyrs killed by the Romans, the seven sons of Channah, and all the other Jews who gave their lives for the sanctification of the Name, may the Merciful One speedily avenge their blood. The following verse applies to them: "Bring in My devotees, who made a covenant with Me over sacrifice" (Tehillim 50:5). Our Rabbis related the following verse to them: "I adjure you, O maidens of Jerusalem, by gazelles or by hinds of the fields" (Shir Hashirim 2:7). They expounded: "I adjure you O maidens of Jerusalem"—the persecuted generations; "by the gazelles"—those who did for Me what I desired, and I did what they desired; "by the hinds of the field"—those who shed their blood for Me like the blood of gazelles and hinds. The following verse also applies to them: "It is for Your sake that we are slain all day long" (Tehillim 44:23).

A person to whom God granted the privilege to rise to the lofty level of dying *al Kiddush Hashem*—for the sanctification of Hashem's Name, although he may not have been a Torah scholar, merits to be in the world to come, even if he was sinful as Yerovam ben Nevat and his colleagues. The Rabbis say of this: " 'No one can approach the high rank of those martyred by the government!' Who are we referring to? We cannot say that this refers to Rabbi Akiva and his colleagues [who were martyrs of the Roman government], because surely they had other claims to eminence. It must be referring to the martyrs of Lydda."

If one did not allow himself to be killed, but under duress transgressed and remained alive, he did not do the right thing. Under duress he desecrated Hashem's Name. However, he does not incur any of the seven penalties enumerated in the Torah, namely: the four death penalties of the human court [stoning, burning, beheading, and strangling]; premature death—*kareis*; divinely caused death; and lashes. There is not a single case in the entire Torah in which a person acting under duress is sentenced to any of these punishments, whether his transgression was minor or major. Only a willful sinner is punished, not one who was forced. As it says: "However, if a person commits [an act of idolatry] high-handedly, whether he is a native born or a proselyte, he is blaspheming Hashem, and that person shall be cut off [spiritually] from among his people" (Bamidbar 15:30). The Talmud is full of statements to the effect that a person acting under duress is not guilty. According to the Torah: "...this case is no different from the case where a man rises up against his neighbor and murders him" (Devarim 22:26). We often read in the Talmud: "According to the Torah, a person who acted under duress, is exempt from punishment." He is not characterized as a sinner or a wicked man, and he is not disqualified [by this] from serving as a witness. Only if he [willfully] committed a sin that disqualifies him from serving as a witness. [All that can be said is that] he did not fulfill the *mitzvah* of *Kiddush Hashem*, but under no circumstances can he be considered as having willfully desecrated Hashem's Name.

Whoever says or thinks that a person should be sentenced to death because he violated a law of which the Sages said that he should give up his life rather than transgress, is completely wrong. It simply is not so, as I will explain. What is meant is that it is a *mitzvah* to offer his life, but if he did not, he is not liable to the death penalty. And even if he was forced to worship idols, he is not liable to *kareis* (be cut off spiritually). He certainly is not executed by order of the court. This principle is clearly stated in Toras Kohanim: "Hashem says [concerning a man who gives any of his children to Molech] 'I will direct My anger against that person'" (Vayikra 20:5). Our Sages comment, "but not if he was forced, acted unwittingly, or was misled." It is clear then that if he was forced or misled he is not liable. We are speaking about a prohibition that, had it been done intentionally, has the stringency of *kareis*. Certainly, if he was forced to commit sins that, when done intentionally, are punishable by lashes, he is not at all liable. The prohibition of *Chillul Hashem* is a negative commandment, [that is not liable to *kareis*]. As it is stated: "Do not desecrate My Holy Name" (Vayikra 22:32). [Surely one who transgresses under duress is not liable.]

It is a known fact that making a false oath is a desecration of Hashem's Name. As it says: "Do not swear falsely by My Name; [if you do], you will be desecrating your God's Name. I am Hashem" (Vayikra 19:12). Still, the Mishnah reads: "One is allowed to vow to murderers, robbers and tax-collectors that what he has is *terumah*, [thereby saving his produce]. Beis Shammai states that one may only use the form of a *neder* (vow). Beis Hillel says that one may also use the formula of *shevuah* (oath)" (Nedarim 3:4).

These things are clearly spelled out. There is no need to bring any proofs to support them; how can anyone say that the law regarding a person who acted under duress and one who acted voluntarily is the same? Our Sages ruled in many cases: "Let him transgress and not give up his life." Now this man [who wrote this response] considers himself to be more worthy than the Rabbis and more scrupulous in the observance of the *mitzvos*. He openly declares his willingness to surrender his life in all cases, and thinks that he is sanctifying Hashem's Name. However, if he would indeed act this way [and surrender his life in every instance], he would be a sinful and rebellious individual. He would bear guilt for his soul, for Hashem said: "Keep My decrees and laws, since by keeping them a person will live" (Vayikra 18:5)—and not die (Sanhedrin 74a).

You have to realize that in all the persecutions that occurred in the time of the Sages, they were ordered to violate *mitzvos* and to perform [sinful] acts, as we are told in the Talmud: they were forbidden to study Torah and to circumcise their sons. They were ordered to have intercourse with their wives when they were ritually unclean. But in the present persecution they are not required to do any forbidden action, only to say something. If a person wishes to fulfill the 613 commandments of the Torah in secret, he can do so. He is not guilty of anything unless he happens to desecrate the Shabbos without being forced to do so. This oppressive regime does not force anyone to do any prohibited act, just to make an oral affirmation [of faith]. They know very well that we do not mean what we say, and that the person making the affirmation is only doing so to escape the king's wrath and to satisfy him with a recitation of meaningless incantations.

If anyone asks me whether he should offer his life or make this acknowledgment, I tell him to acknowledge and not choose death. However if one died a martyr's death rather than affirm the divine mission of "that man" [Muhammad], we can say that he acted righteously. He will receive an abundant reward from Hashem. His position will be in the loftiest levels, for he has given his life for the sanctity of Hashem. However, one should not stay in the country under the rule of that king. [Until he is able to leave,] he should stay at home, do his work secretly, and go out only if it is absolutely essential.

There has never been a persecution as unusual as this, where people are only compelled to say something. Our Rabbis ruled that a person should choose death and not transgress. We cannot infer that they meant speech that does not involve action. One must submit to martyrdom only when he is forced to do something that he is forbidden to do.

A person who is caught in this persecution should conduct himself along the following lines: let him set his sights on observing as many of the *mitzvos* as he can. If he transgressed often or desecrated the Shabbos, he should still not carry what he is not allowed to carry. He should not say to himself: "The transgressions I have made are more grave than [the carrying on Shabbos] from which I am abstaining now." Let him be as careful about observing the *mitzvos* as he can.

A person must be aware of this fundamental Torah principle. Yerovam ben Nevat and others like him are punished for [the grievous sin of] making the calves as well as for disregarding the [comparatively minor] law of *eiruv tavshilin* and similar laws. Don't say that to him applies the rule of "he who has committed two offenses must be held answerable for the more severe one only" (Gittin 52b). This principle applies only to punishments meted out by man in this world. Hashem metes out punishment for minor and serious sins, and He rewards people for everything they do. A person should be aware that he is held accountable for every transgression he committed. He is rewarded for every *mitzvah* he performed. Things are not the way people think.

The recommendation I followed myself, and the advice I want to give to all my friends and anyone that consults me, is to leave those places and to go to where we can practice our religion and fulfill the Torah without compulsion and fear. Let him leave his family and his possessions. The Law of Hashem that He has given us as a heritage is very great. Our commitment to it takes precedence to material values. All thinkers scorn material wealth, which is transitory, but the fear of Hashem endures.

Let us say there were two Jewish cities, one superior to the other in its deeds and conduct, more meticulous with *mitzvos* and more dedicated to their observance. A God-fearing person is required to leave the city where the actions are not quite proper and move to the better city. Our Sages admonished us in this regard, stating: "You should not live in a city where there are fewer than ten righteous residents." They find support for this in the verse [where Abraham pleads with Hashem to spare the city of Sodom, saying,] "Suppose there are ten [righteous people] found there?" And He answered: "I will not destroy for the sake of the ten" (Bereishis 18:32). This is what one should do when both cities are Jewish. Certainly, if a Jew lives in a place inhabited by Gentiles, he must leave it and go to a more favorable place. He must make every effort to do so although he may place himself in jeopardy. He must escape that bad place where he cannot practice his religion properly, and set out until he arrives at a decent place.

The prophets have postulated that he who lives among heretics is considered one of them. They derived it from [the words of King David who said, when he was banished from Eretz Yisrael], "For they have driven me out today, so that I cannot have a share in Hashem's possession, rather I am told, 'Go and worship other gods'" (Shmuel 126:19). You see that [David] equates his dwelling among Gentiles with the worship of other gods. In the same vein, David says: "O Lord, You know I hate those who hate You and loathe Your adversaries" (Tehillim

139:21), and also: "I am a companion to all who fear You, to those who keep Your precepts" (Tehillim 119:63). Similarly, we see that our father Abraham despised his family and his hometown. He ran for his life to escape from the creed of the heretics.

He should make an effort to leave the nonbelievers' environment when they do not force him to follow in their ways. But when they coerce him to transgress even one of the *mitzvos*, he is forbidden to remain in that place. He must leave and abandon everything he owns, travel day and night until he finds a spot where he can practice his religion. There is a big, wide world out there!

The excuse of the person who claims that he has to take care of his family and his household really does not hold water. "A brother cannot redeem a man or pay his ransom to God" (Tehillim 49:8). In my opinion, it is not right to make this claim to avoid the obligation. He should emigrate to a decent place and under no circumstances continue to stay in the land of persecution. Whoever remains there is a transgressor and desecrates Hashem's Name, and is almost an intentional sinner.

There are those who delude themselves into believing that they should remain where they are until King Mashiach comes to the lands of the Maghreb. Then they will go to Jerusalem. I do not know how they will disentangle themselves from the present persecution. They are transgressors, and they cause others to sin. The prophet Yirmiyah had people like them in mind when he said, "They offer healing offhand for the wounds of My people, saying, 'all is well, all is well'" (Yirmiyah 6:14). There is no dependable set time for the coming of Mashiach. One does not know if he is coming soon or in the distant future. The obligation of keeping the *mitzvos* is not dependent on the coming of Mashiach. We are required to engross ourselves in Torah and *mitzvos*. We must strive to achieve perfection in both of them. Then, if Hashem grants us, our children, or grandchildren the privilege to witness the coming of Mashiach, so much the better. If he does not come we have not lost anything. On the contrary, we have gained by doing what we had to do.

A person may be in a place where he sees Torah study coming to an end, the Jewish population declining and gradually disappearing, and he himself unable to practice his religion. He says: "I am going to stay here until Mashiach comes. Then I will be extricated from this predicament." Such a person is guilty of wickedness, destructive callousness, and of wiping out the Jewish faith and ideology. That is my opinion, and Hashem knows the truth.

A person may be unable to fulfill the aforementioned advice [to leave the land of persecution], either because of his fondness for his [native] country or because of his fear of the dangers of a sea voyage. He stays where he is. He, then, must regard himself as desecrating Hashem's Name, not quite deliberately, but almost so. He must consider himself as being scolded by God and punished for his bad deeds. At the same time, he should realize that if he performs a *mitzvah*, the Holy One, Blessed is He, will give him a twofold reward. He did the *mitzvah* for the sake of Heaven, and not to impress others or to be regarded as an observant Jew. In addition, a person's reward for performing a *mitzvah* knowing that if caught, he will lose his life and all his possessions, is much greater than that of a person who fulfills a *mitzvah* without fear. The Torah, referring to a time like the present [when observance of *mitzvos* is done for the sake of Heaven and despite the fact that one's life is in danger], says: "If only you seek Him with all your heart and soul" (Devarim 4:29). Nevertheless, you should not take your mind off your plans to leave the provinces that Hashem is angry with, and do your utmost [to carry them out].

It is not right to shun and despise people who desecrate the Shabbos. Rather, you should reach out to them and encourage them to fulfill the *mitzvos*. The Rabbis ruled that a sinner who willfully transgressed should be welcomed to the synagogue and not humiliated. They based their pronouncement on Shlomoh's advice: "A thief should not be despised for stealing to appease his hunger" (Mishlei 6:30). This means: do not despise sinners in Yisrael when they come secretly to "steal" *mitzvos*.

Ever since we were banished from our land, persecutions have been our fate, as it says: "From our youth it (the persecution) raised us as a father and from our mother's womb it has directed us" (Iyov 31:18). It also says in many places in the Talmud: "a persecution is likely to pass" (Kesuvos 3b). May Hashem put an end to this one.

"In those days and at that time—declares Hashem—the iniquity of Yisrael shall be sought, and there shall be none; the sins of Yehudah, and none shall be found; for I will pardon those I allow to survive" (Yirmiyah 50:12). Let the prophecy be fulfilled speedily in our days. May it be His will. Amen.

Fragment of the *Guide of the Perplexed*

Translated from the Latin by M. Friedlander

That which is impossible has a permanent and constant property, which is not the result of some agent and cannot in any way change, and consequently we do not ascribe to God the power of doing what is impossible. No thinking man denies the truth of this maxim; none ignore it but such as have no idea of Logic. There is, however, a difference of opinion among philosphers with reference to the existence of any particular thing. Some of them consider its existence to be impossible, and hold that God cannot produce the thing in question, whilst others think that it is possible, and that God can create it if He pleases to do so. For example, all philosophers consider that it is impossible for one substratum to have at the same moment two opposite properties, or for the elementary components of a thing, substance and accident, to interchange, so that the substance becomes accident, and the accident becomes substance, or for a material substance to be without accident. Likewise it is impossible that God should produce a being like Himself, or annihilate, corporify, or change Himself. The power of God is not assumed to extend to any of these impossibilities. But the existence of accidents independent of substance is possible according to one class of philosophers, the Mutazilah, whilst according to others it is impossible; it must, however, be added that those who admit the existence of an accident independent of substance have not arrived at this conclusion by philosophical research alone; but it was mainly by the desire to defend certain religious principles, which speculation had greatly shaken, that they had recourse to this theory. In a similar manner the creation of corporeal things, otherwise than from a substance is possible according to our view, while the philosophers say that it is impossible. Again, while philosophers say that it is impossible to produce a square with a diagonal equal to one of the sides, or a solid angle that includes four right angles, or similar things, it is thought possible by some persons who are ignorant of mathematics and who only know the words of these propositions but have no idea of that which is expressed by them. I wonder whether this gate of research is open, so that all may freely enter, and while one imagines a thing and considers it possible, another is at liberty to assert that such a thing is

70

impossible by its very nature; or whether the gate is closed and guarded by certain rules, so that we are able to decide with certainty whether a thing is physically impossible. I should also like to know, in the latter case, whether imagination or reason has to examine and test objects as to their being possible or not; likewise how things imagined and things conceived intellectually are to be distinguished from each other. For it occurs that we consider a thing as physically possible, and then someone objects, or we ourselves fear that our opinion is only the result of imagination and not that of reason. In such a case it would be desirable to ascertain whether there exists some faculty to distinguish between imagination and intellect, [and if so,] whether this faculty is different from both, or whether it is part of the intellect itself to distinguish between intellectual and imaginary objects. All this requires investigation, but it does not belong to the theme of this chapter.

We have thus shown that according to each one of the different theories there are things which are impossible, whose existence cannot be admitted, and whose creation is excluded from the power of God, and the assumption that God does not change their nature does not imply weakness in God or a limit to His power. Consequently things impossible remain impossible, and do not depend on the action of an agent. It is now clear that a difference of opinion exists only as to the question to which of the two classes a thing belongs; whether to the class of the impossible or to that of the possible. Note it.

Gonzalo de Berceo
(Spain, 1190–after 1265)
"The Jews of Toledo"
Translated from the Hebrew by David M. Gitlitz

Gonzalo de Berceo is the first Spanish poet whose name is known. Affiliated to the Catholic Church, he was educated in a monastery and became a deacon in 1220 and a presbyter in 1237. He belonged to the school of *mesters de clerecía*. He wrote in the Castilian dialect of the Rioja region. His books include *Milagros de Nuestra Señora* [*Miracles of Our Lady*], *Martirio de San Lorenzo* [*Martyrdom of St. Lawrence*], and *De los signos que aparecerán antes del Juicio* [*Of the Signs to Appear before the Last Judgment*]. The poem by Berceo that follows is evidence of the anti-Semitic lore of the thirteenth century. It is a call to arms against the Jewish infidels who, in their ingrained evil, repeatedly crucify Jesus Christ. The poem is representative of Berceo's views. In another one by him, about the corruption of Jewish children, he states: "As quick as you can count/ one coin with your thumb,/ this Jew a mound of embers/ and ashes had become;/ not one prayer for his soul/ was said, no psalm was sung;/ instead they cried great curses/ and insults quite a sum."

> In noble Toledo, where the archbishop holds sway,
> toward the middle of August on the holy feast day
> of Christ's glorious Mother, to whom we all pray,
> a great miracle happened, so the people say.
>
> The archbishop himself to God consecrated,
> on the highest altar at mass officiated;
> all the multitude with devotion waited;
> the aisles were full, the choir populated.
>
> The populace devoutly were engaged in prayer,
> like those who for salvation to God their souls bare;

a voice in great anguish resounded in the air,
which troubled all the people who were assembled there.

A pained anguished voice rang out in the sky:
"Listen to me, Christians, and I will tell you why
the Jewish people, deaf of ear and blind of eye,
today against Sir Christ even more than ever vie.

According to the stories in holy Scriptures' lore,
they waged against Sir Christ their persecuting war;
their deeds have hurt me too, they've drilled me to the core
although their wild excesses have injured them still more.

They pitied not the Son to whom no ill was due,
nor His Mother who was forced His agonies to view;
a people so unheedful, who would such evil do,
deserve that their misdeeds on themselves should accrue.

Those false deceitful people, born on an evil night,
have brought old tribulations newly to my sight;
in me they've caused great anguish, my torments they incite;
my Son is on the cross, who of sinners is the light.

Once again to the cross they have affixed my Son;
no one can comprehend how deep my sorrows run;
in Toledo this vile crew has once again begun
to fester; more evil than they are there are none."

All the gathered clergy thereupon this voice did hear,
and all the Mozarabs who were congregated near;
that it was Holy Mary's voice to them was clear,
and that the Jews were doing Her injuries severe.

The archbishop who was singing the mass broke off his song
and spoke to the people who gathered in that throng;

"Believe me, my council, that voice you heard so strong
protested that She suffers from these prideful folk great wrong.

Be advised that the Jews are committing some vile thing
against Jesus Christ, Mary's Son, Holy King;
this causes his Mother renewed suffering;
her anguish is real, it has a truthful ring.

You officials of the city, you leaders gathered here,
you must not ignore all this that you hear;
If you peer into this their tracks will appear;
this foul deed requires that your justice be severe.

Let's go to the chief rabbis' homes; we must not tarry;
we're sure to find there something out of the ordinary;
we have no time for eating, no time for making merry
if we would not incur the wrath of Holy Mary."

The clerics and the people and all their retinues
rushed off headlong together to the district of the Jews;
Jesus Christ was their guide, the Virgin was their muse;
they rapidly discovered the vile treacherous news.

There where the most honored rabbi did reside
they found a wax figure as a man personified;
exactly like Sir Christ it had been crucified:
made fast with large nails, a great wound in its side.

To our great dishonor God's body they scored,
over and over, this whole evil horde;
although with small pleasure they put them to the sword:
as they did was done to them, thanks be to the Lord.

They quickly dispatched all the ones that they caught;
they gave them bad graves, as surely they ought;
they heard the final words and to bad deaths were brought:
that they'd acted rashly these folks were thus taught.

Whosoever should hurt Holy Mary this way,
as these folks were paid thus shall be their pay;
instead let us honor Her, serve and obey,
for Her kind intercession shall aid us one day.

Nahmanides

(Spain, 1195-1270)
Fragment of *Disputation of Barcelona*
Translated from the German by Nahum N. Glatzer

Theological debates between Jewish and Christian religious leaders were a *sine qua non* in the Middle Ages. As Nahum N. Glatzer suggests in the book *The Judiac Tradition* (1969), the four-day debate at Barcelona in 1263, in which Moses ben Nahman (a.k.a. Nahmanides, and known also as Bonastrug de Porta), the rabbi of Gerona, had a leading role, was one of the major religious disputations. There were other disputations, such as those in Paris in 1240, Avila in 1375, and Tortosa in 1413–1414. The other debater in the Barcelona one was Fra Paulo (a.k.a. Pablo Christiani), a converted Jew who had become a Dominican monk; some scholars assume that he taught the Hebrew Bible and rabbinic writings to the scholarly Dominican, Raymond Martini. The disputation was sponsored by King James I of Aragon and was attended by Raymond Martini, Raymond de Peñaforte, the king's confessor, also a Dominican, the Franciscan Peter de Janua, and the aristocracy and representatives of the population. Nahmanides wrote down in Hebrew his impressions. After the debate, he was banished from Aragon by Pope Clement IV. He went to Palestine in 1267, where he died. His account appeared in print first in Wagenscil's *Tela ignea satanae* (1681), together with a Latin translation; both text and translation are corrupt. A more reliable text appeared in Constantinople in 1710. The best edition, on which Glatzer based his translation, is by M. Steinschneider (1860).

Our lord the king had commanded me to debate with Fra Paulo in His Majesty's palace, in the presence of himself and his council, in Barcelona. To this command I replied that I would accede if I were granted freedom of speech, whereby I craved both the permission of the king and of Fra Raymond of Peñaforte and his associates who were present. Fra Raymond of Peñaforte replied that this I could have so long as I did not speak disrespectfully. . . .

Then Fra Paulo began by saying that he would prove from our Talmud that the Messiah of whom the Prophets had witnessed had already come. I replied that before we argued on that, I would like him to show and tell me how this could possibly be true.... Did he wish to say that the scholars who appear in the Talmud believed concerning Jesus that he was the Messiah, and that they believed that he was completely man and truly God in accordance with the Christian conceptions of him? Was it not indeed a known fact that Jesus existed in the days of the Second Temple, being born and put to death before the destruction of that Temple? But the scholars of the Talmud were later than this destruction.... Now, if these scholars had believed in the Messiahship of Jesus and that he was genuine and his religious belief true, and if they wrote those things which Fra Paulo affirms he is going to prove that they wrote, then how was it that they continued to hold by the Jewish faith and their original religious usage? For they were Jews and continued to abide in the religion of the Jews all their days. They died as Jews, they and their children, and their disciples who heard all the words they uttered. Why did they not apostatize and turn to the religion of Jesus as has done Fra Paulo who understands from their saying that the Christian faith is the true faith? ...

Fra Paulo took up the debate and claimed that in the Talmud it was stated that the Messiah had already come. He brought forward that Haggadic story, contained in the Midrash to the Book of Lamentations, about the man who was ploughing when his cow began lowing. An Arab was passing by and said to the man: "O Jew, O Jew, untie your cow, untie your plough, untie your coulter, for the temple has been destroyed." The man untied his cow, his plough, and his coulter. The cow lowed a second time. The Arab said to the man: "Tie your cow, tie your plough, tie your coulter, for your Messiah has been born."

To this I answered: "I do not give any credence at all to this Haggadah but it provides proof of my argument." At this the fellow shouted: "See how the writings of his fellow Jews are denied him!" I replied: "I certainly do not believe that the Messiah was born on the day of the destruction of the Temple and as for this Haggadah, either it is not true or it has another interpretation of the sort called the mystical explanations of the wise. But I shall accept the story's plain literal statement, which you have put forward, since it furnishes me with support. Observe then that the story says that at the time of the destruction of the Temple, after it had been destroyed, on that very day, the Messiah was born. If this be so, then Jesus is not the Messiah as you affirm that he is. For he was born and was put to death before the destruction of the Temple took place, his birth being nearly two hundred years before that event according to the true chronology and seventy-three years previous to that event according to your reckonings." At these words of mine my opponent was reduced to silence.

Master Gilles, who was the king's justiciary, then replied to me with the remark: "At the present moment we are not discussing about Jesus, but the question rather is whether the Messiah has come or not. You say that he has not come, but this Jewish book says that he has come."

To this I said: "You are, as is the practice of those of your profession, taking refuge in a subtlety of retort and argument. But nevertheless I shall answer you on this point. The scholars have not stated that the Messiah has come, but they have said that he has been born. For, for example, on the day when Moses our teacher was born he had not come, nor was he a redeemer, but when he came to Pharaoh by the commandment of the Holy One and said to Pharaoh, 'Thus saith the Lord, Let my people go,' (Exod. 8:1) then he had come. And likewise the Messiah when he shall come to the Pope and shall say to him by the commandment of God: 'Let my people go,' then he shall have come. But until that day comes, he shall not have come, nor [till then] will there be any Messiah at all. For David the king, on the day when he was born, was not a king nor was he a Messiah, but when Elijah shall anoint one to be a Messiah by the commandment of the deity, he [the anointed one] shall be called Messiah and when, afterwards, the Messiah shall come to the Pope to redeem us, then it shall be announced that a redeemer has come."

Hereupon my opponent Fra Paulo urged that the Biblical section Isaiah 52:13, beginning with the words "Behold, my servant shall deal wisely," treats of the subject of the death of the Messiah, of his coming into the power of his enemies, and that they set him among the wicked, as happened also in the case of Jesus. "You do believe," asked Fra Paulo, "that this section is speaking of the Messiah?"

I answered him: "According to the real meaning of the passage, the section speaks only of the community of Israel the people. For thus the prophets address them constantly, as in Isaiah 41:8: 'Thou Israel my servant' and as in Isaiah 44:1: 'O Jacob my servant.'"

Fra Paulo then rejoined: "But I can show you from the statements of the scholars that in their view the Biblical section is speaking of the Messiah."

I replied to this as follows: "It is true that our teachers in the Haggadic books do interpret the servant, in the Biblical section referred to, as indicating the Messiah. But they never assert that he was slain by his enemies. For you will never find in any of the writings of Israel, neither in the Talmud nor in the Haggadic works, that the Messiah the son of David will be slain or that he will ever be delivered into the hands of his foes or buried among them that are wicked."

My opponent, Fra Paulo, returned again to the point discussed, with the assertion that in the Talmud it was distinctly stated that Rabbi Joshua ben Levi had asked Elijah when the Messiah would come and Elijah had given him the reply: "Ask the Messiah himself." Joshua then asked: "And where is he?" Elijah said: "At the gates of Rome among the poor." Joshua went there and found him and put a question to him, and so on. "Now," said Fra Paulo, "if what the Talmud here says be so, then the Messiah has already come and has been in Rome—but it was Jesus who was the ruler in Rome."

I said to him in reply to this: "And is it not plain from this very passage you cite that the Messiah has not come? For you will observe that Joshua asked Elijah when the Messiah would come. Likewise also the latter himself was asked by Joshua: When will the Master come? Thus he had not yet come. Yet, according to the literal sense of these Haggadic narratives, the Messiah has been born; but such is not my own belief."

At this point our lord the king interposed with the question that if the Messiah had been born on the day of the destruction of the Temple, which was more than a thousand years ago, and had not yet come, how could he come now, seeing that it was not in the nature of man to live a thousand years?

My answer to him was: "Already the conditions of discussion have been laid down which preclude me from disputing with you and you from interposing in this debate—but among those who have been in former times, Adam and Methuselah were well nigh a thousand years old, and Elijah and Enoch more than this since these are they who [yet] are alive with God."

The king then put the question: "Where then is the Messiah at present?"

To this I replied: "That question does not serve the purposes of this discussion and I shall not give an answer to it, but perchance you will find him whom you ask about at the gates of Toledo if you send thither one of your courtiers." This last remark I made to the king in irony. The assembly then stood adjourned, the king appointing the time for the resumption of the debate to be the day after next.

On the day appointed, the king came to a convent that was within the city bounds, where was assembled all the male population, both Gentiles and Jews. There were present the bishop, all the priests, the scholars of the Minorities [the

Franciscans] and the Preaching Friars [the Dominicans]. Fra Paulo, my opponent, stood up to speak, when I, intervening, requested our lord the king that I should now be heard. The king replied that Fra Paulo should speak first because he was the petitioner. But I urged that I should now be allowed to express my opinion on the subject of the Messiah and then afterwards, he, Fra Paulo, could reply on the question of accuracy.

I then rose and, calling upon all the people to attend, said: "Fra Paulo has asked me if the Messiah of whom the prophets have spoken has already come and I have asserted that he has not come. Also a Haggadic work, in which someone states that on the very day on which the Temple was destroyed the Messiah was born, was brought by Fra Paulo as evidence on his behalf. I then stated that I gave no credence to this pronouncement of the Haggadah but that it lent support to my contention. And now I am going to explain to you why I said that I do not believe it. I would have you know that we Jews have three kinds of writings—first, the Bible in which we all believe with perfect faith. The second kind is that which is called Talmud which provides a commentary to the commandments of the Torah, for in the Torah there are six hundred and thirteen commandments and there is not a single one of them which is not expounded in the Talmud, and we believe in it in regard to the exposition of the commandments. Further, there is a third kind of writing that we have, called Midrash, that is to say sermonic literature of the sort that would be produced if the bishop here should stand up and deliver a sermon which someone in the audience who liked it should write down. To a document of this sort, should any of us extend belief, then well and good, but if he refuses to do so, no one will do him any harm. For we have scholars who in their writings say that the Messiah will not be born until the approach of the End-time, when he will come to deliver us from exile. For this reason I do not believe in this book [which Fra Paulo cites] when it makes the assertion that the Messiah was born on the day of the destruction of the Temple."

My opponent now stood up and said: "I shall bring further evidence that the Messianic age has already been." But I craved my lord the king to be allowed to speak a little longer and spoke as follows: "Religion and truth, and justice which for us Jews is the substance of religion, do not depend upon a Messiah. For you, our lord the king, are, in my view, more profitable than a Messiah. You are a king and he is a king, you a Gentile, and he [to be] king of Israel—for a Messiah is but a human monarch as you are. And when I, in exile and in affliction and servitude, under the reproach of the peoples who reproach us continually, can yet worship my Creator with your permission, my gain is great. For now I make of my body a whole-burnt offering to God and thus become more and more worthy of the life of the world to come. But when there shall be a king of Israel of my own religion ruling over all peoples, then I would be forced to abide in the law of the Jews, and my reward would not be so much increased.

But the core of the contention and the disagreement between Jews and Christians lies in what you Christians assert in regard to the chief topic of faith, namely the deity, for here you make an assertion that is exceedingly distasteful. And you, our lord the king, are a Christian born of a Christian and all your days you have listened to priests and they have filled your brain and the marrow of your bones with this doctrine and I would set you free again from that realm of habit and custom. Of a certainty the doctrine which you believe and which is a dogma of your faith cannot be accepted by reason. Nature does not admit of it. The prophets have never said anything that would support it. Also the miracle itself cannot be made intelligible by the doctrine in question as I shall make clear with ample proofs at the proper time and place. That the Creator of heaven and earth and all that in them is should withdraw into and pass through the womb of a certain Jewess and should grow there for nine months and be born a small child and after this grow up to be handed over to his enemies who condemn him to death and kill him, after which, you say, he came to life and returned to his former abode—neither the mind of Jew nor of any man will sustain this. Hence vain and fruitless is your arguing with us, for here lies the root of our disagreement. However, as it is your wish, let us further discuss the question of the Messiah."

Fra Paulo then said to me: "Then you do believe that the Messiah has come?"

I replied: "No, but I believe and am convinced that he has not come and there never has been anyone who has said concerning himself that he was Messiah—nor will there ever be such who will say so [concerning themselves]—except Jesus. And it is impossible for me to believe in the Messiahship of Jesus, because the prophet says of the Messiah that 'he shall have dominion from sea to sea and from the river until the ends of the earth' (Psalms 72:8). Jesus, on the other hand, never had dominion, but in his lifetime he was pursued by his enemies and hid himself from them, falling finally into their power, whence he was not able to liberate himself. How then could he save all Israel?

Moreover, after his death dominion was not his. For in regard to the Empire of Rome, he had no part in the growth of that. Since before men believed in him the city of Rome ruled over most of the world and after faith in him had spread, Rome lost many lands over which it once held sovereign power. And now the followers of Muhammad possess a larger empire than Rome has. In like manner the prophet Jeremiah declares that in the Messianic age 'they shall teach no more every man his neighbor, and every man his brother, saying, Know the Lord: for they shall all know me' (31:34), while in Isaiah it is written, that 'the earth shall be full of the knowledge of the Lord, as the waters cover the sea' (11:9). Moreover the latter prophet states that in this time, 'they shall beat their swords into ploughshares . . . nation shall not lift up sword against nation, neither shall they learn war any more' (2:4). But since the days of Jesus up to the present the whole world has been full of violence and rapine, the Christians more than other peoples being shedders of blood and revealers likewise of indecencies. And how hard it would be for you, my lord the king, and for those knights of yours, if they should learn war no more!" . . . Afterwards on the same day I had audience of the king, who remarked: "The debate still remains to be concluded. For I have never seen anyone who was in the wrong argue so well as you have." Then I heard in the palace court that it was the will of the king and of the Preaching Friars [the Dominicans] to visit the synagogue on the Sabbath. So I tarried in the city for eight days.

When they came to the synagogue on the following Sabbath I addressed our lord the king in words that were worthy of the occasion and of his office. . . .

Fra Raymond of Peñaforte rose up and gave a discourse on the subject of the Trinity and asserted that the Trinity was wisdom and will and power. "And had not also the master," he said, "in a synagogue in Gerona assented to what Fra Paulo had said on this point?"

At this I got to my feet and spoke as follows: "I ask both Jews and Gentiles to give me their attention on this matter. When Fra Paulo asked me in Gerona if I believed in the Trinity, I replied: 'What is the Trinity? Do you mean that three material bodies, of the sort that men have, constitute the Godhead?' He said: 'No.' Then I asked: 'Do you mean that the Trinity consists of three subtle substances such as souls or that it is three angles?' He said: 'No.' 'Or do you mean,' I enquired, 'that the Trinity is one substance which is a compound of three substances such as are those bodies which are compounded of the four elements?' He said: 'No.' 'If that is the case' said I, 'then what is the Trinity?' He answered:

'Wisdom and will and power.' To which I replied that I acknowledged that the deity was wise and not foolish, and willful beyond possibility, and powerful and not weak, but that the expression Trinity was entirely misleading. For wisdom in the Creator is not an unessential quality, but He and His wisdom are one, and He and His will are one, and He and His power are one—and, if this be so, the wisdom and the will and the power are one whole. And even if these were unessential qualities of God, the thing which is the Godhead is not three but is one, bearing three unessential qualities."

Then Fra Paulo stood up and said that he believed in the perfect unity of the Deity but that nevertheless there was in that unity a Trinity, and this was a doctrine very profound, for neither the angels nor the princes of the upper regions could comprehend it.

My answer to this was: "It is clear that no person believes what he does not know. Hence it is that the angels do not believe in a Trinity." The associates of Fra Paulo made him remain silent. Our lord the king rose up and he and those with him descended from the place where the prayer-desk was, each going their several ways.

On the morrow, I had audience of our lord the king, whose words to me were: "Return to your city in safety and in peace." Then he gave me three hundred dinars and I took my leave of him with much affection. May God make him worthy of the life of the world to come, Amen.

Alfonso X the Wise
(Spain, 1221–1284)
"Concerning the Jews: *Las siete partidas*"
Translated from the Spanish by Dwayne E. Carpenter

Through the counsel of advisors, King Alfonso X, known as the Wise because of his passion for scholarship, issued his famous code of law, *Las siete partidas*, in which he established what was permitted or not of various inhabitants of the Iberian Peninsula, including the Jews and Muslims. Among other aspects, in this code he offered incentives for conversion. Alfonso X is famous for establishing Arabic and Latin schools. He was often criticized for not making enough effort to convert Muslims to Christianity. The following segment—eleven laws—is devoted to the Jews. For instance, no Jew was allowed to hold an "esteemed position or public office so as to be able to oppress any Christian in any way whatsoever." This code, nonetheless, was not implemented thoroughly. Alfonso X was also responsible for issuing astronomical tablets, the so-called Alfonsine Tables, which two Jewish astronomers prepared on his behalf, and which Columbus used in his journeys.

Jews are a type of people who, although they do not believe in the faith of Our Lord Jesus Christ, nevertheless have always been permitted by the great Christian lords to live among them. Wherefore in the preceding title we spoke of diviners and other men who claim to know the future—showing contempt for God by their desire to be like Him in attempting to know His deeds and secrets—we wish here to speak of the Jews who oppose and insult the marvelous and holy deed He performed when He sent His Son, Our Lord Jesus Christ, into the world to save sinners. And we shall indicate the meaning of the term Jew [*judío*], the origin of this name, and why the Church and the great Christian lords allowed the Jews to live among them; also, in what manner Jews should conduct their lives while they live among Christians and what they are forbidden to do according to our law; which judges may punish them for misdeeds they may have committed or for debts they may owe; how Jews who convert to

Christianity should not suffer disabilities, and what advantage a Jew who becomes a Christian has over those who do not convert, and what punishment those Jews deserve who harm or dishonor Jews who convert; and what punishment those Christians merit who adopt Judaism and what penalty Jews deserve who convert their Muslim slaves.

Religious and Historical Framework

Law 1: "What is meant by the word Jew [judio], what is the origin of the term, and why the Church and the great Christian lords have allowed the Jews to live among Christians"

A Jew is said to be one who believes in and observes literally the law of Moses and who practices circumcision and performs the other requirements of that law. And this name [*judío*] is derived from the tribe of Judah, which was more noble and valiant than any of the other tribes. Furthermore, that tribe possessed another advantage in that from it the Jews were to choose their king. In addition, members of that tribe always struck the first blows in battle. And the reason the Church, emperors, kings, and other princes permitted the Jews to reside among Christians is this: that they might live forever as in captivity and serve as a reminder to mankind that they are descended from those who crucified Our Lord Jesus Christ.

Acceptable Jewish Conduct

Law 2: "In what way Jews ought to conduct their lives while they reside among Christians, and what things they are forbidden to do according to our law, and what punishment those Jews deserve who act in a contrary manner"

Jews ought to conduct themselves meekly and without disorder among Christians, observing their own law and not speaking ill of the faith of Our Lord Jesus Christ which Christians observe. Furthermore, they must take great care not to preach or convert any Christian, praising their own law and maligning ours. And whoever does contrary to this shall die as a result and lose all that he has. And because we heard that in some places the Jews reenacted derisively— and continue to do so—on Good Friday the Passion of Our Lord Jesus Christ, stealing children and placing them on a cross, or forming waxen images and crucifying them when children are unavailable, we order that if we discover from this time forward that such a thing has occurred in any part of our kingdom, and if it can be determined, then all those involved shall be seized, arrested, and brought before the king. And as soon as he has determined the truth of the matter, he shall order the guilty parties to be mercilessly put to death. In addition, we order that on Good Friday no Jew shall dare to leave his quarter; rather, the Jews shall remain there behind closed doors until Saturday morning. And if they do otherwise, we decree that they shall have no claim to reparations for any damage or dishonor done them by Christians.

Jews in Public Office

Law 3: "No Jew may hold any office or position in order to oppress Christians"
Jews were of old most honored and possessed very great privileges over all other peoples, for they alone were called the people of God. But they rejected Him who had granted them honors and privileges, and instead of honoring Him, they scorned Him, putting Him to death most shamefully on the cross. It is reasonable and proper, therefore, that as a consequence of the great error and evil they committed they should lose the honors and privileges they once held. As such, from that day forward when they crucified Our Lord Jesus Christ, they have never had kings or priests from among themselves, as they once did. And the emperors who were formerly rulers of the entire world deemed it right and proper that the Jews should forfeit all the honors and privileges they once enjoyed because of the treason they committed in killing their lord. As a result, no Jew may ever again hold an esteemed position or public office so as to be able to oppress any Christian in any way whatsoever.

Legislation Concerning the Synagogue

Law 4: "How Jews may have a synagogue among Christians"
The synagogue is a place where Jews pray, and they may not construct anew a house such as this in any part of our kingdom without our permission. But those synagogues which they had previously, if they should fall into disrepair, may be restored or rebuilt in that same place where they stood originally,

although they may not be enlarged, nor heightened, nor painted. And if the synagogue is constructed in any other way, it shall revert to the principal church of the locale where it was erected, and the Jews shall forfeit it. And because the synagogue is a house where the name of God is praised, we order that no Christian shall dare to destroy it, nor remove anything from it, nor take anything by force, unless a criminal seeks refuge therein. In this case, he may be removed forcibly and taken before the authorities. Furthermore, we mandate that Christians are forbidden to put animals in the synagogue, or to remain there themselves, or to disrupt the Jews while they are at prayer according to their law.

Sabbath Legislation

Law 5: "Jews may not be summoned to court on Saturday; and which justices may judge them"

Saturday is when Jews pray and remain in their homes and neither conduct business nor engage in any lawsuits whatsoever. And because their religion requires them to observe this day, no one is permitted to summon them or bring them to justice thereon. As such, we decree that no judge may force or constrain Jews to appear in court on Saturday on account of their debts, nor may they be arrested or harmed in any manner on that day, for there are enough other days in the week to seize them and demand those things which may be legally required of them. And Jews are not obliged to answer a summons issued against them on Saturday. Furthermore, we decree invalid any sentence levied against them on that day. But if a Jew wounds, kills, robs, steals, or commits a similar offense deserving of corporal or pecuniary punishment, then judges may properly arrest him on Saturday. In addition, we decree that all suits brought by Christians against Jews and by Jews against Christians shall be tried and adjudicated by our judges in the locales where they reside, and not by the Jewish elders. And just as we decree that Christians may not bring to trial or molest Jews on Saturday, so we order that Jews may not, either in person or by their legal representatives, bring suit against or molest Christians on that day. Furthermore, we decree that no Christian shall dare to seize on his own initiative the property of, or inflict bodily harm on, a Jew; instead, if he has a complaint against him, he must present it legally before our judges. And should anyone be so bold as to coerce a Jew, or steal any of his property, he must indemnify him double the amount.

Conversion to Christianity

Law 6: "Jews shall not be compelled to become Christians; what advantage a Jew possesses who does convert; and what punishment those Jews deserve who harm or dishonor Jews who convert to Christianity"

Neither force nor compulsion in any form may be used to induce a Jew to become a Christian; rather, Christians must convert Jews to the faith of Our Lord Jesus Christ by means of good deeds, the words of Scripture, and gentle persuasion, for Our Lord God neither desires nor loves forced service. Furthermore, we decree that if any Jew or Jewess willingly desires to become a Christian, his fellow Jews shall not hinder him in any way. And if any of them should stone, wound, or kill him because he wishes to convert, or they do this after his baptism, if such a deed can be proved, we order that all of the murderers and accomplices to the homicide or stoning be burned. And if by chance they do not kill the convert, but instead wound or dishonor him, we decree that the judges in the place where the deed occurred pass sentence on the perpetrators of the dishonor so that they make amends for their misdeed. Also, they must receive punishment according to the gravity of their crime. In addition, we order that after any Jews have converted to Christianity, all persons in our kingdom shall honor them and no one shall dare to disparage them or their descendants concerning their Jewish past. And converts shall retain their property, sharing with their brothers and inheriting from their parents and other relatives just as if they were Jews. And they shall have all the offices and honors other Christians enjoy.

Jewish Proselytizing

Law 7: "What punishment a Christian deserves who becomes a Jew"

So wayward is the Christian who becomes a Jew that we order him to be put to death, just as though he had become a heretic. Furthermore, we declare that his property be disposed of in the same manner as we indicated should be done with that of heretics.

Jewish-Christian Social Relations

Law 8: "No Christian, male or female, may reside in the house of a Jew"

We order that no Jew shall dare to have in his house Christian servants, male or female, although Jews may hire Christians to work and care for their lands or to guide them when they must travel through perilous regions. Furthermore, we forbid any Christian, male or female, to invite a Jew, male or female, nor may a Christian receive an invitation from Jews, to eat and drink together or partake of wine made by Jews. In addition, we order that no Jew shall dare to bathe together with Christians. Furthermore, we prohibit any Christian from receiving medicines or cathartics made by a Jew, although he may obtain it on the advice of a knowledgeable Jew, as long as it is prepared by a Christian fully aware of its contents.

Forbidden Unions

Law 9: "What punishment a Jew deserves who lies with a Christian woman"

Jews who lie with Christian women are guilty of great insolence and presumption. As such, we order that henceforth all Jews guilty of having committed such an act shall die. Since Christians who commit adultery with married women deserve death, how much more so do Jews who lie with Christian women, for these are spiritually espoused to Our Lord Jesus Christ by virtue of the faith and baptism they received in His name. And the Christian woman who commits such a transgression should not remain unpunished. We decree, therefore, that if she be a virgin, married woman, widow, or profligate whore, she shall receive the same punishment as the Christian woman who lies with a Muslim, as we indicated in the last law of the title dealing with Muslims.

Slavery

Law 10: "The punishment Jews deserve who hold Christian slaves or convert their captives to Judaism"

Jews shall neither purchase nor hold as slaves Christian men or women. If anyone should act to the contrary, the Christian slave shall be freed and not be required to remit any of his purchase price, even though the Jew was unaware that the slave was a Christian when he purchased him. But if the Jew knowingly purchased a Christian, and used him afterwards as a slave, the Jew shall die as a consequence. Furthermore, we decree that no Jew shall dare to convert his captives, male or female, though they be Muslims or some other barbarous people.

And if anyone, in violation of this decree, should convert his male or female slaves to Judaism, we order that they be freed from those to whom they belonged. And if it should occur that Muslim captives belonging to Jews become Christians, they shall be freed, as indicated in the fourth section [*partida*] of this book, in the title concerning freedom in the laws dealing with this subject.

Distinguishing Marks

Law 11: "Jews must wear distinguishing marks in order to be recognized"

Many errors and offensive acts occur between Christian men and Jewish women and between Christian women and Jewish men as a consequence of their living together in cities and dressing alike. In order to obviate the errors and evils that might result from this situation, we consider it proper and decree that all Jewish men and women living in our kingdom wear some sort of mark upon their heads so that all may clearly discern who is a Jew or Jewess. And if a Jew is discovered not wearing that mark, we order that he pay ten gold maravedis for each such infraction. And if he cannot pay the fine, he shall publicly receive ten lashes.

Moisés de León

(Spain, d. 1305)

Fragment of *The Zohar*

Translated from the Hebrew by Nahum N. Glatzer

Mysticism, it has been said, is a doctrine that attempts to establish an intimate connection between God and man, a break through the world of time and history into one of eternity and timelesness. It has also been defined by F. C. Happold as "a consciousness of the beyond." Jewish mysticism (Kabbalah) flourished in thirteenth-century Spain in reaction, perhaps, to the dryness of Talmudic discussion and the remoteness of rabbis from the community. Gershom Scholem, the scholar of Jewish mysticism, studied its various manifestations, from the first Hassidic movement, to the age of the pseudo-Messiah Shabbetai Zevi and onward into the nineteenth century. Scholem is credited for attributing the authorship of the canonical Kabbalist book, *The Zohar* (first published in three volumes from 1558 to 1560 in Mantua), also known as *The Book of Splendor*, to the Spanish author Moisés ben Shemtov de León, who lived in Guadalajara, Castile, then went to Ávila, and died in the small town of Arevalo. De León studied the works of Maimonides, then turned to Neoplatonism. *The Zohar* is an attempt to explain the whole system of the universe through religious consciousness. In *Major Trends in Jewish Mysticism* (1941), Scholem states that "for centuries it stood out as the expression of all that was profoundest and most deeply hidden in the innermost recess of the Jewish soul."

"Remember the Sabbath Day, to sanctify it" (Exod. 20:8). Said Rabbi Isaac: It is written, "And God blessed the seventh day" (Gen. 2:3); and yet we read of the manna, "Six days ye shall gather it, but on the seventh day, the Sabbath, in it there shall be none" (Exod. 16:26). If there was no food on that day, what blessing is attached to it? Yet we have been taught that all blessings from above and from below depend upon the seventh day. Why, then, was there no manna just on this day? The explanation is that all the six days of the transcendent world derive their blessings from it, and each supernal day sends forth nourishment to the world below from what it received from the seventh day. Therefore he who has attained to the grade of Faith must needs prepare a table and a meal on the eve of the Sabbath so that his table may be blessed all through the other six days of the week. For, indeed, at the time of the Sabbath preparation there is also prepared the blessing for all the six days that shall follow, for no blessing is found at an empty table. Thus one should make ready the table on Sabbath night with bread and other food.

Said Rabbi Hiyya: Because all things are found in the Sabbath it is mentioned three times in the story of Creation: "And on the seventh day God ended his work"; "and he rested on the seventh day"; "and God blessed the seventh day" (Gen. 2:2, 3). Rav Hamnuna the ancient, when he sat at his Sabbath meals, used to find joy in each one. Over one he would exclaim: "This is the holy meal of the Holy Ancient One, the All-hidden." Over another he would say: "This is the meal of the Holy One, blessed be He." And when he came to the last one, he would say: "Complete the meals of the Faith." Rabbi Simon used always to say, when the time of the Sabbath meal arrived: "Prepare ye the meal of the supernal Faith! Make ready the meal of the King!" Then he would sit with a glad heart. And as soon as he had finished the third meal, it was proclaimed concerning him: "Then shalt thou delight thyself in the Lord, and I will cause thee to ride upon the high places of the earth and feed thee with the heritage of Jacob thy father" (Isa. 58:14).

Also mark this. On all festivals and holy days a man must both rejoice himself and give joy to the poor. Should he regale himself only and not give a share to the poor, his punishment will be great. . . . On this days—so we have been taught—the Fathers crown themselves and all the Children imbibe power and light and joy, such as is unknown even on other festive days. On this day sinners find rest in Gehenna. On this day punishment is held back from the world. On this day the Torah crowns herself in perfect crowns. On this day joy and gladness resound throughout two hundred and fifty worlds.

Mark also this. On all the six days of the week, when the hour of the Afternoon Prayer arrives, the attribute of Justice is in the ascendant, and punishment is at hand. But not so on the Sabbath. When the time of the Sabbath Afternoon prayer arrives, benign influences reign, the loving-kindness of the Holy Ancient One is manifested, all chastisements are kept leashed, and all is satisfaction and joy. In this time of satisfaction and goodwill, Moses, the holy, faithful prophet, passed away from this world, in order that it should be known that he was not taken away through judgment, but that in the hour of grace of the Holy Ancient One his soul ascended, to be hidden in Him. Therefore "no man knows of his sepulchre unto this day" (Deut. 36:6). As the Holy Ancient One is the All-hidden One, whom neither those above nor those below can comprehend, so was this soul of Moses hidden in the epiphany of God's goodwill at the hour of the Sabbath Afternoon Prayer. This soul is the most hidden of all hidden things in the world, and judgment has no dominion over it. Blessed is the lot of Moses.

On this day the Torah crowns herself with all beauty, with all those commandments, with all those decrees and punishments for transgressions—in seventy branches of light which radiate on every hand. What it is to behold the little twigs which constantly emanate from each branch—five of which stand in the Tree itself, all the branches being comprised in it!

What it is to behold the gates which open at all sides, and through which bursts forth in splendor and beauty the streaming, inexhaustible light! A voice is heard: "Awake, ye supernal saints! Awake, holy people, chosen from above and from below! Awake in joy to meet your Lord, awake in perfect joy! Prepare yourselves in the threefold joy of the three Patriarchs! Prepare yourselves for the Faith, the joy of joys! Happy are ye, O Israelites, holy in this world and holy in the world to come."

Kings Ferdinand and Isabella

(Spain, 1492)

Edict of 1492

Translated from the Spanish by Jane S. Gerber

Promulgated on March 31, 1492, this edict established the before and after of Jewish existence in Spain. It also announced the consummation of the Christian project of *la reconquista*, devoted to homogenizing Spain under Christian rule at the expense of Jews and Muslims, by then considered unworthy partners. At a request from the Jewish community, the initial July 31 deadline for departure was postponed to August 2 because it coincided with the holiday Tisha B'av. It is important to scrutinize the language the document uses, the rationale it is based on, and the options given to those affected by it. The edict is portrayed as a cure for the "great damage" caused to Christians "by their participation, connection and conversation with the Jews," perceived as treacherous. Also of importance is the question: In its subsequent history, what did Spain lose by having expelled the Jews? By the way, 1492 isn't only the year of Columbus's original voyage across the Atlantic Ocean, but it marks also the appearance of Antonio de Nebrija's first grammar of Spanish, which he called *lengua del imperio*—the language of empire.

Don Ferdinand and Doña Isabel, by the grace of God King and Queen of Castile, Leon, Aragon, Sicily, Granada, Toledo, Valencia, Galicia, Mallorca, Sevilla, Sardinia, Cordova, Corçega, Murcia, Jaén, the Algarve, Algeciras, Gibraltar, and the Canary Islands; [to the] Count and Countess of Barcelona and the lords of Biscay and Molina, Dukes of Athens and Neopatria, Counts of Rosellon and of Sardinia, Marquees of Oristan and of Gociano; to the Prince Don Juan, our dear and beloved son, and to the infantes, prelates, dukes, marquees, counts, masters [of military orders], priors, wealthy men, knight-commanders, governors of the castles and strongholds of our kingdoms and seignories, and to the councils, magistrates, mayors, constables, royal judges, cavaliers, official shield-bearers and good men of the very loyal city of Burgos and of the other cities and villages and places of its bishopric, and of the other archdioceses and bishoprics and dioceses of our reigns and seignories, and to the *aljamas* [communities] of the Jews of the said city of Burgos, and to all the cities and villages and places of our said reigns and seignories, and to all the Jews and their singular persons, thus men and women of whatever age and to all the other persons of whatever legal status, dignity, or preeminence or condition to which that contained below in our letters appertains or may appertain in any manner, health and grace [unto you].

You well know or should know that, because we were informed that in these our kingdoms there were some bad Christians who Judaized and apostatized from our holy Catholic faith, this being chiefly caused by the communication of the Jews with the Christians, in the court that we held in the city of Toledo in the year 1480, we ordered that the said Jews be separated in all the cities, villages, and places of our kingdoms and seignories, and that they be given *juderías* [Jewish quarters] and separate places where they could live, hoping that this separation would remedy [the problem]. Moreover, we have sought and given the order that an inquisition be conducted in the said kingdoms and seignories which, as you know, has been done and is continuing, and on account of it, many guilty individuals have been found, which is notorious. According to which, we are informed by the Inquisitors and by many other religious persons, ecclesiastical and secular, it is evident and apparent that the great damage to the Christians has resulted from and does result from the participation, conversation, and communication that they have had with the Jews, who try always to achieve by whatever ways and means possible to subvert and to draw away faithful Christians from our holy Catholic faith and to separate them from it, and to attract and pervert them to their injurious belief and opinion, instructing them in their ceremonies and observances of the Law, holding gatherings where they read unto them and teach them what they ought to believe and observe according to their Law, trying to circumcise them and their children, giving them books from which to read their prayers, and declaring the fasts that they ought to fast, and joining with them to read and teach them the histories of their Law; notifying them of Passover before it comes, advising them what they should observe and do for it, giving them and taking unto them the unleavened bread and the [ritually] slaughtered meats with their ceremonies, instructing them on the things they should stay away from, thus in the foods as in the other matters, for observance of their Law, and persuading them as much as they can there is no other law nor truth besides it. This is evident from the many declarations and confessions, [obtained] as much from the Jews themselves as from those perverted and deceived by them, which has redounded to the great injury, detriment, and opprobrium of our holy Catholic faith.

Notwithstanding that we were informed of most of this beforehand, and realizing that the true remedy for these injuries and inconveniences was in breaking off all communication of the said Jews with the Christians and to eject them from our kingdoms, we sought to content ourselves in ordering them out of all the cities and villages of Andalusia where it appeared they had done great damage, believing that this would be sufficient, so that the other cities and villages and places of our kingdoms and seignories would cease to do and commit the aforesaid.

And because we are informed that neither that, nor the punishments meted out to some of those said Jews found culpable in the said crimes and transgressions against our holy Catholic faith, will suffice as a complete remedy to obviate and to terminate such great opprobrium and offense to the Christian religion; because every day it is found and made apparent that the said Jews increase their evil and injurious activities where they live and converse, and so as not to grant them more space within which to further offend our holy faith, as much in those whom God has protected as in those who have fallen but have amended and returned to the Holy Mother Church, which, according to the weakness of our humanity and the diabolical suggestion that continually wars against us, which easily could come to pass, unless the principal cause of it be removed, which is to eject the said Jews from our kingdoms. Because whenever some grave and detestable crime is committed by some persons of a group or community, it is right that such a college or community be dissolved and annihilated, and that the minors be punished for the elders, one for the other; and that those who pervert the good and honest living of the cities and villages, and that by contagion could injure others, be expelled from among the peoples, and even for other lighter causes that are harmful to the states, and how much more so for the greatest of the crimes, dangerous and contagious as is this one.

Therefore, we, with the counsel and advice of some prelates, grandees, and cavaliers of our kingdoms and other persons of knowledge and conscience of our Council, having had much deliberation upon it, resolve to order all of and said Jews and Jewesses out of our kingdoms and that they never return nor come back to any of them. Concerning this, we command this letter [Edict] to be given, whereby we command all Jews and Jewesses of whatever age they may be, who live and reside and are in the said kingdoms and seignories, natives and nonnatives alike, who by whatever manner or whatever reason may have come or are to be found in them, that by the end of July of the present year, that they leave the said kingdoms and seignories with their sons and daughters, male and female servants and Jewish domestics, both great and small, of whatever age they may be, and that they dare not return unto them, nor be in them, nor be in any part of them, neither as dwellers, nor as travelers, nor in any other manner whatsoever, upon punishment that if they do not thus perform and comply with this, and are to be found in our said kingdoms and seignories and have come here in any manner, they incur the penalty of death and confiscation of all their belongings for our treasury, and such penalties they shall incur by the very deed itself without trial, sentence, or declaration. And we command and maintain that no one in our said kingdoms, of whatever status, conditions, or dignity they may be, dare to receive, harbor, defend, either publicly or secretly any Jew or Jewess after the said deadline at the end of July has passed, henceforth and forevermore, neither in their lands nor in their homes nor in any other part of our said kingdoms and seignories, under pain of losing all their belongings, vassals, fortresses, and other landed properties and, moreover, to lose whatever sums they may have from us for our treasury.

And so that the said Jews and Jewesses, during the said time until the end of the month of July, may better dispose of themselves, their belongings, and their estates, we hereby take and receive them under our security, protection, and royal guardship; and we assure them and their belongings that, during the said time period until the said day, the end of the said month of July, they may go about in safety, and they may enter, sell, barter, and transfer all their movable and immovable goods, and dispose of them freely at will; and that during the said time period, no evil, injury, or offense be done to their persons nor unto their goods contrary to justice, upon punishment of that which befalls and is incurred by those who transgress our royal security. In like manner, we give permission and authority to the said Jews and Jewesses that they may take out their goods and estate from our said kingdoms and seignories, by sea or by land, provided they do not take out gold, silver, minted money, or other items prohibited by the laws of our kingdoms, except for nonprohibited merchandise or exchange bills.

And, moreover, we command all the councils, justices, governors, cavaliers, shield-bearers, officials, and good men of the said city of Burgos and of the other cities and villages of our kingdoms and seignories and to all our vassals, subjects, and natives that they observe and comply and cause this, our letter and all that is contained in it, to be observed and complied with; and that they give, and cause to have given, all necessary support and help, upon [threat of] punishment by our grace and the confiscation of all their goods and benefits for our treasury. And so that this may come to the notice of all, and no one may pretend ignorance, we command that this letter be proclaimed in the plazas and customary places of that said city and of the principal cities and villages and places of its bishopric by a public crier and before a public scribe. Neither one nor another should do the contrary by whatever manner, upon punishment by our grace and the loss of their offices, and the confiscation of the belongings of whoever does the contrary. And we further command the person who shows them this letter, that they are summoned to appear before us in our court, wherever we may be, within the fifteen days following the day of our summons, upon [threat of] the said punishment, and concerning which we command whichever public scribe was called upon to do this, that he show them signed testimony with his signet in order that we may know how our command is complied with.

[Given in our city of Granada at XXXI days of the month of March, the year 1492 of our Lord Jesus Christ. I the King, I the Queen, I, Juan de Coloma, secretary of the King and Queen, our Lords, which I have written upon their command.]

Fray Luis de León
(Spain, 1528–1591)
"Serene Night"
Translated from the Spanish by Sir John Bowring

Over the years, critics have argued that Fray Luis de León, poet, Biblical translator, and didactic writer, was the owner of an *"alma hebrea,"* a Hebrew soul, since there are unavoidable Hebraic and rabbinical motifs in his oeuvre. Along with Santa Teresa de Jesús (1515–1582) and San Juan de la Cruz (1542–1591), he is part of the triptych of Spanish Christian poets whose *converso* Jewish ancestry palpitated behind their words. The oeuvre by Fray Luis de León is made up of poetry as well as philosophical and religious volumes such as the coded autobiography *Exposición del libro de Job* (1581), and also the treatise *De los nombres de Cristo* (1583). He was influenced by Horace and Virgil as well as by Neoplatonism. The poem "Serene Night," like another poem of his, "Retired Life," is an example of the unconscious—or perhaps overt—drive by descendants of Jews to seek inner peace. Catherine Swietlicki, in her book *Spanish Christian Cabala* (1986), calls attention to the mystical elements in the poem, as they relate to Jewish texts. This poem thus is representative of the tradition of "hidden content" alive in Spain through *conversos* literature.

When yonder glorious sky,
Lighted with million lamps, I contemplate;
And turn my dazzled eye
To this vain mortal state,
All dim and visionary, mean and desolate:

A mingled joy and grief
Fills all my soul with dark solicitude;
I find a short relief
In tears, whose torrents rude
Roll down my cheeks; or thoughts which thus intrude;

Thou so sublime abode!
Temple of light, and beauty's fairest shrine!
My soul, a spark of God,
Aspiring to thy seats divine,
Why, why is it condemned in this dull cell to pine?

Why should I ask in vain
For truth's pure lamp, and wander here alone,
Seeking, through toil and pain,
Light from the Eternal One,
Following a shadow still, that glimmers and is gone?

Dreams and delusions play
With man, he thinks not of his mortal fate:
Death treads his silent way;
The earth turns round; and then, too late,
Man finds no beam is left of all his fancied state.

Rise from your sleep, vain men!
Look round, and ask if spirits born of heaven,
And bound to heaven again,
Were only lent or given
To be in this mean round of shades and follies driven.

Turn your unclouded eye
Up to you bright, to you eternal spheres;
And spurn the vanity
Of time's delusive years,
And all its flattering hopes, and all its frowning fears.

What is the ground ye tread,
But a mere point, compared with that vast space,
Around, above you spread,
Where, in the Almighty's face,
The present, future, past hold an eternal place?

List to the concert pure
Of yon harmonious, countless worlds of light!
See, in his orbit sure,
Each takes his journey bright,
Led by an unseen hand through the vast maze of night!

See how the pale Moon rolls
Her silver wheel; and, scattering beams afar
On Earth's benighted souls,
See Wisdom's holy star;
Or, in his fliery course, the sanguine orb of War;

Or that benignant ray
Which Love hath called its own, and made so fair;
Or that serene display
Of power supernal there,
Where Jupiter conducts his chariot through the air!

And, circling all the rest,
See Saturn, father of the golden hours:
While round him, bright and blest,
The whole empyreum showers
Its glorious streams of light on this low world of ours!

But who to these can turn,
And weigh them 'gainst a weeping world like this,
Nor feel his spirit burn
To grasp so sweet a bliss,
And mourn that exile hard which here his portion is?

For there, and there alone,
Are peace, and joy, and never-dying love,
There, on a splendid throne,
'Midst all those fires above,
In glories and delights which never wane nor move.

O, wondrous blessedness,
Whose shadowy effluence hope o'er time can fling!
Day that shall never cease,
No night there threatening,
No winter there to chill joy's ever-enduring spring.

Ye fields of changeless green,
Covered with living streams and fadeless flowers!
Thou parading serene!
Eternal, joyful hours
My disembodied soul shall welcome in thy bowers!

Luis de Carvajal the Younger
(Mexico, 1567–1596)
"Autobiographical Essay"
Translated from the Spanish by Martin A. Cohen

The quest of Luis de Carvajal the Younger, from his birth in Benavente, Spain, to his death at the stake of the Inquisition in Mexico, is emblematic of the pattern followed by crypto-Jews in the Americas. The one against him, in fact, is one of the most famous inquisitorial cases in the continent. Carvajal was the nephew of the governor of the northern Mexican state of Nuevo León. The uncle was the one who had brought a portion of the family to the other side of the Atlantic Ocean, where it was thought that the Inquisition would be less stern. In the "Autobiographical Essay," which Carvajal began in 1591 or 1592, he chronicles his awakening as a Jew that came from an environment in which only through innuendo were New Christians able to know their true ancestry. The character Joseph in the text is the narrator himself. He chooses the third person as a device to establish a sense of distance and objectivity toward the story. Carvajal was arrested for the first time in 1589, but somehow he convinced his victimizers of his innocence. The final entry of the essay is from 1594, shortly before his second and final arrest. It stands as an invaluable document of the oppression under which so-called Judaizers lived in New Spain, the name that referred to Mexico before it acquired its independence in 1810. In prison, he corresponded secretly with his mother and sister, also incarcerated, by sending them hidden messages which, unfortunately, were intercepted by his opponents and used as evidence against him. The director Arturo Ripstein loosely based his film *El Santo Oficio* (*The Holy Office*) on the essay.

[Written in] Mexico City, New Spain, [by] Joseph Lumbroso, of the Hebrew nation, a pilgrim in Occidental India, in devoted recognition of the favors and boons received from the hand of the Most High, who freed him from the gravest perils, in order that they may be known to all who believe in the Most Holy One and await the great mercies that He employs with sinners.

Awakened by the Spirit Divine, Joseph committed these to writing, along with [the story of] his life until the twenty-fifth year of his wandering, in the form of a brief history.

Before beginning he kneels on the ground before the universal God, the Lord of all mercy, and promises, with the God of truth always before him, to portray accurately everything that he writes below.

In the name of God, Adonay Sevaoth, the Lord of Hosts:

Joseph begins his life at the beginning. It should be mentioned that he was born and raised at Benavente, a city in Spain where he lived until the age of twelve or thirteen. There he began to receive instruction in the rudiments of Christianity from a relative, and he completed these studies in Medina del Campo [to which his family moved from Benavente]. There it pleased God's mercy to shed upon him the light by which he recognized His holiness. [It happened] on a special day, which we call the Day of Pardon, a holy and solemn occasion for us, [which falls] on the tenth day of the seventh month. Since God's truth is so clear and pleasant, all that his mother, his older brother, his older sister, and his cousin from that city had to do was to make mention of it to him [and he understood].

Joseph's father and his entire family emigrated to this land of New Spain, though they first planned to cross over into Italy, where all could better serve, worship, and love the true God. But God's judgments are incomprehensible and just, and the change of plans bringing them to this land must have been God's punishment for one of [his father's] sins, a punishment meted out to his children by God's justice, though not without great compassion, as we shall presently see.

Joseph [who had become] very ill [aboard ship] was removed [when the ship docked] at the port of Tampico. At the same time [another passenger] disembarked, who was best known for his fear of the Lord, our God. He was [also] a famous doctor, and, with God's guidance, he treated Joseph in Tampico until he was cured.

One night, while Joseph and his older brother were sleeping in a small shed housing certain wares that they had brought from Castile, the Lord lashed the port with a hurricane. Its strong and terrible winds uprooted trees and razed most of the buildings to the ground. The building in which Joseph and his brother were sleeping began to shake. The violent wind ripped some of the beams from the roof with such terrible fury that Joseph and his brother instinctively huddled in fear under the delusive protection of their bedclothes. At length, realizing that the collapse of the building was imminent, they arose, drenched and wind-lashed, [and groped their way to the door]. But the wind blew so strongly against the door that, try as they might, they could not open it until God permitted them to pry it partially open by pulling it in the opposite direction. They opened it enough to leave the building before it tumbled to the ground. [In this way] the Holy One came forth in the sight of men to free them from death. Blessed be His most holy name. They went to recuperate in the home of their parents [who] feared that they were dead. On hearing their voices, their loving father received them with tears, thanking and praising the Lord a thousand times.

Shortly thereafter Joseph accompanied his father to Mexico City, leaving his mother, five sisters, and two brothers domiciled—or rather, disconsolately exiled—in Panuco, for they lived in penury in this mosquito-infested and heat-plagued town. When God took his father from this life, Joseph returned to Panuco.

Here God provided him with a Holy Bible, which a priest sold him for six pesos. He read it assiduously in that forsaken land and came to learn many divine mysteries.

One day he came to the seventeenth chapter of [the Book of] Genesis, where the Lord commands our holy father, Abraham, to circumcise himself. The words which say "The soul which is uncircumcised shall be blotted out from the Book of the Living" caught Joseph's eye and struck his heart with terror. Without delay and with the inspiration of the Most High and His good angel, he got up, put the Bible down without even stopping to close it, left the hall in his house where he had been reading, took a pair of blunted and worn shears and went to the ravine at the Panuco River. Burning with desire to fulfill this holy sacrament, without which one cannot be inscribed in the Book of Life, he placed its seal upon his flesh. The shears worked so well that he cut off nearly the entire pre-puce and left only a little flesh. Yet, despite this imperfection, Joseph had no reason to doubt that our Lord would accept his intention. This can be inferred from the Second Book of Chronicles, in the chapter where [Solomon] the wise king of Israel, speaks of his saintly father David's worthy desire, fulfilled by Solomon, to build a temple to the Lord. On the day of its holy dedication, Solomon praised the excellence of the Lord and said that though His supreme Majesty had, through revelation and Nathan's message, forbidden David to build the holy Temple, He accepted David's good intention in place of the deed.

It is worth noting that once Joseph received the seal of this holy sacrament upon his flesh, it served as a bulwark against lust and an aid to chastity. Prior to this he had been a weak sinner, who often merited the stroke of death which the Lord God sent upon a son of our patriarch Judah and his consort Tamar for committing the same sin. [Now] God's mercy was upon him, and, with the holy sacrament of circumcision, he was henceforth delivered from [the perversity of] this sin. The Lord helped him so much that, though he kept looking [for trouble,] like a sick man who always longs for the forbidden, and occasions were not lacking in which he could offend God, it seems that God's hand removed the dangers, because of His boundless mercy. Let us therefore give our thanks to God, for He is good, for His mercy endures forever.

A year after his circumcision [Joseph had a strange adventure]. He [had] accompanied a wretched, blind uncle of his, who was governor, in the name of the king of Spain, of the province called the New Kingdom of León, to some mines recently discovered within that province. He carried with him a small book containing a transcription of the Fourth Book of Ezra, the holy and pure priest and prophet. Joseph's devoted reading of this book had been one of the chief inspirations for his conversion. [And now,] since he did not have the Holy Bible with him in that land of savage Chichimecs, the reading of this book absorbed his leisure hours.

One [September] day—it was the seventh month [according to the Jewish calendar]—his packhorse broke away. Joseph, carrying only harquebus, sword, and dagger, took a brawny horse and pursued it. Two leagues out of town, the horse tired. It was in the midst of a dangerous area; several soldiers had been killed by the Chichimecs there, even near [Spaniards'] houses. When the horse tired and refused to budge, Joseph left its saddle at the foot of a tree, [put fresh priming in the pan,] slid the cover forward, shouldered the gun and started to town on foot.

Night fell on the hilly and pathless terrain before he could determine where he was. He was not a little afraid that some barbarous Indian might chance by and with a single arrow take his life. He was a defenseless target, though he clung for defense to the hope of God's mercy.

Joseph had not breakfasted that day, and though he was not bothered by hunger, he had become terribly thirsty from traveling on foot in the heat of the day without a drop of water. Frenzied with thirst, he had taken his dagger and cut some leaves of the prickly pear, called *nopal* in the Indian language. Since they are naturally moist, they soothed him for a while, but he was so insatiably thirsty that [he took too many] and his mouth and tongue were sore for a week.

Night thus enveloped him. Lost, hungry, thirsty and defenseless in the land of the hostile Chichimecs, he not unnaturally began to fear a horrible death.

By this time he was missed in the town, and his uncle had sent a soldier to a small settlement a half league away to see if he had gone there. When the soldier returned and said no, everyone, especially his uncle, was alarmed, for they feared that he had been killed by [their] enemies. They immediately sent out a search party, composed of a captain and ten men divided into two groups, each with a trumpet and each moving in a different direction. Those who remained in the town, where Joseph was greatly loved, tried to be of help to him in every possible way. One man, who went to string a lantern on a tall tree in the town, fell and broke his legs. It was a gratuitous gesture of affection, for the terrain was so mountainous that the lantern could not be seen [where Joseph was].

Since, as has been said, Joseph was so terrified and anguished, he committed himself to God with heart and soul. As the darkness thickened, his despair and his cries increased. [Then] he heard the blasts of a trumpet echoing loudly through that entire craggy valley. When he realized by this signal that they were looking for him, he fell to the ground and worshipped and thanked the Lord God. Then he got up buoyantly, listened for the sounds, and began to walk in their direction. Soon he heard the trumpet of the second group, but he continued toward the sound of the first trumpet until he could hear his friends talking. Joyously he called to them and they answered. They halted their horses and dismounted, surrounding him and embracing him repeatedly. They put him on a sprightly horse and shot their guns to signal their success. Not long thereafter the entire party assembled and returned to town to an equally joyous reception from the men who had remained behind with Joseph's uncle. Let us give thanks to the Lord of the universe, for He is good, for His mercy with men endures forever. As Saint David said, He is the one who restores to the right path those who have gone astray. He says that when [the children of Israel] lost their way in the wilderness and could not find the road to their dwelling place, and were in addition afflicted with hunger and thirst to the point of death, they cried to the Lord in their distress, and He heard them: He showed them the road and led them to safety. Let us give thanks to Adonai for His goodness and for the miracles He performs for the children of men.

Joseph remained in that region for two years, after leaving his family in the exile of Panuco. His mother and sisters were clad in mourning and [his brothers were] garbed in sadness at the death of their father, who, as has already been said, had died a short while before.

During their father's lifetime, their blind uncle had been introducing his sisters to refined soldiers and officers in an attempt to help them marry well. But their father, who greatly feared the Lord, had opposed such matches and heeded the Lord's most holy commandment prohibiting them. [Now their uncle,] recognizing that as orphans their marital prospects were diminished, [tried all the harder even] before they had removed their mourning garb. The girls endured such poverty that they went about shabby and barefoot a good part of the time. [Yet] they led a chaste and secluded life and virtuously helped their mother.

One day when their minds were far from marriage, they suddenly heard clarions and trumpets at their door. The reason was that the two men whom the Lord had designated as husbands for the orphans, both fearers of the Lord and part of His people, were now arriving. They were rich and prosperous, well dressed and wearing golden chains around their necks. Spurred to come for this good deed by the Lord of Heaven, they had come the seventy leagues separating Panuco from Mexico City expressly to marry the girls and to bring clothes and other gifts to them and their mother. They returned to Mexico City after the wedding, which was celebrated with delight by family and friends. As they congratulated the fortunate mother, many Gentile women, marveling at what had happened, said to her: "What good prayer did you utter [to bring all of this about]?" Like the saintly Sarah, she [answered humbly and] said: "God's mercy is hardly proportional to man's merits, which are always few or none." To the grooms they gave a similar compliment, declaring that they had come to pluck roses from amidst the thorns—roses, indeed, not so much for their beauty, which was slight, as for the virtue and chastity which the Lord had given them. A few days later they all left for Mexico City together, praising the Lord with much joy and gladness: *"Orphano tu eris adiutor"* ["You have been the helper of the fatherless"], says [David to God in a Psalm] and in another *"Pupillum et viduam suscipiet"* ["He upholds the fatherless and the widow"]. Blessed be the Protector of orphans forever.

The news of all this reached Joseph in the battle[-scarred] land he spoke of, [where] his life [was] in great danger because the savage and hostile Chichimecs around him were many and the soldiers with him few. His eyes welled with tears of joy as he thanked the Most High for the good news. As soon as he heard it, he resolved to go to Mexico City at the first opportunity. When the soldiers and the mayor of the town heard of his intentions, they were greatly disturbed and said that if he went away the whole area would be depopulated.

But since His strength surpasses human power, God provided miraculous circumstances for Joseph to leave. The inhabitants of the region, as is usual for battle zones, relied on imports of provisions. [They now] found themselves in dire need of supplies and [were happy that there was] a lull in the fighting and that they had silver to trade. Relying first on God's help [they entrusted Joseph with the mission].

It seemed on the day that Joseph left that the Most High had extricated him from the confinement of [hopeless] chains. And so it was, for in a few short days the Chichimecs flayed and then killed the mayor, in whose house he had stayed. Doubtless Joseph would have met a [similar] end had the Lord, in His loving-kindness, not freed him and removed him from that town. Exalted be His Holy Name forever.

Joseph arrived safely in Mexico City with God's help. He received his mother's blessing and saw his orphaned sisters protected by God. When he had seen them last, they were wearing tattered skirts; now, in their husband's homes, he saw them clad in silk and velvet and bedecked with golden jewels. [And his sisters' husbands] divided the rest of the family between them and gave them shelter. May they be sheltered by the Lord, and may His most Holy Name be extolled alone forever and ever.

But because of their heavy expenditures for the weddings and their subsequent support of so many people, Joseph's brothers-in-law were at the brink of ruin in less than a year. But they never rejected their in-laws. [Yet] as was proper, Joseph and his older brother wished to earn a living for their poor mother and unmarried sisters. The realization that they were poor and without resources grieved them greatly. Despite their outwardly respectable appearance, their necessities were so great that when his brothers-in-law and their wives left for Tasco, Joseph had to take a job as a merchant's bookkeeper in order to make both ends meet. With God's kindness, things soon improved a little.

When Joseph and his older brother were in Mexico City they heard of an old Hebrew cripple who had been bedridden for thirteen years with suffering and its attendant problems. [They went to visit him.] To demonstrate that everyone should love works of charity, God abundantly rewarded their visit, for the cripple presented them with a book which the good Licentiate Morales, who was mentioned earlier, had left for his consolation. Licentiate Morales had kept this cripple in his house for many days and tried to cure him, but when he saw the impossibility of a physical cure, he prepared a book to serve as a salve for his spiritual health. In it, he included a Spanish translation of the holy [Book of] Deuteronomy in the Law of the Most High and also an anthology of a thousand beautiful selections in verse, culled [and translated] from the rich garden of Sacred Writ. [Joseph and his brother proceeded] to make a copy.

One day Joseph and his brother were reading together the chapter containing the curses of the most holy Law when they saw how those true and holy prophecies had been carried out to the letter [among their people] and realized that their way of life was removed from the true path. As they clutched the book of the Law of the Lord they began to lament like a compassionate mother over the dead body of her beloved son.

A few days later, after leaving their mother and sisters with their in-laws in Tasco, Joseph and his brother returned to Mexico City, yearning for the Lord like earth for water. Joseph's brother, who had ardently desired for some time to circumcise himself, carried out his wish during the solemn Passover season. Inspired by God, the brothers went to a barber on one Passover day and rented a razor. Joseph's brother took it, fell on his knees and began to cut off his foreskin, but wounded himself severely. At first the wound did not bleed. The brothers consecrated the act to the Lord their God, sang praises to Him and recited Psalms of His servant, David. A short while later, Joseph's brother sensed the flow of blood. The brothers therefore went to a house which they had rented from an uncle of theirs in a sparsely inhabited area outside the city, and there very cautiously completed the circumcision, all the while fearing that they might be discovered by their hapless uncle, who was blind [in matters of faith].

The house of their refuge was solitary and it contained nothing with which they could stop the [flow of] blood. Without knowing what he was doing, Joseph [decided to] treat it with wine and salt.

When he went to a neighbor and asked for salt to cure a wounded man he got into another serious predicament, because the neighbor said that out of love for God, he wanted to administer it personally to the patient. [Finally he let Joseph have it,] but it did not stop the poor patient's bleeding. It only increased his pain.

Seeing the danger that confronted them, they went to the nearby house of a young man who feared the Lord. When they explained their plight—the situation of the patient with the dripping wound—he graciously welcomed them. Soon, with God's pleasure, the bleeding stopped, but since the wound was large and the cure not administered by a physician, the patient suffered greatly before he recovered, though this furnished him with no small merit to counterweigh his past sins.

When their uncle came to take them to his house and discovered blood-stained cloths, the brothers were terrified. But since it was the Lenten season, they distracted him by saying that they had scourged themselves in penitence and this had brought forth the blood.

When a sister of their uncle, who knew and loved the Lord, learned of this circumcision, she spoke tenderly to Joseph and remonstrated with him because in the time of their need, when they had to cure the wound, they had gone elsewhere [and not come to her].

After removing them from the solitude and mosquitos of Panuco, the Lord showed them further kindness by providing them with many of the holy and devout prayers by which the wise and chosen people of the Lord's ecclesia invoke and praise Him in Jewish synagogues.

This was the way in which the Lord in His holiness took this blessing that is found in the lands where our brothers freely and unobstructedly practice their faith and brought it to the lands of Jewish captivity:

In the Diaspora, in Italy, there lived a servant of the Lord who was extremely poor. Having no trade or occupation by which to support himself or his family, he engaged himself in spiritual affairs and translated the holy prayers I mentioned into the Spanish and Portuguese tongues. He emigrated alone to the New World. An Israelite brother of ours, who at the time was a merchant in Mexico City, told us that this newcomer greatly revered the Lord and abhorred idolatry. He often saw the immigrant running toward his store so fast that he thought something terrible had happened to him. And when he looked for a hiding place, he thought surely he was fleeing from the police. But the reason for these flights was that he had perceived the most abominable idolatry ever heard of or imagined in the world. When he heard the bell that is sounded as [the image of] the crucified one is carried through the streets, he ran to his hiding place to avoid having to kneel down before it.

When this good man returned to Italy he left behind [the book] containing the holy prayers which Joseph and his brother obtained.

After the Lord's boundless mercy had satisfied their most essential need, the spiritual need, His Divine Providence did not fail to repair the material deprivations they suffered. Though they had neither funds nor business knowledge nor acumen, within a year the Lord had given them property worth more than seven thousand pesos. Blessed be He forever and ever who thus provides for the hungry.

In this dilemma the brothers determined to go in the first fleet to Italy in order there to serve the Lord. But it seemed a pity to leave behind a blind brother of theirs who was a Dominican, a preaching friar, and already a master in his order. Wherefore, with determination and concern for him, the two brothers paid him a visit in his monastery, located near the Inquisition's jail, and where at the time he was a teacher of novitiates, to see if they could bring him to the recognition of God's truth and His Holy Law.

After the three had sat down in the friar's cell and conversed for a while, Joseph asked, as if randomly: "Is it really true, as it seems to me I have sometimes heard, that when Saint Moses was holding the tablets of the Law, the Lord God wrote His most holy commandments upon them?" The monk replied. "It is as you say." As he said this, he took the Holy Bible from his bookshelf, found the exact chapter in Exodus, and gave it to Joseph to read. After he had read it, Joseph exclaimed, "As I live, this is—this is really the Law that must be kept."

At this point the hapless friar got up and uttered a great blasphemy. He said that it was good to read the Law but not to keep it, and that although it had been the Law of God, it was superseded. He supported his folly and lie with the very frivolous simile of a king donning a cloak, and then, as it wore out, casting it away and giving it to a page.

He was answered by Joseph's brother, who was older than Joseph but younger than the monk. It should be mentioned here that the three brothers were looking out of a window in the cell that faced the orchard, and through it they could see the sky and the sunset with its brilliant rays.

Said Joseph's brother: "This cloak of the heavens, and this shining sun which God created, have they changed, have they perchance grown old?"

"No," replied the monk.

"So," he retorted, "much less change has there been in God's incorruptible and Holy Law and His word, and even less will there be. We hear this affirmed by your own preachers and scholars, and in the Gospel itself you declare that your crucified one said, 'Do not think that I am come to remove the Law or the Prophets, for their prophecies are holy and true.' Rather he said this: 'It is certainly easier for heaven and earth to be lacking than for one jot or tittle of this Holy Law to be lacking or change.'"

Realizing he must acknowledge the truth of their claim, the benighted priest retreated, saying, "Let's not talk about this any more," and adding: "Blessed be God, who took me out from among you." To which his brothers on either side responded: "Be Thou glorified, our God and Lord, who hast not left us in blindness and perdition like this wretch." The monk said that he deemed his lot happier than theirs and concluded by quoting the Psalms, *"Non fecit taliter omni nationi"* and so on. ["He had not dealt in such a way with any other nation"]. Thus, seeing the truth and unable to deny or contradict it, the miserable, sightless friar was frustrated. And with this the brothers parted.

On another occasion, at Joseph's suggestion, his two older brothers agreed to study for several days and then meet for a discussion of their respective faiths, with the condition that whoever was defeated by the truth of the other's religion must accept it. Though he had said yes, the monk refused to go through with the discussion because he was a cleric, giving the excuse that his law forbade him to investigate or discuss matters of faith. Those wretches think that by shielding their eyes from the light, they can keep from falling into the pits of hell. Rightly did Saint Isaiah marvel at them when he said [in the name of God]: "They are not inclined to stop and say, 'Maybe what I believe is a lie.' I make all men alike, but their sin keeps some blinded."

The fleet was scheduled to depart shortly and the brothers began to look to their affairs. But for the good of the entire family, God in His infinite and divine wisdom and mercy ordained that the Inquisition should now arrest a widowed sister of theirs. She had been accused [of practicing Judaism] by a heretic who was one of our own people and whom a year before she had tried to indoctrinate into the truth of God. On learning of this, the brothers, struck with fright, decided to flee with their mother and [remaining] sisters, but some God-fearing [Israelite] friends with whom they discussed the matter convinced them that it was impossible for them [to take the women along]. After a painful separation which is beyond the power of my words to describe, the brothers therefore went off alone, leaving their family exposed to danger and wending their way to the cadence of their bitter cries and howls. [But] when they reached port, loaded their ship, and were ready to embark, the thought of their mother and sisters exposed to mounting dangers overwhelmed them and made them change their plans. Joseph decided to return home and see what was going on, while his brother would remain behind and await word from him.

Two or three days after arriving home, Joseph went to visit his mother in the evening hours. By day they did not dare to be together, because of what they feared might happen. They were about to sit down to dinner when the constables and notaries of the Inquisition knocked on the door. When they opened it, the Inquisitional officials set guards there, raised ladders, mounted them and came into the house to arrest Joseph's mother. Though wounded with this cruel enemy's fierce stroke, she donned the garb of modesty, bemoaning her troubles yet praising the Lord who had sent them. She was then brought to the pitch-black prison by those ministers of malediction and executioners of our lives.

When her two maiden daughters saw their beloved mother sighing with such pain and sadness that she even moved to compassion the cruel and beastly enemies who were taking her away, they anxiously rushed toward her and cried: "Where are they taking you?" We leave to the prudent reader's imagination the feelings of their lamenting mother as she heard these words.

After she was taken away, her son Joseph was arrested. They found him behind a door, where he had run for refuge out of fear of the atrocious tyrants. They pounced on him, seized him, and carried him to the gloomy, black prison. Joseph uttered nothing except the words: "O God, reveal the truth."

The next day one of his maiden sisters got word to their mother that Joseph had been arrested. A prisoner of the Inquisition was permitted to receive neither visitors nor letters from outside. What his sister did was to put some of Joseph's shirts among the clothes she sent her mother; and as soon as she saw them, she understood. This doubled her affliction, but also her merit.

The night that Joseph was arrested, his older brother returned to Mexico City and sent for him that the two might get together with a younger brother. Then he learned that Joseph had been arrested. This was a severe blow to Joseph's older brother, but he took it like a [true] servant of the Lord God: he prostrated himself on the ground and accepted the divine decree.

With half his family arrested, he was advised to flee the storm. He thought it over and decided to stay. He found a room [which became] his voluntary jail, and remained in it for a full year, waiting to see what the Lord would decree for his family. His companions were the Holy Bible and other sacred tomes which the Lord provided for him, and their assiduous reading absorbed his time.

Nor was Joseph in his prison forgotten by the Lord, his God. Exemplary gifts and favors did he receive from God's most merciful hand.

The Lord is witness that many times in that lonely and dark prison cell, Joseph would think longingly: "Would that in this solitude I were given the companionship of the Psalms of the saintly prophet David. If I read them, I would feel better." He believed that this desire was impossible of fulfillment by human means.

But since for the omnipotent God nothing is impossible, it was fulfilled by His holy decree. At the very time Joseph entertained these thoughts, a

Franciscan friar was arrested [by the Inquisition] and brought to his jail. On a Saturday afternoon, when the savage judges of the Inquisition generally visit the prisoners to comfort them and to minister to their needs (not that this benevolence originates within them, for they are cruel and inhuman, but rather because the Lord our God and Father is pleased to bring the prisoners the solace that comes from sweeping and cleaning their cells for the visit), they came first to the monk. They asked him if he needed anything, and he answered that he would like only a breviary to find consolation in his cell by reciting his customary Divine Office. Then they visited Joseph and, finding him emaciated and depressed, they assigned the monk to him as his cellmate. They brought the monk to Joseph's cell on that very Sabbath afternoon and enjoined him not to reveal that he was a monk.

The two prisoners talked for a while, rejoicing that they had met and would now be together. At dusk the jailer came, opened the cell door and presented Joseph's companion with a breviary. Joseph was overcome with joy and gladness, for he recognized that this was the way in which the Lord his God satisfied his longing, which was to give him a book from which to recite the Psalms as he used to do. He, therefore, gave thanks to God most High for this signal kindness. Let us [all] give thanks to the Lord Adonai, for He is good and supreme and His mercy endures forever. For with one hand He punishes yet [with the other] shows us loving-kindness a thousandfold.

Indeed, through one event we can clearly see what Saint David realized from his learning and travels: "*Secundum multitudinem dolorum meorum in corde meo consolationes tuae laetificaverunt animam meam*" ["When many cares are within me, Your comforts delight my soul"].

It happened in the following way:

When Joseph's long confinement in his cell of agony had made him anxious and depressed, he began to receive special consolations from the eternal God, which for the most part were communicated to him in dreams at night. Once, after a day of fasting and prayer, he no sooner lay down and fell asleep when he heard a voice in his dreams saying: "Be strong and take comfort, for saints Job and Jeremiah are most effectively interceding for you." For a few days he felt better. Then he had another dream, which, judging from what later happened, seems to have been a true and divine revelation. He saw a glass vial, tightly stopped and wrapped outside. It was filled with the sweetest liquid, divine wisdom itself, which is dispensed only in small quantities. Then he heard the Lord

115

commanding Saint Solomon. He said: "Take a spoon, fill it with this liquid and give it to this boy to drink." The wise king began to execute the command. He took a spoonful of that sweet liquid and put it to Joseph's mouth; and as Joseph drank it, he felt greatly consoled. Later, as the reader will be able to observe, this consolation was to come to him again in the world of reality.

Since the imprisonment of Joseph and his mother dragged on and they remained in the hands of such cruel beasts, their fear made them hide their true identity, and they refrained from confessing publicly that they were keepers of the Lord God's most holy Law. For our affliction and travail has reached such a state that if anyone confesses and affirms [this fact] he is subjected by these heretics to exquisite torture and is [then] burned alive. And fear of this is responsible for their denial of their true identity.

One Friday morning, the Inquisitors, in order to determine whether Joseph and his family were practicing Judaism, summoned Joseph's mother for a hearing, as they had done on many previous occasions. Through a small hole which he and his companion had carved with two sheep bones at the threshold of his cell door, Joseph could watch his mother being led to the court of audience.

When the tyrants saw that she continued to deny [that her family practiced Judaism], they decided to subject her to torture. Preceded by the judges, notary, jailer and constable, she was therefore led to the torture chamber, where the torturer was standing, covered from head to toe with a shroud and white hood.

They immediately ordered the patient prisoner to disrobe. They stretched her chaste flesh on the instrument of torture known as the donkey and tied her arms and legs. Then they cruelly twisted the ropes in its iron rings. As the ropes grated her flesh, she heaved the most pitiful sighs, which could be heard by all [the prisoners].

Joseph, on his knees in his cell, heard it all, and that day brought him greater affliction and bitterness than any that had gone before. But he was not without the divine consolation that comes from the hand of the Lord. Blessed be His Holy Name forever. In the midst of that day of affliction, the Lord permitted him to doze off by the door of his cell. On other days, if he fell asleep for a moment, he awoke melancholy and faint, but not that day.

As soon as he fell asleep, he saw the Lord sending him a man who was a paragon of virtue and patience. He was a fearer of God, one of his own people. In his hands he carried a large and beautiful yam. He showed it to Joseph and said: "Look! What a handsome and beautiful fruit!"

To this Joseph replied: "Indeed."

He gave it to Joseph to smell. Joseph blessed the Lord, creator of all, and said to the man: "Indeed, it smells good, indeed." The man then cut the yam in two and said to him: "Now it smells better."

The man then gave Joseph the interpretation. He said: "Before being imprisoned and racked with torture, your mother was whole and she smelled sweet; she was a fruit of sweet savor before the Lord. But now, when she is cut with torture, she exudes the superior fragrance of patience before the Lord."

With this Joseph awoke and was consoled. May the Most High God, who brings consolation to the afflicted, likewise be adored and extolled.

Joseph suffered even more in his cell because his companion's presence prevented him from praying and fasting as he used to. But in that very cell his companion, with the help of the Lord God, was enlightened and converted to the truth of His Holy Law.

This was the way in which, for Joseph's benefit and consolation, the Lord brought healing to his companion:

In their cell stood a wooden cross, before which the poor wretch would kneel and offer his prayers. Once, as the two of them were sitting near their candle, the monk took up the cross or gallows, approached it to the flame and said: "By God, if I should put the cross in the fire, it would burn like any other stick." To which Joseph replied, "Now you see in what you place your trust."

Then they began to converse at length [about matters of religion]. They spoke continually for a week and more, until Joseph's hapless companion came to the recognition of God's truth. Then he rejoiced and sang hymns and praises to the Lord, especially the *Magnus Dominus et laudabilis nimis* which means . . . "Great is the Lord and worthy to be praised." [The monk went on to say:] "Because He deigned to enlighten a sinner like me." And the monk danced and thanked the Creator for having shown him such signal kindness in permitting him to recognize His sacred truth.

All this was ordained by God not only for the salvation of that poor soul but also for Joseph's consolation and relief, because [henceforth] they both kept the Law of Almighty God insofar as they could and they commended themselves to His divine majesty.

One day, when his companion was eagerly and devoutly listening to Joseph tell some of the stories of the Bible, he said: "I wish I had had the opportunity to be enlightened by God's truth before I came to this cell. I wish I had chanced upon it in one of the monasteries where I lived, where they have open libraries with Bibles and many good books."

Joseph's reply was: "Do they keep their libraries open for everyone?"

The monk said: "Yes, and they keep the books out so that anyone may consult them and read them."

Joseph said: "I wish I were put in one of them." Let this be noted in advance for the praise of the Most High and His sacred mercy, for the Lord fulfilled this wish with an extraordinary miracle, as will be seen below.

Once the Most High had enlightened his companion, Joseph lived contentedly in his confinement. He spent his time telling Bible stories to his companion, who listened with rapt attention and devotion. Soon God's truth became so impressed upon this good Gentile's soul that it seemed as if he had been nurtured on it all his life and taught by believing parents. Though he had but so recently been converted, he loathed bacon and lard and the other foods forbidden by the Most High's Holy Law. [He and Joseph adhered] so faithfully [to the dietary commands] that when bacon or sausage or any other forbidden food was served them they agreed to bury it. They would say: "Let us offer the sacrifice," which meant to bury such food and abstain from eating it. As a result they not infrequently suffered hunger in their harsh cell, but when they did they commended it to the Lord and uttered the Psalmist's prayer: *"Miserere mei"* ["Have mercy upon me"].

This happened most often at midday on Friday, for at that time the heretics' entire meal was contaminated.

In short, Joseph's companion comported himself in such a way that he earned the right to be a witness of the true God and his most Holy Law and received the crown of martyrdom [in public when he was burned at the stake], as I shall narrate below.

When Joseph and his family left their prison [duly] penanced and cloaked in the distinctive garb which the enemies of the Law of God require for those who have been convicted of keeping it, the Inquisitors wished to separate the family. They wanted to put each of the women in a different room of a convent that in the company of its idolators they might suffer twice as much as before. But the Lord in His infinite mercy frustrated this plan. He moved the Inquisitor himself to mention it to Jorge de Almeyda, one of Joseph's brothers-in-law, in whose mouth the Lord put the following reply: "Sir, the action you are contemplating should be well considered before you put it into effect. Do not forget that women are extremely curious and impressionable. The [damaging] influence [of these women] upon the nuns might be very difficult to counteract."

This made quite an impression on the enemy. At the Lord's prompting, the Inquisitor changed his mind and, instead of such confinement for life, which is the standard punishment for penitents, he arranged for the women to be given a house where they could all live together—for the sake of the Lord.

Joseph was separated from them and assigned to a hospital, where he was made keeper of the idols—which afflicted him not a little—and employed in other tasks, such as sweeping the floors, which he did after he had moistened them with his tears. But the Lord his God came to his rescue again as He had in all his previous difficulties.

When Joseph despaired of returning to the company of his mother and sisters—he did not even know how he could ask for such a thing—God on High, who was even more grieved, provided a remedy. He ordained that one of Joseph's brothers-in-law find it necessary to take a trip to Tasco and leave Joseph's mother and sisters alone. He [therefore] went to ask the Inquisitor the favor of allowing Joseph to stay with them while he traveled. This was the first step taken by the Most High to remove Joseph from [what he regarded as] his second captivity, where he sat and wept disconsolately because he was forced to eat forbidden foods. Highly exalted be the Most High, who thus came to Joseph's aid in all his difficulties.

When he returned to his mother and sisters, Joseph found that their enemies' threats and some friends' evil counsel had persuaded them to buy and eat Gentile foods, forbidden by the Law of God.

With divine inspiration Joseph changed this. He set before them the example of the saints who preferred to be torn to shreds by cruel tortures rather than eat forbidden foods or even pretend to eat them. But since their hearts were steadfast with their God and Lord—the family had been acting out of fright—little was needed to convince them of their wrongdoing. With many tears and affirmations of their reverence of heaven, they turned again to their God and Lord and added to their merit by rejecting all filthy foods.

As the time drew near for Joseph to return to the hospital where he served, an old monk, a man of great virtue, came to see his mother. The Inquisitor had asked him to be the family's confessor and guardian.

Joseph's mother importuned the monk to secure permission for Joseph to remain on with her and the family. And Joseph received this permission with the requirement that he spend his daytime hours working in a school for Indians which the monk directed. Joseph was given the responsibility of teaching grammar to some of the Indians and helping the monk with his letters and sermons. The Lord his God gave Joseph such favor [in the eyes of] this man that he loved him dearly and cherished him, and not only he but all his staff as well.

Since the carnivorous wolves had confiscated the family's property and left them destitute, the Lord maintained them in their affliction for four and a half years by having the monk support them from his own pocket and from charities of the Church that was so hostile to them. The Lord's performing a miracle for such sinful and wretched people [as Joseph and his family] is even more striking than His performance of a miracle with the innocent and saintly Daniel.

Let us now observe how the Lord in His mercy fulfilled the desire which Joseph expressed to his cellmate when he said: "I wish I were put into one of those libraries." The Lord induced the monk to give Joseph a key to his [private] room in the school, where he kept all his books, a privilege he extended to none of his fellow monks at the school. This kindness from the Lord was soon surpassed by another from His munificent hand. Joseph had been in the school for less than four months when God ordained that the same monk should purchase [Nicholas] de Lyra's *Glosses*, a commentary on the Holy Bible, in four large tomes from the estate of a great preacher of his order who had [recently] passed away. When they were delivered, he went to Joseph, as if looking for compliments and said: "What precious things we are bringing to our school."

With great caution Joseph availed himself of these gifts of God on high. When the monk and all the collegians would go to their quarters to eat, Joseph would remain behind within the [classroom] compound [and steal into the library]. There, by reading the Holy Bible and translating many of its sections into Spanish, he would nourish his spirit, troubled as it was by the thought of [a repetition of the] imprisonment and affliction from which the Lord had so miraculously extricated him.

In his hours of duty, whatever time Joseph had left after teaching his students was consigned by the monk to the arrangement of Oleaster's moralities on the Pentateuch into alphabetical order. This work was so suited to Joseph's temperament and interests that [he realized that] were it not for God's help he could not have obtained it even if he were willing to pay for it with all his blood. Blessed and extolled be the Lord, who satisfies worthy desires. . . .

In this book [of Oleaster's] the Lord revealed to Joseph the holy Thirteen Articles which are the principles of our faith and religion and which are unknown in the lands of our captivity.

One day as Joseph was about to open the door of the monk's room with his key as he had so often done, in order to continue with his translation of the Bible's holy prophecies, he had a presentiment that the monk was coming. The Lord seems to have been warning him. With this premonition he closed the door [and hid himself nearby], thinking: "If the monk comes now, it is a certain sign that the Lord has warned me and is with me." No sooner had this thought crossed his mind when he saw the monk entering his room. Blessed and praised be the Lord!

Joseph longed to find a spring or fountain of water in which to bathe. He thought: "If I had such a privilege in this school, I would lack none other." And the blessed Lord in His infinite mercy satisfied this desire. He ordained that a lay-friar who worked as a gardener in the orchard of that convent, and who was more scrupulous [about his cleanliness] than the rest, should also feel the need of such water for bathing. At this very time the Lord moved him to approach his superior and ask him for permission [—which was granted—] to bring a conduit into the school compound—and to the area where Joseph wanted it! Blessed be the Lord, who alone is good, for His mercy endures forever.

When Joseph, his mother, and his sisters left prison, his older brother, who had been carefully following their fortunes, decided [that it was time for him] to be on his way. Before he left the house which served as his voluntary jail, the Lord performed an extraordinary miracle for him.

In that house lived an Israelite friend who could move about freely. He had the key to the door where Joseph's brother was hiding and he brought him food and drink.

One day the Inquisition sent out an alarm for a concubinary, and when it heard that he might be living next door to the Israelite, it sent to the area a bailiff whom the Israelite knew well to arrest the suspect. [The bailiff looked for the suspect in the house next door], and when he could not find him, he thought that he might have jumped over the wall to the house where Joseph's brother was hiding. The bailiff therefore asked the Israelite to open his door that he might come in and look for the fugitive. The Israelite tried to dissuade him from entering, swearing again and again that the suspect was not there, but to no avail. Fortunately, because it usually took some time to open the door and it was night, the Israelite could stop in Joseph's brother's room and tell him to get out and hide under a staircase. This he did. The bailiff then entered the house to look for his suspect.

After looking all over for him, the bailiff and his party were about to leave when the Lord God worked another of his miracles to demonstrate that a man protected by God is really protected. As the bailiff approached the staircase under which Joseph's brother was hiding, one of his deputies said to him: "Sir, let us look underneath this staircase." But, moved by the Lord [the bailiff answered]: "Forget it, that fellow wouldn't be hiding there." And with this they left, and Joseph's brother came out from under the staircase and went to hide in a room which had already been searched.

He had no sooner done this when the bailiff, who had reached the gate of the house, had a change of heart. He came back and said: "I'll wager that our man is underneath the staircase where I wouldn't look before. I have come back to inspect it." He came in, looked [under the staircase] and was satisfied [that no one was there], and the man protected and freed by the Lord of the world remained free, thanks to His great loving-kindness. May the Lord be extolled forever and ever.

So Joseph's older brother left Mexico City one night. He was accompanied by a younger brother. [Both were] frightened at the prospect of being apprehended by the Inquisition, and determined to die for the Lord if they were. The [Israelite] friend whom we mentioned [above] went with them.

Shortly after they left, word reached Joseph that they had been arrested. He broke into bitter tears and a pall of sadness and melancholy fell over him, his mother, and his sisters. But the report was false: their good God and Lord was preserving and guiding the fugitives. They traveled about four hundred leagues overland in peace and safety until they reached the so-called Port of Horses.

Here, by no small miracle, they came upon an anchored ship whose captain was also a Hebrew and a cousin of the Israelite who accompanied Joseph's brothers. He took them aboard, showered them with presents, and transported them to Spain.

After Joseph had spent several days in tearful sorrow, the Lord sent him the happy news that his brothers had not been arrested and that their precious cargo had arrived at a safe port. Let us again give praise to Adonai, for He is good and supreme. Let us give glory to His Holy Name, for His mercy endures forever.

When the family was imprisoned, one of Joseph's brothers-in-law left for China, but the other remained in Mexico City. After the family had left prison, this brother-in-law continued to help them as he had when they were in jail, and he was always a very obedient son to Joseph's mother. Because God is good and leaves no good work unrewarded, He performed an exemplary miracle for Joseph's brother-in-law, not only to help him but even more [to help] Joseph's mother and sisters.

It seems that after the family had left prison, the Inquisition began to look for Joseph's brother-in-law. The Inquisition's constable called on him, but he refused to go with him and ran away [to Tasco]. Incensed, the Inquisitors sent a warrant for his arrest to a constable in Tasco, who very arrogantly went out to search for him. At this moment the Lord God sent one of the [wild] bulls that roamed in the area against the constable. The bull savagely attacked him, gored him to death, and dragged his body back to his own doorstep.

In this manner, the Lord, God of Israel, permitted Joseph's brother-in-law to remain free. He then stirred his heart to go to Spain to seek liberty for Joseph and his family. He accepted God's mandate with such strong resolve that he spent three and a half years in Spain in quest of this liberty. Finally, with God's help, he attained the necessary document and sent it on [to New Spain], again inspired and aided by the Lord.

I understand now that when Joseph and his family were imprisoned, his other brother-in-law left for China, from whence the Lord brought him back miraculously for the sake of his wife and infant daughter.

In the Orient, Joseph's brother-in-law was often in prison or in danger. The governor of China, moved by personal hatred but even more so by God's design, sent him in his ship to Macao. Since trade there was controlled by the Spanish crown, which had circulated a warrant for the arrest of Joseph's brother-in-law in New Spain, he was apprehended. His ship and all his merchandise were sequestered, and he was bound in chains and sent toward India by ship.

It seems impossible that anyone in such straits could be seen by his wife again. But for the Lord nothing is impossible. One night, in His Holy kindness, He suggested to Joseph's brother-in-law that he file off his chains and take refuge in the ship. Here a friend of his hid him under the deck and brought him food until the day when the departing fleet set sail. And though Joseph's brother-in-law was later arrested and harassed, God soon extricated him from this difficulty and even from the greater ones that he experienced in Manila.

These were occasioned by the enmity which the governor of that island conceived for him. I cannot now go into the reasons for this hatred, because I want to make this story short, since my purpose is to confine myself to the signal benefits and favors which the Lord God of Israel did for Joseph and his entire family.

In order that Joseph's brother-in-law might come back to care for his wife and daughter, the Lord freed him from the governor who, in his capacity as judge, would have unjustly taken his life. And He brought him and his ship to a safe port [in New Spain] at the time when Joseph and his family were still in prison. The news of this unexpected arrival brought great consolation, coming from God's hand, to the entire family, particularly to the man's wife and daughter. For this and for all other consolations may the Lord God of Israel be greatly blessed and adored.

As has been stated above, Joseph's fears that his unmarried sisters would yet be arrested by the Inquisition [proved well founded] . . . and they put the younger one in a building of maximum confinement, where for His glory, the Lord so instructed her that nothing, not even threats of torture, could extract from her any information that would benefit the Inquisitors and hurt her family. From the mouths of sucklings the Lord brings forth praises to confound the enemy and avenger!

Joseph's sister spent more than two years in that building, removed from the companionship of her mother and sisters, who grieved with heavy hearts. Pitiful indeed was the dejection felt by her sisters and especially her loving mother on the occasions when the female warden would bring her to see them and would then take her away. They fervently prayed to the Lord their God to deign to free her and restore her to them.

Adored be His most Holy Name. He heard them at an auspicious moment with His infinite mercy. At the end of two years, when the sentences of Joseph's married sister and the older unmarried one were completed and they were permitted to remove their penitential garb, the God of heaven gave them favor in the eyes of the Inquisitors; they delivered his younger, unmarried sister into their custody at the moment when the girl, as her mother told her to, was about to kneel and pray for this very thing. Thus God, the most liberal Provider, returned all three in freedom and joy to their mother. As their home rang with the happiness of all, so may there ring blessings and praises of the Lord of the heavens, whom the entire family thanked again and again for such favors.

A year after Joseph's captivity, the jailer of the Inquisition told him that the monk who was his cellmate had been rearrested and arraigned on the charge of shattering an idol in the galleys where he was serving his sentence. Joseph was terrified. He was afraid that the monk would try to hurt him—though he had great confidence that with the Lord's help he would be left unscathed. And God, our Lord, immediately performed such a miracle for Joseph that it cannot in all fairness be passed over in silence. Nor can one keep from uttering the praises due to the lofty and sovereign God who protected him.

One night His exalted Majesty revealed to Joseph's mother in a dream what was later to come to pass in reality!

She saw the Inquisitor thrusting a sword at Joseph, but the sword was sheathed. It had been sheathed by the Lord, exalted be His most Holy Name. And this is exactly what happened. When the monk, Joseph's former cellmate, was asked who had taught him, he told the Inquisitors that it was someone who had been his companion in that jail several years before, making it clear by such testimony that he had no intention of letting Joseph get away unharmed. But Joseph's blessed God and Lord saved him. He put the sword in a sheath: When the monk was asked whether he had been taught [Judaism] by his companion before or after the latter's confession, the Lord ordained that the monk should say before. And with this the Lord saved Joseph from the harsh and dark prison. May His most Holy Name be eternally exalted. Amen.

At the same time, Joseph's former cellmate, in the presence of those tyrants, so valiantly professed a belief in the God of Heaven that the like of it has not been seen with any other Gentile in our time. He told them of the mighty acts of the Lord God and [the greatness] of His most Holy Law, and then he said: "The Law which I believe and accept is the true faith and the others are frauds and deceptions of the devil. The king understands this well and so do the filthy Inquisitors, but the Lord hardens their hearts as he did Pharaoh's, for He is determined to take full vengeance upon them when the day of His most holy judgment comes." Though because of this he was subjected to severe trials and afflictions, our God permitted him to pass through them with exemplary patience and faith. Blessed be His most Holy Name forever. Amen.

Three and a half years after Joseph, his mother, and his sisters entered into captivity, an unfortunate event took place involving one of Joseph's unmarried sisters, who was particularly hostile to the idols and idolatries of her hapless, blind neighbors. On a Sabbath of the Lord when they celebrated a festival, she asked her brother Joseph, for the love of God, to take her to the home of a God-fearing Israelite sister. She did this that they might spend the day in the service of the Lord God and might avoid the offense [to God] that would come [by their remaining home, where they did not dare to observe the holy day properly].

She took along a book containing an anthology of passages from Sacred Scripture, which Joseph and his older brother had carefully culled and translated, and other writings attesting to the truth of the Lord our God and His Holy Law. It also included a translation of the Psalms and other holy prayers. This treasure was highly prized by Joseph and his sisters.

On that holy day Joseph's sister put the book in her bosom and took it along for prayer. They left at dawn, happy and singing praises to the Lord God. As evidence of His holy Majesty's loving-kindness, God permitted the book to slip down unnoticed from her bosom and fall on a well-traveled public thoroughfare. When the young girl discovered that the book was missing she was shocked and dispirited and her grief was uncontrollable. She retraced her steps in search of the lost gem, but no trace of it was to be found. Joseph and his two sisters returned home and the rest of the family shared their consternation. Their pain and fright were understandable, since at stake for all of them was nothing less than their lives and what they treasured most in life. They began to regard themselves as arrested and even dead. So great was their fright that were it not for the danger of damning their souls they would have taken their own lives rather than risk falling into the cruel hands of their terrible enemies. In short, every hour they fearfully and bitterly expected the moment of their imprisonment. But, blessed and exalted be the infinite and true Lord God, for He helped them in this difficulty with His accustomed kindness.

Whenever anyone knocked, they thought that the Inquisition's nefarious ministers were at the door to arrest them, and as a result they were in a continuous state of anxiety and trepidation. They purchased only half their usual amounts of oil and other necessities, thinking they would not even be able to finish these.

At the time of these anxieties their Father on high deigned to show His greatness. The mayor of the city was making an inspection tour of bakers and bakeries when, in one of the bakeries, he discovered bread that lacked the required weight [and proceeded to confiscate all the loaves]. Since he knew that Joseph's mother and sisters lived in need, he sent an inspector, staff in hand, to bring them two baskets of bread. Joseph's family lived in such terror that when the Indian maid who served them announced that the authorities were at the door, they were stunned and shaken beyond description. No one dared go down to open the door, for they all feared the blow—a blow which the Lord God turned into mercy.

In short, when they did go down, not a little afraid and expecting imminent imprisonment, they discovered that the mayor, or rather the Lord God Almighty, had sent them his deputy with two baskets full of bread as alms. In this way the Lord filled their houses with His blessing, for they had bread for more than a week. And all their other fears were to be dispelled in a similar manner as the Lord is witness.

In this state of constant anxiety, Joseph used to bore holes in the walls of his house in the middle of the night, and planned to slip out through them and escape when they came to arrest him. But here we can see how vain are the plans of man if the Lord God does not confirm them, and if His divine majesty does not protect a city, in vain does he labor who would protect it.

At the same time Joseph had another terrifying experience. By the will of God most high, the officers of the Crown and the chief constable of the Inquisition happened to clash in the Port of Ulua over the question of institutional priorities. In connection with this, the commissary of the Inquisition for that region came to Mexico City. The commissary at the time was a Franciscan friar and, when he came to Mexico, he naturally went to lodge in the monastery of Santiago, which belonged to his order, while he awaited the start of the discussions.

This Inquisitor had a brother [a Dominican monk] who knew that Joseph used to write and transcribe sermons and other ordinary materials for the Franciscan friars. He asked his brother to get the old monk of the school, in whose care Joseph had been entrusted, to have Joseph copy over a notebook which had been lent him by a fellow monk of his Dominican order. The commissary said he would look into the matter. The Inquisitor agreed to send his brother a note written in Joseph's hand in order to see whether Joseph's handwriting was to his liking.

Joseph [of course], was unaware of what was going on. One day, when Joseph's fears were at their height, the Inquisitor sent for Joseph by one of the monks of the monastery with whom Joseph was not particularly familiar, though he was loved and esteemed by all the monks and all were very friendly toward him. Not without fear and great misgiving Joseph asked the young man: "Who is that with Brother Christopher, our superior?"

He answered: "Brother Christopher is now with the commissary of the Inquisition, on whose errand I have come."

When Joseph heard this, his heart skipped a beat. He suspected that through the commissary the Inquisition was sending for him. You can imagine the fright and panic he was in when he finally resigned himself to going.

He found Brother Christopher and the commissary standing at the convent door. When Brother Christopher saw Joseph he said to the commissary, "Here he is," and even this seemed to confirm Joseph's fears.

The commissary then said: "Let us go up to [my] room." They did, and Joseph's fears received further confirmation when the commissary told him to take pen and paper and write a personal note. Joseph, who knew how well he could write, was terrified, for he not unnaturally suspected that they wanted the note to compare his handwriting with that of the book which his sister had lost. As a result he was plummeted into indescribable distress and anxiety.

Having written this note, Joseph was dismissed. He went home in trepidation—for which the Lord [later] repaid him—and began to think of fleeing for safety. But on this occasion as on others, he experienced the truth of the prophet David's statement that if the Lord does not protect a city, in vain does he wake who would protect it, and if the Lord does not build a city, in vain does he labor who would build it.

A short while later Joseph learned why the commissary of the Inquisition had had him write the note which had induced the anxiety. It was because the monk, who was the Inquisitor's brother, had learned that Joseph was copying papers and sermons for the Franciscan friars. A great preacher in his order had lent the monk a notebook and the latter eagerly wished to have it copied. In order to determine whether Joseph should do the copying for him, he asked the commissary to have Joseph write a note so that he could see his handwriting. When he saw it, he asked his brother the Inquisitor to have Joseph proceed; and the notebook accordingly was forwarded to the old monk who supervised Joseph.

When Joseph realized that his suspicions were groundless, he gave thanks to the Lord. Yet he was perturbed by the fact that the time involved in copying that book reduced the time he could devote to prayer and the service of the Lord his God. But this unbearable situation was turned by the Lord into a means for Joseph's consolation and eventual freedom. For in the very midst of Joseph's anxieties, when he did not even know how to go about seeking his freedom, the Lord was pleased to begin to give it to him. But before I explain how, I shall relate a miracle which the Lord most high performed concerning the notebook [Joseph was copying].

During this time Joseph received word in letters from his brother-in-law [in Spain], informing him that his liberty, mentioned above, had been attained, but for lack of funds, which had to be paid in Madrid, the documents could not yet be [released and] forwarded.

Rather to be freed from a situation that brought anxiety upon him than to obtain these documents [of liberty for himself and his family], Joseph asked the Inquisitor's brother, for whom he was copying the notebook, to help him get permission to move about freely in order to obtain alms [to pay] for his liberty. By command of the omnipotent Lord God, Joseph was given six months' leave.

When Joseph was about to take advantage of this [freedom] he was prevented from so doing by the fact that he had not finished copying the book. He had already arranged with the old monk, his confessor and the school's rector, to pay four Indian scribes to finish it. However—if you want more evidence of the mercies of the Most High, God permitted the old monk to change his mind and for the first time to harden his heart against Joseph. The day after making these arrangements, the rector said to him, with agitation and annoyance: "You must not go. It is unfair for you to leave before finishing the Inquisitor's notebook. A fine thing it is that now that they have given you liberty you scorn them and abandon your work."

Now if Joseph were to finish the notebook by himself, he would need more than his six months' leave which had been given to him. But since he was a captive, he said nothing. He humbly bemoaned his troubles and the fact that they delayed his going into hiding.

On the very day and at the very hour when the monk displayed such hostility and Joseph found himself in that plight, the Lord God sent two of the pages of the Inquisitor on behalf of his brother to pick up the notebook, unfinished though it was, because the preacher who had let the Inquisitor's brother examine it was going away. When the [monk who was the] rector of the school saw this, he was astonished [at Joseph's good fortune] and, inspired by the Lord God, he again favored Joseph as before.

When the provincial of the Franciscan friars learned that Joseph had been granted permission to seek alms, the Lord God touched his heart, and without a word from Joseph, he told his monks to inform Joseph that if he wished he would give him a very favorable letter-patent for the entire province, which would facilitate his being accorded a friendly reception in all the monasteries. Joseph said yes and received the letter as promised.

Then the Lord God moved the heart of the vicar-general, and by God's decree, he gave Joseph fifty favorable letters [of introduction]. The Lord God also gave Joseph favor in the sight of the governor of the Archbishopric, who granted an indefinite extension of Joseph's leave. And since everything was being decreed by God's hand, He moved the Provincial of the Augustinian friars to give Joseph yet another letter that would serve him well in all the monasteries of his order.

Joseph also applied for a letter from the viceroy but believed that it would be impossible to obtain. Since nothing is impossible for the Almighty God who was guiding him, no sooner did Joseph's confessor ask it on behalf of Joseph, his mother, and his sisters, than he was given not one letter, but twenty-five.

Taking these letters and the favor of the Lord his God with him, Joseph left his confinement in Mexico City after four years of anguish and affliction. Yet in the midst of it, he was abundantly aided by the Most High. [Now] wherever he went, God's divine majesty gave him grace. It was no small miracle that he moved his very enemies to shower him with their gifts of money, hens, cheese, corn and other items. Laden with these, he would return to the house of his penance, where his mother and sisters still lived.

Whenever Joseph came to a monastery, he was provided with lodging and offered food, but ever mindful of the Law and commandment of his Lord God, he refused the food to avoid defiling himself, saying that he had already eaten. It often happened, when he left the company and board of these men whom he loathed, that he went to eat his bread among the beasts, thinking it better to eat among horses in cleanliness than in uncleanliness at the tables of his well-bred enemies.

Two months after he first left, Joseph returned to the home of his mother and sisters sound [but not secure], for his heart was still agitated by the fear that his lost book would turn up and lead to an [Inquisitional] warrant for his arrest. He therefore first decided to find out whether it was safe for him to return to his mother's house. He first went to the older of his married sisters, who lived in a separate house with her husband and daughter, and asked her if there was anything new. Since the mercy of the Most High was guiding Joseph along this road of [his] fears, He permitted an occasion to come up in which Joseph would experience fears for his greater good. At his sister's [home] he learned that shortly after he had left, a man had come to his mother's house asking for him and saying that he was a page of the Inquisition's high constable. This had greatly alarmed his mother and sisters and now caused him not a little fright. He debated with himself whether or not he should go into hiding, but the Lord gave him courage to face anything, even death, and he went to his mother's house. It was soon evident that all this had been the prompting of fear, permitted and decreed, like everything else, by God on high that Joseph might recall all His mercies and be able the better to appreciate the gift of liberty that the Lord was about to grant him.

Joseph collected more than eight hundred and fifty pesos in alms from the hands of the barbarous Gentiles. May the Lord God of Israel enlighten them and bring them to a recognition of His holiness, that He may be adored and served by all His creatures. His mighty hand moved them to give Joseph these alms so willingly in most places that it was clear that the alms were coming from the Lord. Then Joseph and his mother received word that the brother-in-law who miraculously escaped from [Mexico City] for this purpose—with God's help—as I have already narrated, had succeeded, with the favor of the Most High, in obtaining the family's restoration to liberty. Again, this news arrived in time to serve as celestial medicine for Joseph's mother, for with its joy the Lord revived her from an illness that had her at the brink of death.

The decrees of liberty came in the first fleet, the one that arrived in this [land of] New Spain around September, 1594. When they came, the Lord had already provided Joseph with sufficient alms to pay for them. But before I tell how, by the Lord's hand and kindness, their penitential garb was removed, it is only proper that I mention two remarkable illnesses that the Lord God inflicted upon Joseph's two unmarried sisters as a most merciful atonement for the entire family, for, like sinning monks, we always need in this life bread and the rod. This is what our holy prophet gave thanks to God for when he said, "*Virga tua et baculus tuus ipsa me consolata sunt*" ["Your rod and your staff, they comfort me"].

The Lord gave the younger girl a throat ailment like quinsy, which lasted more than eight months. The Lord [finally] freed her from that illness by having her throat lanced in several places, but left her with another malady. She was left crippled, and as a result of her treatment, her speech was so impaired that for a few months she could barely make herself understood. But even then the patient girl did not lack divine aid and consolation, because it pleased the Lord to open the understanding of his sister, the one who married Jorge de Almeyda, to everything that the sick girl said. The physician and the surgeon and everyone else, therefore, relied on her to interpret the speech of the sick girl. May the infinite mercy of the Lord God heal her, for she is still an invalid.

To the older unmarried sister, our God, the Lord on High, then gave another very serious and equally perilous illness. Following severe depressions, the girl became mad, and as a result would have endangered not only her own life but the lives of all the rest of the family were it not for the providence of the One who has never abandoned them in their straits and hopefully never will. For in her madness, she has taken the idols in the homes of her heathen neighbors and before their very eyes thrown them out of their windows to be shattered down below. And on top of this she has done things and said things which have brought upon us such fright and danger that only our God and Lord can deliver us, for the glory of His sweet name.

The madness of this poor maiden is such that she babbles ceaselessly, day and night; yet in the course of her occasional gibberish, she utters many bald and lucid truths to the monks and idolatrous nuns who visit her in an attempt to cure her of her sickness.

Two doctors gave her ten stomach cauteries which brought on such pain and fury that she threw things at her mother and sisters and would have killed them, were it not for the grace of God. They have had such a difficult time with the girl that even strangers are moved to pity and compassion and they cry over the family's misfortune as if they were their kith and kin. But they [the members of the family] hope that God on high will extricate them in peace from these crises and bring them to the place where, in recognition of all His kindness and mercy, they may offer a sacrifice of praise in the midst of his servants, for the honor and glory of His most holy name.

The documents freeing Joseph, his mother, and sisters had arrived with the fleet that entered the port of New Spain around September, 1594. Since God our Lord has always led them on the road reserved for His special servants, He ordained that on a Thursday afternoon, on the sixth of October of that year, four days before the news of their liberty reached them, the constable of the Inquisition should come to summon them. This plunged them into the worst predicament imaginable. They bemoaned their lot as if they were already arrested and delivered over to the cruel enemy. But the Lord God, in His great mercy, had decreed that the purpose of the summons was to have them ratify their previous testimony before the Inquisition to the effect that Jacob Lumbroso, Joseph's younger brother [who had escaped from New Spain and] whom the Inquisitors were planning to burn in effigy, studied and kept the holy Law of the Most High. When they had done so, they were sent home, where they joyously celebrated God's merciful deliverance with sacred hymns and songs.

Four days later, which was Monday, October 10, they received the writ of liberty. This was one of the greatest mercies and blessings that [our] wandering and sinning people have ever received from the Lord. So great was the joy it brought that even their non-Jewish acquaintances rejoiced at their cheer, praising God and saying: "Blessed be the Lord God, who [has] had compassion upon you and [has] delivered you from such great travail and affliction."

And because this best suited [God's purpose], they could not [afford immediately to] redeem their penitential garb. Soon God moved a wealthy neighbor of theirs to bond them for eight hundred and fifty pesos. They immediately paid four hundred and twenty of these from the alms that Joseph had collected and took eight months to accumulate the balance. On Monday, October 24, 1594, on the command of God Most High, their penitential garb was removed.

On the same day the Lord performed a great miracle for Joseph. It happened that, at the very moment Joseph went to have his penitential garb removed, a heretic of our own people went before the Inquisitors to accuse one of his [Israelite] brothers [of Judaizing] and also to accuse Manuel de Lucena for having tried to enlighten him and direct him to the knowledge of the Lord God. At that time Joseph was in Lucena's house, though he was not together with him.

Joseph next went to Pachuca to gather some more alms. A week went by after the [heretic's] accusation, when the Lord ordained that the Inquisition arrest the men he had accused. Though the heretic had stated that Joseph was in the same house as Lucena, the Inquisition did not arrest him, because God on High, God Almighty had decided to deliver him with an extraordinary miracle.... May His Holy Name be eternally glorified and praised. Amen.

And because the road along which the Lord God has been leading them has been full of mercies, and His rod has been only the soft scourge of fear, He decreed that on the following Monday, a week after [they had taken off their penitential garb], they should suffer a new blow, one of the most severe yet—though they never suffered any from which the Lord God, in His infinite mercy, did not deliver them in two hours. What this blow was and how it came about are not being recorded for the time being, because the writer is still in lands of captivity, though with the help and favor of the Omnipotent and Almighty Adonay, the God of Israel, he is on the verge of leaving one of the greatest and most dangerous captivities which members of our nation have suffered. Here by the singular kindness of the Lord our God he and his family have been living in a danger no less great than the one which confronted Saint Daniel when he was thrown into the lion's den. The Almighty very miraculously shut the cruel mouths of the [enemies] surrounding him, for had not the Lord our God intervened, he would have immediately been torn to pieces.

Wherefore I humble my heart, worship and glorify God's most holy name and declare that He is good and very great and His mercy is eternal. May it help us and all Israel. Amen.

Francisco de Quevedo y Villegas
(Spain, 1580–1645)
"To a Nose"
Translated from the Spanish by David M. Gitlitz

Along with Lope de Vega and Luis de Góngora, Quevedo was a prolific conceptual poet, satirist, moralist, and novelist whose oeuvre defined the so-called Golden Age of Spanish letters in the sixteenth and seventeenth centuries, an age that, needless to say, was "golden" as a result of the abuses the Iberians engaged in on the other side of the Atlantic Ocean. Quevedo left us with memorable sonnets and dream sequences. He also wrote the picaresque novel *El buscón* (1626), available in English as *The Swindler*, and published *El caballero de la tenaza* (*The Stolid Knight*, 1606), *La hora de todos y la fortuna con seso* (*Everyone's Hour and Intelligent Fortune*, 1645), as well as a series of five *Sueños* (*Dreams*, 1607 to 1621–1622), visions in which, cynically, he imagined hell, death, and the world upside down. A stern xenophobe, Quevedo authored "The Nose" (in Spanish, *"Erase un hombre a una naríz pegado..."*), which might be one of the most anti-Semitic sonnets ever written in Spain, a peninsula known for its anti-Jewish literature. Among modern literati, Quevedo exercised influence over Borges and Octavio Paz.

There was a man suspended from a nose,
Something for all to talk about.
A headsman's pointed blade, a scribes fat pen,
A shark's sharp and most hairy snout,

A twisted and off-center sundial.
A laboratory beaker bent in thought,
An elephant's high-lifted trunk.
The nose that Ovid Naso never sought,

A floating galley's boastful, pushing prow,
Egypt's enshading pyramid,
One whose nasality was infinite,

So fierce, so swollen, it could not be hid,
A dozen nations lie around its base,
It would have been a crime on Annas' face.

Miguel Leví de Barrios
(Spain, 1635–1701)
"One Well-Founded Faith"
Translated from the Spanish by Timothy Oelman

Like that of Luis de Carvajal the Younger, the life of crypto-Jewish poet and play-wright Miguel Leví de Barrios was consumed by contradiction. He was born in Montilla, near Córdova. Little is known of his childhood until 1650, when the Inquisition arrested a relative and the family fled to northern Africa. Eventually he moved to Leghorn, Italy, where he had himself circumcised and acknowl-edged his Jewishness. But then de Barrios moved elsewhere in Europe. For years he divided his time between Brussels and Amsterdam, leading a double life. In Brussels, as *Miguel* Leví de Barrios, he was a captain of horse in the Spanish Army and a declared Christian. Under that identity, he enjoyed the support of prominent political figures. In Brussels he published the volumes of poetry *Flor de Apolo* (1665) and *Coro de las Musas* (1672), in which his Jewish self is tan-gential. In Amsterdam, on the other hand, de Barrios, as *Daniel* Leví de Barrios, he was a member of the Jewish community, married Abigail de Pina, and raised Jewish children. Eventually, he gave up his Brussels side and settled perma-nently in Amsterdam. But he clashed with the Jewish community and also suf-fered mental illness. He was a strong supporter of the pseudo-Messiah Shabbetai Zevi. De Barrios also wrote plays such as *Truth Triumphs in the End.* The last line in the following poem—"he lives secure who puts his trust in you"—from the anthology *Marrano Poets of the Seventeenth Century* (1982), edited by Timothy Oelman, might hold a key to his conflicted identity.

> The giant Philistine thinks to conquer:
> David conquers and breaks his neck in two;
> Daniel in the den sings a thousand hymns:
> all those die who swear he is a criminal.
>
> Proud Haman promulgates the death sentence
> against Mordecai: gallows he erects

and thus allows the Creator on *his* neck
to execute such barbarous intent.

All human power is but a vain shadow:
the most invincible of monarchies
is subject to villainous betrayal.

Oh, how infinite is God's sovereignty!
for, though human affairs are insecure,
he lives secure who puts his trust in you.

Miguel de Unamuno

(Spain, 1864–1936)

"Canción del sefardita"

Translated from the Spanish by Ilan Stavans

The Spanish-American War of 1898 that pushed Spain out of Cuba and Puerto Rico is known in Iberian history as *"el desastre."* It is an experience that marked an artistic generation that is recognized as *"la generación del '98."* One member of this generation was Miguel de Unamuno, a leading philosopher and man of letters born in Bilbao and a professor at the Universidad de Salamanca, where he lived most of his life with the exception of the period he spent in exile as a result of his political opposition to the military leader Primo de Rivera. Unamuno wrote philosophical meditations, newspaper columns, poetry, and novels, such as *Niebla* (1914), *Abel Sánchez* (1917), and *San Miguel Bueno, mártir* (1933), as well as the meditation *Of the Tragic Sense of Life in Men and Nations* (1913). A leading figure in the existentialist movement, he spent his life debating the clash between faith and reason and pondering his belief in Christianity. This little-known poem, number 365 in Unamuno's *Complete Works*, was drafted on August 31, 1928, while Unamuno was in exile in the Canary Islands. It eulogizes Ladino, the language of Jews in Spain, and finds parallels with Spain's language.

> Spanish language, *ladino*ized—
> with it I cry for you, Zion,
> and to you too, hospitable Spain,
> *nest of consolation*;
>
> I shall embrace you fearlessly,
> sweet Sephardic language,
> the legacy of Toledo,
> home to Judah Halevi.

Language of tender romance
used by Rome to guide us
in the quest to fight the trance
that exile became for us.

To my dried lips,
you're the milk and honey
flavored by the wise men
of our New Israel.

Rubén Darío
(Nicaragua, 1867–1916)
"Israel"
Translated from the Spanish by Melanie Nicholson

A dilettante and the leading figure in the esthetic movement known as *Modernismo* in Latin America, which roughly covered the years 1885 to 1915, Rubén Darío was an astonishingly influential poet and man of letters in the Spanish-American language and might be the most important poet in Hispanic culture since Luis de Góngora and Francisco de Quevedo y Villegas. He brought French Parnassianism and Symbolism into the Americas. His books include *Azul...* (*Blue*, 1888), *Prosas profanas* (*Profane Prose*, 1896), and *Cantos de vida y esperanza* (*Songs of Life and Hope*, 1905). Darío produced several poems on Israel and the Jews. For instance, in *Canto a la Argentina* (1914), he included the following lines: "

> Sing out, oh Jews of the Pampa!
> strapping young men of rustic grace,
> sweet Rebeccas of candid glance
> and Rubens with tumbling curls,
> patriarchs with heads of hair
> white and thick as a horse's mane,
> sing, sing out ancient Saras
> and adolescent Benjamins,
> lift the heart's own voice in song:
> 'We have arrived in Zion!'

The poem that follows was also drafted by Darío in Buenos Aires in 1898, at the apex of his talent, as Spain and the United States found themselves at war in the Caribbean. It invokes the image of the Jew as not quite earthly.

> Israel, oh Israel! When will the liquid diamond
> slide from your divine visage into pure blood?

When will the river's wind strike the harp strings
among the assemblies of the Argentine breeze?

When will the tresses of bowed heads
be lifted and stirred by persistent winds?
When will the arm of light give the Wandering Jew
a cup of clear water to slake his thirst?

Israel, oh Israel! That is the hour when the sinful
lark will raise to heaven her song and the great eye
in the deep abyss will be stirred to tenderness.

And when, the saint and the elect having arisen,
Christ our prince will lay his white hand,
will lay his white hand over the red of hell.

Alberto Gerchunoff
(Argentina, 1884–1950)
"A Jewish Gaucho"
Translated from the Spanish by Stephen A. Sadow

Considered to be the "grandfather of Jewish letters in Latin America," Alberto Gerchunoff is the author of the influential *The Jewish Gauchos of the Pampas* (1910), which he published in honor of the first centennial of the Argentine Republic, as a token of appreciation from the Jewish community for the open embrace with which the nation had embraced the Jewish immigrants from Eastern Europe who began to arrive in the late nineteenth century. Gerchunoff began his life speaking Yiddish and Russian, but as soon as he immigrated to South America he switched to Spanish. He became an influential intellectual and leader until World War II, and was a role model for Borges and others in successive literary generations. Other books by Gerchunoff include *Nuestro Señor Don Quijote* (*Our Lord, Don Quixote*, 1913), *El problema judío* (*The Jewish Problem*, 1945), and *Argentina, país de advenimiento* (*Argentina, Forward-Looking Country*, 1952). This autobiographical essay was left unpublished at Gerchunoff's death. It showcases his personal interests at the time of composition of *The Jewish Gauchos*. It was published in English translation in the anthology *King David's Harp* (1999), edited by Stephen A. Sadow.

Moisésville was visibly progressing. Behind the tents the lush horse pastures were giving way, bit by bit, to cultivation, and the furrows were becoming damp and dark. Squeaking carts, drawn by pairs of oxen, brought wire and posts, and the plow creaked while turning over the thick clay. The tame cows and the docile horses decorated our tranquil way of life with their presence, evocative of olden days of peace, the ancient days of the Bible. During the warm mornings the Jews greeted each other as they drew water from the wells, their robust voices covered by the harsh sound of the pulleys. The greetings had something ritualistic and mystical about them in that peaceable and primitive setting.

I had a white mare, agile and fleet, which would arch its neck and gallop backward, under the pull of the bridle, whenever we passed a girl from the colony. An audacious rider already at a tender age, I would lose my way on the outskirts of Moisésville while looking for a lost lamb or for some unexpected rhea tracks.

After midday I would go to the tent of the hunchbacked and lame Jew who taught me Hebrew and then to the synagogue with my father, since I liked to hear the old men's opinions and their interpretations of obscure passages from the texts. A tavern, owned by a Spaniard, had opened close by us. All the farm-workers would meet there, and it quickly became the focal point for the area. Gauchos from nearby ranches, wagon drivers, and passersby would stop off at the rancho, tying their horses to the posts in the *criollo* style, and enter the tavern. More than a few times bitter arguments broke out in it. From behind the counter the Spaniard, raising a club above his head to defend himself against possible attack, would shout them down. The colonists saw this tavern as something evil, and they would not stop telling the town administration's local representative that it should be closed down. After all, something serious had taken place there. A suspicious-looking Jewish fellow, covered with scars, very dark, with shifty eyes and a large curved knife, had stolen a horse from Moisésville; the owner had complained to the authorities; and the police had quickly found the thief and forced him to return the animal. The Jewish fellow, it turned out, was from the outskirts, a slacker, a brawler, and a drunk. After returning the horse, he spent even more time in the tavern, particularly during the afternoons, and never stopped arguing with the other gauchos.

One day, as the colonists were preparing to celebrate Passover, the slacker sat in the tavern from morning to evening, completely drunk. It was getting dark. On the road a few colonists passed by. We were in front of our tent, drinking *maté*, talking about this and that and observing, among other things, that it was foolhardy to live in Moisésville without a gun. But no colonist had so much as a shotgun for shooting partridges. Suddenly a gaucho appeared, brandishing an unsheathed knife. It was an instant at once horrible and terrifying. Shouts of panic heated the air. A moment of terrible confusion passed. Soon I grasped the enormity of our misfortune. I don't know exactly how, but we found ourselves before the town administration.

Laid out on the ground was my father, drenched in blood. Clearly, the horse owner had mistaken him for the thief. In a room inside, women were attending to my suffering mother and my older sister, also in agony, on a pair of cots. The entire distraught colony of Moisésville was on the patio. People had beaten the killer to death; his head lay mutilated and his body torn apart.

My father was buried in the little cemetery of Moisésville. On his tombstone the Jews inscribed an epitaph they had composed in the synagogue, in classical Hebrew: "Here lies Reb Gershun Gerchunoff, beloved for his wisdom, venerated for his extreme prudence, a chosen and just man."

We didn't leave the house for many weeks. In the evening neighbors came over to entertain us, and Pinhas Glusberg, the synagogue's former rabbi, would invariably relate an incomprehensible story about the mythical Russian general Kokoroff, with whom he had had the honor to speak. On the slightest pretext he would intervene, without fail, with the name of the famous officer, who I still can't quite believe existed. Pinhas Glusberg was a little old man, a talker and a dreamer with a poet's imagination. He would ask me. "Don't you see him on autumn afternoons, rising on a distant horizon, a ghost with white wings? Believe me. . . ."

Exhausted by the memory of the tragedy, our family abandoned Moisésville. We moved to Entre Ríos and settled in the Rajíl colony, where we became farmers in the fullest sense. I spent several years there, tilling the land with my brother, guiding the harvester, and caring for the stock. The ox driver, a former soldier with General [Justo José] Urquiza [a *caudillo* who became the largest and wealthiest landowner in Entre Ríos], helped me perfect the art of horse-riding. He also initiated me in the use of the *bola*. Like all Jewish boys in the colony, I looked like a gaucho: I wore widely cut trousers, a large homburg, and boots with ringing spurs; from the horn of the saddle hung a lasso of shining iron rings; and tied to my belt, next to my knife, were *bolas* for hunting.

No Jew of my age could claim to bring a wild yearling down with a jolt better than I. Nor could anyone else stop an unbroken colt in full flight dead in its tracks with a lasso. But my favorite task of all was to take care of the livestock near the stream bordering our land. All the boys in the colony would meet there, presided over by the native ox driver, who, incessantly chewing on his black tobacco cigarette, would invite us to drink *maté* with him.

The ox driver had a special fondness for me. I would praise the songs he sang to the monotonous chords of his broken-down guitar, and at my pleading he would relate his adventures as a heroic soldier. He divided the tasks with the boys: he worked the land, while we planted the seed for the next season's harvest.

In Rajíl my youthful spirit was filled with mythical tales of Indians from nearby regions. Through picturesque, rustic gaucho tales, through simple rhapsodies to Argentina's past, I assimilated the traditions of the place, its collective memories, the imaginary adventures of local warriors. For the first time my heart opened up to the poetry of the countryside, making me aware of the native beauty of Entre Ríos and igniting in me a steady pride in liberty and a love of *criollo* manners. The vast calmness of Entre Ríos, bounded by rivers under a matchless sky, so excited me as to erase my origins and make me an Argentine.

The crops failed the day we saw the approach of a cloud so thick that it blocked out the sun. It was locusts, of course, and hours later both the orchard and the seeded fields were covered with their plague. Men, women, and children all went out with sacks and sugar pans to chase the plague away. The wheat was high, and the orchard was flourishing.

We fought courageously, roaring and shouting. But exhaustion and the locust cloud defeated us, and by the time the sweet, magnificent moon illuminated the colony, only the farmers' sighs and the women's bitter laments could be heard in the saddened huts.

The curse came three years in a row.

But Rajil, like other Jewish colonies, made progress in spite of these disasters. Social life slowly began to stir, and families from different regions quickly formed close ties, overcoming the considerable distances separating them.

The construction of a synagogue and of a school was proposed. Jews convened to deliberate. Since the younger Jews predominated in the assembly, they endorsed the school first. Soon it was established in a large zinc shed, and from all over children were brought in daily, with their lunch pails hanging down.

This was to be the very first school in the area.

I was a good student. I learned the stanzas of the "Himno argentino," the Argentine national anthem, very quickly, During recess my friends would surround me as I repeated the gaucho tales I had heard from the ox driver in Rajíl.

My studies there didn't last long, though. My mother, obsessed with the fatal evening in Moisésville, yearned to leave the region altogether, and her pleading was so compelling that the whole family decided to go to Buenos Aires.

It was 1895, and my uncertain and wandering life had begun. While my mother insisted that I study, it wasn't possible at first, since someone needed to support the family. But how? None of us knew any trade at all, of course. Eventually, I found work in a Jew's business, kneading dough for Passover's unleavened bread. The bakery was far from where we lived, so I had to get up at dawn. At night a Spanish cart driver started me on the Spanish alphabet.

When the season of unleavened bread ended, I once again found myself with no means of support. I had to think about a trade. Soon I entered a mechanic's workshop as an apprentice. I was assigned to a nickel-plating section, among a swarm of shouting young boys who all but drowned out the boss's hoarse voice. I spent the day bent over near a sink filled with chalk, brushing bronzes that I would put in a can of boiling lye later.

My fingers swelled and split open. The days were not as bad as the nights, when I really suffered. Yet in spite of all I liked the mechanic's trade, and when I didn't have work to do in the nickel-plating section, I would go down to the founders' workshop or to the metalworkers' to learn something. After a month I was able to polish pretty well, and I knew how to handle more than a few machines.

I would have stayed in the trade if a shocking event had not convinced my family to pull me out. I am referring to the death of a metalworker, an Italian with enormous, wide shoulders, a rough and good fellow. One morning, on starting the motor, he got his shirt caught in the pulley. I was preparing the lye when I heard a horrifying crash. On the floor I saw his decapitated and mutilated body; an enormous blood stain extended all over the ceiling.

With affectionate insistence my mother persuaded me to leave the mechanic's workshop. I then joined a cigarette maker, from whom I earned fifteen pesos a month and lunch. My boss would pay his workers only after they had filled a certain hourly quota. I learned fast. In three months I was producing a thousand cigarettes a day. The owner didn't keep his word, though, and failed to pay me as promised. So I changed trades yet again and became a ribbon and embroidery maker—a beautiful trade, which I quickly grew to like. I progressed slowly: I spun, learned how to dye silks, knitted random stripes, and became skilled at framing. I was capable of producing a decorated braid less than a centimeter wide.

Soon I was a first-class worker. The factory owner, a jaundiced Jew, near-sighted and quarrelsome, once told me, in the presence of the operators, that I was the most skilled tradesman he had ever known. Meanwhile I kept studying at night. A buddy taught me Spanish grammar, history, and sciences, and a factory friend, a lean and witty Asturian, initiated me in to *Don Quixote*, a book for which I have a singular and profound love.

My aspirations were no longer those of a simple worker: I dreamed of structuring my studies, of taking examinations at the Colegio Nacional; I longed for the glory of a doctorate. No sooner did my day at the factory end than I went to my books, mixing the reading of dry everyday texts with those I sought most: my *Quixote*, *The Thousand and One Nights*, and Victor Hugo's novels. . . .

Over these first serious books I would fall asleep exhausted, and when I half opened my eyes, my mother's angular and wrinkled silhouette would be in front of me. She wouldn't go to bed until she had covered me up, protecting me during those winter nights from the cold wind. A medical student also gave me lessons. But it wasn't easy to study and work simultaneously, and I couldn't leave the shop since I needed to earn a living.

I spent a total of three years in the factory as an ordinary worker. At the end of that period I arranged to work half a day for a third of my salary. This way I could prepare for my exams, which, when the time came, I easily passed.

Now the problem was where to find the money for tuition and books.

A neighbor, the owner of a small store, offered me popular merchandise to sell in the street. This was during the crash of 1899. I would take a bulky sack and go around hawking from sunrise to sunset. I mainly sold the merchandise in the endless port area, but I also spent time on the city's outskirts. And so I walked for long weeks until I collected a paltry sum sufficient for my immediate needs. It was this job that brought me the greatest suffering and humiliation.

I entered the school. I applied myself above all to grammar and history. With a restless character, with exaggerated curiosity, I read enormously, chaotically. I also became interested in public affairs and argued with my classmates about the questions of the day.

That was the time when I obtained my Argentine citizen card, for my trouble, until then, had been not being equal to the others, that is, not being an Argentine. Once, when I told my grammar teacher about this problem, he first laughed heartily and then hugged me affectionately. I was sixteen years old then, two years too young to become a naturalized citizen. The next day, I was called to the school director's little office, where I found my teacher. He put me in a car.

"Where are we going?" I asked timidly.

"Well, my good man!" the director exclaimed, "to make you an Argentine.... Aren't you really one already?"

Once again I passed my exams with high marks. But the question of making a living was still unresolved. I began to give lessons to Jewish workers. But those unpredictable little earnings were clearly insufficient even for the most rudimentary necessities.

The following year I was no longer able to study as a regular student. In vain the school director and my teachers sought work for me. But I could find nothing. Free from the discipline of the program, I again spent many hours in the National Library, poking around books. And so, bit by bit, my interests led me to journalism and literature.

I got to know a number of writers and journalists at public lectures. They grew accustomed to my presence and were quite interested in my views and stories on Jewish life. Soon I became part of the bohemian side of Buenos Aires. This phase lasted for a long time. Happily, neighborhood newspapers and youth magazines began to accept my tentative essays.

One fine day in 1903 I was offered the position of editor-in-chief of *El censor* in the city of Rosario.

Of course, I didn't know how to run a newspaper. It took a great deal of work to acquire the most basic skills. *El censor* was an opposition newspaper, and my articles, virulent like every beginner's, caused a small scandal in town sufficient to make me a man of the press.

The newspaper was forced to close down, and I returned to Buenos Aires armed, fortunately, with a certain professional preparation.

It was then that I joined *El país* and became an effective journalist, able to take on any assignment and do at least a passable job of it. I stayed at this daily for years, but I also collaborated on various periodicals.

My departure from Moisésville and Rajil had not led to my separation from Jewish people. In Buenos Aires the Jewish community was constantly growing, forming a visible nucleus for its intense commercial and industrial activities. Already there were a considerable number of Jews in the high schools and universities, all hardworking and extraordinarily energetic, stubborn, and firm-willed, who didn't take long to distinguish themselves with their scholarly achievements.

Observing this, I conceived a plan to study Jewish life in a free atmosphere, without outside pressure. Wouldn't it be interesting to show Judaism redeemed from the share of slavery, martyrdom, and stoicism that usually plunged it into abjection? I was then the literary critic of *La nación*. Well-placed and calmer than I had once been, I carried out part of my plan in 1910 by publishing a book in which I tried to illustrate the customs of Jewish immigrant farmers in Argentina.

I traveled a lot, edited newspapers in the interior, took over the associate editorship of *La mañana* and later the position of editor in chief of Buenos Aires's *La gaceta*. That, in short, is how I became a full-fledged journalist: wandering from place to place and from one trade to another. Life, in all its hardships, taught me to love being alive. It planted deep in my spirit the feeling of human pain and, more than books had done, shaped my personal ideas. This is why I love the Jewish people, for they know, like no one else, the supreme value of liberty.

In Argentina, Jews, redeemed from injustice and religious stereotypes, will lose their characteristic profile. On this soil they will gradually be freed from the whip of persecution. This can be seen already. From the city and the countryside Argentine Jews are deeply, sincerely patriotic, as are their elders, born in Odessa or Warsaw and immigrants to this land. Argentina can be proud of this and show it to older civilizations. What would the Russian people say about such a transformation, for instance? As I carry out many official functions, I come across Jews who are university professors, which neither shocks nor irritates anyone. These Jews are Argentine citizens; nobody cares which temple they pray in or if they are Catholics or not.

In truth, the Jew lacks religious preoccupation. He is mystical without being dogmatic, exactly the reverse of what anti-Semites think. In an atmosphere of freedom, he is assimilated to the country; he is remade in its essence. The venerable Baron de Hirsch understood this potential well when he founded the agricultural colonies in Argentina, an immense task of practical philanthropy and at the same time a testament to show to the systematic enemies of this small suffering people, dispersed all over the globe.

Neither moneylender nor martyr, the Jew is a free man. No matter what trade he embarks on—laborer of the land, factory worker, financial magnate—in Argentina his status will not change, for this is Palestine for the Jew, a land of liberty, the Promised Land in the Biblical sense of the word.

I don't sing of Jewish life only, though; above all, I'm an Argentine and as such, a man of letters.

Américo Castro
(*Spain, 1885–1972*)
"The Spanish Jews"
Translated from the Spanish by Edmund L. King

Born in Rio de Janeiro, the controversial critic and historian Américo Castro taught at Princeton and Harvard universities for years. His scholarship dealt with literature and history as a means to decipher the Spanish temperament. Castro's books include *España en su historia: Cristianos, moros y judíos* (*Spain in Its History: Christians, Muslims, and Jews*, 1948), *The Spaniards: An Introduction to Their History* (1971), and the anthology of his work, *An Idea of History* (1977). The latter includes essays on Cervantes and Pirandello, and an examination of Don Quixote, *lo barroco* (the baroque) as a literary style, and Sultan Saladin in literature. Castro's thesis is that Spanish culture is to a large extent the result of religious coexistence of Christians, Jews, and Muslims. The following brief entry belongs to Chapter XIII of the influential volume, *The Structure of Spanish History* (1954). It is an example of the sort of psychohistorical meditation Castro undertook throughout his life.

The history of non-Hispanic Europe can be understood without assigning the Jews a position anywhere in the foreground of the picture. This is not the case with Spain. And the primordial, decisive function of the Hispano-Hebrews is in turn absolutely inseparable from the circumstance of their having lived in close articulation with Hispano-Muslim history. The language used by their greatest figures (Maimonides, for example) was Arabic, although they wrote it in Hebrew characters. Their evident superiority to their European coreligionists is correlative to the superior level of Islam as compared with Christendom from the tenth through the twelfth centuries. Without their contact with Islam, they would never have become interested in religious philosophy. No less significant is the fact that only in Spain did the Jews possess an architecture of their own that showed an artistically distinct quality even though it was closely connected with Islamic art. We hear the lovely voice of the Hispano-Hebraic spirit issuing from the synagogues of Toledo and other towns with a firmness and expressive intensity unequaled elsewhere in Europe, where—and this is the explanation—they never felt themselves at home. But the tone of these architectonic expressions—almost totally destroyed—is Islamic; and the poetry, the thought, and the technology of the Hispano-Hebrews are likewise sequels of Arabic civilization. However, I am not going to write a history of the Jews. I am only interested in showing how they fit into Spanish history and what traces they have left in the disposition of its living dwelling-place.

The Jews ejected from their fatherland, that is, Spain, in 1492 felt themselves to be—and how rightly, we shall soon see—as Spanish as the Christians. Let us listen at random to one of them, a certain Francisco de Cáceres, who, like many others, outwardly accepted Christianity and returned to his native land around 1500. The officials of the Inquisition, into whose clutches he happened to fall, asked him why he had gone away. Cáceres answered them with reasons plain and good: "If the king our lord should order the Christians to become Jews or else to leave his realm, some would become Jews and others would leave; and those who left, as soon as they saw their sad plight, would become Jews so they could return to their native place, and they would be Christians and pray like Christians and deceive the world; they would think that they were Jews, and inside, in their hearts and wills, they would be Christians."

Between the tenth and the fifteenth centuries, Spanish history was Christian-Islamic-Judaic, and during those centuries the definitive structure of Hispanic life was forged. It is not possible to break up this history into stagnant pools or to divide it off into parallel, synchronous currents, because each one of the three groups was a part of the circumstances projected by the other two. Nor could we capture this reality merely by gathering together data and events or by objectifying it as a "cultural phenomenon." We must try to feel the projection of the lives of the ones into the lives of the others. For this and nothing else is what their history was. Facts, ideas, and all the rest are inseparable from the lives with which they are integrated. . . .

Just as the kings, nobles, and ecclesiastics entrusted the Jews with the treatment of their aches and pains, so they were also to entrust them with the collection of public income as well as the management and development of other important sources of wealth. We do not realize clearly enough today what it meant to turn over essential branches of the public administration to the Hispano-Hebrews. If the latter had been a normal component of Spanish life, happily articulated in it, their activities as the managerial and banking caste would have had another meaning. Such articulation is historically unthinkable, because the Jew had no honorable place in the Christian idea of the state. England and France expelled the not-very-numerous Jews from their lands in the thirteenth and fourteenth centuries on the initiative of the ruling class. The case of Spain was entirely different. The Jews had remained there in large numbers up to 1492 as serfs of the kings, as enemies of Christianity, and as irritating guests, allowed to share the life of the dominant caste for reasons of necessity and interest. But the politically inferior caste—the Jews—performed functions essential for the collective life in the same way that, as physicians and administrators, they had a place in the private life of those who ruled Spain. The history of every day—not that of the great moments in warfare—came to be something like the product of the Jew's "inferiority" multiplied by the technical incapacity of the Christian—a very uncomfortable situation which disturbed the experience of values and their hierarchy. It is a serious affair when the services that we lend or are lent to us do not mesh with a system of mutual loyalties and common values, as they did where the feudal organization was an authentic reality. In important areas of Spanish life, loyalty and esteem were replaced by the tyranny of the lord and the flattering servility of the Jews, forced to pay this price to subsist.

This false situation was fatal, and equally so was the situation in which the common people had to accept a group whom they hated and despised as their superiors, legally entitled to prey regularly upon their meager resources. And the more evident the superiority of the Jews turned out to be, the worse it became. From such premises it was impossible that there should be derived any kind of modern state, the sequel, after all, of the Middle Ages' hierarchic harmony. The belief *"non est potestas nisi a Deo"* implied a scheme in which all power was founded on justified reason (king or state) related to the right of the individual to govern himself. The genesis of the organization of the state, which reached its culmination in the European nineteenth century, lay in the web of spiritual relationships that, starting with the king, spread downward through graduated levels to the lowliest subject. The feudal system duplicated in the realm of the human the divine organization of the Church. In Spain, however, the inescapable presence of the Moors and Jews in the Christian kingdoms prevented the implantation of the Christian-European social system, fixed by the coordinates of the papacy and the Carolingian Empire. The main paths that were open to the Christian feudal state were obstructed in Spain by the Jew, as necessary as he was foreign. Spain was left outside the feudal system for the same reason that she could bring Castilian prose to flower in texts of high learning, thus in the thirteenth century turning her back on the Latin of Europe. It is almost symbolical that the Pope declined to recognize Alphonse X's indubitable legal rights to the imperial throne.

We may now begin our reflections on the dominating presence of the Jews in the most vital centers of the state organism. It is not known when or how they began to serve as fiscal agents for the Christian kings. During the many centuries of oppression and persecution by the Christians, the Jews became usurers and publicans in violation of the letter and spirit of their own law, because this was the only way they could keep afloat in societies that excluded them from the normal occupations. . . .

Samuel Eichelbaum
(*Argentina, 1894–1967*)
"The Good Harvest"
Translated from the Spanish by Rita Gardiol

Playwright, translator, critic, and author of stories, Samuel Eichelbaum was born in Entre Ríos, Argentina, the child of Russian immigrants. He belongs to the literary generation of Alberto Gerchunoff, the first to infuse Argentine letters with a Jewish sensibility. Eichelbaum is the author of *Tempest from God* and *The Unchanging Traveler*. His plays include *Aaron the Jew* and *No One Ever Knew Her*. He was among the first to handle racial issues openly in his country. "A Good Harvest," Rita Gardiol suggests, appears to be based on a real-life incident. "Some say it is the story of Eichelbaum's father, an unhappy immigrant farmer driven to desperate measures to relocate his family in the city."

For four years now he had been working the two hundred acres of farm land they had given him when he arrived in Argentina from Russia. The Roschpina colony of Entre Ríos was the most cheerful one in the area, but this fact didn't affect his aversion to rural tasks. When he'd sailed for these lands, he'd agreed to accept the farm solely with the goal of getting to America and then later being able to dedicate himself to his trade. Never for a moment had he resigned himself to the idea of working the land. He didn't feel competent enough to do it, nor did he think the countryside was a suitable ambiance for his spirit. On the trip, because of unforeseen events, he had to renounce, for the time being, his desire to settle in the city and dedicate his energies to mechanics, which was the trade that he loved as one loves his chosen work. It had been a trip so full of tragedy that it had totally exhausted him. Upon reaching port in Buenos Aires he no longer had any hopes, plans or desires. He never disagreed with his wife's suggestions, and she never dared to disagree with her mother.

So it was that Bernardo Drugova, to his mother-in-law's great and understandable surprise, without realizing it, turned into a bland and submissive son-in-law. When he didn't oppose his wife's desires, he indirectly obeyed his mother-in-law, since she always exercised total control over her daughter. He took possession of his farm with an indifference that was in visible contrast to the joy felt by other colonizers who had immigrated with him. Farm chores were completely alien to him, but because he had an extraordinary gift for learning manual labor, he very quickly became one of the most expert farmers in the area. Nevertheless, Drugova hated the land. When his wife gave him his first son, it reawakened in him, more intensely than ever, his desire to live in the city. He expressed this to his wife and mother-in-law a number of times and each time, he met with aggressive hostility from the old lady. Although his wife wasn't opposed exactly, neither did she share her husband's desires. Her attitude was one of indifference more from fear of her mother's anger than from a desire to preserve the well-being she might enjoy where she happened to be. Drugova did-n't pursue it. He didn't want to cause his mother-in-law's suffering, because of her age on the one hand and her grumbling disposition on the other. He didn't believe that the stress that the move to Buenos Aires might cause the old woman would be a major and decisive factor in her health, as they wanted him to believe. Nevertheless, he sometimes thought, since both of them said this, it was better not to be too suspicious. Thus Drugova rationalized and kept quiet. For the rest, the old woman knew how to argue skillfully when it came to upsetting her son-in-law's plans:

"Here you have bread and a roof," she would say, "nobly earned bread and an honorable roof. You have no reason whatsoever to reject the destiny you accepted when you started out."

"What would you do in the city? Work in your trade? Every city has a thousand men more competent than you in the same trade."

"It's important to think about the child," he would dare to argue. "We ought to give him a good education. I don't want him to be a laborer like me, ignorant like me."

"Educate him in what is good and honorable, which are the only things that matter. Let him learn to plow and sow the land and he will be good and honorable. Do you think, by chance, that he might become a rabbi? It would be a sin of vanity to aspire to that; a sin as great as if you aspired to make a scholar of him. Aspiring to grandeur is a sin unbecoming to poor people. My love as a grandmother is as great as your love as a father, but mine is sensible and humble. It doesn't need anything grandiose to nourish it. I don't demand anything from my grandson in order to love him."

The discussion would invariably come to an end, thanks to the discreet silence observed by Bernardo, who, although he felt violent sometimes, always managed to control himself.

For a long time, maybe a year, Drugova stopped talking about moving to Buenos Aires. To his wife and mother-in-law it seemed evident that he had abandoned the idea, a supposition doubly pleasing to them: because of the renunciation it implied in itself and the triumph it implied for them. Bernardo worked with such effort that they thought he had completely adapted to his situation. Moreover, the harvest promised to be bountiful enough to complete the well-being which reigned on Drugova's farm, where three enormous stacks, two of wheat and one of oats, stood like hills of gold. The little one, meanwhile, had grown strong and beautiful. The color in his eyes had finally settled and whether it was so or not, the fact was that he seemed to look at the fields with utter indifference, as if his progenitor had transmitted to him his hatred of the land.

In Roschpina, the neighbors had already closed deals for the sale of their harvest. Drugova hadn't done so yet. His wife, on several occasions, suggested that he get on with the threshing, fearing that prices would suddenly suffer a strong drop, as sometimes happened.

"I'm not saying you should be in a hurry to sell it, but I do think you should ready the harvest. You might get a really good offer on condition of immediate delivery, and you would be obliged to refuse it, hurting yourself."

Bernardo, a man of few words, answered such exemplary and sensible observations with silence, communicating the sense of having heeded the advice they always carried.

One morning, long before daybreak, Drugova awakened. He looked around, probably in search of some filter of light that would help him guess the time. He found everything dark, and decided to get up. First he checked on his wife, who was in her usual deep sleep, her dark and muscular arms outstretched, her thick dark hair undone. Two minutes later, from the door of his tool shed, he pensively observed a tenuous and whitish-blue sky announcing good weather. A full moon, pure, limpid, and transparent, adorned everything. Slowly he walked toward the fields. The farm dogs saw their master and followed him, although he tried in vain to stop them. Drugova reached the first shock of wheat, magnificent, unmovable like a house on strong and deep foundations, passed his rough hand over some stalks, as if he wanted to caress them, and felt the soft, pleasant moisture of the dew. Then, almost as if without thinking, he extracted a box of matches from one of his pockets, lit one, and put it as far as he could under the stack, which seemed to shudder at the threat from the insignificant little flame. When the man was sure that his intentions were being carried out, he directed his steps toward the next one, scarcely fifty meters from the first, and repeated the operation. When this was done, he noticed that the first stack of wheat was giving off a thick blackish smoke that thinned out, disappearing entirely at a few meters.

Bernardo started back in haste. Carefully, he undressed and got back into bed. About half an hour had passed when he heard the dogs barking furiously and immediately heard some knocking on one of the window shutters. It was Rogelio, a native servant from the neighboring farm, who had seen the smoke and then came at a gallop to give the warning.

"Don Bernardo, your wheat is on fire! They have set your wheat on fire!"

Drugova's wife woke with a start: "Bernardo, someone has set fire to our wheat."

"I heard," he replied in a dry tone of controlled violence, and started to get dressed while his wife jumped out of bed after thanking Rogelio.

When they went out to the patio, everything was already burned. Both stacks had turned into flames—unattractive because the dawn, which was just now breaking, took away any beauty that might have come from the fire. The woman observed the voracity of the flames; her eyes flooded with tears. As soon as Bernardo appeared, she said in a scarcely audible tone:

"By the time you get there with water, there won't even be a grain left!"

Beside the barn gate to the left, the squalid figure of the servant stood out.

"It seems to have been burning for a while. I rode bareback and came at a gallop as soon as I saw it." And after a silence he added, "How could it have happened, I wonder?"

In his fractured language, Drugova managed to say that this could not be an accident but rather an intentional act. Rogelio commented:

"Can there be Christians so mean-spirited?"

A month later, with what he got from the oats (it was the only stack spared from the disaster), Drugova, his wife, his mother-in-law, and his little son all moved to Buenos Aires.

Federico García Lorca
(Spain, 1898–1936)
"Jewish Cemetery"
Translated from the Spanish by Steven F. White

Federico García Lorca was murdered on an August day of 1936 by right-wing nationalists as the Spanish Civil War unfolded. He was born in Fuentevaqueros, a small town in Andalusía. Andalusian culture is at the heart of his lyrical poetry. In it he sings to the guitar, to gypsies, to bullfighters and knives. He is also known as a playwright for dramas such as *Blood Weddings* (1933) and *The House of Bernarda Alba* (1936). In 1919, García Lorca moved to Madrid. The encounter of metropolitan life made him feel more connected with the Spanish rural folk. He toured Latin America, but only after a 1929 visit to New York, where he was a student at Columbia University. In that period he was influenced by Walt Whitman. The product of that experience is *Poet in New York*, published posthumously in 1940, where he sings to sexual freedom, the anonymous masses, architecture, and nature. His interest in Jewishness was slight, yet *Poet in New York* includes the following poem written on January 18, 1930. It showcases his view of Judaism as a depository of ancient memory. As such, it is a continuation of the vision proposed by Miguel de Unamuno and other Spaniards whose link to Jews was tangential.

The fevers fled with great joy to the hawsers of moored ships
and the Jew chastely pushed against the gate the way lettuce
    grows coldly from its center.

Christ's children slept,
and the water was a dove,
and the wood was a heron,
and the lead was a hummingbird,
and even the living prisons of fire
were consoled by the locust's leap.

Christ's children rowed and the Jews packed the walls
with a single dove's heart
through which all of them wished to escape.
Christ's little girls sang and the Jewish women looked at death
with a pheasant's solitary eye,
glazed by the anguish of a million landscapes.

The doctors put their scissors and surgical gloves on the chrome table
when the feet of the corpses feel
the terrible brightness of another buried moon.
Tiny unscathed pains approach the hospitals
and the dead take off a suit of blood every day.

The architecture of frost,
the lyres and moans that escape from the small leaves
in autumn, drenching the farthest slopes,
were extinguished in the blackness of their derbies.

The dew retreats in fear from blue, forsaken grass,
and the white marble entrances that lead to hard air
were showing their silence broken by sleeping footprints.

The Jew pushed against the gate;
but the Jew was not a port
and the boats of snow piled up
on the gangways of his heart:
the boats that wait in ambush for
a man of water who can drown them,
the boats of the cemeteries
that sometimes blind the visitors.

Christ's children slept
and the Jew lay down in his berth.
Three thousand Jews wept in the galleries of terror
because it was all they could do to gather half a dove among
    themselves,

because one of them had the wheel from a clock
and another a boot laced with talking caterpillars
and another a nocturnal rain burdened with chains
and another the claw of a nightingale that was still alive;
and because the half-dove moaned,
spilling blood that was not its own.
The fevers danced with great joy on the humid domes,
and the moon inscribed in its marble
ancient names and worn ribbons.
Those who dine behind the rigid columns arrived,
so did the donkeys with their white teeth
and the specialists in the body's joints.

Green sunflowers trembled
on the wastelands of dusk
and the whole cemetery began to complain
with cardboard mouths and dry rags.
Christ's children were going to sleep
when the Jew, squeezing his eyes shut,
silently cut off his hands
as he heard the first moans begin.

Jorge Luis Borges
(Argentina, 1899–1986)
"The Secret Miracle"
Translated from the Spanish by Harriet de Onís

Jorge Luis Borges is arguably the most important literary figure from Latin America in the twentieth century. His oeuvre was repackaged by the New York publisher Viking Putnam in the late nineties in three easily manageable volumes: *Collected Fictions* (1998), *Selected Non-Fictions* (1999), and *Selected Poems* (1999). Throughout his life Borges maintained a passion for *lo judío*—things Jewish. In the thirties, in response to an attack, he issued a brief essay entitled "I, a Jew." In it he argues (in a translation by Eliot Weinberger): "Who has not, at one time or another, played with thoughts of his ancestors, with the prehistory of his flesh and blood? I have done so many times, and many times it has not displeased me to think of myself as Jewish. It is an idle hypothesis, a frugal and sedentary adventure that harms no one, not even the name of Israel, as my Judaism is wordless, like the songs of Mendelssohn. The magazine *Crisol* [Crucible], in its issue of January 30, has decided to gratify this retrospective hope; it speaks of my 'Jewish ancestry, maliciously hidden' (the participle and the adverb amaze and delight me)." And he adds: "Two hundred years and I can't find the Israelite; two hundred years and my ancestor still eludes me. . . . What would we think of someone in the year 4000 who uncovers people from San Juan Province everywhere? Our inquisitors seek out Hebrews, but never Phoenicians, Garamantes, Scythians, Babylonians, Persians, Egyptians, Huns, Vandals, Ostrogoths, Ethiopians, Illyrians, Paphlagonians, Sarmatians, Medes, Ottomans, Berbers, Britons, Libyans, Cyclopes, or Lapiths. The nights of Alexandria, of Babylon, of Carthage, of Memphis, never succeeded in engendering a single grandfather; it was only to the tribes of the bituminous Dead Sea that this gift was granted." "The Secret Miracle" is an example of Borges's use of Jewish themes in his fiction. It is a hidden tribute to one of his idols, Franz Kafka.

And God had him die for a hundred years and then revived him and said:
"How long have you been here?"
"A day or part of a day," he answered.

—Koran, II, 261

The night of March 14,1943, in an apartment in the Zeltnergasse of Prague, Jaromir Hladik, the author of an unfinished drama entitled *The Enemies*, of *Vindication of Eternity*, and of a study of the indirect Jewish sources of Jakob Böhme, had a dream of a long game of chess. The players were not two persons, but two illustrious families; the game had been going on for centuries. Nobody could remember what the stakes were, but it was said that they were enormous, perhaps infinite; the chessmen and the board were in a secret tower. Jaromir (in his dream) was the firstborn of one of the contending families. The clocks struck the hour for the game, which could not be postponed. The dreamer raced over the sands of a rainy desert, and was unable to recall either the pieces or the rules of chess. At that moment he awoke. The clangor of the rain and of the terrible clocks ceased. A rhythmic, inanimate noise, punctuated by shouts of command, arose from the Zeltnergasse. It was dawn, and the armored vanguard of the Third Reich was entering Prague.

On the 19th the authorities received a denunciation; that same 19th, toward evening, Jaromir Hladik was arrested. He was taken to an aseptic, white barracks on the opposite bank of the Moldan. He was unable to refute a single one of the Gestapo's charges; his mother's family name was Jaroslavski, he was of Jewish blood, his study on Böhme had a marked Jewish emphasis, his signature had been one more on the protest against *Anschluss*. In 1928 he had translated the *Sepher Yezirah* for the publishing house of Hermann Barsdorf. The fulsome catalogue of the firm had exaggerated, for publicity purposes, the translator's reputation, and the catalogue had been examined by Julius Rothe, one of the officials who held Hladik's fate in his hands. There is not a person who, except in the field of his own specialization, is not credulous; two or three adjectives in Gothic type were enough to persuade Julius Rothe of Hladik's importance, and he ordered him sentenced to death *pour encourager les autres*. The execution was set for the 29th of March, at 9 A.M. This delay (whose importance the reader will grasp later) was owing to the desire on the authorities' part to proceed impersonally and slowly, after the manner of vegetables and planets.

Hladik's first reaction was stark terror. He told himself he would not have shrunk from the gallows, the block, or the knife, but that death by a firing squad was unbearable. In vain he tried to convince himself that the plain, unvarnished fact of dying was the fearsome thing, not the attendant circumstances. He never wearied of conjuring up these circumstances, senselessly trying to exhaust all their possible variations. He lived in infinite anticipation of the process of his dying, from the sleepless dawn to the mysterious volley. Before the day set by Julius Rothe, he died hundreds of deaths in courtyards whose forms and angles strained geometrical probabilities, machine-gunned by variable soldiers in changing numbers, who at times killed him from a distance, at others from close by. He faced these imaginary executions with real terror (perhaps with real bravery); each simulacrum lasted a few seconds. When the circle was closed, Jaromir returned once more and interminably to the tremulous vespers of his death. Then he reflected that reality is not in the habit of coinciding with our anticipation of it; with a logic of his own he inferred that to foresee a circumstantial detail is to prevent its happening. Trusting in this weak magic, he invented, *so that they would not happen*, the most gruesome details. Finally, as was natural, he came to fear that they were prophetic. During his miserable nights, he endeavored to find some way to hold fast to the fleeting substance of time. He knew that it was rushing headlong toward the dawn of the 29th. He reasoned aloud: "I am now in the night of the 22nd; while this night lasts (and for six nights more), I am invulnerable, immortal." The nights of sleep seemed to him deep, dark pools in which he could submerge himself. There were moments when he longed impatiently for the final burst of fire that would free him, for better or for worse, from the vain compulsion of his imaginings. On the 28th, as the last sunset was reverberating on the high barred windows, the thought of his drama, *The Enemies*, deflected him from these abject considerations.

Hladik had rounded forty. Aside from a few friendships and many habits, the problematic exercise of literature constituted his life. Like all writers, he measured the achievements of others by what they had accomplished, asking of them that they measure him by what he envisaged or planned. All the books he had published had left him with a complex feeling of repentance. His study of the work of Böhme, of Ibn Ezra, and of Fludd had been characterized essentially by mere application; his translation of the *Sepher Yezirah*, by carelessness, fatigue, and conjecture. *Vindication of Eternity* perhaps had fewer shortcomings. The first volume gave a history of man's various concepts of eternity, from the immutable Being of Parmenides to the modifiable Past of Hinton. The second denied (with Francis Bradley) that all the events of the universe make up a temporal series, arguing that the number of man's possible experiences is not infinite, and that a single "repetition" suffices to prove that time is a fallacy. Unfortunately, the arguments that demonstrate this fallacy are equally fallacious. Hladik was in the habit of going over them with a kind of contemptuous perplexity. He had also composed a series of expressionist poems; to the poet's chagrin, they had been included in an anthology published in 1924, and no subsequent anthology but inherited them. From all this equivocal, uninspired past Hladik had hoped to redeem himself with his drama in verse, *The Enemies*. (Hladik felt the verse form to be essential because it makes it impossible for the spectators to lose sight of irreality, one of art's requisites.)

The drama observed the unities of time, place, and action. The scene was laid in Hradčany, in the library of Baron Roemerstadt, on one of the last afternoons of the nineteenth century. In the first scene of the first act, a strange man visits Roemerstadt. (A clock was striking seven, the vehemence of the setting sun's rays glorified the windows, a passionate, familiar Hungarian music floated in the air.) This visit is followed by others; Roemerstadt does not know the people who are importuning him, but he has the uncomfortable feeling that he has seen them somewhere, perhaps in a dream. They all fawn upon him, but it is apparent—first to the audience and then to the baron—that they are secret enemies in league to ruin him. Roemerstadt succeeds in checking or evading their involved schemings. In the dialogue, mention is made of his sweetheart, Julia von Weidenau, and a certain Jaroslav Kubin, who at one time pressed his attentions on her. Kubin has now lost his mind, and believes himself to be Roemerstadt. The dangers increase; Roemerstadt, at the end of the second act, is forced to kill one of the conspirators. The third and final act opens. The incoherencies gradually increase; actors who had seemed out of the play reappear; the man Roemerstadt killed returns for a moment. Someone points out that evening has not fallen; the clock strikes seven, the high windows reverberate in the western sun, the air carries an impassioned Hungarian melody. The first actor comes on and repeats the lines he had spoken in the first scene of the first act. Roemerstadt speaks to him without surprise; the audience understands that Roemerstadt is the miserable Jaroslav Kubin. The drama has never taken place; it is the circular delirium that Kubin lives and relives endlessly.

Hladik had never asked himself whether this tragicomedy of errors was preposterous or admirable, well-thought-out or slipshod. He felt that the plot I have just sketched was best contrived to cover up his defects and point up his abilities and held the possibility of allowing him to redeem (symbolically) the meaning of his life. He had finished the first act and one or two scenes of the third; the metrical nature of the work made it possible for him to keep working it over, changing the hexameters, without the manuscript in front of him. He thought how he still had two acts to do, and that he was going to die very soon. He spoke with God in the darkness: "If in some fashion I exist, if I am not one of Your repetitions and mistakes, I exist as the author of *The Enemies*. To finish this drama, which can justify me and justify You, I need another year. Grant me these days, You to whom the centuries and time belong." This was the last night, the most dreadful of all, but ten minutes later sleep flooded him like a dark water.

Toward dawn he dreamed that he had concealed himself in one of the naves of the Clementine Library. A librarian wearing dark glasses asked him: "What are you looking for?" Hladik answered: "I am looking for God." The librarian said to him: "God is in one of the letters on one of the pages of one of the four hundred thousand volumes of the Clementine. My fathers and the fathers of my fathers have searched for this letter; I have grown blind seeking it." He removed his glasses, and Hladik saw his eyes, which were dead. A reader came in to return an atlas. "This atlas is worthless," he said, and handed it to Hladik, who opened it at random. He saw a map of India as in a daze. Suddenly sure of himself, he touched one of the tiniest letters. A ubiquitous voice said to him: "The time of your labor has been granted." At this point Hladik awoke.

He remembered that men's dreams belong to God, and that Maimonides had written that the words heard in a dream are divine when they are distinct and clear and the person uttering them cannot be seen. He dressed; two soldiers came into the cell and ordered him to follow them.

From behind the door, Hladik had envisaged a labyrinth of passageways, stairs, and separate buildings. The reality was less spectacular: they descended to an inner court by a narrow iron stairway. Several soldiers—some with uniform unbuttoned—were examining a motorcycle and arguing about it. The sergeant looked at the clock; it was 8:44. They had to wait until it struck nine. Hladik, more insignificant than pitiable, sat down on a pile of wood. He noticed that the soldiers' eyes avoided his. To ease his wait, the sergeant handed him a cigarette. Hladik did not smoke; he accepted it out of politeness or humility. As he lighted it, he noticed that his hands were shaking. The day was clouding over; the soldiers spoke in a low voice as though he was already dead. Vainly he tried to recall the woman of whom Julia von Weidenau was the symbol.

The squad formed and stood at attention. Hladik, standing against the barracks wall, waited for the volley. Someone pointed out that the wall was going to be stained with blood; the victim was ordered to step forward a few paces. Incongruously, this reminded Hladik of the fumbling preparations of photographers. A big drop of rain struck one of Hladik's temples and rolled slowly down his cheek; the sergeant shouted the final order.

The physical universe came to a halt.

The guns converged on Hladik, but the men who were to kill him stood motionless. The sergeant's arm eternized an unfinished gesture. On a paving stone of the courtyard a bee cast an unchanging shadow. The wind had ceased, as in a picture. Hladik attempted a cry, a word, a movement of the hand. He realized that he was paralyzed. Not a sound reached him from the stricken world. He thought: "I am in hell, I am dead." He thought: "I am mad." He thought: "Time has stopped." Then he reflected that if that was the case, his mind would have stopped too. He wanted to test this; he repeated (without moving his lips) Virgil's mysterious fourth Eclogue. He imagined that the now remote soldiers must be sharing his anxiety; he longed to be able to communicate with them. It astonished him not to feel the least fatigue, not even the numbness of his protracted immobility. After an indeterminate time he fell asleep. When he awoke the world continued motionless and mute. The drop of water still clung to his cheek, the shadow of the bee to the stone. The smoke from the cigarette he had thrown away had not dispersed. Another "day" went by before Hladik understood.

He had asked God for a whole year to finish his work; His omnipotence had granted it. God had worked a secret miracle for him; German lead would kill him at the set hour, but in his mind a year would go by between the order and its execution. From perplexity he passed to stupor, from stupor to resignation, from resignation to sudden gratitude.

He had no document but his memory; the training he had acquired with each added hexameter gave him a discipline unsuspected by those who set down and forget temporary, incomplete paragraphs. He was not working for posterity or even for God, whose literary tastes were unknown to him. Meticulously, motionless, secretly, he wrought in time his lofty, invisible labyrinth. He worked the third act over twice. He eliminated certain symbols as overobvious, such as the repeated striking of the clock, the music. Nothing hurried him. He omitted, he condensed, he amplified. In certain instances he came back to the original version. He came to feel an affection for the courtyard, the barrack; one of the faces before him modified his conception of Roemerstadt's character. He discovered that the wearying cacophonies that bothered Flaubert so much are mere visual superstitions, weakness and limitation of the written word, not the spoken. He concluded his drama. He had only the problem of a single phrase. He found it. The drop of water slid down his cheek. He opened his mouth in a maddened cry, moved his face, dropped under the quadruple blast.

Jaromir Hladik died on March 29, at 9:02 A.M.

Pinkhes Berniker
(Belarus-Cuba-U.S., 1908–1956)
"Jesús"
Translated from the Yiddish by Alan Astro

Born in Belarus, the son of a rabbi, Pinkhes Berniker emigrated to Havana in 1925. He published Yiddish stories. In 1931 he moved to the United States, where he worked as the director of a Hebrew school in Rochester. Several of his Cuban stories appeared in the book *Shtile lebns* (*Quiet Lives*, 1935). It includes the one below, about a Lithuanian Jewish peddler in Cuba who sells images of Christ. The tension between Jewish and Gentile environments and between tradition and modernity is at the core of the tale.

He didn't even take it seriously, the first few times his roommates suggested that he start peddling images of Jesus, of *Yoshke*, as he preferred to call him. He thought they were kidding. How could they have been serious? Were they fools? What could they have meant? How could they possibly think that he should shlep the goyish icons through the streets of Havana? What was he, a boy, a young lad, who knew nothing of the world? How could they imagine that he—a middle-aged Jew with a beard and side curls, who had been ordained as a rabbi, who had devoted all the days of his life to Torah and to divine service— could all of a sudden peddle icons and spread word of Jesus of Nazareth? No, even they couldn't have been serious about that! So he thought, and didn't even try to answer them. He just sighed quietly, wiped the sweat off his face, and sat without moving, sure as he was that they wouldn't bring up any such notion again.

Later, he realized he'd been mistaken. Those roommates of his had been very serious. Not daring to propose the idea outright, they had begun by alluding to it, joking about it. He remained silent, and contrary to their expectations hadn't jumped up from his seat as though he had been scorched. So they began broaching the subject directly, insisting that he not even try any other means of livelihood, even if one were to present itself. He, of all people, was just in the

169

right position to turn the greatest profit from peddling the "gods." No one else could approach his success.

"For every god you sell, you'll clear a thousand percent profit." "And the Cubans love to buy gods." "Especially from you, Rabbi Joseph, who look so much like the bastard, pardon the comparison." "You'll see how eager they'll be to buy from you." "And they'll pay whatever you ask." "Listen to me, Rabbi Joseph, just try it! You'll see! They'll sacrifice everything they have for you! People who don't even need a god will buy one from you!" Thus his roommates urged him to become a god peddler. They couldn't stand to see him half-starved, in total distress, bereft of the slightest prospect for the future. And they really did believe that selling the gods would solve his problems.

The more persistent they became, the more pensive he grew. He didn't answer them, for what could he say? Could he cut out his heart and show them how it bled, how every word they uttered made a sharp incision in it, tearing at it painfully? How could they understand what he felt, if they didn't know how he'd been trained, what his position had been in the old country? He was consumed with self-pity. The world had stuck out its long, ugly tongue at him. Rabbi Joseph, so diligent a pupil that he'd been hailed as the prodigy from Eyshishok, was now supposed to spread tidings of Jesus of Nazareth throughout the world?!

He couldn't resign himself to his lot. Every day, in the blue, tropical dawn, he dragged himself through the narrow streets of old Havana, offering his labor to one Jewish-owned factory after another, promising to do whatever it would take to earn a pittance. He was rejected everywhere. How could they let a venerably bearded Jew work in a factory? Who would dare holler at him? How could they prod him on, ordering him around as necessary? "How could someone like you work in a factory?" "In the Talmudic academy of Volozhin, did they teach shoemaking?" "Rabbi, you're too noble to work here." They looked at him with pity, not knowing how to help.

"Why? Wasn't the great Rabbi Yokhanan a shoemaker?" he asked, pleading for mercy.

"That was then, this is now."

"And what about now? Wouldn't Rabbi Yokhanan still need to eat?" That was what he wanted to cry out, but couldn't. He was already too discouraged. The unanimous rejections tortured him more than the constant hunger. And the charity, the sympathy, offered by all became harder to bear. It wouldn't have humiliated him, had it not been for the presence, in a faraway Lithuanian town, of a wife and three small children who needed to eat. "Send some money, at least for bread." Thus his wife had written to him in one of her most recent letters. And the word "bread" had swelled up and grown blurry from the teardrop that had fallen on it from the eye of a helpless mother.

Joseph recalled the words from *The Ethics of the Fathers*: "If I am not for me, who will be for me?"

"I must harden myself. I must find work!" He called out these words, forcing himself onto the street. Pale, thin, with a despairing mien, he posted himself at a factory door, glancing around helplessly, hoping to catch sight of the owner. From among the workers, a middle-aged Jew ran up to the door and pressed a few pennies into his palm. He froze. His eyes popped out of his head, his mouth gaped open. The couple of cents fell from his hand. Like a madman, he ran from the factory. Late that night, when his roommates returned, he pulled himself down from his cot, stared at them momentarily, and said: "Children, tomorrow you will help me sell the gods." They wanted to ask him what had happened, but glimpsing the pain in his eyes, they could not move their tongues.

Binding both packages of gods together, he left between them a length of empty rope to place upon his neck, thereby lightening the load. He had only to hold onto the packages with his hands, lest they bump into his sides and stomach.

The uppermost image on his right side portrayed Mother Mary cuddling the newborn child, and that on the left showed Jesus already grown. Between the two images he himself looked like the Son of God. His eyes were larger than life and his face paler than ever. Deep, superhuman suffering shone forth from him, a reflection of the pain visited upon Jesus of Nazareth as he was led to the cross.

The day was burning hot. Pearls of sweat shone upon his mild, pale face, and his clothes stuck to his tortured body. He stopped for a while, disentangling his nightmarish thoughts, slowly removing the rope from his neck, straightening his back wrought with pain, and scraping away the sweat that bit into his burning face. He wiped some tears from the corner of an eye.

He saw, far off, the low wooden cabins in the next village. In the surrounding silence, from time to time, there came the cries of the village children. Feeling a bit more cheerful, he slowly loaded upon his body the two packages of gods. Trembling, he strode onward, onward. He was noticed first by the lean, pale children, playing in the street. They immediately stopped their games and stiffened in amazement. The tropical fire in their black eyes burst forth as they caught sight of him. Never had they seen such a man.

171

"*¡Mamá, mamá, un Jesús viene!* A Jesus is coming!" Each started running home. "*¡Mira! ¡Mira!*" The children's voices rang through the village.

From windows and doors along the road women leaned their heads out, murmuring excitedly to one another: "*¡Santa María!*" "*¡Qué milagro!*" "*¡Dios mío!*" They all whispered in astonishment, unable to turn their straining eyes away from the extraordinary man.

Joseph approached one of the houses and pointed to the image of Jesus, mutely suggesting that they buy a god from him. But the hot-blooded tropical women thought he was indicating how closely the image resembled him. Filled with awe, they gestured that he should enter. "*¡Entre, señor!*" said each one separately, with rare submissiveness. He entered the house, took the burden off his neck, and seated himself on the rocking chair they offered him. Looking at no one, he began untying the gods. None of the members of the household dared to sit. Along with some neighbors who had sneaked in, they encircled him and devoured him with their wide-open eyes.

"*¿Tienes hijo?* Do you have a son?" a young shiksa asked, trembling.

"I have two," he answered.

"And are they as handsome as you?" asked another girl, excitedly.

"I myself don't know."

"*¡Mira, él mismo tampoco sabe!* He himself doesn't know!" A strange shame overtook the girls. They looked at each other momentarily, then burst into embarrassed laughter: "Ha ha ha! Ha ha ha!" Their hoarse guffaws echoed throughout the modest home.

"What's going on?" asked the mothers, glancing unkindly toward the men. "Nothing!" said the girls, embracing each other, repeating in passionate ecstasy: "*¡Él mismo tampoco sabe! ¡Él mismo tampoco sabe!* Ha ha ha! Ha ha ha!" Their suffocating laughter resonated, as each tucked herself more closely into her girlfriend's body.

"And what's your name?" One of the girls tore herself from her friend's embrace.

"José."

"What?" asked several of the women in unison.

"José . . ."

"José-Jesús!" The village women began to murmur, winking more than speaking.

One of the shiksas was unable to restrain herself: "And what's your son's name?"

"Juan."

"Juan, Juan," the shiksas began to repeat, drooling. Embarrassed, they pushed each other into the next room, wildly, bizarrely.

There was a momentary silence. Those watching were still under the spell of what had taken place. Joseph, however, was out of patience. "*Nu, ¿compran?* Will you buy already?" he asked, raising his eyes, filled with the sorrow of the world. He could say no more in Spanish, but no more was necessary. Every woman purchased a god from him by paying an initial installment—from which he already cleared a handsome profit—and promising the rest later.

Home he went, with only the rope. All the gods had been sold. He had never felt so light, so unencumbered. He had no packages to carry, and a hope had arisen within him that he would be forever free from hunger and want.

Later, he himself was astonished at how he had changed, at how indifferently he could contemplate Jesus's beard. He went to a Cuban barber and had his blond beard trimmed in the likeness of Jesus.

"Your mother must have been very pious!" said the barber to him, with great conviction.

"How can you tell?"

"When she conceived you, she couldn't have stepped away from the image of Jesus."

"Perhaps." Joseph was delighted.

How could he act this way? He didn't know. The Christian women, his customers in the villages all around, waited for him as Jews await the Messiah. They worshipped him, and he earned from them more than he could ever have dreamed.

They had no idea who he was. He never told them he was a Jew, and he still wondered how he could deny his Jewish background. He learned a little Spanish, especially verses from the New Testament, and spoke with the peasant women like a true *santo*, a saint. And once, when a customer asked him, "*¿Qué eres tú?* What are you?" he rolled his eyes to the heavens and started to say, drawing out his words, "And what difference does it make, who I am? All are God's children."

"And the *judíos*? The Jews?" asked the women, unable to restrain themselves.

"The *judíos* are also God's children. They're just the sinful ones. They crucified our *señor Jesús*, but they are still God's children. Even *Jesús* himself has forgiven them." He ended with a pious sigh.

"And do you yourself love the *judíos*?"

"Certainly."

"*¿De veras?* Really?"

"*¿Y qué?* And what of it?" He put on a wounded face and soon conceded: "My love for them isn't as deep as for the Christians, but I do love them. A sinner can be brought back to the righteous path through love, as our *señor Jesús* said."

"*¡Tiene razón!* He's right!"

"*¡Y bien que sí!* And how much so!"

"*¡Es un verdadero santo!* He's a true saint!" All the women drank his words in.

"And have you yourself seen a real Jew?" Their curiosity couldn't be sated.

"Yes, I have."

"Where?"

"There, in Europe."

"And what did he look like?"

"Just like me."

"Really?!"

"Yes, indeed."

"*¡Si él lo dice, debe ser verdad!* If he says it, it must be true." The peasant women winked to each other, and their faces grew intensely serious, as if in a moment of great exaltation. Joseph fell silent, engrossed in his thoughts. He let the peasant women examine some sample gods, for now he simply took orders, which he filled by mail. In the meantime, he took stock of his situation, how much money he had in the bank, how much he was owed, and how many more thousands he could earn in the coming year, if business improved by just fifty percent. "Who needs to worry?" A smile lit up his face, as he felt these words in his heart: "I give thanks and praise to Thee, Almighty God, who hast given Jesus unto the world."

A new god peddler showed up in the same area. Day in, day out, he dragged himself from one village to the next, stopping at every home. He scraped the scalding sweat off his face and neck as he knocked, trembling, on the hospitable Cuban doors.

"*¿Compran algo?* Will you buy something?" he asked, gesturing broadly. Solidly built mothers and passionate, well-formed daughters looked at him with pity, comforting him and caressing him with the softness of the Spanish tongue and the gentleness of their big, velvety eyes. They gladly offered him a handout but shook their heads at his gods.

"I'm sorry." He got the same answer almost everywhere.

"*¡Compra y no lamentes!* Buy, and don't be sorry!"

"You're right!" answered the women with a slight smile. He stood with his distressed face and heavy heart, looking at the peasant women, unable to understand why they were so stubborn.

A few children gathered around him. They stared at his earnest face, carefully touched the frames of the unveiled images, and began playing with them. "Tell your mother to buy a *santo*!" he said, caressing one of the children. The child stopped laughing. His glance passed from the god merchant to his mother. It was hard for him to grasp what was happening.

"How sweet you are," said the mother, affectionately embracing her now serious child.

"I have a child just like him in the old country," said the god merchant, about to burst into tears.

"*¡Mira, parece una mujer!* He's acting just like a woman!" The peasants were astonished to see the shiny tears forming in the corners of his eyes.

"Should a man cry?" "And he's supposed to be the breadwinner for a wife and children!" "How funny!" A few girls, unable to restrain themselves, laughed in his face. Ashamed, he glanced at their widely smiling eyes, felt his own helplessness, and went away. His feet had grown heavier and his grasp of events slighter. Nonetheless, arming himself with courage, he went from village to village. He knocked on every door and humbly showed his wares: "*¡Compren!* Buy something! If you help me, God will help you. And I sell very cheap!"

But he seldom came across a customer interested in his low prices. Almost everyone was waiting for the *santo*, the holy peddler, who bore a great likeness to God Himself. They dismissed the new god merchant out of hand: "I don't need any." "I'm very sorry." "We've already bought some from someone else." He already knew all their answers by heart.

"Are gods the only thing to peddle?" Such was the bitter question he asked every day of his fellow immigrants.

"Do you know of something better? Food isn't about to fly into your mouth. And what are you going to do with the gods you've already bought?"

"*¡Hay que trabajar!* You've got to work!" exclaimed one of his countrymen, eager to show off his Spanish.

"But my work is in vain!"

"Right now, your work is in vain, but it will pay off in time," said his friends, trying to console him.

"In time, in time!" he muttered nervously, not knowing at whom.

It had grown dark in the middle of the day. The clear, tropical sky had suddenly clouded over. Waves of heat rose from the ground, and the air became closer and denser. At any moment, buckets of rain could fall. *Campesinos*, riding into town, became uneasy, fearful lest the storm catch up with them. So they pushed back their gritty straw hats called *tijanas*, fastened the palm-leaf baskets full of fowl onto one side of their saddles, secured the cans of milk onto the other side, and urged the horses on with all their might. "*¡Pronto!* Faster! *¡Pronto!*"

"Soon there'll be a deluge!" "You'll get soaked with all your gods in the middle of the field." The riders took pity on the poor foot traveler, as they dug their spurs ever more deeply into the sides of their horses. But he scarcely moved his feet, hammering his steps out heavily. It was already past noon, and he hadn't sold a single god.

Arriving at the next village, soaked to the bone, he caught sight of an open door leading into a home full of people. Sneaking in, he put down his pack of gods in a corner behind the door. As he started removing his wet clothes from his even wetter body, he heard a woman speaking: "Here, take five dollars, and send me next week such a San Antonio." "And send me a Jesus by the Well." "I'll take a San Pablo. Take three dollars in the meantime, and I'll pay the rest later." "Make sure you don't forget to send me a Santa María." "And I want a Mother with the Son." The women shouted over each other.

He could hardly believe his ears. He thought that he was dreaming one of his sweet nightly dreams, in which he glimpsed himself amidst circles of peasant women ripping his godly wares out of his hands. He had believed such good fortune was possible only in a dream, but here it was happening for real. "What can this be?" He wondered why he hadn't yet looked into the opposite corner of the room, and he took a few steps towards it.

He stopped in his tracks, stupefied. All his limbs began to shake. He tried to hide his surprise, but never had he seen a man who looked so much like Jesus. "So that's it!" he murmured to himself, as he watched Joseph rolling his eyes from time to time towards heaven, blessing the peasant women as a *rebbe* blesses his Hasidim. "Aha!" He was astonished at the reverence the village women bestowed upon the stranger. "No, no, I could never become such a showman!" He stepped off to one side to keep Joseph from noticing him.

His last bit of hope had run out. "*Y tú, ¿de dónde vienes?* And where have you come from?" The peasant women were surprised to see the new god peddler after Joseph had left.

"From Santo Domingo."

"You've just gotten here?"

"No, I'm already planning to leave."

"Did you see our *Jesusito*?"

"You mean the *vendedor*, the seller of the gods?"

"Yes. Doesn't he look just like Jesus?" asked the peasant women, offended.

"Like Jesus? But he's a *judío*, a Jew!" These words came flying out of his mouth with unusual force.

"*¡Mentira! ¡Mentira!* That's a lie! A lie! You yourself are a *judío*, and a dirty one at that!" The peasant women cried out in unison, pale from emotion.

"*¡Palabra de honor!* I give you my word of honor that he's a *judío*!" The new god peddler couldn't restrain himself when he realized what a terrible impression the word *judío* made on them. But his claims were all in vain. The village women still didn't believe him. He couldn't make them understand. "*¡No, no puede ser!* No, it can't be." "*¡Vamos, vete de aquí!* Come on! Get out of here!" They couldn't stand to hear his words any longer.

He fell silent and left the house, but not the village. He sought out some young men and treated them to a drink. As he sipped the black coffee by the white marble table, he told them that the god peddler with the face like Jesus's, who overcharged their mothers for the pictures they bought from him, was a Jew, a descendent of the ones who had crucified Jesus.

"*¡No hable boberías!* Don't talk nonsense!" "*¿Cómo es posible?* How can that be?" "*¡No me lo diga!* Don't tell me." The young men didn't want to believe him. As their stubbornness grew, so did his. Finally, he told them of the first Jewish commandment. He left twenty-five dollars with the owner of the café and swore that the money was theirs if he had been lying to them. The cash had its effect. It was as though the young men had been touched by fire. All the blood rushed to their faces, and they drank themselves into a stupor.

Joseph hadn't yet arrived at the first house in the village when a lad ran across his path. "*¡Oiga!* Listen, sir, my mother wants to buy something." Hardly able to utter these words, the boy inhaled with difficulty.

"*¡Bendito eres, hijito!* Blessed art thou, my son!" Such was Joseph's gentle answer.

"*¡Por aquí es más cerca!* This way is shorter!" said the little goy as he strode over the field with Joseph trailing behind him.

Soon they were far, very far, from the village. The boy had already pointed out that "right over there" was their house. Although Joseph saw no house "over there," he still suspected nothing, assuming his eyes were not as keen as the little goy's.

"*Oiga, santo, ¿tú eres judío?* Listen, Your Holiness, are you a Jew?" The earth had suddenly brought forth before Joseph's eyes a robust young Cuban. Joseph gazed in surprise. For once, his quick tongue failed him. And when he finally could have said something, it was too late. He was already fully spread out on the ground, with several goyim pinning down his legs, as one held his head and two his arms. He screamed bloody murder, thrashed with his feet, pulled with all his might, but to no avail. They were stronger and did what they had to.

And when they found out he was indeed a Jew, they left him lying there, half-naked in the middle of the field. Every one of them spat in his face, hollered "*Judío*," and ran to the village to tell of this wondrous thing.

The village women refused to believe even their own children. And for a long, long time they wouldn't patronize the new god merchant, for they hoped that *Jesús* would come back. But Joseph never returned.

Julio Cortázar

(Argentina, 1914–1984)

"Press Clippings"

Translated from the Spanish by Gregory Rabassa

An experimentalist whose early career was about dilettantism and whose later work is infused by political commitment, Julio Cortázar was the author of *Bestiary* (1965), *We Loved Glenda So Much and Other Stories* (1983), and *Blow Up and Other Stories* (1985), as well as the magnum opus *Hopscotch* (1963). This story is about the place of the artist in society. It is also a document about the role of Jewish activists in the so-called Dirty War—*la guerra sucia*—in Argentina. A considerable number of *desaparacidos* were of Jewish descent. Thus Cortázar's character, Laura Beatríz Bonaparte Bruschtein, is an archetype.

Although I don't think it's really necessary to say so, the first clipping is real and the second one imaginary.

The sculptor lives on the Rue Riquet, which doesn't seem like a good idea to me, but in Paris you haven't got much choice if you're an Argentine and a sculptor, generally two difficult ways of living in this city. We really don't know each other too well, through snippets of time that stretch back twenty years; when he called me to talk about a book with prints of his most recent work and asked me to do a text to accompany it, I said what it's always best to say in such cases, that he should show me some of his sculptures and then we'd see, or, rather, we'd see then.

I went to his apartment at night, and first there was coffee and some friendly sparring, both of us feeling what is inevitably felt when someone shows his work to another person and that fearful moment comes when bonfires will be lighted or a person has to admit, covering it with words, that the wood was wet and gave off more smoke than heat. And before that, on the telephone, he'd told me about his work, a series of small pieces whose theme was the violence in all the political and geographical latitudes that man inhabits as a man/wolf. We knew some-

179

thing about that, two Argentines, letting the nausea of memories rise up once more, the daily accumulation of fright through cables, letters, sudden silences. While we were talking he was clearing a table; he sat me down in a chair that was just right and began to bring out the pieces, putting them under a carefully placed light, and letting me look at them slowly, and then he turned them gradually; we said practically nothing now, because they had the word and that word was still ours. One after another, until there were ten or so of them, small and filiform, clayish or plaster, born out of wires or bottles patiently wrapped by the work of fingers and spatula, growing out of empty cans and objects underneath that only the sculptor's skill showed me as bodies and heads, arms and hands. It was late at night, all that reached us from the street was the rumble of heavy trucks, the siren of an ambulance.

I was glad that there wasn't anything systematic or too explicative in the sculptor's work, that each piece had something of an enigma about it, and that sometimes one had to look for a long time in order to understand the modality that violence assumed there; at the same time, the sculptures seemed to me to be at once naïve and subtle, in any case without any sense of dread or sentimental exaggeration. Even torture, that last form in which violence takes the place of the horror of immobility and isolation, had not been shown with the doubtful trifle of so many posters and texts and movies that returned to my memory, also doubtful, also ready to hold the images and give them back for who knows what kind of obscure pleasure. I said to myself that if I wrote the text the sculptor had asked me to, if I write the text you ask me to, I told him, it will be a text like these pieces, I'll never let myself be carried along by the facility that all too often abounds in this field.

"That's up to you, Noemí," he said to me. "I know it's not easy, we carry so much blood in our memories that sometimes you feel guilty when you put a limit on it, channel it so it doesn't flood us out completely."

"You're talking to the right person. Look at this clipping, I know the woman who signed it, and I learned other things from what friends told me. It happened three years ago, just as it could have happened last night and can be happening at this very moment in Buenos Aires or Montevideo. Just before leaving to come here I opened a letter from a friend, and he'd sent me the clipping. Let me have another cup of coffee while you read it, you really don't have to read it after what you've shown me, but, I don't know, I'd feel better if you read it too."

What he read was this:

The undersigned, Laura Beatriz Bonaparte Bruschtein, domiciled at No. 26 Atoyac, District 10, Colonia Cuauhtémoc, Mexico 5, D. F., wishes to pass the following testimony on to public opinion:

1. Aída Leonora Bruschtein Bonaparte, born May 21, 1951, in Buenos Aires, Argentina, profession, teacher in literacy program.

Fact: At ten o'clock in the morning of December 24, 1975, she was kidnapped by personnel of the Argentine army (601st Battalion) at her place of employment in the Monte Chingolo slum, near the federal capital.

The previous day that place had been the scene of a battle that had left a toll of one hundred dead, including inhabitants of the area. My daughter, after being kidnapped, was taken to the military headquarters of the 601st Battalion.

There she was brutally tortured, the same as other women. Those who survived were shot that same Christmas night. Among them was my daughter.

The burial of those killed in the fighting and of the civilians kidnapped, as was the case of my daughter, was delayed for about five days. All the bodies, including hers, were transferred in mechanical shovels from the battalion to the Lanús police station, from there to the Avellaneda cemetery, where they were buried in a common grave.

I kept on looking at the last sculpture that had remained on the table, I refused to cast my eyes on the sculptor who was reading in silence. For the first time I heard the ticking of a clock on the wall; it was coming from the vestibule and was the only thing audible at that moment in which the street was becoming more and more deserted; the soft sound reached me like a nighttime metronome, an attempt to keep time alive inside that hole where the two of us were stuck in a way, the duration that took in a flat in Paris and a miserable slum in Buenos Aires, that abolished calendars and left us face to face with that, what we could only call that, all epithets exhausted, all expressions of horror fatigued and filthy.

"'Those who survived were shot that same Christmas night,'" the sculptor read aloud. "They probably gave them sweet rolls and cider, remember that in Auschwitz they passed out candy to the children before sending them into the gas chambers."

He must have seen something in my face; he made a gesture of apology, and I lowered my eyes and looked for another cigarette.

I received official notice of my daughter's murder in Court No. 8 in the city of La Plata, January 8, 1976. Then I was conducted to the Lanús police station, where, after three hours of interrogation, they told me where the grave was located: All they would show me of my daughter were the hands cut off her body and placed in a jar that carried the number 24. What remained of her body could not be turned over because it was a military secret. The following day I went to the Avellaneda cemetery, looking for stake number 28. The inspector had told me that there I would find "what remained of her because one couldn't call what had been turned over to them bodies." The grave was a patch of recently turned ground, twenty feet by twenty, more or less at the rear of the cemetery. I knew how to locate the grave. It was terrible when I realized how more than a hundred people had been murdered and buried, among them my daughter.

2. In view of this infamous situation and one of such indescribable cruelty, in January 1976 I, domiciled on 730 Calle Lavalle, fifth floor, district nine, in the federal capital, bring charges of murder against the Argentine Army. I do it in the same tribunal of La Plata, number 8, civil court.

"You can see, all this is worth nothing," the sculptor said, sweeping his arm through the air. "Worth nothing, Noemí, I've spent months making this shit, you write books, that woman denounces atrocities, we attend congresses and round tables to protest, we almost come to believe that things are changing, and then all you need is two minutes of reading to understand the truth again, to—"

"Shh, I'm thinking things like that right now too," I said with a rage at having to say it. "But if I accepted them it would be like sending them a telegram of support, and, besides, you know very well that tomorrow you'll get up and in a while you'll be shaping another sculpture and you'll know that I'm at my typewriter and you'll think that we're many, even though we're so few, and that difference in strength isn't and never will be any reason to be silent. End of sermon. Did you finish reading? Hey, I've got to go."

He shook his head negatively, pointed to the coffeepot.

As a consequence to this legal recourse of mine, the following things happened:

3. In March of 1976, Adrián Saidón, Argentine, twenty-four years old, employed, my daughter's fiancé, was murdered on a street in the city of Buenos Aires by the police, who informed his father.

His body was not returned to his father, Dr. Abraham Saidón, because it was a military secret.

4. Santiago Bruschtein, Argentine, born December 25, 1918, father of my murdered daughter, mentioned previously, doctor of biochemistry by profession, with a laboratory in the city of Morón.

Fact: on June 11, 1976, at 12 noon, a group of military men in civilian clothes came to his apartment at 730 Calle Lavalle, Apt. 9. My husband, attended by a nurse, was in bed, on the verge of death because of a heart attack and with a prognostication of three months to live. The military men questioned him about me and our children, and added that *"like the Jew bastard you are, you're capable of bringing charges of murder against the Argentine Army."* Then they made him get out of bed, and, *beating him*, put him into a car, without letting him bring along his medicine.

Eyewitnesses have affirmed that the army and the police used around twenty cars for the arrest. We have not heard anything more about him since. Through unofficial sources, we were informed that he died suddenly at the beginning of his torture session.

"And here I am thousands of miles away arguing with a publisher about what kind of paper the photographs should have, the format, and the jacket."

"Bah, pal, just now I've been writing a story where I talk, no less, about the psycho-log-i-cal problems of a girl at the moment of puberty. Don't start up with autotorture, the real kind is quite enough, I think."

"I know, Noemí, I know, God damn it. But it's always the same thing, we always have to recognize that all this happened in another space, another time. We never were and never will be there, where maybe . . ."

(I remembered something I'd read when I was a girl, in Augustin Thierry, perhaps, a story about how a saint, God knows what his name was, had converted Clovis and his nation to Christianity and was describing the scourging and crucifixion of Jesus, and the king rose up on his throne, shaking his spear and shouting: "Oh, if only I could have been there with my Franks!"—the miracle of an impossible wish, the same impotent rage of the sculptor, lost in his reading.)

5. Patricia Villa, Argentine, born in Buenos Aires in 1952, journalist, worked at the Inter-Press Service and is my daughter-in-law's sister.

Fact: Along with her fiancé, Eduardo Suárez, also a journalist, she was arrested in September 1976, and they were taken as prisoners to the general headquarters of the federal police of Buenos Aires. A week after their seizure, her mother, who had taken legal action in the case, was informed that unfortunately it had been a mistake. Their bodies have not been returned to their families.

6. Irene Mónica Bruschtein Bonaparte de Ginzberg, twenty-two years old, artist by profession, married to Mario Ginzberg, construction foreman, twenty-four years old.

Fact: On March 11, 1977, at six in the morning, a joint force of army and police came to the apartment where they lived, taking the couple away and leaving behind their small children: Victoria, two years, six months old, and Hugo Roberto, one year, six months, abandoned at the door of the building. We immediately asked for a writ of habeas corpus, I at the consulate in Mexico City and Mario's father in the federal capital.

I have inquired about my daughter Irene and Mario, denouncing that horrendous sequence of events to the United Nations, the OAS, Amnesty International, the European Parliament, the Red Cross, etc.

Up to this time, however, I have received no news as to their place of detention. I have a firm hope that they are still alive.

As a mother, unable to return to Argentina because of the situation of family perse-cution that I have described, and since legal recourses have been annulled, I ask the institutions and people who fight for the defense of human rights to begin the necessary procedures to return my daughter Irene and her husband, Mario, to me and thus safe-guard their lives and liberty. Signed, Laura Beatriz Bonaparte Bruschtein (from *El País*, October 1978, reprinted in *Denuncia*, December 1978).

The sculptor gave me back the clipping. We didn't say very much because we were dropping from lack of sleep. I sensed that he was glad I had agreed to go along with him on his book, and only then did I realize that he had been doubt-ful up to the last, because I'm known to be very busy, maybe selfish, in any case, a writer deeply involved in her own pursuits. I asked him if there was a taxi stand nearby, and I went out onto the street that was deserted and cold and too broad, to my taste, for Paris. A gust of wind made me turn up my coat collar. I could near my heels clicking in the silence, marking out a rhythm in which fatigue and obsessions so often insert a melody that keeps coming back, or a line from a poem, but which only let me see her hands cut off her body and put into a bot-tle that bears the number twenty-four, only let me see her hands cut off her body, I recovered quickly, rejecting the recurrent nausea, forcing myself to take a deep breath, to think about tomorrow's work; I never knew why I crossed to the opposite sidewalk. There was no need to, since the street opened onto the Place de la Chapelle, where I might be able to get a cab. It made no difference which sidewalk I went along, I crossed because I crossed, because I didn't even have enough strength left to ask myself why I crossed over.

The little girl was sitting on the steps of a porch that was almost lost among the other porches of the tall and narrow houses barely distinguishable from each other in that particularly dark block. That there should be a child on the edge of a step at that hour of the night and in that loneliness didn't surprise me as much as her position, a little whitish splotch with legs tight together and hands covering her face, something that could also have been a dog or some garbage forgotten at the entrance to the house. I looked vaguely around; a truck was pulling away with its weak lights yellow, on the sidewalk opposite a man was walking hunched over, his head sunk in the raised collar of his overcoat and his hands in his pockets. I stopped, took a close look. The child had thin hair, a white skirt, a pink sweater, and when she removed her hands from her face, I saw her eyes and her cheeks and not even the half-darkness could hide the tears, the glow that trickled down to her mouth.

"What's wrong? What are you doing there?"

I heard her breathe deeply, swallow tears and mucus, a hiccup or a pout, I saw her face fully lifted toward me, her tiny red nose, the curve of a mouth that was trembling. I repeated the questions, who knows what I said to her, crouching until I felt her very close.

"My mama," the little girl said, speaking between gasps. "My papa is doing things to my mama."

Maybe she was going to say more, but her arms reached out and I felt her cling to me, weeping desperately against my neck; she smelled dirty, of wet underpants. I tried to take her in my arms and get up, but she drew away from me, looking into the darkness of the hallway. She pointed at something, she started forward, and I followed her, barely glimpsing a stone arch and behind the half-darkness the beginning of a garden. Silently she came out into the open air; it wasn't a flower garden but rather a vegetable patch with low wire fences that marked off planted sections, there was enough light to see the skimpy mastic trees, the poles that supported climbing plants, rags to scare off the birds; toward the center you could make out a low hut patched with zinc and tin cans, from whose small window a greenish light came. There was no lighted lamp in any of the windows of the buildings around the plot; the black walls went up five stories until they merged with a low and cloudy sky.

The little girl had gone directly to the narrow passageway between two vegetable patches that led to the door of the hut; she turned a little to make sure I was following her, and went into the shack. I know that I must have stopped there and half-turned, telling myself that the girl had had a bad dream and was going back to bed, every reason that reason could produce telling me at that moment how absurd and perhaps risky it was to go into a strange house at that hour of the night; maybe I was still telling myself these things when I went through the half-open door and saw the little girl waiting for me in a vague entrance full of old furniture and garden tools. A ray of light filtered through under the door at the back, and the girl pointed to it and, almost jumping over the rest of the entrance, began almost imperceptibly opening the door. Just beside her, face full in the yellowish ray of the opening that was slowly growing larger, I smelled burning, I heard a kind of muffed shriek which was repeated over and over, interrupted then taken up again; my hand pushed on the door and I took in the foul room—the broken stools and beer and wine bottles on the table, the glasses, and the table covering of old newspapers, beyond that the bed and the naked body gagged with a dirty towel, her hands and feet tied to the iron bedstead. His back to me, sitting on a bench, the girl's papa was doing things to her mama; he was taking his time, slowly lifting his cigarette to his mouth, letting the smoke out of his nose slowly while the lighted end came down to rest on one of the mama's breasts, remained there for the duration of the gagged shrieks under the towel wrapped around her mouth and face except for the eyes. Before understanding, accepting being part of that, there was time for the papa to withdraw the cigarette and bring it up to his mouth again, time to enliven the lighted end and savor the excellent French tobacco, time for me to see the body burned from the stomach to the neck, the purple or red splotches that went up from the thighs and the sex to the breasts, where now the lighted end rested again with a careful delicacy, seeking an unscarred spot on the skin. The shriek and the shudder of the body on the bed that creaked under the spasm were mixed with things, with acts that I didn't choose and which I will never be able to explain to myself. Between the man with his back to me and myself there was a broken-down stool, I saw it rise up in the air and fall at an angle onto the papa's head; his body and the stool rolled onto the floor almost at the same second. I had to jump back not to fall too. I had put all my strength into the motion of raising the stool and hitting him; that strength immediately abandoned me, leaving me a staggering simpleton. I know that I looked for support without finding it, that I looked vaguely behind and saw the door half-open, the little girl no longer there and the man on the floor a confused splotch, a wrinkled rag. What came afterward I could have seen in a movie or read in a book, I was there as if not being there, but I was there with an agility and an intent that in a very brief time—if it happened in time—led me to find a knife on the table, cut the bonds that held the woman,

186

pull the towel from her face, and see her get up silently, perfectly silent now as if that were necessary and even essential, look at the body on the floor as it began to contract from an unconsciousness that wasn't going to last, look at me wordlessly, go to the body and grab it by the arms while I held its feet. With a double lift we laid it out on the bed, tied it with the same cords, quickly reset and knotted, tied him and gagged him in that silence where something seemed to vibrate and tremble with an ultrasonic sound. What follows I don't know, I see the woman still naked, her hands pulling off pieces of clothing, unbuttoning pants and lowering them into wrinkles at the feet, I see her eyes on mine, a single pair of wide-open eyes, and four hands pulling and tearing and undressing, vest and shirt and shorts, now that I have to remember it and have to write it, my cursed state and my harsh memory bring me something else indescribably lived but not seen, a passage from a story by Jack London where a trapper in the north struggles to win a clean death while beside him, turned into a bloody thing that still holds a glimmer of consciousness, his comrade in adventures howls and twists, tortured by the women of the tribe who horribly prolong his life in spasms and shrieks, killing him without killing him, exquisitely refined in each new variant, never described but there, like us there, never described and doing what we must, what we had to do. It's useless to wonder now why I was involved in that, what was my right and my part in what was going on under my eyes that without doubt saw, that without doubt remember how London's imagination must have seen and remembered what his hand was incapable of writing. I only know that the little girl wasn't with us after my entry into the room, and that now the mama was doing things to the papa, but who knows whether only the mama or whether once more they were gusts of night, pieces of images coming back out of a newspaper clipping, the hands cut off her body and put in a bottle that bore the number twenty-four through unofficial sources we found out that he died suddenly at the beginning of the torture session, the towel over her mouth, the lighted cigarettes, and Victoria, two years and six months old, and Hugo Roberto, one year and six months, abandoned at the door of the building. How could I know how long it lasted, how could I understand that I too, I too even though I thought I was on the right side, I too, how could I accept that I too there on the other side from the cut-off hands and the common graves, I too on the other side from the girls tortured and shot that same Christmas night, the rest is turning my back, crossing the garden patch, bumping against a wire fence and scratching my knee, going out onto the freezing and deserted street and getting to La Chapelle and almost immediately finding the taxi that took me to glass after glass of vodka and a sleep from which I awoke at noon, lying across the bed and fully clothed, with my knee bleeding and that perhaps providential headache that straight vodka brings on when it passes from bottleneck to throat.

I worked all afternoon. It seemed inevitable and frightening to me that I was capable of concentrating to such a degree; at dusk I phoned the sculptor, who seemed surprised at my early reappearance. I told him what had happened to me. I spat it out in a single flow of words that he respected, although at times I could hear him coughing or trying to get a question in.

"So you see," I told him, "you see I haven't taken too much time to give you what I promised."

"I don't understand," the sculptor said. "If you mean the text about—"

"Yes, that's what I mean. I just read it to you, that's the text. I'll send it to you as soon as I make a clean copy, I don't want it around anymore."

After two or three days that had been lived in a haze of pills and drinks and records, anything that could be a barrier, I went out to buy some food; the refrigerator was empty and Cuddles was mewing at the foot of my bed. I found a letter in the mailbox, the sculptor's thick handwriting on the envelope. There was a sheet of paper and a newspaper clipping. I began to read while I walked toward the market and only afterward did I realize that when I had opened the envelope I had torn and lost a piece of the clipping. The sculptor was thanking me for the text for his album, unusual but to all appearances very much like me, far removed from the usual things in albums, although that didn't bother him any more than it bothered me. There was a postscript: "A great dramatic actress has been lost in you, although luckily an excellent writer has been saved. The other afternoon I thought you were telling me something that had really happened to you, then by chance I read *France-Soir*, from which I have taken the liberty of clipping the source of your remarkable personal experience. It's true that a writer can argue that if his inspiration comes from reality, and even from the crime news, what he is capable of doing with it raises it to another dimension, gives it a different value. In any case, my dear Noemí, we're too good friends for you to have felt it necessary to prepare me in advance for your text and unfold your dramatic talents on the telephone. But let's leave it at that; you know how much I appreciate your collaboration and I'm very glad that. . . ."

I looked at the clipping and saw that I had inadvertently torn it; the envelope and the piece stuck to it were thrown away somewhere. The news item was worthy of *France-Soir* and its style: an atrocious drama in a suburb of Marseilles, the macabre discovery of a sadistic crime, ex-plumber bound and gagged on a cot, the corpse, et cetera, neighbors furtively aware of repeated scenes of violence, small daughter missing for several days, neighbors suspecting abandonment, police looking for mistress, horrendous spectacle offered to the—the clipping broke off there; when the sculptor had licked the envelope too abundantly he had done the same thing as Jack London, the same as Jack London and as my memory; but the photograph of the shack was intact and it was the shack in the vegetable patch, the wire and the zinc sheeting, the high walls surrounding it with their blind eyes, neighbors furtively aware, neighbors suspecting abandonment, everything there slapping me in the face from the bits of the news item.

I caught a cab and got out on the Rue Riquet, knowing that it was stupid and doing it because that's how stupid things get done. In broad daylight it had nothing that matched my memory, and even though I walked along looking at every house and crossed over to the opposite sidewalk as I remembered having done, I couldn't recognize any entranceway that looked like the one from that night; the light fell onto things like an infinite mask, porches but not that porch, no access to an inner garden, simply because that garden was in the suburbs of Marseilles. But the little girl was there, sitting on the steps of some entrance or other, she was playing with a rag doll. When I spoke to her she ran off to the first door; a conciérge came out before I could call to her. She wanted to know if I was a social worker, certain that I had come for the little girl whom she had found lost in the street; that very morning some gentlemen had been there to identify her, a social worker would come to get her. Although I already knew it, before leaving I asked what her last name was, then I went into a café and on the back of the sculptor's letter I wrote the end to the text and went to slip it under his door, it was proper that he should know the ending, so that the text accompanying his sculptures would be complete.

Jacobo Timerman
(*Argentina, 1923–1999*)
Fragment of *Prisoner without a Name*
Translated from the Spanish by Toby Talbot

Arguably the most influential Jewish book from Latin America in the second half of the twentieth century is *Prisoner without a Name, Cell without a Number* (1981), by journalist and editor Jacobo Timerman. The following segment is Chapter 3. Made into a mediocre TV movie with Liv Ullman and Roy Scheider, the volume is a meditation on freedom and justice that chronicles the tension between the author and the military junta in Argentina in the late seventies. Timerman was placed under house arrest. International pressure eventually allowed him to leave the country and move temporarily to Israel. He also authored the controversial *The Longest War: Israel in Lebanon* (1982), as well as *Chile: Death in the South* (1987) and *Cuba: A Journey* (1990).

When I founded *La Opinión*, I had been a political journalist for newspapers, magazines, radio, and television for twenty-four years. The first issue of the newspaper appeared on May 4, 1971, and I was arrested in April 1977. During that interval in Argentina, six presidents governed—so to speak. Sanctions against *La Opinión* took place under all these regimes in the form of judicial *de facto* measures, bomb assaults at my home and office, the murder or disappearance of one of my journalists, and finally my arrest and the army's confiscation of the newspaper. The most subtle form of sanction was economic, for Argentina—though this is not commonly known—is a country whose economy is almost seventy percent government-controlled, and advertising from government agencies constitutes a decisive portion of the revenue a newspaper requires to ensure its financial solvency. Successive administrations suspended government advertising in *La Opinión* whenever an article provoked them. One government invented a Machiavellian stratagem: it induced the association of newspaper distributors, which it controlled, to request a larger number of copies of *La Opinión* than the market could absorb. In the event the newspaper refused, the distributors were released from their distribution agreement with it; if the newspaper complied, delivering this inordinate quantity of unneeded newspapers resulted in excessive production costs. Whenever such economic sanctions took place, *La Opinión* turned to its readers, increasing its price until it became the most expensive newspaper in the country, but one that remained, unlike the others, independent of public or private advertising.

La Opinión, curiously enough, was a moderate newspaper. It was often compared to *Le Monde*, but in relation to the ideological position of the French daily, one could say that *La Opinión* was a typically liberal newspaper. Every day it committed what in Argentina was construed as a capital sin: it used precise language to describe actual situations so that its articles were comprehensible and direct. Might one claim that *La Opinión* was attacked for semantic reasons? Not so, though semantics is the method employed in Argentina to avoid seeing problems in their total dimensions. Newspapers write virtually in code, resorting to euphemisms and circumlocutions, speaking in a roundabout way, as do leaders, politicians, and intellectuals. One might have the impression that Argentina is a rich heir dissipating its inherited fortune—in this instance, the wealth derived from the generations that ruled between 1860 and 1930—but trying as hard as possible to conceal the fact that the fortune is dwindling and nobody is making any effort to restore it. In this sense, *La Opinión* was genuinely provocative. On more than one occasion it published news stories that had appeared in other papers but were completely incomprehensible to those outside the informed inner circle, and explained these articles so that the average reader could understand them. Actually, it was an explanation of a news item that had appeared five days before in a provincial paper, without measures having been taken against that paper, that led to President Isabel Perón's ten-day suspension of *La Opinión*. Similarly, President Videla suspended *La Opinión* for three days for having published an explanation of an article that had appeared in a Jesuit magazine, although that particular issue of the Catholic journal was not even confiscated.

The Argentine rulers wanted to be viewed like Dorian Gray, but *La Opinión* was the mirror hidden above, which appeared daily on the streets, presenting Dorian Gray's true face.

The semantics of the three governing factions that rule Argentina—the Perónists, trade unions, and armed forces—constitutes one of the oddest processes in political practice. In essence, this is not unprecedented, considering the accumulated experience of fascism and communism with propaganda, slogans, and the structuring of a reality contradictory every step of the way to actual events. But fascism and communism are political phenomena of great magnitude and encompass nations of vast geopolitical and international interests. The semantic process of these ideologies tends to create not only an inner reality within its own territories but also an agile and flexible instrument for international penetration. But why should such a phenomenon occur in a country that is relatively small, practically devoid of demographic or economic growth, containing 25 million inhabitants on 3 million square kilometers who could live peacefully off its existing wealth and enjoy greater ease than even the Swiss?

During a meeting of the International Monetary Fund, a Brazilian economist who I'm sure prefers to remain anonymous defined the different economic groupings in the world as follows: 1) the developed countries; 2) the undeveloped countries; 3) Japan, which occupies a category of its own, inasmuch as these small islands, despite their lack of natural resources and raw materials, have become an industrial power with a permanent demographic boom; and 4) Argentina, because the Japanese work and save for years in order to be able to live one day like the Argentines, who neither work nor save.

Juan Domingo Perón used to say that: "Violence from above engenders violence from below"—a statement that could be found in any Harvard, MIT, or Hudson Institute study on the aggressive feelings of populations with meager resources. A liberal statement, a sociological equation, which in an organized country might lead merely to a polemic on the ways in which such aggressiveness can be eliminated through housing, education, or public health programs. In Argentina, however, Perónist youth understood at once what Perón was saying: he approved of violence and terrorism, and would lend his support to any murder, kidnapping, or assault that fit into his goals for the conquest or reconquest of power.

Another statement epitomizing an important political clue to the last ten years in Argentina was taken by Perón from Pericles: "Everything according to measure, and yet in harmony." I found this same phrase in an article by Nahum Goldman that was published in *La Opinión*. A serene saying, tranquil-sounding, not hard to understand and appreciate, it justifies a political process meticulously carried out so as to produce the smallest possible number of critical situations. But Perónists and all Argentines understood immediately what it signified: anyone opposed to the tactical methods established by Perón would be executed by the boys, pushed from below by the violence from above. Those boys who, logically, regarded Pericles' statement as a kind of revolutionary strategy no different from Fidel Castro's phase in the Sierra Maestra or Mao Zedong's in the Yenan Mountains. "Measure" referred to Perón's orders and "in harmony" to the machine gun.

Another of Perón's statements in his infinite semantic creativity was: "Reality is the only truth." This might be construed as an incitement to careful, meticulous scrutiny of data culled from reality in order to discover peaceful, moderate paths toward a political solution. In practice, however, it formed the basis for Perónist intolerance of any solution outside the ken of its own followers, schemes, or totalitarian rigidity and the justification of utterly irrational acts in the economic, cultural, and political spheres. In fact, the only admissible reality was Perónism, since that was the majority, and the only truth was the Perónist way of life.

The form of combat devised by the other political parties was also a semantic process: to negotiate without contradicting, to await the inevitable crisis and deterioration of officialdom rather than exert any opposition that might induce a crisis which could explode like a grenade in Argentina's face. The anti-Perónist newspapers employed euphemisms to present their criticism, euphemisms that were comprehensible to the parties involved in the game but not to the readers. *La Opinión*, however, was attempting (or perhaps flirting daily with) suicide to expose the true face of Dorian Gray.

A similar instance occurred with the military government following the defeat of Peronism. The revolt against the Perón presidency found its principal proponent in *La Opinión*, for we insisted on the need to fill the vacuum in which the country dwelt. Military leaders were prepared, according to long conversations between them and editors of *La Opinión*, for a revolution to take place in order to terminate the violence of both left and right, to enforce sanctions against corruption, to curb terrorism through legal channels, and to overcome the danger of superinflation. The whole nation longed for peace. During Isabel Perón's last year of rule, *La Opinión* voiced these principles day after day; and finally in March 1976, when the army seized the government, the entire country, including the Perónists, breathed a sigh of relief.

But once again semantics ran parallel to a reality that daily contradicted it. General Videla's government strove to accomplish peaceful acts; it spoke of peace and understanding, maintaining that the revolution was not aimed against anyone in particular or any special sector. But military leaders hastily organized their personal domains, each one becoming a warlord in the zone under his control, whereupon the chaotic, anarchistic, irrational terrorism of the left and of fascist death squads gave way to intrinsic, systemized, rationally planned terrorism. Each officer of a military region had his own prisoners, prisons, and form of justice, and even the central power was unable to request the freedom of an individual when importuned by international pressure. Every individual whose freedom was solicited in the years 1976 to 1978 by the central power, the Catholic Church, or some international organization immediately "disappeared." It was usually necessary to track down the individual in question in a clandestine prison and then submit a petition indicating the hour, day, and place that he'd been seen alive.

Whenever the government was forced to admit repressive excesses, the wording of its self-criticism tended to suggest merely that a certain ward of prisoners had gone one night without food. Whenever a military officer referred to those who'd "gone away forever, it sounded rather like a melancholy remark intended to recall those who'd emigrated to distant lands and continents to rebuild their lives. The semantic process could acquire even sudden clownish overtones. When Thomas Reston, a spokesman for the U.S. State Department, expressed his government's concern over attacks on the headquarters of certain organizations that defended human rights in Argentina, the reply given by one of the ministers indicated that the Argentine government was likewise concerned and, at the same time, wished to protest the existence of the Ku Klux Klan in the United States. Newspaper, radio, and television commentators reinforced this attitude. How to explain that the Ku Klux Klan did not form part of the North American government and occupied no seat in President Carter's cabinet, whereas in Argentina the moderates of the military revolution had thus far been unable to gain control over repression or over, in many instances, the official operation of parallel justice from their local version of the Ku Klux Klan.

If *La Opinión* succeeded in surviving between March 1976 and April 1977, the first year of military government, it was because army moderates decided that this journal, critical but not antagonistic, opposed to terrorism but supportive of human rights, ought to survive. The continued existence of *La Opinión* was a credit abroad; it backed the philosophy of future national reconstruction, it upheld the thesis of national unity, and was committed on a daily basis to curbing extremist excesses. The moderates, in those early years, comprised a minority in the armed forces, and only their political acumen enabled them to retain a foothold in the ongoing process. Political parties, virtually all civil institutions, the Catholic Church, and Western governments maintaining the most satisfactory relations with Argentina all calculated that the best strategy was patience—to wait for time to pass and the extremists to weaken, and in the meantime not to impose excessive demands on the moderates.

On paper, this approach was not implausible. Elections seemed inevitable. But in my position as editor-in-chief of *La Opinión*, every day I had to confront that distinction between extremists and moderates when relatives of those who had disappeared would show up and assume that *La Opinión* could assist in finding them. More than once I had to explain that an article in *La Opinión* could mean a death sentence; nonetheless, their loneliness and the dearth of news made them believe that printing an article on a disappearance was advantageous. At least it fortified them in their solitude and for the upcoming struggle. On balance, I'm unable to weigh the results. I know that I saved the lives of some and believe others were killed merely because *La Opinión* demanded knowledge of their whereabouts. But in the long run the battle, it seems to me, had to be fought, so that at least there *was* a battle, embryonic as it might be. Some people hold that the only possible response to totalitarian repression—whether fascist or communist—is to go underground or into exile. Both of these solutions were contrary to my philosophy. I thought it necessary at the time to go one step further: to attack the leaders of extremist military groups directly. It may have been one such group, unbeknownst to President Videla and the central government, that kidnapped me.

How was one, then, to judge the moderates? They were, are, and will always be opposed to all excesses. Yet they opposed none of these. Was this due to lack of strength? They simply said they were allowing the unavoidable to occur. I recall a remark made by the chief of the Army General Staff to a diplomat who intervened on my behalf when I was arrested: "Timerman isn't delinquent, but it's best not to meddle in the affair. Don't get involved." Hence support of the moderates, acknowledging their immobility and the enormity of extremist excesses, constituted a veritable leap into a vacuum. This attitude elsewhere had provided Hitler with a free hand for seizing power in Germany and had empowered the communists in Cuba to take over the youthful, romantic revolution of the Sierra Maestra against Fulgencio Batista's dictatorship.

The moderates, in my opinion, had to be supported by way of public pressure rather than patience. The Western governments did not view the situation similarly, nor did the Church, the Argentine political parties, or other Argentine newspapers. Nonetheless the fact that this impunity was at least disputed has gone on record. At present it's hard to determine the significance of the policy of *La Opinión*, although this will certainly be clearer in the future when we have a better perspective.

One might say that my present freedom is a result of the patience exercised by the moderates. My own belief is that the concessions made on my behalf by the moderates toward the extremists have been harmful to Argentina on an international scale, for the case should have impelled the moderates to wage a more militant battle against the extremists, particularly since they would have been joined in that battle by an army minority plus a popular majority, political parties, and civil institutions. I believe the moderates would have won the battle, and Argentina would have been saved some years of tragedy.

I was kidnapped by the extremist sector of the army. From the outset, President Rafael Videla and General Roberto Viola tried to convert my disappearance into an arrest in order to save my life. They did not succeed. My life was spared because this extremist sector was also the heart of Nazi operations in Argentina. From the very first interrogation, they figured they had found what they'd been looking for for so long: one of the Sages of Zion, a central axis of the Jewish anti-Argentine conspiracy.

Question: Are you Jewish?
Answer: Yes.
Question: Are you a Zionist?
Answer: Yes.
Question: Is *La Opinión* Zionist?
Answer: *La Opinión* supports Zionism since it is the liberation movement of the Jewish people. It considers Zionism to be a movement of high positive values, the study of which can shed light on many problems related to building national Argentine unity.
Question: Then it *is* a Zionist newspaper?
Answer: If you wish to put it in those terms, yes.
Question: Do you travel to Israel often?
Answer: Yes.
Question: Do you know the Israeli ambassador?
Answer: Yes.

My first interrogation took place after I'd been standing for several hours with my arms handcuffed behind my back, my eyes blindfolded. It was a sort of revelation for the interrogators. Why kill the hen that lays the golden eggs? Better to exploit him for the most important trial against the international Jewish conspiracy.

That's what saved my life. From that moment on, my arrest was officially recognized. The moderates tried for two years to get me released, and even thirty months later, when my freedom had been obtained, it was exploited as a pretext by the extremists to attempt a revolution to expel the moderates from power. A revolution that concluded in a ridiculous farce in the city of Córdoba—a forty-eight-hour uprising with no fighting, no bloodshed, only surrender.

Seen in this light, one could say that the moderates were correct. I think they were not. They could have combatted the extremists much sooner; they had, and in fact still have, greater strength than they imagine, and thousands of lives might have been saved. On the other hand, it's hard to talk about tactics when countless innocent people lost their lives.

My life was saved because the Nazis were overly Nazi; because they believed, as they informed me, that World War III had begun and that they enjoyed every conceivable impunity. One of the interrogators, known as Captain Beto, told me: "Only God gives and takes life. But God is busy elsewhere, and we're the ones who must undertake this task in Argentina."

Salomón Isacovici
(Romania-Ecuador, 1924–1998)
Fragment of *Man of Ashes*
Translated from the Spanish by Dick Gerdes

The book *Man of Ashes* (1990) has been marred by controversy since its inception. Its authorship was put into question by Juan Manuel Rodríguez, whom Salomón Isacovici hired to complete the volume. Isacovici is a native of Sighet, Rumania, also the native town of Elie Wiesel. He emigrated to Quito in 1948. Discussion of *Man of Ashes* appears in the essay "Novelizing the Holocaust?" (*The Essential Ilan Stavans*, 2000) and in "The Rights of History and the Rights of Imagination," by Cynthia Ozick (*Quarrel and Quandary*, 2000). The following is Chapter 19, which is placed toward the end of Isacovici's book. It discusses his impressions of Quito and its population. As such, it addresses a topic almost absent from the considerable literature of the Holocaust: its impact in Latin America.

Just before descending into Quito, the plane had throttled back and seemed to glide over the city. We had to skirt around gargantuan mountains that seemingly had risen out of the ground only yesterday and were now covered with intensely green vegetation. We started our landing by circling the city. I could even see the Spanish roof tiles on the houses and, as we looked down from above, the separations between the houses looked like trenches. I thought that the city must have been under siege, started to think that I had just left Europe looking for peace and here I was about to land in a city at war. But I calmed down once I was on the bus with Frida and her brother and discovered that those divisions were simply adobe walls between the lots.

Reunited with Frida, I was able to forget some of my problems, among them my lost suitcase. When we got to her parents' apartment, I had expected to get the cold shoulder, but it didn't turn out that way at all. Her family was hospitable and courteous. I imagined that by then they had given some serious thought to our relationship. Such a long trip and having come from so far away was proof enough that our love for each other had grown much more than they had imagined since the first time I had asked for their daughter's hand in marriage.

That same day I found a cheap place to live on the corner of Tarqui and 12 de Octubre streets. I knew practically no Spanish; what I did know I had learned from the bullfighters who crossed the Atlantic with me on the *Yagielo*. I could sing a few lines of "*Se va el caimán, se va el caimán, se va para Barranquilla,*" but despite those few words, which wouldn't even get me a job singing in a bar, I hardly understood anything.

From the very beginning, I was taken by the accent of the people of Quito: they seemed to whistle as they talked, as if they were mumbling some prayer between their teeth. And people would always say hello and shake hands. Humble people would tip their hats to me on the street and courteously murmur "*patruncito*"—master—upon which I would nod and smile because I had no idea what they were saying to me. The lack of communication was going to be a serious problem.

But the most serious problem was my dire economic situation. My suitcase had been lost in Panama and, without exaggerating, I had little more than the shirt on my back. I had four dollars and two cartons of American cigarettes on me. The Romanian sailor had given me the cigarettes. By selling them I could pay my first month's rent, but I still had to eat and buy some clothes, razor blades, soap, and shoes. Basically, I could make it for two months, so I had to find work immediately. Not knowing the language was a big disadvantage. By communicating with gestures and practically wearing out my only pair of shoes, I finally landed my first job in Ecuador. I began as a welder for the Ecuadoran Iron and Steel Company; I also taught soldering and chroming classes to young apprentices. While learning the language, all I could do was utter monosyllables and make mistakes. After a month on the job I received a small raise.

The Ecuadorans were very friendly and hospitable. Practically no one knew about what had happened in Europe, so no one asked me about my past. Since I was obsessed with trying to forget about what I had left behind, I turned myself entirely over to my work. I had decided to spend two extra hours a day at work, meaning that along with the raise I had received, my weekly salary was going up.

In order to learn a new language, I had to start speaking it; I began to talk as much as I could with those fine people. Since I would mix French and Romanian with Spanish, my coworkers would laugh and enjoyed listening to me talk. After four months I could speak with some fluency, but I still had a foreign accent. By then I was able to understand what the phrase "*se va el caimán*" meant.

It wasn't long before the Goldstein brothers, German immigrants who owned a soap factory, hired me as a salesman. I figured that by leaving the steel company and doing sales work, I could earn more through commissions and eventually save enough to start my own business. The soap factory was nothing more than two halves of a metal barrel with handles welded to the sides that hung from a tripod and under which a wood fire would heat the basic ingredients inside—coconut oil and caustic soda.

Within two weeks the number of orders I had secured from neighborhood stores had far outstripped the factory's ability to meet them. That same week, I demanded that the Goldstein brothers put their books in order and pay me the commissions that had come due. They gave me a pittance of what they owed me, rebuked me, and then fired me.

Stimulated by the apparent success of their soap factory, I decided to start one of my own. So I hired a guy who was working for the Goldsteins, but I offered him a better salary and a share in the sales. Of course, he came to work for me immediately. I rented a space and called my business venture the "Universal Soap Company."

I bought a barrel and cut it in half. One half was for preparing the first-class soap and the second barrel was for the speckled second-grade soap, to which we would add the dregs of the first-grade soap. I constructed a collapsible box that I lined with galvanized zinc to prevent corrosion from the caustic soda. That box was used to prepare the soap mixture. Then I built a tool to cut the soap into bars and also molds to give them an attractive shape. I copied the image of a small fish from a glass ashtray that would be molded into one side of the bar, and on the other side would appear the name of my company. I made the molds out of scrap aluminum. I poured the cast metal into clay molds I made with my own hands. They came out looking perfect.

Once everything was ready to go, my employee and I began to mass-produce bars of soap. We would let the soap mixture cool in the collapsible box, where the paste would begin to solidify. Then we would cut the soap into pieces, press them into the individual molds, and out would come the bars of soap that looked to me like bars of gold. We would let them harden in the sun.

The next morning I was out on the streets of Quito plying the wares I had made with my own hands. Very few store owners would pay me cash on the barrelhead; just about all of them offered only a small advance up front and then agreed to a long-term payment if they were to accept the merchandise. Within the month I went broke because I had no working capital to buy the raw materials. Once again I was back on the street without a job or a cent to my name. I managed to earn a little here and there doing part-time soldering jobs for different welding shops.

Nevertheless, Frida's parents finally agreed to set a date for our marriage. I saved every cent I could in order to have enough money to rent a house and purchase furniture and utensils. Frida had been working as a seamstress. When we would take walks through the main park, La Alameda, near the center of town, we never discussed Europe; it was as if it had never existed.

Finally, the big day had arrived: January 23, 1949. The wedding took place in a restaurant, and about eighty people attended. Except for Frida's family, I didn't know anyone there. Someone had loaned me a suit and a pair of shoes, the latter of which didn't fit me at all. I think, other than the immense happiness I felt when Frida became my wife, the most imposing impression I have of my wedding was the intense pain of sore feet that made me remember the "Death March."

Our honeymoon lasted one day, less time than it took for the aches and pains in my feet to go away. I escorted my wife to Tarqui and 12 de Octubre streets as if to the most luxurious hotel in the world. The next morning I was already at my new job. As it turns out, I had met a veterinarian at the wedding, and after talking for a while, we became friends. When I told him I was unemployed, he said I could work for him on his farm in Conocoto. And so it was that on the second day after getting married I became a farmer. I could have earned good money, but it only lasted six weeks, and once again I found myself without work. Frida was making only little money as a seamstress. I felt guilty that I was unable to support her and even more ashamed that I had to hit the streets again in search of part-time work as a welder. I was best at utilizing the mechanics I had learned in Sighet and later in Paris; but industial jobs were scarce and even a skilled worker's chances were almost nil.

After four months of marriage, I found a stable job as a tractor driver and administrator of a *hacienda* way up on a mountain called Pasochoa. The salary was great, and we got all the milk we wanted. Working in the countryside fortified my spirits. The beauty of the landscape was breathtaking. The snowcapped mountain peaks reminded me of my homeland near the Carpathians.

My job consisted of overseeing the *hacienda* staff, including a foreman and twenty-two Indian peons and their families who worked on the land in exchange for small parcels of land. Basically, they worked for nothing and they were required to do menial tasks for the foreman, Segundo, who acted as the head of their families. Work was assigned to every family member regardless of their age or sex.

Up there on those high, barren plateaus, where the wind would sweep fiercely down the rocky gorges and craggy terrain, the spectacular vistas seemed to be in harmony with nature—except for the poverty-stricken condition of the unfortunate Indians. Their faces, like scorched adobe cracked by the harsh sun, their unabated hunger, their innumerable diseases, and their servility to the boss—all filled me with the same anxiety that I felt in the concentration camps. These were human beings living out their death. The twenty-two families were scattered about the bleak, cold wilderness where only a little straw would grow. They lived in mud huts covered with straw roofs and no ventilation. They would enter through a minuscule doorway, seeking warmth; there, they lived in squalor among lice and pestilence. Their wretchedness was comparable only to those who had been dispossessed of everything, namely, the inhabitants of the Nazi concentration camps. Like those prisoners, no peons rebelled, no one would dare to look a white person in the eye. They were always staring at the ground and seemed resigned to endure any kind of insult and to carry out the orders of the heartless foreman.

Segundo, a fierce *mestizo*, was the absolute authority among the Indian peons on the *hacienda*. He assigned the work not only the way he saw fit but also according to the relationships he had established with each one of them. The treatment they received depended upon the sympathy or disdain he held for them, which, in turn, depended on the gifts and contributions they would make to him. The gifts ranged from chickens, eggs, and guinea pigs to a daughter of one of the peons.

The children of the peons were required to work as servants in the house of the *hacienda* owner. Just as I had been unable to fathom how some of the most advanced civilizations in Europe could inflict cruelty on my people, I simply couldn't believe that such deplorable conditions—anonymity, poverty, and slavery—could still exist in contemporary times.

The local medicine man—Juancho Quispe—was the only person who demonstrated any concern for the Indians' well-being. He would prescribe liquor and herbs, taken from the barren plateaus, to the sick and agonizing people. He'd grind up the ingredients to make tonics or rub them on their ailing bodies.

That world was really disheartening, even though one tends to become indifferent, to look the other way, or simply cease to see when he has to face misery up close. Wanting to help in some way, I would buy them medicines—powdered sulphate, iodine, pills—in order to cure their illness. But the foreman reprimanded me, saying I couldn't heal Indians with white man's medicine because they only believed in Quispe's ways of healing.

The suffering I had experienced in the camps was no different from what they were living, except that they didn't know any better, nor did they strive to improve their situation. But they had to know life could be better; they were aware of how the foreman lived and they had seen the owner's house, yet their state of peonage made all that seem no more than an impossible dream. You never saw them smiling. When they drank they would fall into a drunken stupor and lose consciousness; cheap booze didn't make them happy either.

Their faces, seemingly sculpted by fire, were as expressionless as rocks. Never once did they tell me about their suffering or misfortunes. They never dared to question the foreman's orders. Despite the harsh treatment and the constant abuse, they still trusted Segundo more than they did me because I was a white man. To be white created a barrier between two worlds, and there was nothing I could do to win them over.

On the weekends they would walk down to the nearby town of Amaguaña in order to buy salt, animal fat that they called *mapahuira*, and unrefined sugar. While in town, they would sit on the ground, bundled together in their frayed ponchos, around a barrel of *chicha*, a fermented corn drink. Groups of Indians would line up to buy it by the bucketful and drank the alcohol from a wooden cup that they passed along from one to the other until they became stupefied. *Chicha*, which was prepared in a wooden barrel, required corn, cane sugar, and ammonium, making it a highly toxic drink. By nightfall they were stumbling all over the place; the women, reeling and tottering like sacks of grain with their babies strapped to their backs, would stagger back to their huts into which they would tumble and fall asleep on the dirt floor. On Mondays they were useless because they were still unable to get up and go to work.

Suffering from lack of nutrition since birth and having to start working at an early age, both men and women were worn out and ancient by the time they reached thirty years of age. Those who looked old were simply early-to-middle-aged men and women who had been consumed by the endless suffering, abuse, poor food, and endemic sickness.

Typically, a peon would earn barely pennies a day, women even less. That miserable salary was complemented by what they managed to raise on their plot of barren land, where hardly anything would grow—their guinea pigs, a few chickens, and perhaps a sheep or two. The land was as destitute as they were and, in order to fertilize it, they would pilfer manure from the cattle stalls. Then they would plant a little barley, potatoes, and corn. Their principal food was toasted corn and broad beans. When I tilled the land on the *hacienda*, their children would follow behind and compete with the buzzards for the fat white grub worms that they would take home, fry, and eat. That "delicacy" was called *cucaito*.

Happiness did not figure in anyone's life on those high, bleak, barren plateaus. Even though I had always enjoyed working on the land, there wasn't much that could induce me to smile. But one of the most enduring memories I have of that era was learning that Frida was pregnant. Amid the joy of knowing that we were going to have a child, I pondered my situation and worried about the lack of medical assistance for Frida in that godforsaken place. But I couldn't just quit my job; there was nothing else that paid so well. While I spent a lot of time worrying, Frida's abdomen began to expand. The abundant rainfall that year gave new impetus and hope to the *hacienda*.

Meanwhile, Segundo was doing everything possible to get my administrative position on the *hacienda*. To him it meant the power to pillage the *hacienda* brazenly and unscrupulously; naturally, the peons had no part to play in that power struggle.

Finally, it came time for Frida to leave the *hacienda* and go back to live with her parents in Quito, in the event there were any emergencies during the pregnancy. I stayed on, and Segundo's harassment didn't let up. One night I thought an earthquake had occurred. All around the house the ground was shaking, as horses stampeded. Every night Segundo and a group of peons would run the horses around the house to frighten me and to thwart my sleep. A light sleeper because of the nightmares of the past, I would wake up at the drop of a pin. Images of the Nazi destruction would pop into my mind as if they had been fired by catapults. One day I ordered a shotgun from Quito. The day it arrived, I loaded it and waited for the onslaught of the horses that same night. Then I walked out onto the brick patio and fired two shots into the air, for that's all it took to rid myself of the Riders of the Apocalypse. Nevertheless, Segundo's harassment didn't let up: he really wanted my job.

One day I had to inspect a cornfield, and I left the mule I used for getting around the *hacienda* tied to some bushes. Nearby, there was grass for him to graze on. Once I had finished surveying the area, I went back to my mule and climbed on. Nervous to begin with, the animal was spooked by a bird, and began to buck. The saddle slipped, and suddenly I was holding onto the animal's stomach for dear life as he galloped like a bat out of hell. My right foot was caught in the stirrup. The mule headed full speed for the *hacienda*. I fell to the ground, and the animal just kept on dragging me across the tilled soil until he reached a fence. As the mule jumped it, I grabbed a fence post and held on. The saddle came off the mule.

My entire body was battered and bruised. The peons had loosened the cinch in order to make me fall. In great pain, I slung the saddle over my shoulder and walked back to the *hacienda*. I told one of the servants to catch the mule and tie it to a post. I was so angry that I found a strap and gave the animal a good thrashing. Suddenly a sharp pain pierced my hip. The servant helped me get into bed, where I remained for several days unable to move.

During my third day of immobility, Quispe came around to see me and for the next two days he gave me massages. Then he said: "Get up, *patrón*." As if by magic I stood up, and within days I was completely well.

During my convalescence, I received a message to return to Quito immediately because Frida was about to give birth. I went down to Amaguaña and took a bus to the capital. On the way, I was able to observe all the *haciendas* in the Los Chillos Valley, one of the most beautiful areas of the entire world. It reminded me so much of my homeland! Then I thought about my family and that soon I was going to be a father and start my own. I looked up at the sky. Clouds were floating by. "They see me," I said to myself, "and while they wouldn't be happy with my present situation, this is what life is all about and I'm ready to do whatever it takes for my new family."

When I arrived, Frida was already in the delivery room. I stood vigil in a waiting room with white walls and haggard people. After two hours of waiting I received the news that my son Roberto had been born. I took care of everything at the hospital and went back up to the *hacienda*. As I traveled back to those desolate, barren mountains, I thought about how my son's birth was going to change my life.

Frida was unable to join me for a while. Loneliness was like a nostalgic cloak that enveloped me. Even though I didn't like it, I had to immerse myself in my work to make time pass quickly. Six weeks later, Frida and Roberto were able to join me at the *hacienda*. The adobe walls and the frosty plateaus were not the best of environments for them, but Frida never complained. She had told me once that she would follow me to the end of the world, and even though that line sounded like something out of a movie, she meant it.

One day I ordered the peons to plow a particular stretch of land on a hill for planting barley. One of them wouldn't obey and said something nasty to me in Quechua, upon which I popped him so hard that he went rolling down the side of a ditch. I was afraid that I had killed him. As I ran down to help him, I prayed that he wasn't dead.

I reached the bottom. The Indian, Nieves, looked up at me and began to scurry away on all fours. I was relieved when I saw that he was still alive. But that incident made me think about the type of life I was leading on the *hacienda*. I was a long way from what we call civilization, the salary wasn't anything to brag about, and I lived in a hostile environment. I climbed up a hill and looked out over the fields where the peons were working. They were plowing with teams of oxen, gripping the handles of the plows as the steel blades attempted to penetrate the hard clay. The earth didn't want to yield. The rays of the sun bounced off their stolid faces, and apathy was the only expression that could be discerned.

I rode my bay horse back to the *hacienda*. Frida was surprised to see me return so early. I told her what had happened and about my decision to leave. Frida, who hadn't complained once for over a year and a half, jumped for joy. We immediately began packing the few things we owned, and then spent a peaceful last night on the *hacienda*.

By six o'clock in the morning we were already heading down to Amaguaña. Avelino Gualachico, the only peon who ever trusted me, carried our belongings on his back. Two other peons brought along a dozen chickens. By the time we reached Amaguaña, however, only a few were still alive. The peons had broken their necks so that I would have to give them away, which is what I did.

On Monday I went to the office of the *hacienda* owner, who lived in Quito. I asked for my salary for the last twenty days that I had worked on the *hacienda*.

While he was courteous to me, he sent me away without paying me, saying that I had abandoned my job and broken our contract. That was in March 1951.

The tormented peons and the foreman who was always exploiting them had made me see reality. I had sought refuge at the end of the world and I had wanted to forget the past, but I had come to understand that the past is never completely swept away and forgotten. It is with us always, for better or for worse. Suffering and misery were as much a part of those barren plateaus as the past in my soul. The past can never be forgotten or erased permanently, it only allows for certain distractions. Simply put, I had seen up close another facet of humanity, just as terrible as the concentration camps, even though the situation was relatively unknown by most people and of little concern to others. In much the same way that no one wanted to recognize the existence of the concentration camps in Europe, Ecuadorans were denying the fact that some of their fellow citizens were being tortured by the stinging whip of exploitation.

Was God aware of how those forgotten people were subjected to annihilation? Or was it like the concentration camps, where everyone just looked out for themselves? I didn't have an answer. At that moment when the setting sun had painted a yellowish tinge on the hills around Pasochoa, it suggested the majestic presence of a superior being whose hand touched every one of us. But for what purpose?

Marshall T. Meyer
(U.S.-Argentina, 1928–1993)
"Thoughts on Latin America"

An outspoken rabbi and human rights activist, Marshall T. Meyer was the founder of the Seminario Rabínico Latinoamericano in Buenos Aires. He was also on the faculty at the University of Judaism in California, and was in the eighties the head of the Congregation B'nei Yeshurun on the Upper West Side of Manhattan. The following speech delivered in the mid 1980s to an American Rabbinial assembly, is representative of Meyer's political stance, and of his view of Judaism as a religion that travels beyond geographical borders, languages, and ideologies. As he states it himself, his views often brought him enemies, and he was derided by his opponents as "a Communist Rabbi."

Colleagues, I am a refugee in my own country at the present moment. I am still in deep cultural shock even though I have had the opportunity of living and working at the University of Judaism for the past six months. Had anyone told me that it would be so difficult to immerse myself in the idiom and the realities of American culture and American Judaism despite my repeated visits over the years, I never would have believed it.

I have returned after a quarter of a century in Latin America. In this country I have visited and spoken in scores of cities, and I never cease to marvel at the extraordinary ignorance in the United States of America, on the part of Christian and Jew alike, about what is happening south of the border. And this is so in spite of the fact that day by day Latin America is occupying a more prominent part of our daily newspapers, in spite of the fact that if certain policies are continued we may be on our way, God forbid, to yet another war which could engulf an entire continent.

Let me sketch some sort of background upon which we can grapple with some of the issues tonight. I will try to do this as briefly as possible. Central and South America, for most North Americans, constitute one huge landmass populated by "those people down there in our backyard." Those "people down there" do not consider themselves in anybody's backyard. Those "people down there," according to any serious demographic prognosis, within fifteen years will represent 500 to 550 million people against a combined population in the United States and Canada of some 290 million people. Those "people down there," Christians, Jews, communists, atheists, agnostics, secularists, and so forth, by and large have one thing in common: they dislike intensely the United States of America and its policy with regard to Central and South America in particular, and with regard to all Third World countries in general.

We cannot describe Central and South America as one huge landmass. There are enormous cultural, historical, and socioeconomic differences. There are even differences in the types of Spanish spoken. Brazil, with a population of 130 million people, speaks Portuguese. The combined resources of the Amazon Basin dwarf the natural resources of North America. There are ethnic differences of enormous proportions in different countries due to differing percentages of Indians and *mestizos*. There are variegated historic backgrounds from country to country. The Catholic Church, although by far the greatest religious force in Latin America, is merely a *pro forma* Catholicism in some countries; in others it is a profound spiritual reality, and in still others popular superstition. The presentation of the Church as monolithic is a glib statement made by non-Catholics who are not acquainted with Catholic history or society.

In the Chile of today, under the military dictatorship of the murderer Augusto Pinochet—who does not receive much criticism from the current administration in this country—the cardinal is aggressively opposed to the fascist government, as he has been since Pinochet took power. (Chile has a Jewish population of about twenty-five thousand.) Since 1964, the Brazilian cardinal, Don Helder Camerra, has fought Figuereido and the military regime, as well as other fascist dictatorships. On the other hand, the Argentine hierarchy of the Roman Catholic Church was apologetic during the entire period of the Nazi fascist military dictatorship and sided with the government against the people and against many of its own priests and nuns.

There are also enormous economic and industrial differences. It makes no sense to think that Paraguay is similar to Argentina, or that Argentina has a great deal in common with Honduras, or to think that Chile is the same as Venezuela.

The enormous distances separating the countries and the difficulties in communication help to make the problems, whether they be economic, sociopolitical, or psychological, very complicated and difficult to understand. North

American Jewry is no exception to the generalization that I have presented. We, too, understand very little about the countries to our south. We know so little about Latin American Jewry.

Let's explore some demographic facts. In 1959, when my wife Naomi and I arrived in Buenos Aires, there were some 850,000 Jews in all of Latin America, including Central America. According to the *American Jewish Yearbook* of 1962, 721,000 Jews lived there. The Jewish population of Central and South America, according to U.O. Schmelz and Sergio Della Pergola of the Hebrew University in the *Yearbook* of 1984, is 495,000.

Practically every country, with the exception of Mexico, Costa Rica, Panama, and Venezuela, has dropped anywhere from one-third to one-half of its Jewish population, and not precisely because of *aliyah*. Since *hokamat ha-medinah*, the entire Central and South American number of *olim* (without counting *yordim*) has been some 80,000. That's all. The Jewish population of Uruguay was 45,000 to 48,000 in 1959. It is listed in the *Yearbook* of 1984 as 30,000. It is actually much closer to 22,000. Basically, we are dealing with an area that has few if any scientific demographic studies. Consequently, the numbers are more like "guesstimates" than the product of such studies.

What is happening now with regard to Jewish religious movements in Central and South America? Orthodoxy has nowhere near the power that it has in North America. Most of the Jews who came to Central and South America were secularists. The one single power above all others that maintains Jewish identity is the existence of the State of Israel. Let there be no doubt about it. The Zionist organizations and their political party structures in each and every one of these countries are by far the most important single force responsible for Jewish identity and unity.

I remember stating at the United Synagogue Convention in 1960 that: "The least important institution the Jewish life in Latin America is the synagogue." I doubted at that time whether there was a *minyan* to say *kaddish* for the synagogue, which was dying as an institution.

Reform Judaism practically did not exist. There were twenty or twenty-five rabbis for the entire continent of 850,000 Jews, and the only rabbis who had university education were those few who had been ordained at West European rabbinical seminaries. These dedicated survivors were the individuals really responsible for the maintenance of something congruent and organic with regard to religious Judaism. Most of the Sephardic rabbis had little or no secular education in the countries from which they came.

The Conservative movement in South America at the present time is by far the most important force in religious Judaism. During the last High Holy Days, the graduates and the students of the Seminario Rabínico Latinoamericano served over 110,000 Jews. The Seminario was founded in 1962. It is now officially an affiliate of the Jewish Theological Seminary of America. There are some thirty students in rabbinical school. Each of them, of course, has his university title (*licenciatura* in Spanish, which is almost the equivalent of a Master's degree). There is no such thing as a B.A. degree. One enters directly into a professional school from high school. Thus our rabbinical students include lawyers, doctors, and engineers. The last few years of their studies are spent in Israel, and the *senikhah* is given in Buenos Aires. We have two secondary schools in the Seminario, as well as a number of other departments. A total of 450 students are studying at the Seminario Rabínico Latinamericano today in all its departments.

The Bet El community started with some ten families. It now has over one thousand families and two rabbis. There are about 150 to 160 *b'nai* and *b'not* yearly. There are over 150 weddings each year. The congregation, *barukh kashem*, on any given Friday night numbers well over a thousand people, the vast majority of whom are twenty-five years old or younger. Many years ago, we started Camp Ramah in Argentina. There is now a Camp Ramah in Chile. In practically every country in Latin America there are such camps (although not all of them are called Ramah), and these camps were founded and are directed by graduates of the Seminario. When we arrived, it was quite obvious that there was little to read in Judaica. Thus we were forced to go into translating and publishing. Happily, during the twenty-five years, we have published over seventy volumes, which include the entire bilingual liturgy with many original liturgical creations.

As a result of the vitality of Zionism, all of the Conservative congregations are very Zionist in their programming. From Bet El, the Seminario, and Camp Ramah in the past twenty-five years, over 1800 families have gone on *aliyah*. As a matter of fact, there is a desperate need for Spanish-speaking Conservative congregations in Israel.

Israel is so important for our congregation that nobody can become a member of Bet El who is not a regular donor to the United Jewish Appeal [UJA]. We have been willing to lose members over this issue. That is to say, if you ask for tickets for the High Holy Days (which are not for sale) you have to have your receipt from the UJA. This is also true of celebrating weddings or *b'nai* and *b'not mitzvah* at Bet El. There are a number of other ideas which we have implemented there that we have found to be extraordinarily attractive to the youth.

The rich do not sit in the front row, nor do the rich necessarily have light. Pews or seats are not for sale. All tickets for the High Holy Days are free to those who have paid their dues. Tickets are placed into an urn, and all *aliyot* to the Torah as well as seating arrangements are drawn from the urn. One receives an honor, including opening the Ark, not because he or she has been a big donor, but because he or she was lucky enough to be chosen in the drawing. I suggest that this is one of the basic reasons why the youth came back to the synagogue or found the synagogue in the first place. They found a genuine equality and not the typical running after the wealthy. Of course, this alone does not explain the phenomenon. More important is an egalitarian, participatory, spiritually vibrant service, *conducted by the young people themselves*.

I am almost proud to say that there has never been a president of Bet El, or of the Seminario, who was a millionaire. Many people have given their time and their efforts in raising money. But many people have often had to leave their positions as president or as members of the board of directors because of the severe economic difficulties which they were experiencing. In no way, of course, was there ever a prejudice *against* the wealthy.

Central and Latin America today are involved in a most delicate process; the gradual democratization of the continent. And here I am going to touch upon something that will be controversial. It has to do with the Pope. First of all, what has the Pope to do with all of this? He is openly against "liberation theology." On each and every visit that he has made to the South American continent, he has made false comparisons of Marxism and liberation theology. With all of his goodness and loving-kindness, he seems more afraid of the word "communism" than he is of the fact that millions of Catholics are oppressed, undernourished, illiterate, and sick.

Liberation theology is a theological school of thought that has been born out of hunger, oppression, illness, underemployment, and downright slavery. This is a very serious issue confronting everyone today. It has been argued in this country that Nicaragua may have to be invaded because we cannot afford to have a communist regime in our "backyard." Just about every possible and imaginary argument is being used, including the fact that there is anti-Semitism in Nicaragua (where there are three Jews and, search as I did this summer, I could not find one of them). Why isn't anyone speaking the truth of what happened under Somoza? Why aren't we reading about Stroessner in Paraguay now? If the three million Paraguayan slaves rise up tomorrow, will we have to invade them too?!

The problem is that the Jew, because of his economic interests, because of his industrial activities, evidently seems to be more comfortable with the military dictatorships which afford "stability" than with the popular movements of the exploited. Unless this changes, it will blow up in our faces.

There is a class struggle in South America today. As a result of my association with human rights, I have been called the Pink Rabbi, or the Communist Rabbi. I have been called almost everything. Of one thing I am certain, Jews can become involved in the democratization. Jews have the potential of getting involved in the overthrowing of the fascist regimes and in the stabilization of the popularist democratic governments throughout the area. I believe that the future of the Jews in Latin America will depend upon their participation in these democratic processes. This is definitely opposed to the policies of the administration in Washington. Anti-Semitism in Nicaragua is a bogus issue. It does not exist *today*. The whole idea that the synagogue in Managua, Nicaragua, was taken over is a misunderstanding, to say the least. I spent an entire evening with the Junta in Managua. They offered me the keys to the synagogue. "Find some Jews, rabbi. The synagogue is yours." The Managua synagogue was not even listed as such. Its overhead costs were paid for by an individual, a member of whose family is now on the West Coast, going from synagogue to synagogue speaking about anti-Semitism in Nicaragua. I have in my possession a copy of a telex that was sent by the former American ambassador to Nicaragua to the State Department, denying the allegation of anti-Semitism and stating it to be absolutely ridiculous.

There is a question of socioeconomic proportions with tremendous political undertones in this area, but it is not a question of east and west in Latin America. It is a question of north and south.

Many Jews are becoming involved in a type of liberation theology. One could make a strong case that the first liberation theologians were the Prophets of Israel. Actually, the first Prophet who taught liberation theology was Moses, if I am not mistaken. The foundation of the *Jewish Movement of Human Rights in Argentina* is just that type of phenomenon. Those Jews who are living in Latin America have to make a decision: whether to back fascist military dictatorships, and therefore run the risk of what happens to them when the dictatorships are overthrown by the exploited, downtrodden people who suffer malnutrition, illiteracy, and the lack of proper medical care (just to list only the prime examples of their extraordinary pain), or to work for authentic democracy. Democracy, not Russian totalitarianism.

The present administration in Washington is trying to leave out the Contadora countries from the process of peacemaking in Central America. Contadora represents Mexico, Panama, Venezuela, and Colombia. The combined foreign debt of the Latin American countries is hundreds of billions of dollars. The International Monetary Fund is pressuring for an arrangement. The greatest pressure that is facing Argentina today is economic. Dr. Alfonsin, the president of Argentina, is a genuinely noble human being, a democrat, a pluralist, a light for South America. Argentina is not the only country in an unbearable economic squeeze. We as Americans must be conscious of the possible consequences of those economic pressures.

If the United States moves into Nicaragua, ladies and gentlemen, and if, as a form of fighting back, the Latin American countries default on the *interest* of those billions, the entire Western banking system could crack within twenty-four hours, and what happened to the lira and the shekel and the peso might happen to the dollar as well.

When we first arrived in Argentina, there were 82 pesos to the dollar. The rate of exchange is now 48 million pesos to one dollar. (They have dropped six zeros, so it is 480 pesos.) Only Argentina beats Israel in the rate of inflation. Last year, it was over eight hundred percent. As you all know, inflation is not an economic problem alone. It eats into the very warp and woof of a society. It changes the philosphy and the values of a society. Why on earth would you save a penny? What is the value of work if the money that you make today cannot buy enough bread for tomorrow? This is something that we must understand. You cannot require the repayment of this money without breaking the backbone of these countries, throwing them back under fascist dictatorships. The only countries that the administration is backing today are the fascist dictatorships. And I think this should be clearly stated.

Why is this a Jewish problem? As a rabbi, I felt obliged to visit prisons and to try to comfort parents of the disappeared people, be they Christian, Jew, or agnostic. Why? Behind what little I have done in human rights (which is such an endless task) there was and is one basic idea: if we are to take the Prophets seriously, we cannot negate history and return to a "golden ghetto." I have tried to respond to life in this jungle as I believe a rabbi should respond. The problems are ours because Amos, Isaiah, and Hosea taught us that they are ours, taught us that there is only one mankind as there is only one God. And this is the basis of liberation theology. Why should so few have so much and so many starve? This is a Jewish question. This is a Biblical question. I bleed with people when I see them hungry and crawling for safety. That is why I am so active in the Sanctuary movement. I have heard too many Jews say: "What do I have to do with a Guatemalan? I do not speak Spanish. Why should he be in my synagogue? He is a Roman Catholic. Let the churches take care of it!"

Do you remember the plethora of arguments and articles that appeared about the silence in the churches during the Second World War? What did they say? "What do I have to do with a Polish Jew? He speaks Yiddish. Let the Jews worry about him." Unless the synagogue becomes sensitive to the needs of *all* peoples who are hungry and downtrodden, unless we are capable of feeling for *everybody* who is being persecuted, what right do we have to think that the world will take notice when we scream out only on anti-Semitic issues? God forbid that these cries for aid and help on the part of the refugees from Central America be met with silence in the synagogues! We will not be roundly applauded for what we do, but I believe more in the Judge of all judges who will call us to task for repeating the silence because of which we suffered the loss of one-third of our people.

This Jewish involvement in liberation theology and human rights is obviously political as well as religious. My own participation in the human rights movement does not stem from any partisan politics, neither in North America nor in South America. My response, with every ounce of strength I possess as a Jew who professes his faith, emanates from my understanding of Judaism. We were slaves in Egypt and we taught the world to strike out for freedom.

"Proclaim liberty in the land to all the inhabitants therein." We are supposed to know what that means. God knows we suffered enough in the Holocaust, and there certainly is something somewhere written about the word *shalom* in our Bible. Somewhere we can find the concept of the sanctity of life. Somewhere? On every page of our sacred texts!

What is the future of Jews in South America and Central America? If I could push a magic button which would transfer the Seminario and all of its affiliates to Israel, I would push that button. Today there are over forty-seven congregations affiliated with the Seminario Rabinico Latinoamericano. This is the Conservative presence in Latin America, over twenty percent of the Jewish population of the continent. I repeat: if I could push the button and all of those people would go to Israel, I would do it. But they are free to go just as you and I are free to go, and they choose to stay, just as so many of us here choose to stay.

If they are going to stay, then their future will depend upon the democratization of this part of the world. Please God, I would like to see it achieved by peaceful means. But the people of Chile have a limit to their suffering, and those of you who haven't seen children die of starvation except on television can't really appreciate my words. I don't wish it on you. Nor do I wish it on you to be present when people find out that their child has disappeared. Let me briefly attempt to tell you what it means to be a "disappeared person." You wait at home for your mother or father if you are young, or for your sister. Or you wait for your son or your daughter and at about 11:00 the front door is blown open by the blast of a machine gun. The traffic has been cut in front of your house. Six or eight people dressed as I am dressed now, very barely in uniform, walk in. They smash your wife over the head with the butt of a rifle; they slam you against the wall and ask you where your son or daughter is. You say that she is in night school, that he is in medical school. And you start to pray in any language or in any religious tradition that you have or that you don't have, that he or she won't show up. They destroy everything in your apartment and they steal everything that they can get their hands on, and if they don't get everything the first time, the next morning a truck comes by and takes it away.

Lo and behold, if you wait long enough, your son comes home. He was at his girlfriend's house or at his uncle's house for dinner. And the first thing that happens is that his arm is grabbed and broken and he is kicked in the back just to make sure he doesn't do anything to escape. And you scream out: "Where are you taking him?" "We want to look into his record to see what he has been up to." "But he is seventeen years old, she is nineteen years old, he hasn't been doing anything, she is not involved in politics." "Don't worry, if he hasn't done anything, he'll be back in two or three days."

You rush to the police but the police have no record of anything, and they say there must be some error. You go to the Ministry of the Interior. You go to the army, the navy, the air force and you get the same answer. You go to your lawyer and you ask him to write a *habeus corpus* and he says: "I am afraid to write a *habeus corpus* because my colleagues are disappearing and I've seen it happen in front of my eyes." You call up your own brother or your own sister and beg them to come over, saying: "They have destroyed us." The answer: "I'm worried about my own children." I've seen families destroyed. They still don't talk because there people whose children or parents disappeared were pariahs in their own families and in their own communities.

You may have read about "the mad mothers," women who have the names of their missing sons and daughters embroidered on their white bandannas and who walk in silence every Thursday at 3:30 P.M. around the obelisk in the Plaza de Mayo. When the mothers of the Plaza de Mayo came to services at my synagogue, very few people were walking with them. You could count them on a few fingers.

You know what it means when someone you love comes home late. How does your heart react when you have been waiting for *six or seven years*, waiting to receive a cadaver over which to say *kaddish*? One man came into my study, rolled up his sleeve and showed me the numbers. "For this I was saved from Auschwitz? Rabbi, I have a *halakhic* question. They took my two sons. Do I have a right to say *kaddish*?" I answered: "Are you asking me as a rabbi?" "Yes." He had me by the throat at this point. I said: "If you can't prove that he's dead and it's only been a couple of months, you've got to wait." "How can you ask me to wait any longer?" He is still waiting.

After Dr. Alfonsín became president of Argentina, within five days he founded the National Presidential Commission for Missing People. When he called and invited me to participate in that commission, which was a plenipotentiary commission with documentation allowing its members to go into every military installation in Argentina, the military turned green because I was an American Citizen *and a rabbi*! If it is true that not one Jew was arrested solely because he was a Jew, it is also true that when he was in prison he was triply or quadruply tortured because he was a Jew. People started coming to the synagogue in greater numbers, increasingly greater numbers—to cry, to weep, or to hear a word that attacked the government, a word of protest.

It was then, at a meeting of the board of directors of my synagogue, that someone said he was frightened for the entire congregation. "We can't allow the mothers to come here all the time." To the everlasting dignity and nobility of the board of directors, their answer was: "This synagogue will always be open to those who want to enter, and our rabbi will always have the freedom of the pulpit to say what he feels must be said."

I believe, ladies and gentlemen, that the future of Jewry in Latin America will depend exclusively upon our capacity to give a congruous answer as a Jewish community there. And here we must act as their brothers, not turning our backs on them, speaking with them, and showing that the United States of America has human beings in it who are not imperialists considering them merely a daisy or a weed to be plucked from their backyard.

Insofar as the synagogues will remain true to the vocation of justice and righteousness, insofar as we will follow the teachings of Torah and the Prophets, then there will be a future, if this galaxy and indeed this planet has a future. So when we speak of Central and South America, know that there are half a million of our brothers and sisters there in addition to another 500 million people who are also our brothers and sisters; and not only there, but throughout the world. If we are faithful to the noblest ideals of our beloved Judaism, we will know how to respond.

Mario Vargas Llosa
(Peru, 1936–)
Fragment of *The Storyteller*
Translated from the Spanish by Helen Lane

Mario Vargas Llosa is a novelist, playwright, essayist, political commentator, and presidential hopeful whose books include *Conversation in the Cathedral* (1969), *The War of the End of the World* (1981), *In Praise of the Stepmother* (1988), and *The Feast of the Goat* (2000), as well as *Making Waves* (1997). His interest in Jewish characters is limited to a single novel: *The Storyteller* (1987). Loosely based on the life of Isaac Goldemberg (see the corresponding Goldemberg entry), it relates the odyssey of Saúl Zuratas, a Peruvian Jew with a dark birthmark on his face, who, when his studies in anthropology in Lima leave him dissatisfied, decides to disappear into the jungle to become part of an aboriginal tribe on the verge of extinction. The following fragment, from early in the novel, is a portrait of Zuratas. Vargas Llosa has also written essays on the Middle East and on anti-Semitism.

Saúl Zuratas had a dark birthmark, the color of wine dregs, that covered the entire right side of his face, and unruly red hair as stiff as the bristles of a scrub brush. The birthmark spared neither his ears nor his lips nor his nose, also puffy and misshapen from swollen veins. He was the ugliest lad in the world; but he was also a likable and exceptionally good person. I have never met anyone who, from the very outset, seemed as open, as uncomplicated, as altruistic, and as well-intentioned as Saúl; anyone who showed such simplicity and heart, no matter what the circumstances. I met him when we took our university entrance examinations, and we were quite good friends—insofar as it is possible to be friends with an archangel—especially during the first two years that we were classmates in the Faculty of Letters. The day I met him he informed me, doubled over with laughter and pointing to his birthmark: "They call me Mascarita—Mask Face. Bet you can't guess why, pal."

That was the nickname we always knew him by at San Marcos.

He came from Talara and was on familiar terms with everybody. Slang words and popular catchphrases appeared in every sentence he uttered, making it seem as though he were clowning even in his most personal conversations. His problem, he said, was that his father had made too much money with his general store back home; so much that one fine day he'd decided to move to Lima. And since they'd come to the capital his father had taken up Judaism. He wasn't very religious back in the Piura port town, as far as Saúl could remember. He'd occasionally seen him reading the Bible, that, yes, but he'd never bothered to drill it into Mascarita that he belonged to a race and a religion that were different from those of the other boys of the town. But here in Lima, what a change! A real drag! Ridiculous! Chicken pox in old age, that's what it was! Or rather, the religion of Abraham and Moses. *Pucha*! We Catholics were the lucky ones. The Catholic religion was a breeze, a measly half-hour Mass every Sunday and Communion every first Friday of the month that was over in no time. But he, on the other hand, had to sit out his Saturdays in the synagogue, hours and hours, swallowing his yawns and pretending to be interested in the rabbi's sermon—not understanding one word—so as not to disappoint his father, who after all was a very old and very good man. If Mascarita had told him that he'd long since given up believing in God, and that, to put it in a nutshell, he couldn't care less about belonging to the "Chosen People," he'd have given poor Don Salomón a heart attack.

I met Don Salomón one Sunday shortly after meeting Saúl. Saúl had invited me to lunch. They lived in Breña, behind the Colegio La Salle, in a depressing side street off the Avenida Arica. The house was long and narrow, full of old furniture, and there was a talking parrot with a Kafkaesque name and surname who endlessly repeated Saúl's nickname: "Mascarita! Mascarita!" Father and son lived alone with a maid who had come from Talara with them and not only did the cooking but helped Don Salomón out in the grocery store he'd opened in Lima. "The one that's got a six-pointed star on the metal grill, pal. It's called *La Estrella*, for the Star of David. Can you beat that?"

I was impressed by the affection and kindness with which Mascarita treated his father, a stooped, unshaven old man who suffered from bunions and dragged about in big clumsy shoes that looked like Roman buskins. He spoke Spanish with a strong Russian or Polish accent, even though, as he told me, he had been in Peru for more than twenty years. He had a sharp-witted, likable way about him: "When I was a child I wanted to be a trapeze artist in a circus, but life made a grocer of me in the end. Imagine my disappointment." Was Saúl his only child? Yes, he was.

And Mascarita's mother? She had died two years after the family moved to Lima. How sad; judging from this photo, your mother must have been very young, Saúl. Yes, she was. On the one hand, of course, Mascarita had grieved over her death. But, on the other, maybe it was better for her, having a different life. His poor old lady had been very unhappy in Lima. He made signs at me to come closer and lowered his voice (an unnecessary precaution, as we had left Don Salomón fast asleep in a rocking chair in the dining room and were talking in Saúl's room) to tell me:

"My mother was a Creole from Talara; the old man took up with her soon after coming to this country as a refugee. Apparently, they just lived together until I was born. They got married only then. Can you imagine what it is for a Jew to marry a Christian, what we call a goy? Not you can't."

Back in Talara it hadn't mattered because the only two Jewish families there more or less blended in with the local population. But, on settling in Lima, Saúl's mother faced numerous problems. She missed home—everything from the nice warm weather and the cloudless sky and bright sun all year round to her family and friends. Moreover, the Jewish community of Lima never accepted her, even though to please Don Salomón she had gone through the ritual of the lustral bath and received instruction from the rabbi in order to fulfill all the rites necessary for conversion. In fact—and Saúl winked a shrewd eye at me—the community didn't accept her not so much because she was a goy as because she was a little Creole from Talara, a simple woman with no education, who could barely read. Because the Jews of Lima had all turned into a bunch of bourgeois, pal.

He told me all this without a vestige of rancor or dramatization, with a quiet acceptance of something that, apparently, could not have been otherwise. "My old lady and I were as close as fingernail and flesh. She, too, was as bored as an oyster in the synagogue, and without Don Salomón's catching on, we used to play Yan-Ken-Po on the sly to make those religious Sabbaths go by more quickly. At a distance: she would sit in the front row of the gallery, and I'd be downstairs, with the men. We'd move our hands at the same time and sometimes we'd fall into fits of laughter that horrified the holier-than-thous." She'd been carried off by galloping cancer, in just a few weeks. And since her death Don Salomón's world had come tumbling down on top of him.

"That little old man you saw there taking his nap, was hale and hearty, full of energy and love of life a couple of years ago. The old lady's death left him a wreck."

Saúl had entered San Marcos University as a law student to please Don Salomón. As far as Saúl was concerned, he would rather have started giving his father a hand at *La Estrella*, which was often a headache to Don Salomón and took more out of him than was right at his age. But his father was categorical. Saúl would not set foot behind that counter. Saúl would never wait on a customer. Saúl would not be a shopkeeper like him.

"But why, Papa? Are you afraid this face of mine will scare the customers away?" He recounted this to me amid peals of laughter. "The truth is that now that he's saved up a few shekels, Don Salomón wants the family to make its mark in the world. He can already see a Zuratas—me—in the Diplomatic Corps or the Chamber of Deputies. Can you imagine!"

Making the family name illustrious through the exercise of a liberal profession was something that didn't attract Saúl much either. What interested him in life? He himself didn't know yet, doubtless. He was finding out gradually during the months and years of our friendship, the fifties, in the Peru that, as Mascarita, myself, and our generation were reaching adulthood, was moving from the spurious peace of General Order's dictatorship to the uncertainties and novelties of the return to democratic rule in 1956, when Saúl and I were third-year students at San Marcos.

By then he had discovered, without the slightest doubt, what it was that interested him in life. Not in a sudden flash, or with the same conviction as later; nonetheless, the extraordinary machinery had already been set in motion and little by little was pushing him one day here, another there, outlining the maze he eventually would enter, never to leave it again. In 1956 he was studying ethnology as well as law and had made several trips into the jungle. Did he already feel that spellbound fascination for the peoples of the jungle and for unsullied nature, for minute primitive cultures scattered throughout the wooded slopes of the *ceja de montaña* and the plains of the Amazon below? Was that ardent fellow feeling, sprung from the darkest depths of his personality, already burning within him for those compatriots of ours who from time immemorial had lived there, harassed and grievously harmed, between the wide, slow rivers, dressed in loincloths and marked with tattoos, worshipping the spirits of trees, snakes, clouds, and lightning? Yes, all that had already begun. And I became aware of it just after the incident in the billiard parlor two or three years after our first meeting.

Every so often, between classes, we used to go over to a run-down billiard parlor which was also a bar, on the Jirón Azángaro, to have ourselves a game.

Walking through the streets with Saúl showed how painful a life he must have led at the hands of insolent, nasty people. They would turn around or block his path as he passed, to get a better look at him, staring wide-eyed and making no effort to conceal the amazement or disgust that his face aroused in them; and it was not a rare thing for someone, children mostly, to come out with some insulting remark. He didn't appear to mind, and always answered their abuse with a bit of cheerful repartee. The incident as we entered the billiard parlor didn't provoke him, but it did me, since by nature I'm a far cry from an archangel.

The drunk was bending his elbow at the bar. The moment he laid eyes on us, he came staggering over and stood in front of Saúl with arms akimbo. "Son of a bitch! What a monster! What zoo did you escape from?"

"Well, which one would you say, pal? The only one around here, the one in Barranco, of course," Mascarita replied. "If you dash right over, you'll find my cage still open."

And he tried to make his way past. But the drunk stretched out his hands, making hex signs with his fingers, the way children do when they're called bad names.

"You're not coming in here, monster." He was suddenly furious. "With a face like that, you should keep off the streets. You scare people."

"But if this is the only one I've got, what do you suggest I do?" Saúl said, smiling. "Come on, don't be a drag—let us by."

At that, I lost my patience. I grabbed the toper by the lapels and started shaking him. There was a show of fists, people milling round, some pushing and shoving, and Mascarita and I had to leave without having had our billiard game.

The next day I received a present from him. It was a small bone shaped like a diamond and engraved with a geometric design in a yellowish-brick color. The design represented two parallel mazes made up of bars of different sizes, separated by identical distances, the larger ones seemingly nestled inside the smaller ones. His brief accompanying letter, good-humored and enigmatic, went something like this:

Hi pal,
Let's see if this magic bone calms that impetuosity of yours and you stop punching poor lushes. The bone is from a tapir and the drawing is not the awkward scrawl it appears to be—just a few primitive strokes—but a symbolic inscription. Morenanchiite, the lord of thunder, dictated it to a jaguar, who dictated it to a witch-doctor friend of mine from the forests of the Alto Picha. If you think these

symbols are whirlpools in the river or two coiled boa constrictors taking a nap, you may be right. But, above all, they represent the order that reigns in the world. Anyone who lets anger get the better of him distorts these lines, and when they're distorted they can no longer hold up the earth. You wouldn't want life, through your fault, to fall apart and men to return to the original chaos out of which Tasurinchi, the god of good, and Kientibakonri, the god of evil, brought us by breathing us out, now would you, pal? So no more tantrums, and especially not because of me. Anyhow, thanks.
Ciao,
Saúl

I asked him to tell me more about the thunder and the tiger, the distorted lines, Tasurinchi and Kientibakori. He had me hanging on his words for an entire afternoon at his house in Breña as he talked to me of the beliefs and customs of a tribe scattered through the jungles of Cusco and Madre de Dios.

I was lying on his bed, and he was sitting on a trunk with his parrot on his shoulder. The creature kept nibbling at his bright red hair and interrupting him with its peremptory squawks of "Mascarita!" "You be still now, Gregor Samsa," he soothed him.

The designs on their utensils and their cushmas, the tattoos on their faces and bodies, were neither fanciful nor decorative, pal. They were a coded writing that contained the secret names of people and magic formulas to protect things from damage and their owners from evil spells laid on them through such objects. The patterns were set by a noisy bearded deity, Morenanchiite, the lord of thunder, who in the middle of a storm passed on the key to a tiger from the heights of a mountain peak. The tiger passed it on to a medicine man, or shaman, in the course of a trance brought on by ayahuasca, the hallucinogenic plant, which, boiled into a brew, was drunk at all Indian ceremonies. That witch doctor of Alto Picha—"or, better put, a wise man, chum; I'm calling him a witch doctor so you'll understand what I'm talking about"—had explained to him the philosophy that had allowed the tribe to survive until now. The most important thing to them was serenity. Never to make mountains out of molehills or tempests in teapots. Any sort of emotional upheaval had to be controlled, for there is a fatal correspondence between the spirit of man and the spirits of Nature, and any violent disturbance in the former causes some catastrophe in the latter.

"A man throwing a fit can make a river overflow, and a murder make lightning burn down the village. Perhaps that bus crash on the Avenida Arequipa this morning was caused by your punching that drunk yesterday. Doesn't your conscience trouble you?"

I was amazed at how much he knew about the tribe. And even more so as I realized what a torrent of fellow feeling this knowledge aroused in him. He talked of those Indians, of their customs and myths, of their surroundings and their gods, with the respect and admiration that were mine when I brought up the names of Sartre, Malraux, and Faulkner, my favorite authors that year. I never heard him speak with such emotion even of Kafka, whom he revered, as he did of that tribe of Indians.

I must have suspected even then that Saúl would never be a lawyer, and I suspected also that his interest in the Amazonian Indians was something more than "ethnological." Not a professional, technical interest, but something much more personal, though hard to pin down. Surely more emotional than rational, an act of love rather than intellectual curiosity or the appetite for adventure that seemed to lurk in the choice of career made by so many of his fellow students in the Department of Ethnology. Saúl's attitude toward this new calling, the devotion he manifested for the world of the Amazon, were frequently the subject of conjecture on the campus of the San Marcos Faculty of Letters.

Was Don Salomón aware that Saúl was studying ethnology, or did he think he was concentrating on his law studies? The fact was that, even though Mascarita was still enrolled in the Faculty of Law, he never went to class. With the exception of Kafka, and *The Metamorphosis* in particular, which he had read countless times and virtually knew by heart, all his reading was now in the field of anthropology. I remember his consternation at how little had been written about the tribes and his complaints about how difficult it was to trace down material scattered in various monographs and journals that did not always reach San Marcos or the National Library.

It had all begun, he told me once, with a trip to Quillabamba during the national holidays. He had gone there at the invitation of a relative, a first cousin of his mother's and an uncle of his, who had emigrated from Piura to that region, had a small farm, and also dealt in timber. The man would go deep into the jungle in search of mahogany and rosewood, hiring Indians to clear trails and cut down trees. Mascarita had gotten on well with the Indians—most of them pretty well Westernized—and they had taken him with them on their expeditions and welcomed him in their camps up and down the vast region irrigated by the Alto Urubamba and the Alto Madre de Dios and their respective tributaries. He spent an entire night enthusiastically telling me what it was like to ride a raft hurtling through the Pongo de Mainique, where the Urubamba, squeezed between two foothills of the Cordillera, became a labyrinth of rapids and whirlpools.

"Some of the porters are so terrified they have to be tied to the rafts, the way they do with cows, to get them through the gorge. You can't imagine what it's like, pal!"

A Spanish missionary from the Dominican mission in Quillabamba had shown him mysterious petroglyphs scattered throughout the area; Saúl had eaten monkey, turtle, and grubs and gotten incredibly soused on cassava masato.

"The natives of the region believe the world began in the Pongo de Mainique. And I swear to you there's a sacred aura about the place, something indefinable that makes your hair stand on end. You can't imagine what it's like, pal. Really far out!"

This experience had consequences that no one could have envisaged. Not even Saúl himself, of that I'm sure.

He went back to Quillabamba for Christmas and spent the long year-end vacation there. He returned during the July vacation between terms and again the following December. Every time there was a break at San Marcos, even for only a few days, he'd head for the jungle in anything he could find: trucks, trains, jitneys, buses. He came back from these trips full of enthusiasm and eager to talk, his eyes bright with amazement at the treasures he'd discovered. Everything that came from there interested and excited him tremendously. Meeting the legendary Fidel Pereira, for instance. The son of a white man from Cusco and a Machiguenga woman, he was a mixture of feudal lord and aboriginal *cacique*. In the last third of the nineteenth century a man from a good Cusco family, fleeing from the law, went deep into those forests, where the Machiguengas had sheltered him. He had married a woman of the tribe. His son, Fidel, lived astride the two cultures, acting like a white when with whites and like a Machiguenga when with Machiguengas. He had several lawfully wedded wives, any number of concubines, and a constellation of sons and daughters, thanks to whom he ran all the coffee plantations and farms between Quillabamba and the Pongo de Mainique, putting the whole tribe to work and paying them next to nothing. But, in spite of that, Mascarita felt a certain liking for him:

"He uses them, of course. But at least he doesn't despise them. He knows all about their culture and is proud of it. And when other people try to trample on them, he protects them."

In the stories he told me, Saúl's enthusiasm made the most trivial happening—clearing a patch of forest or fishing for gamitana—take on heroic dimensions. But above all, it was the world of the Indians, with their primitive practices and their frugal life, their animism and their magic, that seemed to have bewitched him. I now know that those Indians, whose language he had begun to learn with the help of native pupils in the Dominican mission of Quillabamba—he once sang me a sad, repetitive, incomprehensible song, shaking a seed-filled gourd to mark the rhythm—were the Machiguengas. I now know that he had made the posters with their little drawings showing the dangers of fishing with dynamite that I had seen piled up in his house in Breña, to distribute to the whites and *mestizos* of the Alto Urubamba—the children, grandchildren, nephews, bastards, and stepsons of Fidel Pereira—in the hope of protecting the species of fish that fed those same Indians who, a quarter of a century later, would be photographed by the now deceased Gabriele Malfatti.

With hindsight, knowing what happened to him later—I have thought about this a lot—I can say that Saúl experienced a conversion. In a cultural sense and perhaps in a religious one also. It is the only concrete case I have had occasion to observe from close at hand that has seemed to give meaning to, to make real, what the priests at the school where I studied tried to convey to us during catechism through phrases such as "receiving grace," "being touched by grace," "falling into the snares of grace." From his first contact with the Amazon jungle, Mascarita was caught in a spiritual trap that made a different person of him. Not just because he lost all interest in law and began working for a degree in ethnology, or because of the new direction his reading took, leaving precisely one surviving literary character, Gregor Samsa, but because from that moment on he began to be preoccupied, obsessed, by two concerns which in the years to come would be his only subjects of conversation: the plight of Amazonian cultures and the death throes of the forests that sheltered them.

"You have a one-track mind these days, Mascarita. A person can't talk with you about anything else lately."

"*Pucha*! That's true, old buddy. I haven't let you get a word in edgewise. How about a little lecture, if you're so inclined, on Tolstoy, class war, novels of chivalry?"

"Aren't you exaggerating a little, Saúl?"

"No, pal. As a matter of fact, I'm understating. I swear. What's being done in the Amazon is a crime. There's no justification for it, whatever way you look at it. Believe me, man, it's no laughing matter. Put yourself in their place, if only for a second. Where do they have left to go? They've been driven out of their lands for centuries, pushed farther into the interior each time, farther and farther. The extraordinary thing is that, despite so many disasters, they haven't disappeared. They're still there, surviving. Makes you want to take your hat off to them. Damn it all, there I go again! Come on, let's talk about Sartre. What gets my back up is that nobody gives a hoot in hell about what's happening to them."

Why did it matter to him so much? It certainly wasn't for political reasons, at any rate. Politics to Mascarita was the most uninteresting thing in the world. When we talked about politics I was aware that he was making an effort to please me, since at that time I had revolutionary enthusiasms and had taken to reading Marx and talking about the social relations of production. Such subjects bored Saúl as much as the rabbi's sermons did. Nor would it be accurate to say that these subjects interested him on the broad ethical grounds that the plight of the Indians in the jungle mirrored the social iniquities of our country, inasmuch as Saúl did not react in the same way to other injustices closer to home, which he may not even have noticed. The situation of the Andean Indians, for instance—and there were several million of them, instead of the few thousand in the Amazon jungle—or the way middle- and upper-class Peruvians paid and treated their servants.

No, it was only that specific expression of human lack of conscience, irresponsibility, and cruelty, to which the men, the trees, the animals, and the rivers of the jungle had fallen prey, that—for reasons I found hard to understand at the time, as perhaps he did, too—transformed Saúl Zuratas, erasing all other concerns from his mind and turning him into a man with a fixation. With the result that, if he had not been such a good person, so generous and helpful. I would very likely have stopped seeing him. For there was no doubt that he'd become a bore on the subject.

Occasionally, to see how far his obsession might lead him, I would provoke him. What did he suggest, when all was said and done? That, in order not to change the way of life and the beliefs of a handful of tribes still living, many of them, in the Stone Age, the rest of Peru abstain from developing the Amazon region? Should sixteen million Peruvians renounce the natural resources of three-quarters of their national territory so that seventy or eighty thousand Indians could quietly go on shooting at each other with bows and arrows, shrinking heads and worshipping boa constrictors? Should we forgo the agricultural, cattle-raising, and commercial potential of the region so that the world's ethnologists could enjoy studying at first hand kinship ties, potlatches, the rites of puberty, marriage, and death that these human oddities had been practicing, virtually unchanged, for hundreds of years? No, Mascarita, the country had to move forward. Hadn't Marx said that progress would come dripping blood? Sad though it was, it had to be accepted. We had no alternative. If the price to be paid for development and industrialization for the sixteen million Peruvians meant that those few thousand naked Indians would have to cut their hair, wash off their tattoos, and become *mestizos*—or, to use the ethnologists' most detested word, become acculturated—well, there was no way round it.

Mascarita didn't get angry with me, because he never got angry with anyone about anything, nor did he put on a superior I-forgive-you-for-you-know-not-what-you-say air. But I could feel that when I provoked him in this way I was hurting him as much as if I'd run down Don Salomón Zuratas. He hid it perfectly, I admit. Perhaps he had already achieved the Machiguenga ideal of never feeling anger so that the parallel lines that uphold the earth would not give way. Moreover, he would never discuss this subject, or any other, in a general way, in ideological terms. He had a built-in resistance to any sort of abstract pronouncement. Problems always presented themselves to him in concrete form: what he'd seen with his own eyes, and the consequences that anyone with an ounce of brains in his head could infer from it.

"Fishing with explosives, for example. People assume it's forbidden. But go have a look, pal. There isn't a river or a stream where the mountain people and the Viracochas—that's what they call us white people—don't save time by fishing wholesale with dynamite. Save time! Can you imagine what that means? Charges of dynamite blowing up schools of fish day and night. Whole species are disappearing, old man."

We were talking at a table in the Bar Palermo in La Colmena, drinking beer. Outside, the sun was shining, people hurried past, jalopies honked aggressively, and inside we were surrounded by the smoky atmosphere, smelling of frying oil and urine, typical of all the little cafes in downtown Lima.

"How about fishing with poison, Mascarita? Wasn't that invented by the tribal Indians? That makes them despoilers of the Amazon Basin, too."

I said that so he'd fire his heavy artillery at me. And he did, of course. It was untrue, totally untrue. They did fish with barbasco and cumo, but only in the side channels and backwaters of the rivers, or in water holes that remained on islands after the floodwaters had receded. And only at certain times of year. Never in the spawning season, the signs of which they knew by heart. At those times they fished with nets, harpoons, or traps, or with their bare hands. You'd be goggle-eyed if you saw them, pal. On the other hand, the Creoles used barbasco and cumo all year round, and everywhere. Water poisoned thousands of times, decade after decade. Did I realize? Not only did they kill off all the fry at spawning time, but they were rotting the roots of trees and plants along the riverbanks as well.

Did he idealize them? I'm sure he did. And also, perhaps without meaning to, he exaggerated the extent of the disasters so as to reinforce his arguments. But it was evident that for Mascarita all those shad and catfish poisoned by barbasco and cumo, all the paiche destroyed by the fishers of Loreto, Madre de Dios, San Martín, or Amazonas, hurt him neither more nor less than if the victim had been his talking parrot. And, of course, it was the same when he spoke of the extensive tree felling done by order of the timber men—"My uncle Hipólito is one of them, I'm sorry to say"—who were cutting down the most valuable trees. He spoke to me at length of the practices of the Viracochas and the mountain people who had come down from the Andes to conquer the jungle and clear the woods with fires that burn over enormous areas of land, which after one or two crops become barren because of the lack of humus and the erosion caused by rain. Not to mention, pal, the extermination of animals, the frantic greed for hides and skins which, for example, had made of jaguars, lizards, pumas, snakes, and dozens of other species biological rarities on the point of vanishing. It was a long speech that I remember very well on account of something that cropped up at the end of the conversation, after we had polished off several bottles of beer and some cracklings (which he was extremely fond of). From the trees and the fish his peroration always circled back to the main reason for his anxiety: the tribes. At this rate they, too, would die out.

"Seriously, Mascarita, do you think polygamy, animism, head shrinking, and witch doctoring with tobacco brews represent a superior form of culture?"

An Andean boy was throwing bucketfuls of sawdust on the spittle and other filth lying on the red tile floor of the Bar Palermo as a half-breed followed behind him, sweeping up. Saúl looked at me for a long while without answering.

At last he shook his head. "Superior, no. I've never said or thought so, little brother." He was very serious now. "Inferior, perhaps, if the question is posed in terms of infant mortality, the status of women, polygamy or monogamy, handicrafts or industry. Don't think I idealize them. Not in the least."

He fell silent, as though distracted by something, perhaps the quarrel at a neighboring table that had flared up and died down rhythmically since we first sat down. But it wasn't that. Memory had distracted him. Suddenly he seemed sad. "Among the men who walk and those of other tribes there are many things that would shock you very much, old man. I don't deny that."

The fact, for instance, that the Aguarunas and the Huambisas of the Alto Maranón tear out their daughters' hymen at her menarche and eat it, that slavery exists in many tribes, and in some communities they let the old people die at the first signs of weakness, on the pretext that their souls have been called away and their destiny fulfilled. But the worst thing of all, the hardest to accept, perhaps, from our point of view, is what, with a little black humor, could be called the perfectionism of the tribes of the Arawak family. Perfectionism, Saúl? Yes, something that from the outset would appear as cruel to me as it had to him, old buddy. That babies born with physical defects, lame, maimed, blind, with more or fewer fingers than usual, or a harelip, were killed by their own mothers, who threw them in the river or buried them alive. Anybody would naturally be shocked by such customs.

He looked at me for a good while, silent and thoughtful, as if searching for the right words for what he wanted to say to me.

Suddenly he touched his enormous birthmark. "I wouldn't have passed the test, pal. They'd have liquidated me," he whispered. "They say the Spartans did the same thing, right? That little monsters, Gregor Samsas, were hurled down from the top of Mount Taygetus, right?"

He laughed, I laughed, but we both knew that he wasn't joking and that there was no cause for laughter. He explained to me that, curiously enough, though they were pitiless when it came to babies born defective, they were very tolerant with all those, children or adults, who were victims of some accident or illness that damaged them physically. Saúl, at least, had noticed no hostility toward the disabled or the demented in the tribes. His hand was still on the deep purple scab of his half face.

"But that's the way they are and we should respect them. Being that way has helped them to live in harmony with their forests for hundreds of years. Though we don't understand their beliefs and some of their customs offend us, we have no right to kill them off."

I believe that that morning in the Bar Palermo was the only time he ever alluded, not jokingly but seriously, even dramatically, to what was undoubtedly a tragedy in his life, even though he concealed it with such style and grace: the excrescence that made him a walking incitement to mockery and disgust, and must have affected all his relationships, especially with women. (He was extremely shy with them; I had noticed at San Marcos that he avoided them and only entered into conversation with one of our women classmates if she spoke to him first.) At last he removed his hand from his face with a gesture of annoyance, as though regretting that he had touched the birthmark, and launched into another lecture.

"Do our cars, guns, planes, and Coca-Colas give us the right to exterminate them because they don't have such things? Or do you believe in 'civilizing the savages,' pal? How? By making soldiers of them? By putting them to work on the farms as slaves to Creoles like Fidel Pereira? By forcing them to change their language, their religion, and their customs, the way the missionaries are trying to do? What's to be gained by that? Being able to exploit them more easily, that's all. Making them zombies and caricatures of men, like those semi-acculturated Indians you see in Lima."

The Andean boy throwing bucketfuls of sawdust on the floor in the Palermo had on the sort of sandals—a sole and two cross-strips cut from an old rubber tire—made and sold by peddlers, and a pair of patched pants held up with a length of rope round his waist. He was a child with the face of an old man, coarse hair, blackened nails, and a reddish scab on his nose. A zombie? A caricature? Would it have been better for him to have stayed in his Andean village, wearing a wool cap with earflaps, leather sandals, and a poncho, never learning Spanish? I didn't know, and I still don't. But Mascarita knew. He spoke without vehemence, without anger, with quiet determination. He explained to me at great length what counterbalanced their cruelty (the price they pay for survival, as he put it): a view of Nature that struck him as an admirable trait in those cultures. It was something that the tribes, despite the many differences between them, all had in common: their understanding of the world in which they were immersed, the wisdom born of long practice which had allowed them, through an elaborate system of rites, taboos, fears, and routines, perpetuated and passed on from father to son, to preserve that Nature, seemingly so superabundant, but actually so vulnerable, upon which they depended for subsistence. These tribes had survived because their habits and customs had docilely followed the rhythms and requirements of the natural world, without doing it violence or disturbing it deeply, just the minimum necessary so as not to be destroyed by it. The very opposite of what we civilized people were doing, wasting those elements without which we would end up withering like flowers without water.

I listened to him and pretended to be taking an interest in what he was saying. But I was really thinking about his birthmark. Why had he suddenly alluded to it while explaining to me his feelings about the Amazonian Indians? Was this the key to Mascarita's conversion? In the Peruvian social order those Shipibos, Huambisas, Aguarunas, Yaguas, Shapras, Campas, Mashcos represented something that he could understand better than anyone else: a picturesque horror, an aberration that other people ridiculed or pitied without granting it the respect and dignity deserved only by those whose physical appearance, customs, and beliefs were "normal." Both he and they were anomalies in the eyes of other Peruvians. His birthmark aroused in them, in us, the same feelings, deep down, as those creatures living somewhere far away, half-naked, eating each other's lice and speaking incomprehensible dialects. Was this the origin of Mascarita's love at first sight for the tribal Indians, the "chunchos"? Had he unconsciously identified with those marginal beings because of the birthmark that made him, too, a marginal being, every time he went out on the streets?

I suggested this interpretation to him to see if it put him in a better mood, and in fact he burst out laughing.

"I take it you passed Dr. Guerrita's psych course?" he joked. "I'd have been more likely to flunk you, myself."

And still laughing, he told me that Don Salomón Zuratas, being sharper than I was, had suggested a Jewish interpretation.

"That I'm identifying the Amazonian Indians with the Jewish people, always a minority and always persecuted for their religion and their mores that are different from those of the rest of society. How does that strike you? A far nobler interpretation than yours, which might be called the Frankenstein syndrome. To each madman his own mania, pal."

I retorted that the two interpretations didn't exclude each other. He wound up, highly amused, giving free play to his imagination.

"Okay, supposing you're right. Supposing being half-Jewish and half-monster has made me more sensitive to the fate of the jungle tribes than someone as appallingly normal as you."

"Poor jungle tribes! You're using them for a crying towel. You're taking advantage of them, too, you know."

"Well, let's leave it at that. I've got a class." He said goodbye as he got up from the table without a trace of the dark mood of a moment before. "But remind me next time to set you straight on those 'poor jungle tribes.' I'll tell you a few things that'll make your hair stand on end. What was done to them, for instance, in the days of the rubber boom. If they could live through that, they don't deserve to be called 'poor savages.' Supermen, rather. Just wait—you'll see."

Apparently he had spoken of his "Mania" to Don Salomón. The old man must have come around to accepting the fact that, rather than in halls of justice, Saúl would bring prestige to the name Zuratas in university lecture halls and in the field of anthropological research. Was that what he had decided to be in life? A professor, a researcher? That he had the aptitude I heard confirmed by one of his professors, Dr. Jose Matos Mar, who was then head of the Department of Ethnology at San Marcos.

"Young Zuratas has turned out to be a first-rate student. He spent the three months of the year-end vacation in the Urubamba region, doing fieldwork with the Machiguengas, and the lad has brought back some excellent material."

He was talking to Raúl Porras Barrenechea, a historian with whom I worked in the afternoons, who had a holy horror of ethnology and anthropology, which he accused of replacing man by artifacts as the focal point of culture, and of butchering Spanish prose (which, let it be said in passing, he himself wrote beautifully).

"Well then, let's make a historian of the young man and not a classifier of bits of stone, Dr. Matos. Don't be selfish. Hand him on to me in the History Department."

The work Saúl did in the summer of '56 among the Machiguengas later became, in expanded form, his thesis for his Bachelor's degree. He defended it in our fifth year at San Marcos, and I can remember clearly the expression of pride and deep personal happiness on Don Salomón's face. Dressed for the occasion in a starched shirt under his jacket, he watched the ceremony from the front row of the auditorium, and his little eyes shone as Saúl read out his conclusions, answered the questions of the jury, headed by Matos Mar, had his thesis accepted, and was draped in the academic sash he had thus earned.

Don Salomón invited Saúl and me to lunch, at the Raimondi in downtown Lima, to celebrate the event. But he himself didn't touch a single mouthful, perhaps so as not to transgress the Jewish dietary laws inadvertently. (One of Saúl's jokes when ordering cracklings or shellfish was: "And besides, the idea of committing a sin as I swallow them down gives them a very special taste, pal. A taste you'll never know.") Don Salomón was bursting with pleasure at his son's brand-new degree.

Halfway through lunch he turned to me and begged me, in earnest tones, in his guttural Central European accent: "Convince your friend he should accept the scholarship." And noting the look of surprise on my face, he explained: "He doesn't want to go to Europe, so as not to leave me alone—as though I weren't old enough to know how to look after myself! I've told him that if he insists on being so foolish, he's going to force me to die so that he can go off to France to specialize with his mind at rest."

That was how I found out that Matos Mar had gotten Saúl a fellowship to study for a doctorate at the University of Bordeaux. Not wanting to leave his father all by himself, Mascarita had refused it. Was that really the reason why he didn't go off to Bordeaux? I believed it at the time; today I'm sure he was lying. I know now, though he confessed it to no one and kept his secret under lock and key, that his conversion had continued to work its way within him until it had taken on the lineaments of a mystical ecstasy, perhaps even of a seeking after martyrdom. I have no doubt, today, that he took the trouble to write a thesis and obtain a Bachelor's degree in ethnology just to please his father, knowing the while that he would never be an ethnologist. Though at the time I was wearing myself out trying to land some sort of fellowship that would get me to Europe, I attempted several times to persuade him not to waste such an opportunity. "It's something that won't come your way again, Mascarita. Europe! France! Don't throw a chance like that away, man!" His mind was made up, once and for all: he couldn't go, he was the only one Don Salomón had in the world, and he wasn't going to abandon him for two or three years, knowing what an elderly man his father was.

Naturally I believed him. The one who didn't believe him at all was the one who had secured him his fellowship and had such high academic hopes for him: his professor, Matos Mar. The latter appeared one afternoon, as was his habit, at Professor Porras Barrenechea's to exchange ideas and have tea and biscuits, and told him the news:

"You win, Dr. Porras. The History Department can fill the Bordeaux fellowship this year. Our candidate has turned it down. What do you make of all this?"

"As far as I know, it's the first time in the history of San Marcos that a student has refused a fellowship to France," Porras said. "What in the world got into the boy?"

I was there in the room where they were talking, taking notes on the myths of El Dorado and the Seven Cities of Cibola as set down by the chroniclers of the Discovery and the Conquest, and I put my oar in to say that the reason for Saúl's refusal was Don Salomón and his not wanting to leave him all by himself.

"Yes, that's the reason Zuratas gives, and I wish it were true," Matos Mar said, with a skeptical wave of his hand. "But I'm afraid there's something far deeper than that. Saúl's starting to have doubts about research and fieldwork. Ethical doubts."

Porras Barrenechea thrust his chin out, and his little eyes had the sly expression they always had when he was about to make a nasty remark.

"Well, if Zuratas has realized that ethnology is a pseudoscience invented by *gringos* to destroy the Humanities, he's more intelligent than one might have expected."

But this did not raise a smile from Matos Mar.

"I'm serious, Dr. Porras. It's a pity, because the boy has outstanding qualities. He's intelligent, perceptive, a fine researcher, a hard worker. And yet he's taken it into his head, can you believe it, that the work we're doing is immoral."

"Immoral? Well, when it comes right down to it, who can tell what you're up to there among the good old *chunchos*, under cover of prying into their customs?" Porras laughed. "I myself wouldn't swear to the virtue of ethnologists."

"He's convinced that we're attacking them, doing violence to their culture," Matos Mar went on, paying no attention to him. "That with our tape recorders and ballpoint pens, we're the worm that works its way into the fruit and rots it."

He then recounted how, a few days before, there had been a meeting in the Department of Ethnology at which Saúl Zuratas had flabbergasted everyone, proclaiming that the consequences of the ethnologists' work were similar to those of the activities of the rubber tappers, the timber cutters, the army recruiters, and other *mestizos* and whites who were decimating the tribes.

"He maintained that we've taken up where the colonial missionaries left off. That we, in the name of science, like them in the name of evangelization, are the spearhead of the effort to wipe out the Indians."

"Is he reviving the fanatical *Indigenista* movement to save Indian cultures that swept over the campus of San Marcos in the thirties?" Porras sighed. "I wouldn't be surprised. It comes in waves, like flu epidemics. I can already see Zuratas penning pamphlets against Pizarro, the Spanish Conquest, and the crimes of the Inquisition. No, I don't want him in the History Department! Let him accept the fellowship, take out French citizenship, and make his name furthering the Black Legend!"

I didn't pay much attention to what I heard Matos Mar say that afternoon amid the dusty shelves covered with books and busts of Don Quixote and Sancho Panza in Porras Barrenechea's Miraflor house in the Callé Colina. And I don't think I mentioned it to Saúl. But today, here in Firenze, as I remember and jot down notes, this episode takes on considerable meaning in retrospect. That fellow feeling, that solidarity, that spell, or whatever it may have been, had by then reached a climax and assumed a different nature. In the eyes of the ethnologists—about whom the least that could be said was that, however shortsighted they might be, they were perfectly aware of the need to understand the jungle Indians' way of seeing in their own terms—what was it that Mascarita was defending? Was it something as chimerical as the recognition of their inalienable right to their lands, whereupon the rest of Peru would agree to place the jungle under quarantine? Must no one, ever, have the right to enter it, so as to keep those cultures from being contaminated by the miasmas of our own degenerated one? Had Saúl's purism concerning the Amazon reached such extremes?

The fact was that we saw very little of each other during our last months at San Marcos. I was all wrapped up in writing my thesis, and he had virtually given up his law studies. I met him very infrequently, on the rare occasions when he put in an appearance at the Department of Literature, in those days next door to the Department of Ethnology. We would have a cup of coffee, or smoke a cigarette together while talking under the yellowing palms outside the main building on campus. As we grew to adulthood and became involved in different activities and projects, our friendship, quite close in the first years, evolved into a sporadic and superficial relationship. I asked him questions about his travels, for he was always just back from or just about to set out for the jungle, and I associated this—until Matos Mar's remarks to Dr. Porras—with his work at the university or his increasing specialization in Amazonian cultures. But, except for our last conversation—that of our taking leave of each other, and his diatribe against the Institute of Linguistics and the Schneils—I think it is true to say that in those last months we never again had those endless dialogues, with both of us speaking our minds freely and frankly, that had been so frequent between 1953 and 1956.

If we had kept them up, would he have opened his heart to me and allowed me to glimpse what his intentions were? Most likely not. The sort of decision arrived at by saints and madmen is not revealed to others. It is forged little by little, in the folds of the spirit, tangential to reason, shielded from indiscreet eyes, not seeking the approval of others—who would never grant it—until it is at last put into practice. I imagine that in the process—the conceiving of a project and its ripening into action—the saint, the visionary, or the madman isolates himself more and more, walling himself up in solitude, safe from the intrusion of others.

I for my part never even suspected that Mascarita, during the last months of our life at San Marcos—we were both adults by then—could be going through such an inner upheaval. That he was more withdrawn than other mortals or, more probably, became more reserved on leaving adolescence behind, I had indeed noticed. But I put it down entirely to his face, interposing its terrible ugliness between himself and the world, making his relationship with others difficult. Was he still the laughing, likable, easygoing person of previous years? He had become more serious and laconic, less open than before, it seems to me. But there I don't quite trust my memory. Perhaps he went on being the same smiling, talkative Mascarita whom I knew in 1953, and my imagination has changed him so as to make him conform more closely to the other one, the one of future years whom I did not know, whom I must invent, since I have given in to the cursed temptation of writing about him.

I am certain, however, that memory does not fail me as far as his dress and his physical appearance are concerned. That bright red hair, with its wild, uncombed tuft on the crown of his head, flaming and unruly, dancing above his bipartite face, the untouched side of it pale and freckled. Bright, shining eyes, and shining teeth. He was tall and thin, and I am quite sure that, except on his graduation day, I never spotted him wearing a tie. He always wore cheap, coarse, cotton, sport shirts, over which he threw some bright-colored sweater in winter, and faded, wrinkled jeans. His heavy shoes never saw a brush. I don't think he confided in anyone or had any really intimate friends. His other friendships were most likely similar to the one between the two of us, very cordial but fairly super-ficial. Acquaintances, yes, many, at San Marcos, and also, doubtless, in the neighborhood where he lived. But I could swear that no one ever heard, from his own lips, what was happening to him and what he intended to do. If in fact he had planned it carefully, and it hadn't just happened, gradually, imperceptibly, the product of chance circumstances rather than the result of personal choice. I have thought about it a lot these last years, and of course I'll never know.

Angelina Muníz-Huberman

(Mexico, 1936–)

Fragment of *The Merchant of Tudela*

Translated from the Spanish by Claudia Lucotti

Angelina Muníz-Huberman is the author of, among other books of fiction and nonfiction, *Enclosed Garden* (1988), *Dulcinea Encantada* (*Enchanted Dulcinea*, 1992), and *Las Confidentes* (*The Confidants*, 1997). She has been instrumental in uncovering the crypto-Jewish heritage in Mexican culture in particular, and Hispanic civilization in general, as is displayed in her anthology *La lengua florida: Antología sefardí* (*The Florid Tongue*, 1989). *El mercader de Tudela* (*The Merchant of Tudela*, 1998) is a postmodern novel about the twelfth century Jewish traveler Benjamin of Tudela (see entry on Benjamin of Tudela). This chapter comes early in the book, setting Tudela's quest in perspective.

How to explain to himself and to the others that he, Benjamin bar Jonah, was to abandon his studies of the Torah and the Halachah and embark on an adventure like the one that was about to begin?

How to tell his beloved teachers and father that he was to give up being a rabbi to become a merchant?

Who would believe that the Angel of Truth had appeared in a dream to illuminate his path and tell him that he must change his life and become a merchant of precious stones and cloth and make a long journey to the ends of the earth where he would find what he was meant to find?

Benjamin bar Jonah could not answer these questions to himself, and he did not worry about not being able to do so. During his studies he had learnt that the most important things always remained unanswered. That the most difficult things could never be deciphered. And that knowledge was unending. The world was fluid matter for interpretation. This is why he was better at asking questions than at answering them.

Benjamin bar Jonah had made his decision. The Angel's call could not be put off. He would start on his journey accompanied by rich merchandise. He himself would carefully cut some jewels of circular design just as he had learnt from the old jewelers. He would get the Moorish looms to weave cloth of silver and of gold for him, and brocades of complicated design in all the tones of the rainbow, and wool carpets with just one knot and angular patterns in the shape of a hook, all in a row. He would look for those who polished gems to burnish edges and facets so that they reflected the light as never before. He would ask the illuminators of manuscripts to prepare books with the loveliest illustrations they could think of. He would order new essences, oils, kohl powder, and prodigious ointments from the perfume sellers. And goblets, jugs, jars, dishes, and bowls from the glassworkers. In special pots decorated with a symbol representing eternity and boxes shaped like prisms he would place the finest spices and herbs picked in the mountains for medical purposes. In wooden chests covered with ivory plaques full of floral motifs he would stow away the precious stones. He would go with the best blacksmiths and leather workers in the whole kingdom to order daggers and poniards of steel, gold plate, enamel, and ivory; wooden sheaths covered with embossed leather; baldrics made of silk and silver. He would order solid coffers made of finely carved walnut to put his precious merchandise in. He would get hold of mules young and strong to carry the loads and a pair of Arab steeds for him to ride. He would find a good muleteer who knew the way and who owned a wagon in good condition to transport his possessions.

He would probably spend a year performing these tasks. He would study the routes and prepare a detailed map. He would travel from one community to another and in each he would obtain information on how to reach the following.

Benjamin bar Jonah's first task was to recall the dream in which the Angel of Truth, *Malach ha-emet*, had appeared to him. Recall it and write it down, for this was not Benjamin bar Jonah's first prophetic dream, and dreams are made of ethereal, volatile stuff.

Dreams come and go: they are free and escape our memory. We frequently forget about them, except for the small reminders related to some minor unimportant action. Benjamin knew this. Benjamin who, time and time again, used to go over Joseph's story and his dreams when imprisoned in Egypt.

A certain minor unimportant action or a movement performed every day was all Benjamin needed to test his memory, and he made an effort to remember, detail by detail, the images of his dream. If he only remembered a sensation: "I know my dream was a sorrowful one for when I move my hand I am filled with sadness. And as moving one's hand is not a sign of sorrow, this must be because in my dream the hand was related to some sad deed: perhaps with a rejection which pained some other person who appeared in the dream and whom I also cannot remember. Thus, being awake only revives the feeling of sorrow when I move my hand. And my sorrow increases to double its size because I cannot learn its true origin." If he only remembered that sensation, his day was a sad and solitary one. But if the sensation was of another kind such as joy or euphoria, even though he could not recall the exact events, his day was filled with peace and activity, and he felt content with himself and filled with joyful expectations.

The dream of the Angel of Truth, *Malach ha-emet*, was not a forgotten dream but one which is remembered afterwards with the greatest clarity and the most revealing precision. This is what Benjamin bar Jonah noted down in his *Book of Dreams*:

I stood in the midst of a meadow of newly sprouted vegetation. The sunlight was very very clear. In the distance, some pale grey mountains faded away, and this was a landscape I had never seen before. One or two trees with silver leaves barely gave any shade. I knew something was going to happen and I was waiting for it to occur. The light began to increase, and the landscape and the mountains disappeared. A floating circle of even more intense golden light formed itself in the centre of the sunlight. There appeared a figure impossible to describe, of great beauty and radiating light. I could not say whether it was a human or an angelic figure, or even if it was abstract or geometrical. It was like a combination of all four. Or perhaps it was formed by delicate waves which went from the human to the angelic, to the abstract, to the geometric. Though the figure moved gently, I also seem to remember that it appeared static, as if painted on a piece of wood covered with a sheet of silver and gold. If the figure could have a face, that face would smile at me, and if it had a mouth, from it the following words would issue forth:

Thou shalt take thy belongings and journey forth to places of thy choice, as long as thou losest not the thread, the helping hand, the sacred roof.

Thou shalt carry The Book *close to thy heart.*

Thou shalt open it on the exact page.

The page that never flies away.

So that thou lettest it fly.

The blank page.

So that thou writest it as it should have been written.

Remember that thou hast been chosen so that, once again, the holiness of the written letter shall not be forgotten.

That written letter that thou must maintain in black fire upon white fire.

Remember that thou hast been chosen so that, once again, your people, strangers among other peoples, shall not be extinguished and forgotten.

Remember that thou shalt lose thy way, and the return journey will be painful.

Remember that thou hast been chosen, once again, so that one life will save many lives.

Then, silence ensued. A melodious silence which was full of the music of the spheres. Inaudible. The light became more intense and the prodigious image impossible to define of the Angel of Truth, *Malach ha-emet*, enveloped the rest of the landscape as if the sand and the trees with silver leaves had never existed. Everything slowly faded. If I had not awoken immediately (in my dream) and had not at that moment written down the dream and the complete message (in my dream itself), I would have forgotten it soon after. But at that very moment I knew. The dream had to be remembered and the dream was forcing me to change my life. That was why I had written down my dream in my dream.

In this way, Benjamin of Tudela was able to remember the dream he had written down in his dream and then note it down in his *Book of Dreams*. Having performed this task, all that was left to do, while he gathered his merchandise, was to talk with his father and teachers and tell them about the change in his life.

"Yes, I understand. I also dreamed with embarking on a journey and with the words of the Angel who was calling me. But I did not dare. I did not know if they were true. You were about to be born and I would not have forgiven myself if I had abandoned your mother. I preferred the warmth of my home, hearth, good soup, thick clothes, and pages and pages to study. I forgot the dream when you, a newborn babe, let out your first cry. And I never thought of it again, until now when you tell me about this same dream."

Benjamin bar Jonah still has his doubts. If life is tranquil in Tudela, his small city of Navarre, if the walks through the gardens and vineyards of Mosquera are delightful, what makes him want to travel to the unknown, to other lands and other seas, other tongues and other faces: dangers, wars, treason, disease?

A desire for adventure and a feeling of curiosity about the Angel of Truth's command once again confirm his first impulse. Yes, he will travel. Yes, he will dedicate the rest of his life to going on pilgrimage. Already within him there boils that feeling of unrest which belongs to those who cannot live too long in one same place. To those who need a new bed and new sheets. Chairs of new leather and wide backs. Other landscapes outside the window. And something,

something he desires very much. Something that he does not know very well what it is but that he desires intensely, with a beating heart, with an unexplained nostalgia. Something he has searched for but still has not found.

Going on a journey is also a form of knowledge. He will hear the teachings of the enlightened rabbis, and discussing different matters with them will be most profitable. The teachings of Maimonides are transmitted from one person to another. He who owns a copy of one of his manuscripts knows himself to possess a treasure, and magnanimously lets those who do not have one read it. There are also those who secretively create their own interpretations of the Holy Texts and call these new versions the Tradition, the Reception of the Letters, or the Kabbalah. One of the initiated is called Abraham ben Isaac and from him will he hear wise words and prophecies never expressed before.

The one he does not know how to say goodbye to is the embroiderer, hidden behind a veil, who prepares lace and cloth of gold for him. Alucena, the daughter of the Moorish weavers from whom he has ordered part of his merchandise, possesses the color of emeralds tinged with sunlight in the only visible part of her face: her eyes.

Those eyes now accompany Benjamin bar Jonah and they appear to him in light and shade, in the frame of a door, in the beams of the roof, in the pages he will read on Friday evening, in the carefully folded philacteries. Eyes detached, eyes that only possess movement and changing shades of color. Eyes that speak, that hear. Eyes that are the letter *ayin*: *ayin*-eye: eye-letter.

"Where do these eyes come from?" he asks Alucena, and she smiles with her eyes. "Embroider these eyes for me on the rich cloth I will take with me, as I cannot take you." "And why can't you take me?" says Alucena.

Benjamin tried to stiffle a gesture of surprise and has remained quiet. For days he has thought about Alucena's words. What was it she meant? That it was he who could not take her or that it was she who could not go with him? Or that it was the others who would not let them go off together? But the first thing to think about was whether they would go off together. He had simply said that for the sake of saying it, but her question was in earnest. Could a real situation emerge from a simple question? From something unexpected? Why had a negation been returned to him as a question? He had taken it for granted that he could not take her with him. She had made him doubt.

To be able to see Alucena's eyes every day: that was what taking her with him would mean. But, how would he perform this? Impossible. Neither in dreams,

243

nor when he awoke at dawn, nor after drinking the sanctified wine, nor when under the effects of a fever could he imagine a way to take her with him.

Benjamin bar Jonah continued getting everything ready and he pushed away the image of Alucena: Alucena's eyes. He would go to her house to pick up the richly embroidered pieces of cloth only when they were ready. Meanwhile, he concentrated on reading the Only Book: the Book which enclosed total wisdom but that he still did not know how to free.

Benjamin bar Jonah had been brought two beautiful Arab steeds: a white one and a black one, just as he had asked for. Every day he approached them, stroked them, fed them apples out of his hand. Then he rode them in turns, crossing the gates of the city and galloping cross-country. He named the white one Aleph and the black one Beth.

Little by little he collected his merchandise. Little by little his father and his teachers began to accept the idea of his departure. The Angel had not appeared again to him in dreams, and Benjamin interpreted this as a good sign, a form of showing his approval for the way Benjamin was obeying his commands.

The moment of departure arrived. He gathered all his fellow travelers and spoke to them for a long time so as to agree upon the first part of their journey. The muleteer asked him for permission to take along a young apprentice who only asked to be given his meals.

On the last Sabbath, in the synagogue, Benjamin received the blessing of the elders. He was asked to read verse 18:18 from the Book of Exodus. "Thou wilt surely wear away, both thou and this people that is with thee: for this thing is too heavy for thee; thou art not able to perform it thyself alone."

And he was entrusted to God.

On leaving the synagogue, Benjamin bar Jonah lifted his eyes to heaven: a great *Aleph* appeared among the brilliant stars: he knew that the Angel of Truth had signed the covenant.

Rosa Nissán
(Mexico, 1939–)
Fragment of *Like a Bride*
Translated from the Spanish by Dick Gerdes

Rosa Nissán is the author of two related novels, *Like a Bride* (1992) and *Like a Mother* (1996), which chronicle the life of Oshinica, a Sephardic Jew in Mexico in the late twentieth century. (The novels appeared in English in a single volume in 2002.) Nissán is the first modern Sephardic author to use large amounts of Ladino—Judeo-Spanish—in her fiction. Nissán has also written stories and a travel book about Israel. In 1993 the Costa Rican director Guita Schyfter made a successful film adaptation of *Like a Bride*. The following chapter of the novel is entitled "Moshón's Bar Mitzvah."

That was the first time I'd ever seen my grandfather carry the Holy Book and the rolls that contain the Torah, which is covered in velvet with gold lace around the edges. Some have a carved wooden cover with inlaid colored stones. There is no object more sacred. My mother and grandmother, who were sitting in the front row, were crying. When a boy reaches thirteen years old, he becomes a man and joins the community, with rights and obligations. Even though he was nervous, his presentation came off well. After having heard him recite it so many times, I also knew it by heart. Well, I think he skipped a line, but no one noticed:

"Dear rabbis, dear parents, dear grandparents, it is an honor for me . . ." and he went straight through it without taking a breath except at the end.

"I want to thank my parents who have made sacrifices for my education, and I promise to take care of them and my brothers and sisters for the rest of my life." (I liked that part the best because it's good to have a brother who'll take of me when I become a spinster.)

Even though my grandfather would deny it, I saw him crying; so was my dad. Assisted by the rabbis, Moshón read from the Torah, and then he walked up and down the central aisle carrying the sacred book. It made him happy that everyone went up to him to touch and kiss the book while he held it. Perhaps he'll never have the opportunity to do it again, but we knew how he felt. I was so proud of my brother because he was the most important person that day, and the ceremony was in his honor. And he's so handsome, too! He's the best looking of all of us; at least my friends think so.

My father almost laughs to hear him read Hebrew. He even acts like a child in first grade, because he's forgotten it. After it was my brother's turn to read from the Torah, I could tell he did it better than any of them, and no one laughed at him like they did at home. When they called upon him to carry the sacred book, I got emotional, because my family never manages to do anything for the synagogue. My dad isn't rich, so he doesn't donate much or even volunteer in the community. He pays his dues and he's a good Jew.

It was one of the few times that my grandpa's face lit up: every few moments he'd ask Moshón proudly: "Tell me, son, what makes a good man?"

"The three P's: plain, potent, and proper!" my brother responded with grit. He's lucky he doesn't have to be good-looking. That's where I have to shine. The good thing is that I'm pretty attractive, especially if I push up my nose with my finger. But if I had blue eyes, I'd *really* be good-looking. And straight hair doesn't help.

The invitations to Moshón's *bar mitzvah* were beautiful: they even included a full-length black-and-white picture of him wearing his *tallith* with Zion in the background. The words were in Spanish on one side and Hebrew on the other. I don't know why they did it like that, because no one around here can read Hebrew. It was great to see his picture on a hundred invitations; now he's famous.

My mom invited almost everyone who came; she has lots of friends who care about her because she always helps them with their problems. Her two best friends came, along with members of the mother's club at school because she helps out there, too. Games were set up everywhere, even in the bedrooms. The guests brought lots of presents. Everyone on my father's side came: his sister and her husband and my grandparents. No one from Lagunilla Market or Chapultepec came.

I went to get a washbowl and a pitcher of water while my sister got a towel. We took them to the dining room for the men to wash their hands. The eldest of the family, my grandfather, was first. I set the bowl down, and when he stretched out his hands, I poured water over them; then my sister quickly handed him the towel. Each man took his turn, starting with the eldest and going down in age, according to our law. Moshón had always insisted on being included in the ritual, and every year we would chide him, saying no, not you! And we'd leave him standing there with his hands sticking out; but this year my grandfather wouldn't let us ignore him.

"Eugenia, why do you do that to your brother? He is a man now, for he just turned thirteen years old," exclaimed my grandfather.

I was furious. While I poured, letting the water barely trickle over his hands, my proud brother just laughed. We got settled around the table, and the prayers continued. They prayed and prayed. No wonder we seem boring, it just went on and on.

We're hungry!

Oh, God, Moshón really irritates me!

"The wine, Luna! Bring on the wine!"

I think they're about to finish; they usually end with wine. The silver goblet with a star and the Hebrew letters engraved on it sat next to my grandfather. He has used it at celebrations ever since I was born. Swaying back and forth, he ends with an "Amen!"

His squeaky voice and the frown on his face are his way of scolding us for fighting over who gets to sit next to him. But, with respect, we watch him slowly fill up the goblet and then slowly put it to his mouth, scrutinizing our every move. He takes a sip, pauses, and then passes it to my dad, who follows him in age, but since he's sitting at the other end of the table, we pass the goblet along from one to the other. After he takes a sip, he gives it to my uncle and then to my grandmother, but just when she raises the goblet to her lips, my grandfather says, "No, wait, it's Moshón's turn."

Then it goes from my grandmother to my mother, from my mother to my aunt, from my aunt to me, and finally to my sisters, who are at the tail end of the line. Then he cuts up the bread that's next to his plate, sprinkles a little salt on it, and gives a piece to each one of us without stopping his prayers. When he finally takes off his cap and cracks a smile, we can begin talking. And that is the moment when Uba knows she should give my grandfather a bowl of soup and put the plates of rice and avocado on the table. Since I'm sitting next to him, we share a piece of avocado. Then he jokes with me, and everyone has to listen; no one else is allowed to talk.

All the women must get up to help, because the table belongs to the men.

"Moshón, you can't have my place. See, Mommy, that's why I don't like to serve."

"Luna, sit down, tell us the story about when we first came to Mexico," exhorted my grandfather. "Come to the table and talk to your grandchildren. Sit down, Oshinica, listen to your grandmother."

"No? Okay... the first one to come to this continent was my cousin Isaac," said my grandfather. "He wrote to us and said there was electricity, lights, and money by the shovelful. In Jerusalem, people were poor, and then there were the Turks. So, we bought two tickets—second class—on a boat, and we came here."

"And I boiled eggs and potatoes," interrupted my grandmother, "and I packed some cans of sardines and fruit to last us several days. We couldn't eat just anything, you see, it had to be kosher."

"The ship took us to Veracruz," my grandfather continued, "and we had made arrangements to meet with Isaac in Mexico City. So we took the train, but when we arrived, he wasn't at the station. We waited until night came on, and when we saw that he wasn't coming, we managed to communicate with a taxi driver, thanks be to God. We asked him to take us to the Jewish neighborhood. He asked someone who told him it was La Lagunilla, so he took us there. We drove around until we saw a man on the road changing a tire. The taxi driver said, 'Hey, friend, I think they're from your country, they don't know anyone here, what should I do with them?' The man wiped his brow, looked at us, and said he was Jewish. He offered to take us to his home. We stayed with his family for about a month, and then we found a room in the neighborhood where the store is today. Did you know, Moshón, that we lived in Number 3?"

"And do you know who that man is? Why, it's Mr. Behar," said my grandmother, smiling. "He's your grandfather's best friend; he had the store next to ours, and now his grandson looks after it."

"And that's how we got here," my grandfather concluded. "Then we opened a stall at the market, and my son and I started selling dresses."

"It's true, isn't it, Mother, that after we arrived you sent me to school wearing my white tunic?" asked my father. "In Israel they didn't wear pants, and we had brought only clothes that we had worn back there. We didn't know what else to bring. I attended a school that was on República de Chile, and at first I only spoke Hebrew. They made fun of me until one day I hit one kid so hard that no one ever bothered me again. That's why I always say you have to defend yourself or else they'll walk all over you. But I made some really good friends, and even today some still come around and say hello. Efrén—the guy who sells kosher chickens on Medellín Street—well, he studied with me."

"Do you remember, Mom," I said, "the day Dad left me in charge of the stand? I wanted to go home, and when he didn't come back soon, I did it in my pants."

"That's the breaks, child, because there was no way you could have left the business unattended," he said with a laugh.

Alicia Freilich
(Venezuela, 1939–)
"Recollections of a Criolla Zionist"
Translated from the Spanish by Joan E. Friedman

Alicia Freilich is a journalist, activist, and Zionist in Caracas and the daughter of a correspondent for the Yiddish-language newspaper *The Forward*. She also teaches literature at the Universidad Central de Caracas. Freilich is the author of the novels *Legítima Defensa* (*Legitimate Defense*, 1984), *Cláper* (1987), and *Colombina descubierta* (*Columbus's Sister Discovered*, 1991). The essay that follows, written for the anthology *King David's Harp* (1999), is a display of her unabated enthusiasm for Jewish life in Venezuela.

This time it seemed very different. For all the other military coups the radio had played "funeral music," as the Venezuelan public called those endless selections of classical music. The was no doubt that this was different, very special. Máximo and Rebeca, tense and tearful, ears glued to the set, counted with their fingers as a distant voice counted off: yes, no, yes, no, yes.

Suddenly a brief silence. Then enthusiastic applause. Then screams, tears, and laughter. When she embraced me, Rebeca said between sobs, something like: "The majority of the world voted for the partition of Palestine. The English are leaving. Venezuela voted yes! At last we have a piece of land!! But this happiness will cost us a lot of blood."

Spoken in November of 1947, the last sentence sounded more like sour grapes yet was so typical of our ancestral rite, according to which each joy should be tempered by mourning because of what happened two thousand years ago with the Fall of the Second Temple, during the reign of Titus the Roman. There was more to it, of course. Much more. It was what we knew, suffered, and learned through bitter experience: for the Jews as a people, happiness is never free, continuous, or long-lasting.

And yet for that singular moment, the children of the house, Perla, two years old, Miriam, three, and I, Alicia, eight, all enjoyed the unusual festive mood. In our home, for as long as anyone could remember, even at the modest birthdays and frugal Sunday dinners with *paisanos*, always, between bites of *lekach* (sweet cake), sips of tea with lemon, and sweet Yiddish melodies coming from the RCA Victrola, the conversation since forever had always been the same: Germany, Poland, ghettos, crematoriums, in other words: HOLOCAUST.

As of May 1948, with the official declaration of Israel's independence, the lively sounds of the Hora, and the waving of the little blue-and-white flags with their Star of David, "Hatikvah," the national anthem, was sung out loud. Not even the Arab invasion that took place only hours after the establishment of the Jewish National Homeland could erase the smiles from the faces of adults and children in their daily and communal activities, thus mitigating that heavy and sad atmosphere that pervaded the entire previous decade.

That infantile and adolescent Zionism marked forever our generation of *judíos criollos*, that is, the firstborn in Venezuela. We were children of immigrants of the pre- and postwar Europe of 1939. From that moment on, we understood that our small and simple life *here* gravitated around great and complex events taking place in a *there* where Israel, the United States, Russia, and other powers met, unconcerned about us.

It was no accident that my father became a self-taught journalist for the *Forward* in New York and several Israeli dailies; nor that Miriam, and I, and now my youngest son, took up that profession with the goal of fighting for human rights. From the very beginning, at the back of that very small, dark, and narrow store, to the very last day of World War II, the Freilichs devoured and saved every *Universal* as well as any foreign newspapers they could find.

The radio, always on with news accounts sandwiched in between delightful sitcoms and adventure and love stories, the parental voices commenting on Zionism and Jewish culture, and the eloquent oratory of those in charge of collecting funds for the Zionist campaigns (which to this very day so ably manages the guilt feelings of the Diaspora) were the three forging elements of that Zionism, injected into us day by day from the War of Independence to the Sinai War. This experience was totally auditory until the fifties, when television invaded our privacy and destroyed part of the fantasy.

At the Moral y Luces, Herzl Bialik, the first Jewish high school in Venezuela, we were constantly reminded of the need to reconcile our "first duties" as Venezuelan descendants of the Liberator Simón Bolívar with our ancestral and therefore automatic duties toward the father and founder of political Zionism and the major poet of the Hebrew language. The most prepared Jewish primary and secondary school educators were able to find refuge in our school because they were for the most part democrats who had been repressed by the dictatorship of General Marcos Pérez Jiménez. This made it easy for their young liberal students to hold onto their Zionism as a Jewish national liberation movement, which they saw as going hand in hand with that of the Algerians, the Irish, and the Cubans.

From the routine of that traditional homey Judaism, without excessive or obsessive religious practices, we all became one with a democratic Israel, a nation built on a secular, tolerant, nationalistic ideology. And so it functioned from the fifties until the beginning of the eighties. It continued through the Camp David Accords, my years at the Universidad Central de Venezuela, and my career teaching Spanish and literature as well as enjoying the great honor of being the first former student of the Jewish high school to return as one of its instructors.

With other Jewish graduates of the Venezuelan Republic, democratic as of 1958, I witnessed the victorious Six-Day War (which seemed, in appearance at least, to give Israel secure borders) and the surprise of the Yom Kippur War (which began to undermine that security). We lived through a visual, idealized, and reactive Zionism in the face of a growing virulent Latin American anti-Semitism based on Castro's revolutionary catechism.

The international left ended our honeymoon by hiding its Catholic-based anti-Jewish agenda behind what they called Marxist anti-Zionism. Of course, our answer in defense was equally violent.

I formed part of a small group, improvised for the emergency, to answer the challenge publicly. Ours was a unilateral point of view, the same point of view that in another place and time made Golda Meir answer: "Who are the Palestinians? I am a Palestinian." Ours was justified paranoia, for being *accused* of Zionism at that point carried the same pejorative weight as that *"dirty Jew"* of forever. In addition, we suffered from a crass emotional ignorance that blocked our vision of reality. It is always so hard, if not impossible, to accept (the singularity of) someone else's nationalism. It is the cause of all conflict, all battles. We were brought up in the belief that Israel was built on an empty territory where a few natives with turbans rode peacefully on their camels. Suddenly it became clear that the presence of the Jewish state had reactivated an incipient Palestinian identity to the point of becoming a manipulable nationalism, repressed and ready to explode, unable to admit the possibility of either coexisting with or being neighbors of the Israelis.

It was as if our silk-paper Zionism had lost its innocence, understood its original sin, and, in the face of ever-growing Arab intransigency of *no recognition, no dialogue, no peace*, found itself enmeshed in a change too difficult to assimilate. Thus our diminutive and admired David reverted into a gigantic and repulsive Goliath who heartlessly smashes its fragile adversary. This stereotype persists and weakens the soil of Zion since the Sabra and Chatila episodes of 1982.

Twenty years earlier, I had understood my need to *feel* Israel with my own hands, before starting out my married life with Jaime Segal Kuperstein, a Romanian survivor of a Russian work camp during Hitler's war. He had arrived in 1947 with his parents, Ana and Aaron, and his sister, Silvia. He became a neurologist. We created a family of four, blessed by two children: Ernest Israel, an opthalmologist, and Ariel Yehuda, a journalist, historian, and writer.

That trip to a touristic and fashionable Israel with its epic and romantic image, all the best of the novel *Exodus*, and the image of the kibbutz as a fountain that destroyed the malarial swamp, affected me less than my other voyage. The other one had been toward freedom of spirit, away from relatives and friends of my parents, all escapees of Nazi Europe. Here in Israel, on the one hand, you had all pioneers, grateful for the miracle of survival, needy of a new planet that would sincerely learn to respect and integrate the Jew and would feel shame for its original complicitous silence; on the other hand, their children, born in Israel, strong realists, unbelieving and arrogant, ready to kill to survive, did not in the least believe in *divine miracles* or in a humanitarian conscience. In both cases and complementing each other, Zionism was idealistic and practical, supernatural and ordinary.

This human contact plus the horrifying tales that I had personally heard from the lips of Aunt Guta and Uncle Abraham Hirshbein, Auschwitz survivors, constitute the *materia prima* of my intellectual, polemical, and passionate Zionism, which I tried to share and communicate in numerous articles published in the newspapers *El nacional* and *El universal* and in the magazine *Resumen*.

In the following fifteen years, no longer teaching in classrooms, alternating ideological purpose, and through many articles, I dealt with other matters of Venezuelan and world affairs. I did book reviews, news pieces. I interviewed some figures who were sacred cows, others who were newsworthy, and even some who were totally unknown. Part of that journalist work was collected in *Triálogo*, *Cuarta dimensión*, *Entrevisados en carne y hueso*, *La venedemocracia*, and *Legítima defensa*.

In 1974, five years after I began this editorial journalism, the Venezuelan government granted me the Francisco de Miranda Award in recognition of my efforts. Later, in my mature years, my father's mental health caused a complete turnaround. Alzheimer's disease, the illness of forgetting, devastated my father for ten years until his death in 1991. The long and intermittent psychoanalysis I underwent to deal with some of the stirred-up neuroses had many hard moments from which I emerged with the desire to rescue, through literature, parallel lives.

Thus my first novel, *Cláper*, was conceived. Published in 1987, it has had three printings. An English translation was published in 1998. In it I narrate in a bifurcated first person, biographical fragments of my progenitor and of myself in order to expose lyrically the dramatic contrast that conflicted us as "grand-children" of the Holocaust and complicit witnesses to Zionism. The fixed point of my existence has always been somewhere in between *shtetl* values transported to South America and acquired ones needed to survive amid the customs and influences of the Gentile world.

The situation in the Middle East, always a part of our daily bread, became even more so after the war with Lebanon. With the trauma of the Intifada, the conflictive character has become more pronounced, and a new lens shows Zionism divided between *followers* and *spectators*.

There were premonitions, of course, since 1967, even with that sensational, heroic Zionism that General Moishe Dayan commanded. A million nationalist Palestinians scattered in Gaza and the West Bank of Jordan, fed blind anti-Israeli intolerance by Arab leadership, is a lethal combination now culminating explosively in the detention camps and prisons, fertile ground for sowing more Hamas-type terrorism. And Israel, in the midst of full economic expansion, is also in the midst of agonizing debates and ideological chaos. She is half liberal and secular, a fifth Palestinian semi-occupied, and the rest Jewish nationalistic. The right, of course, feeds the fires of the religious militants, whose extremism, identical to that of the Muslims, led to Rabin's assassination. For the very first time and with no remorse, with sincere Biblical faith, one Zionist kills another, a democratic prime minister of the state of Israel. Our God lost his *oneness* and dictates to the anointed assassin, the holy messianic annihilating his brother.

Zionism is wounded to its very core. It admits two autonomous states, one Jewish, one Palestinian. Reality proves, even to moderate Arabs, that this is the only way to begin a difficult but necessary peace.

Perhaps this hurtful perception of imminent historical suicide, two Jewish people radicalized by opposing Zionisms, as happened to the kingdoms of Israel and Judea and led to the destruction of the First Temple of Jerusalem by the Babylonians, among other more personal reasons, led me to write my second novel, *Columbina descubierta*, in 1991. I created the novel with a difficult, cryptic prose, a hermeticism that paradoxically favored the most dissimilar interpretations, all very valid. It merited in 1992 the prestigious Mexican Fernando Jeno Award. The novel is based on the theories of the Spanish thinker Salvador de Madariaga, according to whom Christopher Columbus was a *marrano*, militantly Jewish, as were all the financial supporters of his first voyage. All were persecuted by the Inquisition headed by Torquemada, himself a descendant of *conversos*, converts to Catholicism, who gladly gave himself to the task of annihilating hidden Jews. My protagonist, Binhich (which in Hebrew means "knowledge") Colón, has to become several different characters to survive in this century, and her lunatic alienation was my metaphor for asking (myself) if Zionism and the Holocaust, the two pillars that bear the biography of the contemporary Jews, were indefensible delusion.

It is only now, at a sufficient distance, that I detect the authentic unconscious motivation that led me to create the novel on such secret foundations and under such a labyrinthine poetic covering. That is how I projected and at the same time covered up my profound fear of the reactions I would elicit from the fanatics in my very own community today.

So now, in the midst of the cybernetic era, one has to ask oneself about the future of Zionism. Before our perplexity, phobic because impotent, the Israel of our deepest love, the Israel of the Constitution, not the Israel of manipulated Sacred Scriptures or the Israel of resented ethnicities. But Israel the original, the pristine, which granted citizenship and nationality on the bases of *humane* laws, this Israel might seem on the contrary to be heading toward a theocracy with its apartheid of a powerful minority exterminating any unusual traces of its very particular Biblical reading.

What then shall be the thread that binds once again our feeling of belonging? How does one say, after five thousand years of history, "Who am I?" Or worse: "What am I?"

In Sarajevo, there is a seven-hundred-year-old Spanish-made Haggadah. After enduring horrible reincarnations, it arrived in Bosnia where it survived in synagogues, churches, and mosques. A short time ago it was saved from burning after heavy Serb bombing of the main library. Now, this original tome, with its magnificent illustrations recounting Jewish liberation from Pharaonic slavery, is jealously guarded in a secret place by the Bosnian Islamic police. It is considered an emblem, a talisman of survival miraculously preserved.

Could this Song of Freedom that we chant yearly at Passover be the text and symbol of Zionism for the third millennium?

Homero Aridjis
(Mexico, 1940–)
"Sepharad, 1492"
Translated from the Spanish by George McWhirter and Homero Aridjis

Born in Michoacán, Mexico, to Mexican-Greek parents, Homero Aridjis is a novelist, newspaper columnist, diplomat (he has been Mexico's ambassador to the Netherlands and Switzerland), the president of International PEN and, especially, a polyphonic poet. His books include *Before the Kingdom* (1963), *Blue Spaces* (1969), *Living to See* (1977), *Second Expulsion from Paradise* (1990), and *A Time of Angels* (1994). In 2002 New Directions released *Eyes to See Otherwise: Selected Poems 1960–2000*. The following sixteen-part poem chronicles Aridjis's quest for the Sephardic past in the Hispanic world. It is the same topic he developed in his novels *1492: Life and Times of Juan Cabezón de Castilla* (1990) and its sequel, *Memorias del Nuevo Mundo* (*Memoirs of the New World*, 1991).

> *For Pharaoh will say of the children of Israel,*
> *they are entangled in the land, the wilderness hath shut them in.*
>
> —Exodus 14:3

> *And the Lord said unto Moses, wherefore criest thou unto me?*
> *speak unto the Children of Israel that they go forward.*
>
> —Exodus 14:15

I

In the alleys of the walled city,
drunken soldiers pronounce your name badly.
On the treacherous summer roads,
a lascivious pack of Moors
attacks your virgin girls; like fauns
with their budding breasts wrapped in rags

they flee, tumbling into the nets of others.
The light of all your yesterdays throbs in your eyes;
kings, monuments to the forgettable,
offer you their hostile friendship.
You travel on foot beside your weary love,
you contemplate a day as clear as knotless cedar.

II

Going forth, you fall back.
Words, chattels, whole cities—
somewhere you forget them.
Your bag is full of the holes
you spill out of.
You go, loaded with what you cannot carry,
there being nothing to take.
The day has given everything bar an ending
and still has everything to give.
The eyes fixed ahead turn back
with nothing to turn back to. I
would give gold for nothing to give.

III

Rest from the road at dawning,
many weary before setting to.
Pay no heed to the dreams that build around you,
the serpent of forgetting bites at your heels
and sadnesses tie you to the land.
Jettison the longing,
if your shadow weighs too heavy on the ground,
pluck it from you, cast it out
of you, to whom these streets belonged,

these bodies,
these years
in a city that today expels you.

IV

There are centuries where nothing happens
and years in which whole centuries pass,
the body of a man unfolds in time
and his hand reaches down through the millennia.
The day's fierce colors
are filled with stabbings
and the children's faces cobbled over by history.
The walls of life are battered through,
man is a bolt of lightning in his own heavens;
roll over any stone and it turns up tombs and temples,
tug open this door and swollen rivers pour forth.
Man is in his moment of unremembering.

V

The hard road of goodbye has begun,
you dwindle in the eye of those, stopped
in the doorway of a house, receding.
Take a weight off your body, brush away your dust,
do not admit to the urgings that spur you to injury,
nor flay the flanks of your children
to get anywhere too soon:
no exile is worse than the one within us.
Though fallen in your estate you are not naked,
spread the sun that burns between your two coldrife souls,
the two halves of you: one going, one staying.
The whole air of exile is yours.

VI

Don't puff up in the mirror of yourself,
many waxed ecstatic at shapes they saw
sleepy-eyed, only to raise an eyelid
and see an ass braying in their faces.
Ward off dreaming whilst still awake,
it leads only to shadows of what lives.
Beyond the kings and their provisions,
far from all inquisitors and their human
curs there is a kingdom of limitless love.
High above the night they shut you
into, the light feet of the rain play
on the sods of something unrepeatable.

VII

Even without a memory, they say, you will die
of homesickness, drown in thirst by the water's edge;
mired dreams will steal out to meet you,
your own footsteps in the streets make you reel;
the one-eyed ire blots out the good eye,
allowing blind justice to slaughter you.
The City of Generations is yours no more,
devout ghosts will be sired on your daughters,
heretics of blood and shadow.
Those who expelled you are mere reflections
in the mirror of That One who is no-place. Only That One,
who speaks not, exists. Only to him, The One I see not, do I
    look.

VIII

In Sepharad, we settled our debts,
quit our estates, exchanged houses for asses;

our daughters of twelve and up married off,
so they might cross over adversity
in the shadow of their husbands.
From the moment of the Expulsion Order
our goods were seized.
We had no rights as persons to be spoken
to in public or in private.
The Bibles, synagogues, and cemeteries
were confiscated by the dogs of God.
From the early morning we took the road into exile
as far as the closed off night of history.

IX

Before leaving Sepharad, we were already departed,
on foot and on horseback; by ass and by cart
far from ourselves we arrived by hard stages,
along roads hardened for hooves, along carriageways and
    King's ways,
even on wrong roads we walked all the while into exile.
The Sun, the Moon, the dust and the streams kept up with us,
without ever lying down, we rose early in wide open country.
The night carter rested from his fatigue,
but not us. Even in death we kept on walking.
In the mountain thickets the *marrano* promised us
a mass of maravedis and marvels.
We got only a grave trodden on by men.

X

Cast out from Sepharad, which cast itself out,
expelled we were from the squares of the faithful,
their religious and secular festivals, but not their fires;
lice-ridden, naked, and bare of foot,
our daughters ravished, our sons stabbed

by the Moors along every road,
the gates of the Inquisition opened for us.
The tolls and taxes paid to King Ferdinand,
covered the cruzados for the King Joao of Portugal,
who collected us into his kingdom to sell,
with our God and our history upon our backs
we left a Sepharad which had cast itself out.

XI

A new Moses shall come with a shining countenance,
he shall sing the ancient desert hymn,
shall lift up his rod and reach out his hand,
through the midst of the dry sea
shall the children of Sepharad pass.
The water shall stand as walls to right and left,
the bitterness depart, without ever wetting us.
Safe and sound, through the red water we will go
singing as we others, years before, went through.
Over the kings and the inquisitors of this world
the waves of justice will close.
The light that opens our eyes will last a thousand years.

XII

From their graves dug up by the dogs of God,
from the black boxes where the ashes go
into autos-da-fé—the bull rings where
the body dead, judges for the Holy Office
free the soul into its frenzy—,
unable to do anything, our grandsires watch us
set forth into exile from Sepharad.
Their lips sealed into a silence
longer than the rope that lashes us to life,

eyes lashed to a dream greater than the dream of death,
God's name blurted out by clods of men, the dead
are known only to the clay.

XIII

This land of exile is a lump of salt
from which I sup my own thirst,
these eyes that mis-see are a human hunger in me.
With love's hangdog head, enshrouded in you
my today is your no-day, and in us both, no-I am.
These bygone fields no longer know me,
shadow and unshadow war over your body;
this abode of mine gone, I have no place in the world.
The light that lights my way burns.
A tower of fire am I in the terrifying squares
where commonfolk crowd in to see
the doomsday drama of my passion.

XIV

Shut into the dungeon of their devotion
they give me nothing to eat or drink,
but the darkness is all mine.
Men, not the land, exile me;
in Burgos, they hound me out of Burgos,
in Vitoria I am forbidden to eat;
in Seville they turn me into a fiery statue. I,
and the others, the Caballerías, the Lunbrosos
have no place in the world of men.
Besides, what does exile amount to, if for those who step by
here—cobblers, tailors, physicians, menders—
their stay only comes to a day.

XV

Like a procession of shadows along
the serpent of history, of forgetting,
we see the shape of exile on the sea.
In the port of Santa Maria, the rabbi raises his rod,
holds forth his hand to part the waters
to preserve us from ourselves.
But the sea does not open in two halves,
does not close over the Inquisitors,
the horizon ill-omens plague and starvation
and the sight of the ships alone saddens the expelled.
The reality of exile sinks home:
men's justice is unbearable.

XVI

You who drove your cart over the ocean, your boat over the
        land,
gave credence to the rabbi when he preached: "This exile
        comes from God."
The exile comes not from God, but men—
neighbors, friends, your own kin.
Vain words those of the prophet
who swore he'd lead us to a promised land,
lead us, rich and hugely honored, out from Sepharad.
The king took possession of the only paradise we had: our life,
took our keys to the gate: the present,
took for his own what we searched for: a dream.
On the tablets of the afterlife and time,
his name is engraved in gold;
ours is graven in ashes.

Ariel Dorfman
(Chile-U.S., 1942–)
Fragment of *Heading South, Looking North*

An émigré intellectual and Distinguished Professor at Duke University, Ariel Dorfman is best known for his Broadway play *Death and the Maiden* (1992), which was directed for the silver screen by Roman Polanski. Dorfman, a poet, essayist, and novelist, is the author of numerous books, among them *How to Read Donald Duck: Imperialist Ideology in the Disney Comic* (1975), *Widows* (1981), *The Last Song of Manuel Sendero* (1987), *Some Write to the Future* (1991), *The Nanny and the Iceberg* (1999), and *Blake's Therapy* (2001). The essay that follows comes from his memoir *Heading South, Looking North*(1998), in which Dorfman chronicles his bicultural, bilingual education—part in Spanish, part in English—in a Chilean Jewish family with strong leftist views. This is Chapter 2: "Dealing with the Discovery of Life and Language at an Early Age."

I was falling.

It was May 6, 1942, and the city was Buenos Aires and I had only just been born a few seconds ago and I was already in danger.

I did not need to be told. I knew it before I knew anything else. But my mother warned me anyway that I was falling, the first words I ever heard in my life, even if I could not have registered them in my brain, the first words my mother remembers being pronounced in my presence. Strange and foreboding that of all the many words attending the scattered chaos and delirium of my birth, the only shrapnels of sense my mother snatched from extinction and later froze into family legend should have been that warning.

It was not intended as a metaphysical statement. My mother had been dosed with a snap of gas to ease her pain as she labored, and when her newborn baby had been placed on a nearby table to be cleaned, she thought in her daze that it was slanted and the boy was about to roll off, and that was when she cried out. "*Doctor*," she called, and my uncomprehending ears must have absorbed the meaningless sound. "*Doctor, se cae el niño, se cae el niño*," she told the doctor that I was falling, the boy was about to fall.

She was wrong about my body and right about my mind, my life, my soul. I was falling, like every child who was ever born, I was falling into solitude and nothingness, headlong and headfirst, and my mother, by her very words, by the mere act of formulating her fear in a human language, inadvertently stopped my descent by introducing me to Spanish, by sending Spanish out to catch me, cradle me, pull me back from the abyss.

I was a baby: a pad upon which any stranger could scrawl a signature. A passive little bastard, shipwrecked, no ticket back, not even sure that a smile, a scream, my only weapons, could help me to surface. And then Spanish slid to the rescue, in my mother's first cry, and soon in her murmurs and lullabies and in my father's deep voice of protection and in his jokes and in the hum of love that would soon envelop me from an extended family. Maybe that was my first exile: I had not asked to be born, had not chosen anything, not my face, not the face of my parents, not this extreme sensitivity that has always boiled out of me, not the early rash on my skin, not my remote asthma, not my nearby country, not my unpronounceable name. But Spanish was there at the beginning of my body or perhaps where my body ended and the world began, coaxing that body into life as only a lover can, convincing me slowly, sound by sound, that life was worth living, that together we could tame the fiends of the outer bounds and bend them to our will. That everything can be named and therefore, in theory, at least in desire, the world belongs to us. That if we cannot own the world, nobody can stop us from imagining everything in it, everything it can be, everything it ever was.

It promised, my Spanish, that it would take care of me.

And for a while it delivered on its promise.

It did not tell me that at the very moment it was promising the world to me, that world was being disputed by others, by men in shadows who had other plans for me, new banishments planned for me, men who were just as desperate not to fall as I had been at birth, desperate to rise, rise to power.

Nor did Spanish report that on its boundaries other languages roamed, waiting for me, greedy languages, eager to penetrate my territory and establish a foothold, ready to take over at the slightest hint of weakness. It did not whisper a word to me of its own imperial history, how it had subjugated and absorbed so many people born into other linguistic systems, first during the centuries of its triumphant ascendancy in the Iberian Peninsula and then in the Americas after the so-called Discovery, converting natives and later domesticating slaves, merely because the men who happened to carry Spanish in their cortex were more ruthless and cunning and technologically practical than the men who carried Catalán or Basque or Aymará or Quechua or Swahili inside them. It did not hint that English was to the north, smiling to itself, certain that it would father the mind that is writing these words even now, that I would have to surrender to its charms eventually, it did not suggest that English was ready to do to me what Spanish itself had done to others so many times during its evolution, what it had done, in fact, to my own parents: wrenched them from the arms of their original language.

And yet I am being unfair to Spanish—and also, therefore, to English. Languages do not only expand through conquest: they also grow by offering a safe haven to those who come to them in danger, those who are falling from some place far less safe than a mother's womb, those who, like my own parents, were forced to flee their native land.

After all, I would not be alive today if Spanish had not generously offered my parents a way of connecting with each other. I was conceived in Spanish, literally imagined into being by that language, flirted, courted, coupled into existence by my parents in a Spanish that had not been there at their birth.

Spanish was able to catch me as I fell because it had many years before caught my mother and my father just as gently and with many of the same promises.

Both my parents had come to their new language from Eastern Europe in the early years of the twentieth century, the children of Jewish émigrés to Argentina—but that is as far as the parallel goes, because the process of their seduction by Spanish could not have been more different.

And therein lies a story. More than one.

I'll start with my mother. Hers is the more traditional, almost archetypical, migratory experience.

Fanny Zelicovich Vaisman was born in 1909 in Kishinev. Her birthplace, like her life itself, was subject to the arbitrary fluctuations of history: at that time, Kishinev belonged to Greater Russia, but from 1918 was incorporated into Romania and then in 1940 into the Soviet Union—only to become, after the breakup of that country, the capital of the republic of Moldavia. If my mother had stayed there, she would have been able to change nationalities four times without moving from the street on which she had seen the first light of this world. Though if she had remained there she would probably not have lived long enough to make all those changes in citizenship.

Her maternal grandfather, a cattle dealer, was murdered in the pogrom of 1903. Many years later, I heard the story from my mother's Uncle Karl, in Los Angeles, of all places. It was 1969 and he must have been well over eighty years old, but he cried like a child as he told us, tears streaming down his face, speaking in broken English and lapsing into Yiddish and being semi-translated by my mother into Spanish so Angélica and I would understand, his pain imploding like a storm into the mix of languages, unrelieved by the passing of time: how his mother had hid with him and his sisters and brothers in a church, how they had listened for hours while the Cossacks raged outside—those screams in Russian, those cries for help in Yiddish, the horses, the horses, my great-uncle Karl whispered—and how he had emerged who knows how many centuries later and found his father dead, his father's throat slit, how he had held his father in his arms.

It was that experience, it seems, that had led the family, after aeons of persecution, finally to emigrate. Australia was considered, and the United States, but Argentina was selected: Baron Maurice de Hirsch's Jewish Colonization Association had helped to open the pampas to Jews anxious to own land and cultivate the prairies. Two brothers of my grandmother Clara set out, and when they wrote back that the streets of Buenos Aires were paved with gold, the rest of the family started making plans to leave as well. Only Clara's mother was unable to emigrate: her youngest daughter would not have passed the tests of the health authorities in Argentina, apparently because she had had meningitis, which had left her seriously retarded. Which meant that both of them, mother and daughter, lived their lives out in Kishinev until they were killed by the Nazis. According to my mother, the old woman went out into the streets the day the Blackshirts drove into town and insulted them and was shot on the spot; and though I would love this story to be true, love to have a great-grandmother who did not let herself be carted off to a concentration camp and forced her foes to kill her on the same streets where her husband had been slaughtered, I have often wondered if this version is a fantasy devised more to inspire the living than to honor the dead.

What is certain is that my mother was saved from such a fate by departing with her parents. At the age of three months, she found herself on a boat from Hamburg bound for an Argentina that, devoid as it might be of pogroms, nevertheless had enough Nazis and Nazi lovers to force her, thirty-six years later, into her next exile. The ambivalent attitude of the host country toward the Jews was presaged in two run-ins my mother had with the Spanish language at an early age.

When she was six years old, my mother recalls, she had been sent to her first school. In the afternoons, private piano lessons were offered, and my grandmother Clara insisted that her child take these, perhaps as a way of proving how genteel and civilized the family had become. On one of the first afternoons, my mother was by herself in the music room waiting for the teacher, when the door slammed shut. From the other side, a mocking chorus of Argentine children started shouting at her in Spanish. She tried to open the door but they were holding it tight. *"No podés,"* they taunted her. You can't open the door, because you're a Jew, *"porque sos judía."* Definitely not the first words she ever heard in Spanish, but the first words she ever remembers having heard, the words that have remained in her memory like a scar. You talk funny, they said to her. You talk funny because you're a Jew.

She probably did talk funny. Yiddish had been the only language her family spoke in Argentina for years. It is true that my mom's father, Zeide, forced himself to learn some rudimentary Spanish: a week after arriving in Argentina, he was peddling blankets house-to-house in Buenos Aires, starting with the Jewish community, and was soon knocking at the doors of Spanish-speaking goyim as well, prospering enough to eventually start a small shop. But his wife, at least during those first years, was inclined to stay away from the new life, from the new language: almost as if Clara feared, clutching her baby daughter to her, that out there the Cossacks were still lurking, ready to attack.

Instead of the dreaded Cossacks, another military man passed briefly through the family's life and inadvertently convinced my Baba Clara, several years before those anti-Semitic school brats refused my mother entry into the community, that Argentina was truly willing to welcome the immigrants.

One day, an Argentine colonel emerged from his brother's residence, next door to the Zelicovich house. He stepped into the torrid heat of the Buenos Aires summer and there, on the sidewalk, he saw his little niece playing with a pretty, blond-haired, foreign-looking girl—my mother, who was probably three years old, maybe four, who had by then picked up a smattering of Spanish from the neighborhood kids. The colonel advanced, reached out with one hand toward his Argentine niece and with the other did not take out a gun and shoot my mother but clasped her small hand and trundled both of them off to the corner for some ice cream. An irrelevant incident, but not to Baba Clara: my mother's mother, upon seeing the colonel go off with the children so amiably and then return with prodigal ice-cream cones, was amazed beyond belief. She said she lifted her hands to heaven to thank the Lord. An army officer, any member of any army, was a devil, a potential Jew-killer: that such a man should invite a child from the Tribe of Israel to share sweets with his niece was as miraculous as the czar quoting the Torah.

My mother does not remember the colonel or the little friend or the ice cream. What she has consigned to memory is the reaction of her mother. What she remembers is her mother's voice that very night, recounting in Yiddish the marvels of Argentina and its love of the Jews to her skeptical sister Rosa. Or was it on a later occasion? Because Clara repeated the same story over and over again through the years. Paradoxical that it should have been in Yiddish, because the story registers and foretells the defeat of Yiddish, how kindness forced it to retreat, her offspring's first tentative, independent steps into a world where Yiddish was not necessary. A world that would demand of my mother, as it demands of all immigrant children, that she abandon the language of her ancestors if she wanted to pass through that door those children would soon be trying to slam shut. I believe this story has abided in the family memory so many years because it is foundational: the prophetic story of how my mother would leave home and assimilate, escaping from that ghost language of the past into the Spanish-echoing streets.

Streets where my father, many years down the road, was waiting for her.

By then, fortunately for me, they both spoke Spanish. I can almost hear him now convincing her to marry him in the one language they both shared, I try to eavesdrop so many years later on the mirror of their lovemaking, listening to how they conceived me, how their language coupled me out of nothingness, made me out of the nakedness of night, *la desnudez de la noche*.

My father's trail to the wonders of the sleek Spanish he murmured in her ears had not been as direct and simple as my mother's. Rather than the normal relay race of one language replacing the other, it had been a more convoluted bilingual journey that he had taken.

To begin with, he had emigrated not once but twice to Argentina; though perhaps more crucial was that he came from a family sophisticated in the arts of language, a sophistication that would end up saving his life several times over.

Adolfo was born in 1907 in Odessa, now Ukraine, then Greater Russia, to a well-to-do Jewish family that had been in the region for at least a century and probably longer. As well as Russian, his father, David Dorfman, spoke English and French fluently, as did his mother, Raissa Libovich, who also happened to be conversant in German after three years of studying in Vienna. All those languages, but no Yiddish: they considered themselves assimilated, cosmopolitan, it was not due to any pogrom. In fact, the 1903 pogrom where my mother's grandfather died had been beaten back in Odessa by the Jewish riffraff and gangsters immortalized later in Isaac Babel's writings. Their expatriation derived from a more trite and middle-class problem: in 1909, at about the time my mother was being born across the Black Sea, David Dorfman's soap factory had gone bankrupt and he had been forced to flee abroad to escape his creditors. Of that venture, only a seal, used to stamp certain particularly fragrant epitomes of soap, remains in my father's possession: "Cairo Aromas," it gradly proclaims in Russian. But my grandfather, rather than heading for the mythical Cairo of the seal, set off for the more distant and promising Buenos Aires of history. And one year later his wife and three-year-old Adolfo followed him.

Some years later—it was 1914 by then, and the child was six—Raissa and her son were headed back to Russia, purportedly on a visit to the family, though persistent rumors mention another woman, whom David might have been scandalously visiting. Whether or not the gossip is true, what is certain is that my grandmother and my father picked the worst time to go back: they were caught in the eruption of the First World War and then in the Russian Revolution. The reasons for their staying on have always been nebulous. "We were going to beat those Prussians in a matter of months, it was going to be a picnic," my baba Pizzi told me half a century later, when she and the world knew that it had been anything but a picnic. "And," she added, "you always think it's about to end and then it doesn't and you wait a bit more and you've invested so much hope in believing that it'll all finish tomorrow that you don't want to give up that easily." Pizzi would tell me this in English on my visits to Buenos Aires, before I myself would experience what it is to believe that something terrible will end soon, before my own exile would teach me that we spend a good part of our lives believing things will get better because there is no way we can imagine them, wish to imagine them, getting worse. My exile—when I fled Buenos Aires after fleeing Chile; my exile—when the phone rang in Amsterdam with the news that Pizzi had died, and I learned that banishment does not take from you only the living but takes their death from you as well. Pizzi had died and I had not been there, I would never sit by her side again and ask her about the past, the steps of Odessa and the *Potemkin*, the Russian secret police raiding the house, never again be able to ask her about the day my father had brought my mother home to be introduced as his future wife, never again discuss with my favorite grandparent the difficulties of being a woman journalist in Buenos Aires, never again hear her painstakingly translate into English for my benefit the stories for children she wrote for the Argentine Sunday papers and had herself translated from Russian into Spanish, as she had translated *Anna Karenina* for the first time into Spanish, never again hear from her lips the tales of how they had survived the hardships of the war, how she had spent those years alone with her son, preparing to return to the land where her husband awaited them.

And then the revolution had come. Like so many Jews at the time, she fervently supported it. But how to make a living with everything in turmoil? While her son went to school with the bullets flying and the walls splattered with red slogans and the city changing hands overnight—she kept a home for him, and food on the table, and managed to put him through school, and it was all due to her languages; that's what kept them alive. And she was so proficient at them that she started working with Litvinov and ended up serving the most prominent Bolshevik Jew of them all, Trotsky, acting as one of his interpreters at the peace talks with the Germans at Brest Litovsk, where the fate of the Soviet Union was decided. She remembered how he had paced up and down on the train as it sped through the Ukraine to the meeting: How much to give up, how much to concede, how much to pay for peace and the time to build a new army, a new society?

And while she was translating German into Russian in order to survive, her husband, half the world away, was patiently translating from Russian into Spanish in order to bring her and the boy safely to Argentina. When the revolution broke out, it became almost impossible to get people safely out of the newly formed Soviet Union, but my grandfather had hit on a plan: there was a flood of immigrants steaming into Argentina and the police needed people who could interpret for them and help streamline the process, and David found a job with them, hoping that his new post would strengthen his assertion that his faraway wife and son were de facto Argentine citizens and should be helped to exit from Ukraine. Incredibly, he managed to convince some official in the Argentine government to intervene, and more incredibly, somebody in the frenzied Soviet Foreign Minstry listened, and that is how Raissa and Adolfo managed to take the last ship—at least so goes the family legend—to leave Odessa at the end of 1920. My father remembers a stowaway: the Red Army soldiers coming on board and the young man's fearful eyes when he was discovered, the stubble on his face, the look of someone who knew he would die—and then they hauled him away, dragged him back to that glorious Odessa of my father's youth, that Odessa now of danger and death.

It's hard to be sure, but there's a good chance, my father says, that he and his mother would not have outlived the terrible year of 1921. The civil war, the famine, the plague decimated Odessa and so many other cities in the country: most of Raissa's family, left behind, died. And among the dead was Ilyusha, Adolfo's older cousin. To the fatherless boy, Ilyusha had been a protector, an angel, a brother for seven lonely years. That cousin of his had let my father tag along as he plunged into the turmoil and romance of the revolution. My father's participation had not gone beyond carrying a mysterious black bag that Ilyusha always wanted near him, a bag that contained nothing more dangerous, it seems, than poems and pamphlets, but it was the first social activism of my father's life, and he was never to forget it. Ilyusha's memory was to haunt him through the turbulent twenties and into the thirties, as Argentina itself began to head for what seemed a revolution of its own.

Spanish received my father with open arms, a smoother welcome than my mother's. Either because he had already had previous experience with the language as a child or because his parents were polylingual themselves, he was soon speaking and writing Spanish brilliantly, so well that, soon after graduating from the university, the Russian émigré Dorfman wrote and had published the first history of Argentine industry, becoming his country's leading expert on the subject. More books, many articles and essays followed, all of them focusing on Argentina and its tomorrow, all of them in Spanish: apparently an absolute commitment to his new land and language.

My father was bilingual and remains so to this day. That he kept his Russian intact can be attributed to his having spent his formative years in Odessa, to the fact that Russian contained within its words the full force of its nationhood and literature and vast expanses—unlike the language that my mother discarded, a Yiddish that occupied no territory, possessed no name on the map of nations, had never been officially promoted by a state. But my father's retention of Russian may signal something else: a doubleness that did not plague my mother. She rid herself of Yiddish as a way of breaking with the past, bonding forever with the Argentina that had taken her by the hand the day when she was three and offered her an ice cream in Spanish. She could easily segregate her first, her original language, relegate it to the nostalgia of yesteryear, a gateway to a land that no longer existed except in the shards of hazy family anecdotes. Her monolingualism was a way of stating that Yiddish had become irrelevant to the present, to her present.

My father could never have said that of Russian. The language of his youth, the language his parents spoke with him at home, was to embody for many in my father's generation—in Argentina and all over the world—the language in which the future was being built: the first socialist revolution in history, the first socialist state, the first place on the planet where men would not exploit men. Always vaguely leftist and rebellious, by the early 1930s my father had joined the Communist Party and embraced Marxism. Like many men and women his age, he saw no alternative to what he was sure were the death throes of capitalism reeling from the Depression. It is one of the ironies of history that those ardent internationalists who were so suspicious of nations and chauvinism and proclaimed that only the brotherhood of the proletariat of all countries would free mankind should have ended up subjecting their lives, ideas, and desires to the policies and dictates of one country, the Soviet Union. They perceived no contradiction: to defend real socialism in the one territory where it had taken power would mean sustaining a state that, by its shining example—and later by armed force—would help bring freedom and equality and justice to every corner of the globe.

And the Moscow trials? And Stalin's purges? And the famine and destruction of the peasantry? And the Kronstadt massacre? And the gathering bureaucratic power of a new elite speaking in the name of the vast masses?

Few communists at the time protested or even seemed to care. My father was no exception. Though I have wondered whether my father's love affair with the Soviet Union was not also buttressed and even hardened by his romance with Russian, the circumstance that the language that had caught him as he fell into the abyss of birth happened to be the very language that he believed was destined to redeem the whole of fallen humanity. The language of his dead cousin, the language of the streets of Odessa, the language of the revolution: my father's past was not something to be thrown away, as my mother threw away her Yiddish. It could coexist with his Argentine present and inseminate it and bring together the two sides and periods of his life, Russia and Latin America, to create a nationless future, socialism in Argentina.

But there is, in fact, no need for this sort of pop psychology, no need to resort to linguistic explanations for my father's blind adoration of the Soviet Union. History was furnishing reasons enough: the consolidation of Mussolini and the rise of Hitler and then the Civil War in Spain convinced innumerable revolutionaries to swallow their doubts (if they had any) and embrace the one power ready to stand up to the Nazis. And even after my father was expelled from the Party at the end of the 1930s—but not, I am sad to report, because of ideological or political differences but due to a slight divergence about some abstruse question of internal democracy—even then, even after the Hitler-Stalin Pact of 1939, he adhered steadfastly to Marxist philosophy and politics.

Up to the point that when I was born in 1942 my father gave me a name I would disclaim when I was nine years old, for reasons that will be revealed: the flaming moniker of Vladimiro. In honor of Vladimir Ilyich Lenin and the Bolshevik Revolution, which, my father felt, was fast approaching the pampas.

What was really approaching those pampas was fascism—at least, a deformed and mild Criollo version of it. A year after my birth, in June 1943, the military, headed by General Ramírez, toppled the conservative government of Ramón Castillo. It was a pro-Axis coup, and behind it was the enigmatic figure of then-Colonel Juan Domingo Perón.

My father would soon run afoul of these men. When the new military government took over the Universidad de la Plata, where my father taught, he resigned indignantly, sending them a letter of protest, *à la* Emile Zola. A copy, unfortunately, does not exist: but I have been told that in it my father insulted the military, their repressiveness, ignorance, clericalism, extreme nationalism, and, above all their infatuation with Franco, Hitler, and Mussolini. The authorities reacted by expelling him from his position (a first in the history of Argentina) and then decided to put him on trial, demanding that his citizenship be revoked. I have taken out the old boxes in my parents' Buenos Aires apartment and leafed through the yellowed progovernment tabloids of the day, and there they are, the headlines calling for the "dirty Jew-dog Dorfman" to be shipped back to Russia, "where he belonged."

History does repeat itself, first as tragedy and then as farce: almost half a century later, ultraconservative anti-Semitic right-wingers in the United States would suggest that I do the same thing, following me around with signs screeching VLADIMIRO ZELICOVICH [*sic*] GO HOME TO RUSSIA whenever I gave a lecture about Chile at a university, waving copies of a twenty-minute speech Jesse Helms had delivered against me on the Senate floor, brimming with information provided to him by the Chilean Secret Police. But those people in America in the 1980s couldn't do anything to me. The men who threatened my father in Argentina in 1943 were somewhat more powerful.

Again, my father was falling.

But this time it wouldn't be Russian that would catch him, save him. Or the Russians, for that matter. It would be their archrivals.

Before he could be jailed, my father skipped the country on an already-granted Guggenheim Fellowship. My anti-imperialist father fled in December of 1943 to the United States, the most powerful capitalist country in the world, protected by a foundation built with money that had come out of one of the world's largest consortiums. Money that had come from tin mines in Bolivia and nitrate in Chile and rubber plantations in the Congo and diamonds in Africa saved my Leninist dad.

But the Americans were preparing Normandy, and Stalingrad was raging, and Auschwitz was burning Jews and homosexuals and Gypsies, and Roosevelt had created the New Deal, and anyway, even if my father had not been able to offer himself all these expendiently progressive reasons for journeying to the center of the empire, there was a more practical one: he had to escape. And America was the only place he could go.

And therefore the place where, over a year later, in February of 1945, the rest of the family joined him.

First, we hopped across Latin America, Santiago and Lima and Cali and Barranquilla, and then finally Miami, each flight delayed for a day or two because of the war, as if Spanish was saying goodbye to me very slowly, as if it were reluctant to let me depart on what would end up being a bilingual journey. Though what may have been most significant about that initial trip north was that the first night of my first exile was spent in the neighboring country just across the Andes, the place that still symbolizes the South for me, there, in that city of Santiago de Chile which was to become my home so many years later. *Wondrous* may be a better word than *significant*: that my first night in that city should have been in a hotel, the Carrera, facing the Presidential Palace of La Moneda, where I was to spend so many nights in the last days of the Allende Revolution, looking out onto the plaza, catching a glimpse of men behind the windows of that hotel looking back at me, perhaps from the very room where I had slept as an infant. A mysterious symmetry which would have been even more amazing if I had died at La Moneda—because, in that case, my first childhood voyage to Santiago could have been construed as truly premonitory, that two-and-a-half-year-old child visiting the site of the murder that awaited him twenty-eight years in the future.

If the gods existed and if they were inclined to literary pastimes, they would have organized precisely that sort of ending for their enjoyment, they would have taken my life and harvested one hell of a metaphor. Fortunately, in this case at least, nobody powerful enough to intervene was playing a sick practical joke on me.

Instead, I was the one playing jokes—on my mother and older sister, who spent most of the one afternoon they had for sightseeing shut up in that hotel room searching for the baby shoes, my only pair, that I had mischievously hidden in a pillowcase. With such skill and malevolence, according to my mother, that we almost missed the chance to tour the city before it grew dark. I like to think that the boy I used to be knew what he was doing, that he was in fact trying to intercept my innocent eyes from seeing Santiago for the first innocent time, from crossing the path of Angélica, the woman of my life, who was that same afternoon breathing those very molecules of air under those same mountains. I like to think he recognized Santiago, he had heard the city or its future calling quietly to him to wait, to hold himself in reserve, to hide the shoes. Or maybe it was the city that recognized him.

New York, however, did not recognize me at all. Or maybe sickness is a form of making love, tact, contact, the winter of New York seeping into the lungs of the child still immersed in mind, if not body, in the sultry heat of the Buenos Aires summer, New York blasting that child inside his simulacrum of a snowsuit, inside the garments that had been hastily sewn together by his mother in the remote southern tip of the hemisphere to simulate a snowsuit, New York claiming that child, telling him that things were not going to be easy, no hiding shoes in this city, no guided tours: in this city we play for keeps, kid.

Our family descended from the train onto the platform in Grand Central Station, and there was no one there to greet us but the cold. We had crossed the South of the United States during the night. I have no memory, again, of that trip, except that years later, when I read Thomas Wolfe and his long, shattering train ride to the home toward which the angel was fruitlessly looking, the home he said you could never return to, I felt a shudder of acknowledgment—I had been on that train, I had crossed that U.S. South leaving my own Latino South. So I do not remember the moment when I stepped for the first time in my life onto the concrete of the North, there in New York, holding my mother's hand.

My father was not there waiting for us.

He appeared fifteen minutes later, explained that he had made a mistake or the train had arrived at a different platform, but my mother felt something else was wrong, she felt the mix-up was ominous, because my dad was distant, unfamiliar, his eyes avoiding hers. What my father could not bring himself to tell her was that just before our arrival, at around the time I was hiding my shoes in a Chilean pillow, he had been conscripted into the U.S. Army, and unless he could get a deferment or change his 4A classification, he would be off to the European Front and my mother, who didn't know a word of English, would be stranded in a foreign city with two small children, forced to live on a fifty-dollar-a-month GI salary. Four days later, still without telling his wife the truth, my father departed early from the hotel where we were lodged and reported for duty in downtown Manhattan, fully expecting to return in uniform to break the news to my mother; the uniform would tell the news he dared not utter himself. He showered with dozens of other conscripts, he slipped into the army clothes and then, at the very last moment, was informed that he had been reclassified because the sort of work he was doing at the newly established office of Inter-American Affairs had been deemed "essential." David Rockefeller, who had created that office in the State Department to fight the advance of fascism in Latin America, had intervened. Again, the tricks and treats of history: a Republican saved my philocommunist father from being sent to war against the allies of the fascists he had just escaped from back home. The point is that my father was able to make a cheerful trip back uptown and tell my mother the reason why he had seemed so remote since our arrival, assure her there was nothing to worry about, from now on happy days would be here again.

But they wouldn't, at least not for me, at least not immediately.

The first order of business was to move out of our prohibitively expensive hotel, not easy in a New York where no new housing had been built since the start of the war. A savvy Uruguayan friend suggested my parents read the obituaries in the newpapers and nab a vacated apartment. Implausibly, that stratagem worked. They rented what in the folklore of the family would always be called *la casa del muerto*, the Dead Man's House. It was, according to my mother, the most depressing, run-down joint she had ever inhabited: a two-room dump, airless under a weak dim bulb hanging like a noose from the ceiling, with small slits of windows gaping onto a gray desolate inner courtyard, three beds in each room, as if several people had died there, not just one.

That was the place, the house of death. That's where I caught pneumonia one Saturday night in February of 1945, when my parents had gone out by themselves for the first time since we had arrived in the States—and I carefully use that verb, to catch, aware of its wild ambiguity, still unsure, even now, if that sickness invaded me or if I was the one who invited it in. But more of that later.

To save his life, that boy was interned in a hospital, isolated in a ward where nobody spoke a word of Spanish. For three weeks, he saw his parents only on visiting days and then only from behind a glass partition.

My parents have told me the story so often that sometimes I have the illusion that I am the one remembering, but that hope quickly fades, as when you arrive at a movie theater late and never discover what really happened, are forever at the mercy of those who have witnessed the beginning: *te internaron en ese hospital*, my mother says slowly, picking out the words as if for the first time, *no nos acordamos del nombre*, there is a large glass wall, it is a cold bare white hospital ward, my parents have told me that every time they came to see me, tears streamed down my face, that I tried to touch them, I watch myself watching my parents so near and so far away behind the glass, mouthing words in Spanish I can't hear. Then my mother and my father are gone and I turn and I am alone and my lungs hurt and I realize then, as I realize now, that I am very fragile, that life can snap like a twig. I realize this in Spanish and I look up and the only adults I see are nurses and doctors. They speak to me in a language I don't know. A language that I will later learn is called English. In what language do I respond? In what language can I respond?

Three weeks later, when my parents came to collect their son, now sound in body but in all probability slightly insane in mind, I disconcerted them by refusing to answer their Spanish questions, by speaking only English. "I don't understand," my mother says that I said—and from that moment onward I stubbornly, steadfastly, adamantly refused to speak a word in the tongue I had been born into.

I did not speak another word of Spanish for ten years.

Isaac Goldemberg
(Peru–U.S., 1945–)
"The Jew's Imprecise Sonnet"
Translated from the Spanish by Stephen A. Sadow and Jim Kates

Isaac Goldemberg, poet, novelist, playwright, and editor, lives in New York City. Born in Peru, he is the child of a Jewish father and an Indian mother. His divided self is reflected in the semi-autobiographical novel *The Fragmented Life of Don Jacobo Lerner* (1984). His books also include the novel about soccer, *Play by Play* (1986), and the collection of poems, *La vida al contado* (1992). This poem, representative of Goldemberg's mixed heritage and conflicted soul, is part of the anthology *Self-Portraits and Masks* (2002).

> Jesus, you have forgotten my America, come one day and be born in these crazy lands.
> —Carlos Pellicer

For God's sake, don't even dream, Jesus,
of being born into my other promised land.
This Jew implores you, groveling.
As well as the Peruvian who flays me

For being the son of a camel. No. A burro.
A burro offered up on your wooden cross
used by the Jew to strip skin from my carcass
for being the imprecise son of a camel and burro.

Jesus, pay no attention to that poet
who calls you from the depths of your Christian
being to be born in these crazy parts.

I swear by the God of Abraham, of you,
that you may not sacrifice for my Peruvian
what you have given abundantly for my Jew.

280

Tino Villanueva
(Mexico-U.S., 1945–)
"At the U.S. Holocaust Museum, Washington, D.C."

A prominent Chicano poet whose artistic roots—the clash between literature and politics—date to the Civil Rights era, Tino Villanueva was born and raised in Texas. He is on the faculty of Boston University. His books include *Shaking Off the Dark* (1984), *Scene from the Movie "Giant"* (1993), and *Chronicle of My Worst Years/Crónica de mis años peores* (1994). He also edited an influential anthology, *Chicanos* (1985). This poem is a testament of Villanueva's visit, as a non-Jew, to the hallways of the U.S. Holocaust Museum. It was originally published in *Partisan Review* and reprinted in *Hopscotch*.

I. Before Our Eyes

We've had it told to us before;
We've seen annihilation, *Vernichtung*
at the movie house in town.
Videos reveal the same declensions of rage,
speech acts crowds shall act upon—
no principles governing reflection,
words shattering glass, building up the
circumstances of the fire,
the same conclusion mortality demands.

Now before our eyes how darkly different
when a deep terrain of text persists with artifacts;
and photographs, each one a cell of time made real.
We turn, and make our way on cobblestones,
pounded out from Mauthausen,
and through a freight car walk along once more,
fitting facts in place—:

281

what led up to what; how a people lived
keeping at their tasks which came to be their lives
with the etched impression of their
history taking place,
until one day: were seized
and carted off in trains like perishable goods
squeezed into the mind-dark of enclosure,
breath coming hard.

Great god,
what geography of pain we are walking through.
What a season of convincing clouds that
hang like smoke, as when the soul,
unassailable,
has found release through manumission.
And what indecent will of those who
saw no cause to care, foreshadowing, therefore,
the concentric rush of time running out.

This is fact: the harsh articulation
of someone's life that, in the end,
will end too soon.

II. The Freight Car

We move on, affirming the proximity of everything,
eyes breaking open to the light: installations here,
photographs and objects there, the visual details of
time kept dying. Suddenly: an intractable fragment
of truth—a freight car brought, finally, to a halt

on the same illicit logic of rails. No stench now;
human grime gone, washed away by water and soap
and the varnish of time. Still it affronts: the tight
seal of steel and wood, a prisonhouse suffocatingly
small, nonsequent, disconnected from the event.

If steel and scarred wood could recount their story
from memory, could beg forgiveness or bring back
the dead, then my hand might not flinch at their
touch as I enter, enter the past: One evening
a cantor was singing before a full congregation,

true worship known by heart. Peacefulness in
the infinite and the lightness of candlelight
breathlessly still when a muster of men from a
shadow realm broke forth, cutting off the prayer.
Cantor, families and friends by the thousands,

hundreds of thousands, were led to the station,
rabid soldiers barking out orders, firing pistols
in the air, dogs bringing up the right flank. So
many helpless immortals so far from their dwelling,

clutching their garments, huddled like the bundles
they carried, unable to run away from their names.
To think they leaned where I'm standing, squatted
or kneeled, dark-stricken, their children driven
to tantrums; or stood where they could against

steel-dug-into-wood, no heaven above them, no earth
below. Some in their places fell mute, were confused,
riddled with fright when the train screeched, jolted
forth, shimmied and swayed and pulled out. Others
kept faith and for them the summit of sky remained

whole: still others felt death beginning to sink
into them—everyone drawing a breath: breath in,
breath out, holding their breath, sighing, inhaling-
exhaling full breaths, half-breaths, gasping with
all complexities of thirst. Long after Treblinka,

"Water," I hear them cry. "Water, air. I step
out, looking back as I move away with the crowd.
One freight car at a standstill, uncoupled from its
long concatenation of steel dissolved into this
artifact: the summation of all that advances no more.

III. The Photographs

To look
into devastated eyes is not enough; to touch
the photographs is not enough.
Even if their breath could reach me,
I could utter nothing among the ruins
written with light.
But someone such as I, a nobody in all of this,
has come to see (this much the heart allows):
what man has done to man, human acts of the profane,
and the defeated countryside.

Led to camps
by the uniform substance of hate,
one by one they held
still enough to be caught in the strict regulation
of natural or flat light. I read it in their eyes:
reluctance seeking its own landscape
with so much night to come. To myself I say:
this face, or that face had a name:
Joseph, Daniel, or Hannah,
but oh, you are a number—
sharp alchemy scored on skin.
I pray your soul remained intact until the end.

(Print after print: I am carried away by destruction
exhausted into fact, forgetting
the persecuted who escaped; who from the

edges of the battlefield were saved, here by a
timely neighbor, a benevolent baker; there by a
factory owner, a farmer, or by decent Catholic nuns
—reflexive acts of the unsung.)

Then there was Ejszyszki (A-shish-key), 1941:
a village of 4,000 that could not find the
doors to exodus—slaughtered in two days.
I touch the photographs of how it was
before it ended in a great field of darkness . . .
and my body shrieks.
Five decades, and in another country,
I am too late in a blazing nightmare
where I reach out,
but cannot save you, cannot save you.
Sarah, Rachel, Benjamin, in this light you have risen,
where the past is construed as present.
For all that is in me: Let the dead go on living,
let these words become human.

I am your memory now.

Alcina Lubitch Domecq
(Guatemala-Israel, 1953–)
"Résumé Raisonné"
Translated from the Spanish by Ilan Stavans

A frugal *ficctionalist* influenced by Borges and Italo Calvino, Alcina Lubitch Domecq is the daughter of a Holocaust survivor and a Guatemalan mother. She is the author of two sparse books: *El espejo en el espejo: o, La noble sonrisa del perro* (*The Mirror's Mirror: or, The Noble Smile of the Dog*, 1983) and *Intoxicada* (*Intoxicated*, 1984). Her stories have been translated into several European languages. She lives in Jerusalem. The autobiographical essay that follows, originally published in *The Literary Review* (Fall 1999), serves Lubitch Domecq to reflect on her *mestizo* self. She explores issues of guilt and silence in the so-called "Second Generation," the children of those who lived beyond the Nazi atrocities of 1939 to 1945.

1953–1961

I was born in Guatemala City. My father was a Holocaust survivor whose arrival in Central America was arranged by a distant cousin connected at some point to the Alliance Israélite Universelle. After the liberation of Auschwitz, Papa spent a few weeks wandering around in the Pale. He stayed briefly in Lodz (where he met an idol of mine, Isaiah Spiegel, at the time retrieving from memory the stories included in *Ghetto Kingdom*), then made his way to Lyon, worked a few weeks in a Paris shoe factory, and eventually sailed across the Atlantic. His arrival point was Havana, where he lived for three months toward the end of 1946. Then his cousin managed to bring him to Guatemala, where Papa's name changed from Ya'akov Yehoshua Lichtenshtein to Jacobo Lubitch and where, willy-nilly, he began working as an assistant in an optician's office. My mother, Josefina Domecq Pérez, a non-Jew, was from a wealthy Spanish family with ties to Mexico's wine industry. She was nineteen when she got pregnant with my brother Elías, twenty when I was born, and twenty-four when my youngest sibling, Nicolás, came into the world. By all accounts, Papa met Mama at a *quinceañera* (Sweet Fifteen) party. She was immediately struck by the serial number tattooed on his arm. Their betrothal was not met with welcoming eyes by Mama's family. Thus the wedding was remarkably small: fewer than a dozen guests, mostly her friends; Papa's cousin refused to participate, accusing my father of betrayal. Up until his death in about 1969, he disapproved of *die goye*.

The house I was raised in during the first nine years of my life was a large, beautiful *hacienda*. I can still picture its endless corridors and exuberant gardens, manicured weekly by Don Lupe, the *portero*. The property belonged to the Domecq family, and we shared it with Abuela Clotilde and the strict Tía Refugio, whose changing moods the children learned to fear from early on. Papa changed jobs regularly. For several years, he worked at a hat factory in downtown Guatemala City—I remember its elevated shelves filled with elegant *sombreros de fieltro*. But he made little money. Still, we lived an opulent life with servants and nannies, sponsored in full by Mama's family. My brother Elías and I had an English teacher, Señora Krieger, very strict in manners, who came to the house twice a week to give us private lessons. I also had a swimming teacher, Damián Pissá (his name will not abandon me, although the silhouette of his face has), whom we met every Saturday at an indoor swimming pool in a northern district of the city.

I spent my *niñez*—somehow the Spanish word rings truer—running up and down the *hacienda* alleyways, climbing trees in the yard, and frolicking in a river bend that crossed the southern section of the property. But my childhood was not happy. Ever since I can remember, Papa's sickness loomed in the background. The Holocaust had left a deep scar in him. He never talked about what he had gone through. But it was clear his suffering had been unbearable. He hardly ever smiled and detested seeing himself reflected in the mirror. He refused to shave. Mama would trim his beard in the garden every two or three months, while he sat in a reclining chair. He combed his hair in the kitchen. And his clothes were always disheveled and poorly matched. He was an outright nonobservant Jew, for he had lost all faith in G-d during the Holocaust; but in his physical appearance, he eerily resembled an orthodox Hassid, those I've come to despise since my *aliyah*. I always remember him as shadowy, erratic, waggish: though he wasn't severe, his facial gestures were always rigid; on occasion he would smile at us children, but his smile would invariably come out as contrived, forced, unintended. For many years, I was sure his anger was directly targeted at me. And so did Elías. All photographs of his past vanished during the war—all except two. Someone in Israel sent them to us by mail, and somehow I ended up storing them in a bedroom drawer. I'm not sure he ever knew I had them. Alone at night, when he and Mama were away, I would study them carefully, figuring out the link between his calamitous past and his discomforting present. In one of these photos Papa, still a child of around eight or nine, is on a tricycle, smiling at the camera, without one of his front teeth; in the other, he stands next to one of his aunts—Pearl Lichtenshtein (1898–1944), I believe— and you can see in his expression the rascal he once might have been. But all this joyful spirit was lost forever. Lost many times over.

On one occasion, when I was about the same age as he is in the tricycle photo, I saw a portrait of Adolf Hitler in a history book. Mama explained to me that he was the leader of the Nazi army that killed all of Papa's family. I was mesmerized. Somehow, it didn't seem possible that a man so gallant would perpetrate so much evil. Hitler's facial expression was enigmatic: he smiled at me. Was this smile stolen? Had he taken it away from Papa? I vividly remember telling myself that if I ever saw Hitler walking on a downtown street, I would first ask him. And if he refused to answer, I would call the police. My brother Elías laughed. His laughter hurt me.

"Hitler is dead, silly!" he would say.

"But what if he isn't? What would you tell him if you all of a sudden saw him on the sidewalk?"

"In Guatemala? Silly."

"Of course. Where else? Do you know how many Nazis fled to Brazil when the American soldiers were about to capture them?"

"How many?"

"Hundreds. Or perhaps more."

"To Guatemala?"

"Yes. Señora Krieger told me many speak Spanish now. Not German anymore...."

"Well..."

"Well what? Can you imagine Hitler stopping at our door? What would you do?"

"What would I do? I would kill him," Elías would answer.

And I got scared by his reply. "No, don't do that.... Don't kill him! You would end up in jail! And I don't want you in jail. Jail makes people sad."

"And what would you do, Alcina?"

But I would fall dumb and have no answer. What would I *actually* do if I ever saw Hitler?

Shortly before we left Guatemala, Papa was placed in a psychiatric ward. We children were not told why, for we were supposed to be protected from such horrible endings. It took me many, many years to put the puzzle together. When I was born, he had begun talking to himself. At the hat store, he would stand alone for hours in his office, staring at the wall. He would see in his customers' faces a resemblance to his siblings and friends before the war, and would talk to them about incidents that had happened many years ago. His cousin tried to help. He recommended that Mama take him on a long vacation. She arranged a trip to Spain, but Papa refused to go. *"No mientras Franco, el Mussolini español, nos dé la bienvenida"* (not while Franco, the Spanish Mussolini, is there to welcome us). He said—and often repeated—that everything was alright. And for a while things did seem okay. After a couple of brief psychotic incidents at the store, he returned to normal. Mama got pregnant again, this time with Nicolás. It was when Nicolás, barely two years old, was run over by a car and died in the hospital that Papa lost total control. He couldn't bear the tragedy. In his view, the driver had been a Nazi. He had been spying on our family and was ready to kill his children one by one. He asked Mama to move, and we did, to a small apartment in Calle Corregidor. But Papa's paranoia got worse. He was sure people were following us. He didn't want us to go out, to attend school. I didn't find out anything about the collapse of his partnership with his cousin. And I only remember slightly his erratic behavior. In my eyes, he had suddenly become alive, and I loved him more than ever for talking to me directly, for making sure I was fine, for not wanting me to go to school so that I could play with him at home. *Mi niña*, I remember him saying in Yiddish, *ales ken ich ton far dir, myn shayne, myn liebe.* Obviously, in my childhood mind only a small fraction of what he said and meant was understandable.

Why Mama married him is still a puzzle to me. The family legend has it that she got pregnant with Elías and her own mother, a devout Catholic, forced them to become husband and wife. But this explanation cannot quite satisfy me: as a young man, Papa might have been a caring lover; he might have wanted to stick to life by marrying such a wealthy and attractive woman; but there is an aspect in my mother's character, one I can easily trace in my own behavior, that serves as a key to the enigma: her messianism. She was obsessed with the way in which Jews had been treated by the Nazis. Spain's expulsion of the Jews was a constant theme in our family conversations—what a mistake it was, how much Spaniards had lost, how the nation's "ticket to becoming modern" had thus been delayed for centuries. In her view, the Holocaust and the 1492 expulsion were symmetrical events in history, and at least in her life she wanted to set the record right. So she married Papa to amend the world. In doing so, of course, she lost her only chance for happiness and pushed us all into an abyss.

Nicolás—*Nicolasito*—died in June 1961, and Papa was finally declared "incapable of civil conduct" at the end of that year. Abuela Clotilde and Tía Refugio capitalized on the occasion and forced Mama into a divorce. Enraged, she took Elías and me to Mexico, where we settled in the Polanco district. We never saw Papa again. I wish we had, though. Guatemala for me is a sad country.

1962–1981

We lived in Mexico until 1972, but I never learned to love it. Mexicans are friendly and warm, but I arrived at a time of enormous spiritual upheaval in my life and had little interest in my surroundings. Mama was reticent, uncommunicative. She felt she had betrayed Papa and was in constant struggle with my grandparents about returning to Guatemala. They forbade her to do so. Instead, they sponsored her lavish trips abroad—to Europe, Asia, the Middle East—while Elías and I were left with an endless number of nannies and enrolled in day schools where teachers struggled hopelessly to integrate us into the classroom. Mama insisted that we attend Jewish school, and so my grandparents sent us to Escuela Yavneh, where Elías stayed until his graduation. I, instead, was a more troublesome case and was transferred to various other schools. My last two years of high school were at Colegio Israelita, in Colonia Narvarte.

My adolescence was thoroughly influenced by what I lived through in Mexico. We lived in the Polanco district, not far from Chapultepec Park, where the wealthy Jewish community ostentatiously parades its riches. As a result of Papa's breakdown, I felt a deep need to understand his past—and my Jewishness. But my surroundings offered me few clues. Those who surrounded me were not inclined to intellectual reflection. Even the holiday of Yom Kippur was performed in a theatrical, treacherous fashion: it was more about high fashion than about atonement and repentance; in the main synagogue of Acapulco No. 70, where Mama took me and my brother, Jews would show up in fancy leather jackets and expensive cars. I was thirsty for knowledge about the

Holocaust, but since Mexico had only marginally participated in World War II, there was no serious debate about its tragic consequences. As a result, my longing to unravel Papa's dementia only deepened.

In my late teens, I began to socialize only with non-Jews, especially with a dance troupe I got acquainted with, whose rehearsals took place in the Teatro de la Danza, behind the Auditorio Nacional. I also got involved in a theater workshop directed by Hugo Hiriart. (He first introduced me to Ilan Stavans.) My first literary attempts were sophomoric poems I published in a magazine put out by a small group of Jewish dissidents, *Odradek*, a title inspired by an imaginary animal invented by Franz Kafka.

Then I traveled to London, Spain, Rome, and, eventually, Israel. Mama had by then remarried—a non-Jew, a mechanic whose overwhelming love for her made him go through a painful conversion to Judaism that included the ritual of circumcision at thirty-seven years of age—and Elías was enrolled in engineering school at the Universidad Nacional Autónoma de México. I had saved some money while working at a multimedia company, putting together audiovisual shows for big companies like Coca-Cola and Kodak. In London I stayed at a friend's apartment. My friend's mother was a high-powered set designer in the West End, and she took us to parties and cocktails and introduced me to Harold Pinter and Eugène Ionesco. I was so impressed by Ionesco, a Romanian absurdist, that I began reading everything he had ever written. I even memorized *The Bald Soprano* in full. I had the good fortune, during one of his short stays in London, to work for him as an assistant for a couple of summer weeks, organizing his papers and correspondence. Thanks to Ionesco, I came to understand the true purpose of art: to fluster and disturb, to do what reality had forced on Papa—an explosion!

I stayed a total of fifteen months in Europe. In Las Ramblas of Barcelona, I became reacquainted with my mother's family. And by sheer accident I met Ilan Stavans again, first in Toledo and then in Salamanca, at the home of a mutual friend whose name I again cannot invoke but whose generosity is long-lasting. On my departure, he gave Stavans and me a copy of the same book, Enrique de Murger's *Escenas de la vida de Bohemia* (*Scenes of Bohemian Life*). I still have my copy, with its solid red hardcover and embossed golden title and the following Spanish inscription:

> *¡Adios, Cruel Tierra Inconstante!*
> *Azote humano, sol helado*

Cual solitaria alma errante
Inadvertido habré pasado.

Goodbye, Cruel Inconstant World!
Human scourge, frozen sun
A solitary errant soul
I will have passed unnoticed.

At that time Stavans and Zuri Balkoff, a BBC correspondent, had begun to conceive their collaborative novel, *Talia in Heaven*, and we talked about the plot and its ramifications in detail. When I left them, Stavans promised to send me a copy in six months, but he took over three years. I was dumbfounded by it: much of what we had jointly imagined had materialized, described in a meticulous, almost mathematical prose. With lightning speed, I wrote a preface, and the volume was finally published in 1989.

In Italy I wandered around from one museum exhibit to another, adding to my diary, drafting possible short stories, without a goal in sight. I wandered until my money ran out. It is at that point that I decided that, rather than return to Mexico, where no one waited for me, I would wander a bit more. And so I took a boat across the Mediterranean to Greece and on to Haifa. I arrived in 1975, shortly after the spaceship *Voyager* was launched into orbit and before Israeli commandos rescued a hijacked Air France plane in Entebbe, Uganda. Israel for me was a revelation. Papa had considered making *aliyah*, immigrating to Palestine, but changed his mind and instead traveled to Central America. Thus from my arrival on, I was struck by what his life would have been had he opted for the first choice. For one thing, I wouldn't have been alive; fate is nothing but a chain of accidents. This casualty concerned me far less, though, than the landscape I was witnessing: natural and human. The soil felt as if it was mine; I sensed that I had belonged to it long before I had arrived. At a volunteer office, I was placed in Ma'ale ha-Chamisha, a kibbutz not far from Jerusalem, where I began cleaning the kitchen and milking cows. These menial jobs would have been unacceptable to me in Mexico, but in Israel I was prepared to do them without complaint. After all, the kibbutzniks immediately embraced me as one of theirs; they realized I was a wandering soul in need of permanent shelter. And that, precisely, is what they gave me.

I lived in the kibbutz almost seven years, becoming part of the larger family. Mama and Elías came to visit me on occasion. I kept writing in Spanish while at the same time I immersed myself in an Ulpan to learn Hebrew. This made my redemption all the more complete. Hebrew for me is a tongue of spirituality, much more solid than Spanish or any other Diaspora language. Recently, at the request of my friend David Grossman, I have begun writing in it—a piece for *Ma'ariv*, a story, not much. I've learned its syntax well, but I confess to still feeling alien to it. The tongue became more pedestrian, less elevated in 1979, with my brief three-year marriage to a kibbutz member. My daughter Yael Bathya was born in 1980. I brought her to Mexico with me when she was two. My divorce was painful, if anything because my ex-husband was always around—working the fields, chatting at breakfast in the cafeteria, organizing the self-defense squads. Grossman, although not a kibbutznik, has been quite supportive. Hearing him talk about Jewish literature in the privacy of an afternoon walk, particularly about the work of Eastern Europeans, is a source of inspiration.

It is during those difficult months that most of my novel *El espejo en el espejo: o, La noble sonrisa del perro* was written. The fragmented plot circles around the misadventures of a girl lost on a battlefield. The ubiquitous public images of Israeli independence and the Six Day War stuck in my mind. But the mood of the volume is much more introspective and reflexive. I conceived it as the search for a lost father figure, a meditation on pain and desolation. It was released in 1983. I had sent it to Salomón Laiter, a novelist friend in Mexico. He embraced it from the beginning and persuaded the publisher Joaquin Diez Canedo to bring it out. My gratitude is immense.

1982–1995

I returned with Yael to Mexico to promote it and stayed with Mama and her new husband in the Tecamachalco district. I had intended my visit to be brief, but it ended up lasting half a decade. Money was not an issue, since my maternal grandfather had died a year before, and both my brother Elías and I had each inherited a large sum of money. With it I bought an apartment in Colonia Hipódromo, not far from my grandmother, and a *pied-à-terre* in Jerusalem. I began to socialize with Esther Seligson. And I tried to write more.

Literature for me is a most strenuous, painful endeavor. It takes me months, at times years, to complete a short story. Thus, as I look back at *The Mirror's Mirror*, I am astonished by how quickly it was born—thirteen months altogether. Critics have compared it to Borges and Calvino, but I trust it is closer to the oeuvre of Isaiah Spiegel, the inimitable Ida Fink, and Lamed Shapiro, in particular, the scene in which Teresa is raped and "savaged" by an enemy soldier. The novel was born during an in-between period sparked by inspiration, one from which I've never been able to recuperate. I suffer from a terrifying inferiority complex: as soon as I finish a tale, I'm convinced of its worthlessness, and so I tear it up. Each word, each comma emerged out of a deep struggle with forces within that I'm unable to control. As a result, I have often tried to give up writing, but I can't; I need literature as much as I need food and love. I write to explain the ghosts of my past, to come to terms with Papa's tragic existence and its aftermath; I write to understand the coincidences that have made me who I am. My fiction, consequently, is always about origins and about the magic that surrounds us. In 1987, after a long struggle and just before I resettled in Israel, I finished *Intoxicada*. Many of the stories in this volume began as novels, but I simply gave them up: their images were too excruciating, too sharp. That readers can identify with them puzzles me but also satisfies me: What ought we to do with pain if not transform it into art? Isn't that the only way to overcome suffering? What does silence mean for a writer? When Primo Levi is told by a Gestapo soldier at Auschwitz, "There is no 'why' here!" what ought the survivor do if not turn the why into a statement on the possibilities of life? I have returned to Guatemala once or twice in my adulthood. My only purpose: to look for traces of Papa. Elías had a vague recollection of the name of the ward he had been sent to: Florista or Floresta; but it proved to be mistaken. I returned to our *hacienda*: it had been abandoned since the late seventies, when a guerrilla group had kidnapped an important businessman in the neighborhood and dropped his body a few blocks away. I wandered from one psychiatric hospital to another looking for clues. But I found none. Not only had he abandoned me, he had been swallowed by anonymity.

I began studying the *Sefer ha-Zohar* with Esther Seligson. She introduced me to Angelina Muñiz-Huberman, whose teaching opened my eyes to Mexico's Sephardic ancestry. Her volume *Enclosed Garden* opened my eyes to a universe inside me. In 1989 I brought Yael back to Ma'ale ha-Chamisha. Soon after, I began studying Kabbalah in earnest at various yeshivas. Judaism has a derogating approach to women: we are wise when it comes to earthly knowledge but inept in intellectual matters. Time and again my studies were interrupted by obstructing rabbis refusing to allow me to sit in their learning rooms. But Orthodox women are not as passive as secular Jews want to believe; they organize themselves, and so I got involved in a number of marginal learning groups. As I immerse myself in religious matters, I realize how literary the Jewish religion is: the written word is sacred, and the mysteries of the universe are all hidden in it. Not only is the Bible filled with extraordinary tales, but so is the work of G-d's progeny—the Talmud and Gemara. My own books are filled with anecdotes, but they are deficient in style and structure. I often wished I had not written them. Silence, I often think, is my true language.

And yet, I write....Alone, to myself. I write in spite of all the suffering it unravels. And I will continue to do so even if I don't ever show the product to others. In all honesty, I might never bring out another book again. Still, literature places me firmly on the ground. It gives weight to my being. Not surprisingly, I find it quite difficult to stay in a single place for long: in 1993, after Mama died of breast cancer, I sold my apartment in Mexico; and since then I've also sold the *pied-à-terre* in Jerusalem. Only in literature I find a home—silent, eclipsed, but a home nonetheless. Last time I saw Angelina Muñiz-Huberman in Israel, in 1991, I asked her: Is writing worth the effort?

"Perhaps not," she replied. "But do we have a choice?"

"Silence," I responded.

"Nature is silent...words are human. And only words can be *personalized*."

She is right: To write is to erupt.

Marjorie Agosín
(Chile-U.S., 1955–)
Fragment of "Dear Anne Frank"
Translated from the Spanish by Richard Schaaf, Cola Frazen,
and Mónica Bruno

A poet and human rights activist, Marjorie Agosín teaches Spanish at Wellesley College, Massachusetts. She is a descendant of European Jews who fled the Holocaust and settled in Chile. Agosin was born in the United States. Her parents returned home to Santiago, where she lived for the next sixteen years. She has lived north of the Rio Grande since 1972. She is the author of *Scrapes of Life: Chilean Women and the Pinochet Dictatorship* (1987), *Zones of Pain* (1989), *Happiness* (1993), and *A Cross and a Star: Memoirs of a Jewish Girl in Chile* (1995). The following poem is part of a volume of the same title released in 1998 in which Agosín establishes a lyrical dialogue across time with Anne Frank.

I

Under the fall of night
amidst noises watching, stalking,
in the darkness as dark as heads of war,
I have you calling me, Anne Frank, I hear us calling
each other. Among the shadows,
thresholds open
letting you come in, Anne, emaciated, transformed
like a demon.

II

You embrace me.
You tell me how you saw women marching naked, ceremonious

through fields of poppies;
how you saw your father making signs behind the wire beyond
the smoke.
then you ask me:
where did I leave my red chiffon dresses,
and if I too keep a diary that I can show you.

III

There is no one here in this house, Anne,
not even the guardians of dreams.
Only you and I watching each other, without recognizing each other,
With history's equivocal gaze,
and you tinge with blood the room and windows,
this perverse dusk,
this bloody canvas.

Ruth Behar
(*Cuba-U.S, 1956–*)
"The Hebrew Cemetery of Guabanacoa"

A MacCarthur Fellow and an anthopologist on the faculty at the University of Michigan, Ruth Behar is the author of *Translated Woman: Crossing the Border with Esperanza's Story* (1993) and *The Vulnerable Observer: Anthropology that Breaks Your Heart* (1996). She left her natve Cuba as a little girl. Since the nineties, she has been active in the movement to reconcile the two Cuban halves after the Fidel Castro revolution of 1958 and 1959—the population inside Cuba and the exiled population in Miami and elsewhere. In 1994 she coedited with Juan León the anthology *Bridges to Cuba/Puentes a Cuba*. Behar has also produced an autobiographical TV documentary, *Adió Kerida*. This poem is representative of her persistent search for Jewish origins.

Outside of Havana
are the Jews
who won't leave Cuba
until the coming
of the Messiah.

There is the grave
of Sender Kaplan's father
a rabbi's grave
encircled by an iron gate
shaded by a royal palm.

There is the grave
in Hebrew letters
that speak Spanish
words of love and loss.
Ay kerida, why so soon?

There is the grave
with a crooked
Star of David.
There is the grave
crumbled like feta.

I go searching
for the grave
of my cousin
who was too rich
to die.

I despair.
I've promised a picture
to my aunt and uncle.
They're rich now in Miami
but not a penny for Fidel.

And then I find it—
the grave of Henry Levin
who died of leukemia
at age twelve
and money couldn't save him.

Poor boy,
he got left behind
with the few living Jews
and all the dead ones
for whom the doves pray.

I reach for my camera
but the shutter won't click.
Through ninety long miles
of burned bridges I've come
and Henry Levin won't smile.

I have to return another day
to Henry Levin's grave
with a friend's camera.
Mine is useless for the rest
of the trip, transfixed, dead.

Only later I learn
why Henry Levin
rejected me
a latecomer
to his grave.

My aunt and uncle were wrong.
Henry Levin is not abandoned.
Your *criada*, the black woman
who didn't marry to care for him,
tends his grave.

Tere tells me she can't forget
Henry, he died in her arms.
Your family left you, cousin,
so thank God for a black woman
who still visits your little bones.

Ilan Stavans
(Mexico-U.S., 1961–)
Fragment of *On Borrowed Words*

Ilan Stavans, a native of Mexico, is the Lewis-Sebring Professor in Latin American and Latino Culture at Amherst College, Massachusetts. He is the author of *The Hispanic Condition* (1995), *Art and Anger* (1996), and *The Riddle of Cantinflas* (1998), and editor of *Tropical Synagogues* (1994) and *The Oxford Book of Jewish Stories* (1998). In 2002 Routlege published *The Essential Ilan Stavans*, an anthology of essays and stories that includes pieces on the Subcomandante Marcos, Alberto Gerchunoff, Walter Benjamin, and Jewish memory. The following personal essay is from *On Borrowed Words: A Memoir of Language* (2001), in which Stavans reflects on the role that language and identity played in his Mexican-Jewish education. His fragment is from the second chapter, entitled "The Rise and Fall of Yiddish."

> In Yiddish the boundary between comedy and tragedy,
> and between fact and fiction,
> is always a thin and wavering line.
>
> —Irving Howe

Bela Stavchansky, a small, imposing old lady known among her grandchildren as Bobe Bela—and, in the jargon of Mexico's Ashkenazic Jews, as *La Bobe*—utters delicious Yiddish sentences to herself in the dark. She is not alone in her one-bedroom apartment. María—a.k.a. Mari—her temperamental maid, is around. But the two are always fighting: in polite Spanish, Bole Bela asks for something—a glass of hot tea with a sugar cube, a Tylenol, her daily dose of vitamins; Mari, in a terrible mood, won't answer, though. So Bela switches languages. This is a recurrent strategy: when in distress, return to your homeland: your first tongue. Bela talks to herself, and thus, to the ghosts of her past. Or else, she calls her beloved second child, my father Abremele. Generally, it is an answering machine she gets on the other end. *"H-o-l-a, h-a-b-l-a B-e-l-a ... Abremele, quiero hablar*

301

contigo. Háblame." Is her voice on tape already? Must she press a particular number? Will her Abremele listen to her? These machines are magic. How do they work? Do they have a genie inside? She might simply wait until somebody answers the phone, for she surely prefers a living person. Why should she talk to a machine? She needs company, a voice to listen to. So she calls again hours later. "Abremele *chulo*," she says, carefully avoiding Mari's name so as not to announce her intentions, "*vos ken men ton mit di goye? Zi redt mir nisht.*" The maid is driving her crazy, she says. She does not answer her queries and is always in a bad temper. And then again an hour later. And again. Soon Abremele will listen patiently to her complaints, first on tape, then live through the miracle of phones from Bela's apartment in Colonia Polanco. He can't avoid them. He is used to them. "You've had her for almost twenty years, Mami," he replies. "Will you finally fire her? Who will help you? You're alone. Your three children are too busy. . . . Do you want to move to the *heischel*?" he wonders, referring to the Jewish Home for the Elderly in Cuernavaca, Morelos, also known as *moishe-zkeinim*, some fifty-five miles south of Mexico's capital. "I will take you whenever you want."

Bela isn't ready. She is eighty-four but looks at least a decade younger. Her buoyancy is her most admirable quality: wrinkled as a prune, but with a drive as spirited as an Olympic champion. No, life is not finished yet. There is still more, much more to see, to read and to appreciate. Her eyes are tired all right, and her bones are heavy. She has lost her hearing, so Abremele must shout on the phone for her to understand. "What? I don't understand," and he tries again, but she doesn't register. "*Zog es mir in Yiddish?*" switch to Yiddish, she suggests, for Yiddish is *der mame-loshen*, the language of stomach and soul. It is also the language of the dead. And if the dead can understand it, why shouldn't she? My father complies, only to realize what he has known all along: Bela is really not interested in conversation; dialogue is too exhausting an enterprise for her, too demanding. Three, four fixed ideas are all she has in her mind, and nothing in the world, not even a major catastrophe, will change them. Mari is not her problem. It's her restlessness, the isolation that comes with old age. "*Ya he pasado de la tercera a la cuarta edad. No sirvo. . . . Estoy descompuesta,*" she tells him: I'm useless, I'm damaged, I have reached a point of no return. She isn't, obviously. She might be losing it, but she is as vigorous as a horse: every day she walks a few blocks to the supermarket, in the afternoons she plays poker with friends, on Friday nights she attends services at a nearby synagogue, and on weekends she visits her children and grandchildren.

"Abremele, *zug mir, main liebe kind*: ¿Y *qué con Ilán*? Has he written back?"

"What do you mean, 'What is with Ilan'? *Está ocupado*. He is busy, Mamá, just like all of us. He has a family to attend, and . . . "

Not always have I been a jewel in Bela's crown. For years I wasn't good enough. What kind of money does a writer earn? Isn't it like acting? Can he support a family? Look at your father. Didn't he have problems raising his family? Your cousins in Israel and Philadelphia, ah, they do have solid professions, don't they? Nevertheless, since my essays have begun appearing in national newspapers, since my name circulates among her friends—*Dain liebe einikel, Bela!*—I'm the grandchild she thinks about.

"Did he get my package? You haven't told me . . . " she wonders.

"Of course he did," he replied impatiently.

More than a month ago, she sent to my New York address a package that included some correspondence and a tightly wrapped bound notebook. MI DIARIO, she titled it, my diary, though it has no daily entries to speak of. She also calls it, in broken Spanish, *un chico relato*, a brief tale. It has a total of thirty-seven pages, all typed in capital letters. My mother did the secretarial work: Bela would give her a pile of handwritten pages; my mother transcribed it meticulously and sent it back; then Bela revise the typed version once, twice, until fully satisfied. She began writing it around 1980 and finished it thirteen years later.

"So, has he read it?" Bela is anxious to hear my reaction, for I am, as of late, the literary genius in the family, and whatever I say goes.

"He has it, Mamita, he has, believe me. I'm sure he'll write you directly. In due time."

And I do, of course, in a matter of days. I cannot cherish her diary enough, so important is it for me. I have reread it three, four, five times, trying to find meaning between the lines. The style is undeliberately loose, chaotic, repetitive, ungrammatical, and it pays no attention to accents and punctuation. Nevertheless, it is invaluable in its warmth, conviction, and clarity of vision. Bela is overwhelmed by nostalgia, uncritical of her past. How could she not be? What else could one expect from a self-made woman whose schooling didn't reach beyond second grade?

Why did she write her *diario*? So as not to waste her memory, I tell myself at first. So as to turn her life into an asset for future generations. What if all of a sudden she became an amnesiac? Or is this a gimmick to manipulate the family's collective memory? The more I think of it, the better I realize that the "why did she write it" is the wrong kind of question. Don't all of us want to leave a mark, set the record straight before time runs out? Don't we all dream of changing the world at least a bit by solidifying our place in it? History (with a capital H) doesn't claim her as a hero. She grew up, escaped Poland before Hitler invaded, settled in Mexico, prospered, had children and grandchildren.... Nothing intrepid about it, except for the feeling, so deep in her heart, that we are what our words say we are, and *tsuzein* is different from the Polish *byc*, the Hebrew *leiyot*, and the Spanish *ser*.

Bobe Bela dedicates her diary not only to me but to my wife and one-year-old son as well: "*Dedico mi [diario] [o un chico relato] de mi juventud a mis queridos nietos, Ilan, Alison y Josh, como recuerdo de Bobe Bela.*" She dedicates it in Spanish, though. I wonder why. And not only is the dedication in Spanish, but so is the entire narrative. This, in fact, is the most urgent question I have, the one I would love to discuss with Bela. Why not in Yiddish, her mother tongue, the tongue in which instinctively she sobs and screams? I know the answer, of course: she wants to be read, understood, appreciated; she is eager to reach not only me but my wife and, sometime in the future, my children as well. I don't for a second doubt the truthfulness of her *diario*. But her words have been modified— or, shall I say, betrayed—have they not? And yet I won't raise the issue in my letter. First, because as susceptible as she is, my remarks will surely be misunderstood. She might suspect that implicit in my query is a censure of her written Spanish, although that is the last thing I would dare to imply. Her Spanish is pidgin all right—broken, ungrammatical—but it is hers all the same: it has style, it has pathos, it has power. It is the tongue of an immigrant—embryonic, wobbly, in constant mutation. It came to her at age nineteen, when alone, scared to death, she crossed the Atlantic and settled in Mexico. She appropriated the language so that I, thirty years later, could make it my own. So I don't dare to question her. Who am I to dispute her choice of language? A guardian of *der mame-loshen*?

Háblale, Ilan ... *Orale*. She wants to know what you think!

And what do I think? I treasure the text, for sure. I have read segments of her *diario* to Joshua. As I wander through its descriptions, I seize, with amazement, the scope of her existential journey, for Bela is a natural polyglot: aside from Yiddish she was fluent in Polish and Russian, and with time she learned a broken English and a bit of Hebrew as well: seven languages, including Spanish. She was born in 1909, in Nowe Brodno, now a suburb of Warsaw. When she emigrated to Mexico in 1930, she made a conscious decision never to use Polish and Russian again. Astonishing, I tell myself: most people have trouble even pronouncing a second tongue, but Bela was verbally so rich, she could afford to give up two languages. Rich, obviously, is the wrong adjective, for her rejection of Polish and Russian didn't come as a result of a surplus of words. Instead, it was a matter of survival, a brusque but healthy attitude she forced herself to take so as to achieve the only available peace of mind she could dream of: she was a youngster, ready to begin her new life, her past needed to be overcome, even erased, if survival was to be achieved. Not only a new country and a new culture but a language was on the horizon when she left Nowe Brodno.

Poverty was not a curse but a state of mind. "When you don't know what you're missing," she once told me in broken Spanish, "you aren't really missing it, are you?" Bela's maiden name, Altschuler, means in German "old-synagogue attendee." Perhaps the family originated in Provence in the thirteenth century and later on moved to Prague and from there to Galicia in the Austro-Hungarian empire. They were lower middle class. Her father, Yankev Yosef, owned a garment store with a pretentious English name: Sklep Manufactory. It was a two-story building with wooden floors and also functioned as the family's home. I visualize its pallid colors, not unlike the settings of an Andrzej Wajda film. Every time a customer entered through the front door, a bell would announce his arrival. A little window allowed Bela's mother to see from the kitchen, who it was. On the first floor was the kitchen separated from the store by a door through which entering customers could be seen and heard, as a small bell announced anyone stepping in. At the kitchen's center was a charcoal oven. Dovidl, Bela's younger brother, whom I would later on hear about as Tío David, would sleep next to the oven, for there was never enough room upstairs for two adults and eleven children. A back room behind the store functioned as a bunker: preserves, blankets, and extra clothes were stored in case an anti-Semitic attack occurred, and, I also conjecture, a sharp ax often used to cut wood. (A pistol might have been of use, of course, but Polish Jews were not allowed to possess weapons.) In the rear of the building was a kitchen, with a small furnace and a bed for one of the seven children. Bela and her sister Reisl slept on the second floor.

Fear, *el miedo*, is the unifying message throughout Bela's *diario*. In the first part alone the words *el antisemitismo* appear a total of seventeen times, more than any other proper noun. Nowe Brodno was infested with it. I picture the town through Bela's childish eyes, artificially, realizing it is but a figment of my imagination, a hazy marketplace of noise and odor, silhouettes shuffling around, orthodox Jews confabulating in a corner, automobiles gaining attention, horses carrying milk and butter. Nowe Brodno was divided in half by Bialolenska Street, a commercial road, wide, newly asphalted by the Polish authorities, on which Sklep Manufactory was located. The street reminds me of Isaac Babel's Odessa in "Story of My Dovecot," a haunting tale I've reread a thousand times, if only to evoke a past I'm convinced I had a share in, a story where *el miedo* is described in such a subtle, indirect way that the reader is left thinking, after the last line is over, if life for the Jews on the banks of the Baltic Sea and in Central Europe in general was ever about anything else.

The Altschulers were urban dwellers. The women, it seems, were much more cosmopolitan and enlightened than their male counterparts. They took care of business while their husband prayed at the synagogue. I'm tempted to describe them, anachronistically, as *maskilim*, a term that traditionally applied to the enlightened male Jewish establishment from the eighteenth century onward; perhaps not full-fledged intellectuals, but attentive listeners to the voices of the mind. While the men believed the universe is filled with angels and demons, the women were hard-nosed and utilitarian. They looked down on the *shtetl*, as most others in Nowe Brodno did, approaching it as too parochial, too confined to a medieval superstition that the *Haskalah*, as the Jewish "Age of Reason" is called in Hebrew, had painstakingly struggled to overcome.

I confess to feeling insecure. Am I portraying them as more educated than they really were? Was superstition not an essential element in their husbands' daily life? When, as a child, I would visit Bela at her previous apartment, in Colonia Hipódromo, I would hear more than I could ever digest about fanatical beliefs: at a dinner table, the saltshaker should not be passed from hand to hand, as the Devil thus spreads his influence, as he does, too, when Jews whistle, so *nunca chifles* . . . ; and if a sibling is ever lying flat on the ground, never jump over him, for *la muerte lo condenará* . . . , the Angel of Death might quickly follow. . . . I am still perplexed at the way in which Bela, along with other women of her generation, conveyed these superstitions to me. Was there not a hint of irony in their tone? Or were they convinced that evil forces, *Yetzer ha-Rah*, could suddenly overwhelm us all? Is this too literal an approach: females as practical, males as somewhat fanatical? In the Mexico of my childhood, Jewish men were out making money to support the family, whereas women stayed at home. But this was only a superficial division, for women had the upper hand when it came to family business. Even after a discussion occurred, *di yiddishe mame* ruled, never through easy-to-understand sound bites but through forceful persuasion that left no room for doubt.

Gender issues might not have been aired, but morality was, and in a way that turned it into the topic of conversation *sine qua non*: Does the individual bring on his own downfall or is everything predestined? Are we free to battle the forces of darkness? Are they a test the Almighty lays out for us? The Altschulers were not a conflicted crew: society was moving forward toward a less mystical, more scientific future; religion played a role in their daily routine, but it was clear, from the children's various interests, that ideology could soon replace it as the next generation's idol worship. Nowe Brodno, I read in Bela's *diario*, was some forty miles away from Warsaw. To get there one took a train to cross Prague, a small district, and then crossed the Vistula River. The trip could take hours, but the closeness of the capital, with all its financial and cultural attractions, made life in provincial Nowe Brodno bearable. This proximity to the center of Polish culture allowed for a sense of superiority, a kind of distinction nurtured by the modernity that surrounded them. And it marked Bela's views: in spite of the tricks destiny held in store for her, she would strive to educate herself, to elevate her soul, to be above others, particularly above the Gentile peasantry, whose illiteracy she perceived as a prison.

On Friday night, when the cleanup was over, a white tablecloth was spread on the table by Reisel and Bela. It was *Shabes*. The candlesticks would be placed at the center, surrounded by *khales*, the traditional bread rolls. Bela's mother was short, obese, and blue-eyed. She knew arithmetic, which made her a *khukhem*, a wise woman. She took care of the store's finances and often traveled with her son Gil to Warsaw to buy merchandise. In Warsaw she also bathed in the *mikveh*. Bela's father, on the other hand, was a *Hasid* belonging to a mystical sect tied to the emanating glory of the Ba'al Shem-Tov. He prayed twice a day and spent long hours reading the Talmud. But he was a family creature, just like my own father: he woke up early every morning to prepare tea for his wife, which he took to her bed; next he cooked breakfast for the entire family; in the afternoon he fixed tea with *chicoria*; a loyal husband, it seems, and a trusted father....

The Altschulers didn't last long in Nowe Brodno. A pogrom convinced Shaul to move, and he took the family to nearby Puttusk, apparently a more protected and peaceful town, where one of Bela's older siblings had established himself with his wife and newborn baby. But the general sense of insecurity—*el miedo*, yet again—soon reached Puttusk as well, and both Bela and her older brother Gil were victims of physical attacks. By then Bela was already an ardent Zionist and often spent her free hours disseminating propaganda at public meetings. Once, a gang of young Poles caught up with her after school. They pushed her aside, ridiculed her in public, rudely pulled her long ponytails, and screamed at her: "Pig Jew. Why don't you move to Palestine, where you and your putrid friends belong, and help in the cleansing of Poland?" This scene is conveyed in Bela's *diario* with enormous pathos but without embellishment, in a matter-of-fact fashion. The words Pig Jew—*puerco judío*—seem written in fire.

I can see why Bobe Bela would become a Zionist. She has never really talked to me about her adolescent ideologies, and her narrative is silent on this issue. Abraham, my father, has told me that her Zionist dreams were short-lived. "I don't believe she ever truly considered moving to Palestine, like some of her friends did," he says. It wasn't only a matter of emigration, though. For her, Palestine was not, I trust, a Jewish state in the future, but an alternative in the present: an escape, a safe heaven. Many years later, in the late seventies, her oldest grandchild would emigrate to Israel. With time she would go visit him. But Israel, in her eyes, was too rough, too ironbound. Could she ever have moved there for good? She is, she always was, a diasporist—a guest, a renter of someone else's property. Still, she paints herself as a restless, committed feminist whose family poverty made it impossible for her to enter institutions of higher learning and thus become a leader of her own people. An accurate picture? Impossible to know. Other women of not so dissimilar backgrounds did excel: Emma Goldman, Golda Meier, Dvora Baron. Bela's father hired a *lerer*, a Yiddish teacher, whose responsibility it was to instruct the children in religious and secular subjects. But she was ambitious, she wanted more—to the point, as she puts it, of ingratitude. In one scene, Bela has a terrible fight with her parents, which she soon after regrets, for not allowing her to study in a respected Warsaw school. In another, she suggests a number of possible plots for novels she could have written, had she received the proper education. Memoirs are subjective, manipulative, driven by our desire to improve our prospects in human memory, and as rudimentary as it is, Bela's is no exception. Her flattering self-portrait is in sharp contrast to the domineering, exploitative, conservative lady she has always been, at least within family circles.

True, her literary interests are obvious. She is, and has been since I can remember, a voracious reader, if not a versatile debater. She is an avid borrower of library books from the CDI, the Jewish sports and entertainment center in Mexico's capital, and the librarians know her simply as Señora Stavchansky. They see her regularly and are even ready to send her titles home on request, should she be unfit to make the journey from Colonia Polanco to the northern edge of the city. She reads everything, in Yiddish, Spanish, and, with difficulty, English: from the weekly *Der Shtime* to Chaim Potok's novels, from Sholem Asch to Saul Bellow, even though, as she confessed to me once, *Humbold's Gift* made absolutely no sense to her. I once gave her a Spanish translation of *My Life as a Man*, by Philip Roth, as a birthday present. She hated its open sexuality, its condescending tone. "Too dirty," she announced as she returned it to me. She was not an enthusiastic fan of Bashevis Singer, but in her eyes Singer was a champion of the Yiddish language in a post-Holocaust era, and thus needed to be read, even in translation, if only to pay homage to a culture that is no more. In private, though, she believed him too erotic as well. (She didn't know, nor did I tell her, that Singer was publishing stories in *Playboy* at the time.) Bashevis's older brother, Israel Joshua, was more akin to her spirit. She adored *The Brothers Ashkenazi*, which she read in Yiddish, as well as *The Family Carnovsky*, a novel we were made to read in junior high. When in 1978 Isaac Bashevis Singer was awarded the Nobel Prize for Literature, Bela was thunderstruck with excitement, as if she herself had been the recipient of the Stockholm honor. She immediately called me: "What joy, Ilancito!" she said.

Deep inside, she is sentimental and even melodramatic, and her descendants are well aware of it. The most beloved present she ever received was a seventy-five-minute video—kitsch in its most tangible incarnation—made by her three children, Tío Isaac, my father, and Tía Elenita, on the occasion of her eightieth birthday. A sequence of stills, first in black and white and then in color, juxtaposed to real-life sequences of Bela having breakfast, Bela at the beauty salon, Bela in the park, Bela smiling to—and for—her grandchildren, is accompanied by bubblegum music. I wasn't present when she received it at a sumptuous *fiesta*, but heard all about it: Bela wept inconsolably, her life parading before her toward the happiest of endings. Her love of melodrama was revealed in her one and only icon: Danielle Steele. She has read every single one of Steele's sagas of love and money. For a time, she would try to persuade me to read at least one. What Bela liked about them was their emphasis on feelings and the conflicted passions they described, and the fact that the sex scenes were never too explicit. So infatuated was she with Danielle Steele that, much as her father, a G-d-fearing *Hasid* at the turn of the century, sought the helpful advice of erudite rabbis in time of trouble, so did the vulnerable Bela turn to Steele. When Galia, her youngest granddaughter, suddenly ran away with a Gentile, a *sheigetz*, in Bela's Yiddish terminology, she wrote a long, tortured letter to Steele asking for guidance. She asked me if this would be proper. She was eager to know if novelists of her stature occasionally responded to their fan mail. And she asked if I could provide her with Steele's address. To me, the whole situation was painfully comic. I was torn: I loved Bela with all my might, but I felt she was doing herself a disservice by seeking help from so cheap a writer. Still, all she asked for was an address, not my own advice. Did my sense of intellectual superiority need to intrude? Who was I to stop her? Had not Bela succeeded in rebuilding her life from scratch? In the end, I gave her the address of Danielle Steele's publisher in New York and told her not to expect too much: authors of her stature responded to their mail, but not directly; they did it through a secretary, who probably had three or four standard letters sent out to millions all over the globe. In the end, I was wrong, of course. Not only did Danielle Steele write back to Bela, she actually composed a long and detailed letter about Galia's escapade. She asked Bela to be patient and, more important, to allow the young of today to seek their own path without intrusion. Steele obviously took my grandmother's pain quite seriously and, in her reply, made her the happiest woman on earth.

The other icon she worshipped, and wished she had corresponded with, was Sholem Aleichem—Pan Sholem Aleichem—about whom I heard her talk at considerable length while growing up. No doubt my own passion for *Tevye the Dairyman* was a result of her influence. Several times Bobe Bela took me to see, in 1974, "*Violinista en el tejado*," the Spanish adaptation of *Fiddler on the Roof*. The lead actor was the legendary Manolo Fábregas, a megastar on the Mexican stage and the child of refugees of the Spanish Civil War. The melodies of the syrupy show still cling in my mind: "*Si yo fuera rico, yaddah, yaddaaaah daddah daddah daaaah....*" Bobe Bela obviously thought we would all get a strong dose of *Yiddishkeit* by listening to an imposing Gentile actor portray Sholem Aleichem's character in a way that recalled Anthony Quinn in *Zorba the Greek*. I wasn't as attuned then to the delicacies of translation as I would later become, but even then it struck me as fanciful that a completely Gentile cast would talk about *dybbuks* and *shlimzals*. Could a goy teach *Yiddishkeit*?

Bobe Bela often reminisced about public readings by the author of her favorite characters—Tevye himself, as well as Motl Peyse, Menachem Mendle, and Shayne Shayndl—delivered to cheering crowds in Warsaw and all through Galicia. In Nowe Brodno, these gatherings were a catalyst of sort for the Jewish community, illuminating moral values in a rapidly changing time. Sholem Aleichem, in a way, was a rabbi, a spiritual leader: in an age of secularism, when hordes of Jews abandoned tradition, he, more than any other Yiddish fabulist (Isaac Leib Peretz, Sholem Asch, Itzik Manger) articulated the dilemmas of ideology and faith with the kind of humor people found utterly irresistible. He died in 1919, around the time Bela turned ten years of age, and was buried in Brooklyn. The last years of his life had been marked by dislocation, as the First World War exiled him, first to Denmark, then to the United States. She was sorry not to have attended a reading, for as her *diario* silently acknowledges, she nourished the dream of one day becoming a writer herself: a prestigious one, capable of hypnotizing big audiences with enchanting tales of love and treason. Truth is, she had neither the imagination nor the verbal dexterity to accomplish this goal. I cannot recall a single occasion on which she told me a story. Nor can I remember her having a disposition toward the "plotlines of our convoluted world," as Charles Dickens once put it. Her dream, I think, was a result of a distinguished career as reader: Bela, after all, would devour full books in a matter of days, although she hardly reflected on them with others; it was, clearly, her way of escape, of inhabiting a reality far better than the one that fate had bestowed on her. And well, if she only had the talent and opportunity to shape that imaginary reality, to make it her own, she would be a far happier person.

For Bela in essence was sour and unforgiving. The strategy of abandoning Polish and Russian in order to begin a new life is, at first sight, a survivor's triumph. But it also denotes an uncompromising approach to the past: pain and unpleasantness ought to be ignored, eliminated from memory, nullified. This approach permeated her whole existence. My father would often complain of not having the chance to discuss anything remotely painful with his mother. When he was a boy, she had several miscarriages. Or most probably, they were abortions. He and Tío Isaac would be given money and sent out to the movies in a nearby theater. They knew, of course, their mother was undergoing some sort of operation—in my mind, I picture buckets of blood—but after returning home, not a word would be uttered about it. Silence reigned. Can I blame Bela for censoring her past? Isn't immigration, by definition, a search for a different self? History, in her view, was a cruel monster ready to obliterate everything in its path.

Of Bela's six siblings, three perished under the Nazis. Their individual stories are heartbreaking. I invoke them frequently, puzzled by the way human affairs are ruled by accidents. What else, if not randomness, explains her survival?...

Aboard the transatlantic boat, *Sparndam*, Bela found few other Yiddish speakers, but when she landed in Tampico, the verbal, social, and natural landscapes changed dramatically. Mexico: How did she end up in such an alien, exotic, "uncivilized" locale? How were these ports of entry chosen? What made Herschel, Bela's older brother, travel to Rio de Janeiro? And what made their sibling Gil choose the ancient land of the Aztecs? How on earth did they know about these unlikely places in the misnamed *Nuevo Mundo*? At that time *shtetl* dwellers and other Eastern European Jews were emigrating to North and South America, especially to New York and, to a lesser extent, to the Argentine Pampas, thanks in large degree to the encouragement of philanthropist Baron Maurice de Hirsh. But other nations of the Americas were also actively seeking immigrants at the turn of the century. In Buenos Aires since the mid-nineteenth century, a debate on the backwardness of the countryside had established that the only way to "civilize" the nation was by developing consmopolitan urban centers as much as possible. Immigrants were perceived as agents of progress and capitalism and, in spite of a strong feeling of anti-Semitism sponsored by the Catholic Church, the doors were opened to the Jews. They settled in small communes in central Argentina, such as Moisésville and Rajíl. By the second generation, though, most of them had moved to Buenos Aires and other major cities. Brazil, too, had opened the doors to Eastern European Jews. By 1915, Argentina had around 26,000, whereas Brazil had approximately 18,000. In the Southern Hemisphere, these were the largest magnets for Yiddish-speaking immigrants, followed, in descending order, by Mexico, Cuba, Colombia, and Peru.

It is next to impossible—*un acertijo*, a puzzle—to track down why Bela ended up in Mexico. Or so it seems to me. Was it because it was close to the United States, and a different destination at a time when Yiddish-language Eastern European dailies were wondering, in loud editorials, how many immigrants America could really digest? Or was it a comment by a forgotten friend, a chance encounter, or was it a small newspaper advertisement, perhaps, in the corner of the section devoted to opportunities abroad? What is unquestionable was that the U.S. immigration quota was restricting entry for Jewish immigrants, and an alternative needed to be found. This quota, in fact, made Bela and her descendants Mexican, did it not? At the heart of her rebirth across the Atlantic was a negation: *Thou shall not be American.*Whatever it was, I cannot avoid describing it as *ain tzufal*, *un accidente*: the enigma of arrival as an accident of fate. In her memoir, Bela's arrival in Tampico is described in astonishing detail. As the vessel approached the port, she saw from afar the many shanties, *las chozas y casuchas.* The town was rustic and primitive. Nothing like Warsaw in sophistication. She disembarked from the *Sparndam* and was exposed, for the first time, to a different type of *mujik*: the *mestizo.* Repeatedly, I have tried to visualize these first few minutes—the shock, the disquieting confusion. It appears, at least at first sight, as if Bela's past, tense and miserable, was replaced by a destiny equally tense and miserable.

She would often invoke the wise Ecclesiastes: *nada hay nuevo bajo el sol*, there is nothing new under the sun. Often she thought of returning to Nowe Brodno and her parents and friends. How could she not? The chaos, the anxiety came to her in the syncopated rhythms of Spanish, a language that at first overwhelmed Bela. It was too guttural. But it was hers: to survive, she would need to master it, to make it her own. One day, she would need to feel as if Polish was nothing but a loose thread in her past, a memory. One day she would think: What is *nostalgia* in Polish? And she would not be able to come up with the right word, for it had rescinded to depths she would no longer be capable of reaching.

In only a few weeks she realized Tampico was unworthy of her, and so she decided to move onto Ciudad de México, *the* commercial and cultural magnet for the entire region. The railway system had been built more than thirty years before but the revolution of 1910 impeded its updating, so it took her twenty-eight hours to reach the capital by train. She quickly found room and board and soon felt embraced by the vigor and enthusiasm of a thriving, Yiddish-speaking Jewish community. Bela quickly realized her potential: she would marry and multiply, prosper and reign.

The Jewish presence in the city was limited to a handful of neighborhoods. A tour today through the downtown Calle Justo Sierra, near the cathedral, where the Sephardic Temple Monte Sinaí still stands, not far from its Ashkenazic counterpart, Nidje Israel, on the adjacent Calle Revillajijedo, allows the visitor to stand on the sites where the Holy Office of the Inquisition publicly burned a handful of crypto-Jews who in 1492, when Cristóbal Colón found an alternative course across the Atlantic in his search for the Indies, sought to escape the intolerance of Spain. These Sephardic immigrants arrived some three centuries before the Ashkenazic newcomers. But is it right to describe them as *imigrantes judíos?* On the street, Bela and her peers were often described as *rusitos* and *polacos*. Their identity stood out. In contrast, their Iberian counterparts blended more easily: they looked Spanish. The long and fruitful cohabitation of Muslims and Christians in the peninsula had darkened their skin but and in many cases had also lessened, if not altogether erased, their piety. Their fate was tragic, though. Three hundred years later, what was left of their traditions and costumes? Could many still call themselves Sephardim? Were they familiar with Ladino—Judeo-Spanish, also known as *judesmo*—a dialect that recalls old Spanish and Portuguese but is written in Hebrew characters? How many *conversos* settled in *Nueva España*, New Spain, as Mexico was known during colonial times, it is impossible to know. In most historical accounts, the number oscillates between three and four thousand. A substantial minority among them were *marranos* (in Hebrew, *annusim*), that is *conversos* whose devotion to the Jewish faith, kept in secrecy, was still strong. . . .

The arrival of the Ashkenazim from Russia and Eastern Europe in the last couple of decades of the nineteenth century was seen as an altogether new beginning. The two waves couldn't have been more different. In the sixteenth century religious persecution and purity of blood—*la pureza de sangre*—brought them to this *refugio* far away from Europe, but while the *marranos* arrived in disguise and the *conversos* had already given up their Judaism, their successors, the Ashkenazim, also victimized as a result of their faith, never hid their religious affiliation. They didn't need to. In an era of freedom and openness after the 1910 revolution, peaceful, fruitful cohabitation of marginalized groups was the approach taken by the Mexican government. In fact, President Plutarco Elías Calles, in office during the Second World War, after an approach by the Alliance Israelite Universelle and other international organizations, publicly invited Jews to settle in Mexico. His rationale was simple: Jews were catalysts in emerging capitalist societies, and Mexico, in the first quarter of the twentieth century, after the bloody revolution of 1910, was hoping to leave behind its feudal past and become a stable and strong economy. But the groundwork for Mexico's Jewish community took place earlier, in distinct periods and from disparate geographies—between 1880 and 1930, when immigrants arrived from Eastern Europe, and in the sixties and later, when a wave arrived from the Mediterranean, from what once was the Ottoman Empire—Syria, Lebanon, the Balkans, northern Africa, and the Middle East. By the time Bela set foot in Tampico and, subsequently, in Ciudad de México, a thriving community was already awaiting her.

The first Ashkenazic synagogue and *mikveh* were built in 1890, and Bela discovered the much-needed refuge from her solitude, the hot Club Centro on Calle Tacuba No. 15, where community activities of all sorts—weddings, balls, parties, theater, poker, and so on—could be planned. Between 1910 and 1920 some three thousand arrived, and the number increased by three times during the next decade. Since most immigrants were socialists, communists, and Bundists, among their first projects was the building of a Yiddish-language day school (which they did in 1924), a Jewish Comintern (a.k.a. *Der Yiddisher Centraler Comitet*), and a number of philanthropic organizations that might allow Eastern European Jews to climb the social ladder. Their success was tremendous: in only a matter of decades, many *shtetl* dwellers opened a variety of businesses, from jewelry to leather, brewing, and clothing, and became quite wealthy. Culture flourished in every respect, and a couple of Yiddish dailies—*Der Shtime* and *Der Veg*, which I fondly remember reading—served as organs of cohesion....

In her *diario*, Bela describes in emotional detail how she met, on Calle Tacuba No. 15, her beloved Srulek Stavchansky, a *centavo*less Ukrainian immigrant from Khaschevate, a small milling town southwest of Lwow, and of course a Yiddish speaker as well. She remembers the first phone call she received from him and the sunny Sunday afternoon in Alameda Park, when Srulek asked to marry her and kissed her—in her Spanish, *se me declaró*. In my imagination, Diego Rivera's painting "Sunday at the Alameda Central" includes them both, next to each other, just behind José Guadalupe Posada. The description of the kiss is narrated briefly, as if Bela, at the time of writing, was conscious of the potential eroticism of the scene, dirty in her eyes, and thus decided to repress it as best she could. Exactly four months after her arrival, they became engaged. Their marriage took place in 1930, also at the Club Centro on Tacuba No. 15. Her brother Gil, still in Tampico, was unable to attend the wedding but helped the young couple financially. Their poverty, nonetheless, was abysmal. They shared a house with another family and struggled to make ends meet. Zeyde Srulek had arrived with only his most basic belongings, but he was a lucky fellow: he borrowed money to buy shoe laces and shaving blades, and when he sold these, he bought a lottery ticket. He became a winner and used the money to buy a hardware store on the busy corner of calles Academia and Corregidor. His luck did not last long, though. Hardship forced him to sell it, and he became an employee. They moved to Tampico, where Gil, still in good terms with them, helped him open a children's clothing store. The couple prospered and multiplied. Tío Isaac was born. No *mohel* was available in town, and one had to be brought in from Veracruz to perform the ritual circumcision. After a year the family returned to Ciudad de México, where Srulek opened an animal food store, Molino El Venado, the predecessor of the Forrajera Nacional, S.A., which my father would inherit on his father's death. They moved to a newly built home in the eastern section of Colonia Anzures and then to another, more modern one in the nearby Colonia Portales, both Jewish bastions. It wasn't until Bela's children were married that the Jewish community as a whole gravitated north to more affluent neighborhoods like Polanco, Las Lomas, and Tecamachalco, where politicians and the *nouveau riches* settled.

Bela kept her children close to her. She trained them to be first Jewish and then Mexican, and exhorted them to embrace Spanish as their mother tongue while keeping Yiddish as "the Jewish, i.e., intimate language." As was common, they met Gentiles only in the neighborhood, for kids were sent to Jewish schools and afterschool programs. This separation generated in them—and in their entire generation—an ambivalent sense of identity. What made them Mexican? And how did they distinguish themselves from other Jews? This duality was, and still is, much more accentuated among Mexican Jews than in their counterparts in the United States and, I dare say, even in Brazil and Argentina. Yiddish, among Ashkenazim, was the umbilical cord with Europe, one never fully cut. Spanish made them native citizens with full civil rights, but mixed marriages were few and contact with Catholics and other immigrants was minimal. In short, it was an insular mentality.

All this, needless to say, was destined to change as I was growing up. The ambiance persisted, the nostalgia for *shtetl* life, but the term *shmaltz* had become ubiquitous. It was clear the *shtetl* had not been a *paradise* after all. It was crowded with ruffians and criminals. Praying to G-d? Devoting one's whole life to tradition? Well, a portion of the population did, but the place was stern, miserable, cold. At first the Holocaust, the fatal blow to Yiddish as a living vehicle of communication—how many languages in history have perished so suddenly, in the span of five to six years?—elevated the *shtetl* to the stature of lost kingdom. But the State of Israel emphasized the idea that Jews were not ethereal beings but flesh-and-blood citizens, militaristic, down to earth. And as Mexico struggled to modernize by opening itself up to the world, it was clear that Jews could no longer be aloof, unconcerned, apathetic. They were part of the nation, just like everyone else, with misgivings about their *mexicanidad* perhaps—what Mexicans call *malinchismo*—but fully responsible for their actions. None of Bela's children finished a college education, but others in their generation did, my mother included. And while the Jewish day schools, by definition private, keep a close eye on early education, college was the place where exposure to the outside world was inevitable. The result is clear: divorces increased, interreligious marriages were more common (two of Bela's nine grandchildren—my brother Darián included—married Gentiles), and the degree of Jewish participation in Mexican public life increased considerably. Whereas not a single Jew of Bela's generation held a high-ranking government job, several did a generation after, and many more in my own.

The Colegio Israelita de México (aka Der Yiddisher Shule in Mexique), in Colonia del Valle, which I attended from kindergarten to high school—a total of fifteen years—embodied the views on history, education, and culture sustained by Bela's immigrant generation. From outside, nothing about the building signaled its Jewishness: it had no letter signs, no insignias. It must have had more than a thousand children enrolled. Its ideology was decidedly Bundist: secular in vision, embracing culture as the true religion. Rosh Hashana, Yom Kippur, Succoth, and other Jewish holidays were celebrated, but in a nonmilitant fashion. What made us Jews, we were told, was not G-d but the intellectual and spiritual legacy carried along for three millennia. The immolation of the Jewish people was not stressed—suffering wasn't a ticket to superiority.

Yiddish class, our link with the past, was obligatory. It met every day, sometimes even twice. At a time when, in the Jewish world at large, the number of speakers whose average age was around fifty made it a less used language than Serbo-Croatian, we were taught how to read, write, and speak it fluently. Students attended lectures in Yiddish and were assigned history volumes in Yiddish too. I remember submerging myself in long novels by Israel Joshua Singer, Sholem Ash, and Sholem Aleichem. And I read innumerable Hassidic tales and Holocaust poems as well. Understandably, a majority of the student population saw this as a nuisance: Why study Yiddish, a dying tongue? They attended in their exams almost mechanically and quickly forgot what they had learned the moment they exited the classroom. But for me Yiddish was a passion: I loved its cadence, its hallucinatory beat. At fifteen or sixteen, I fervently reread passages from *Die Mishpokhe Carnovsky* and *Kiddush ha-Shem* at home and memorized poems. I especially recall a melancholy march by Hirsh Glik that became the hymn of the United Partisan Organization in 1943 and has become a memorial for martyred Jews:

Never say that you are going your last way,
Though lead-filled skies above blot out the blue of the day
The hour for which we long will certainly appear,
The earth shall thunder 'neath our tread that we are here!

זאָג ניט קיין מאָל אַז דו גייסט דעם לעצטן וועג,
כאָטש הימלען בלייענע פאַרשטעלן בלויע טעג,
קומען וועט נאָך אונדזער אויסגעבענקטע שעה–
ס׳וועט אַ פויק טאָן אונדזער טראָט–מיר זיינען דאָ!

From lands of green palm trees to lands all white with snow,
We are coming with our pain and with our woe,
And where'er a spurt of our blood did drop,
our courage will again sprout from that spot.

פון גרינעם פּאַלמענלאַנד ביז ווייסן לאַנד פון שניי,
מיר קומען אָן מיט אונדזער פּיין, מיט אונדזער וויי,
און וווּ געפֿאַלן ס׳איז אַ שפּריץ פון אונדזער בלוט,
שפּראָצן וועט דאָרט אונדזער גבורה, אונדזער מוט.

For us the morning sun will radiate the day,
And the enemy and past will fade away,
But should the dawn delay or sunrise wait too long,
Then let all future generations sing this song.

ס׳וועט די מאָרגנזון באַגילדן אונדז דעם היינט,
און דער נעכטן וועט פֿאַרשווינדן מיטן פיינד,
נאָר אויב פֿאַרזאַמען וועט די זון אין דעם קאַיאָר–
ווי אַ פּאַראָל זאָל גיין דאָס ליד פון דור צו דור.

This song was written with our blood and not with lead,
This is no song of free birds flying overhead,
But a people amid crumbling walls did stand,
They stood and sang this song with rifes held in hand.

דאָס ליד געשריבן איז מיט בלוט און ניט מיט בליי,
ס׳איז ניט קיין לידל פֿון אַ פֿויגל אויף דער פֿריי, -
דאָס האָט אַ פֿאָלק צווישן פֿאַלנדיקע ווענט -
דאָס ליד געזונגען מיט נאַגאַנעס אין די הענט!

I also sought out Yiddish films of the twenties, thirties, and forties. If a copy was available, I showed it in a cinema club I organized every Wednesday at the school auditorium. I loved watching Maurice Schwarz and Molly Picon. So feverish was my enthusiasm that I began to dream myself into Sholem Aleichem's stories.

Yiddish, for me, was truly the mother tongue, whereas Spanish, the street language, the one I most often used, was the father tongue. The duality was not artificial: Jewishness (though not Judaism, at least not then) was in my heart and soul. There was nothing cerebral about it: it was, I was taught, the source of endurance, the fountain of life. Spanish was also taught at school, of course, and so was Hebrew, although the latter was introduced fairly late. Zionism didn't become the predominant dogma until I was about to leave school. This brought along the slow demise of Yiddish and the triumphant embrace of Hebrew as the language of the Jewish people of today and tomorrow. But Hebrew felt constructed to me, artificial. On Monday mornings students sang the Mexican and Israeli anthems and pledged allegiance to the two flags. And yet, although I learned it fast, I couldn't quite feel comfortable with its cadence: Zionist patriotism seemed foreign. It wasn't really mine. . . .

Bobe Bela's journey parades slowly in front of my eyes, as if I was watching the long video movie made when she turned eighty. Smiles, tears, feuds—the melodrama of everyday life: Tío Isaac first became a travel agent, then a jewler, and finally a respected painter; Tía Elenita, Bela's daughter, married a leather manufacturer; a grandson became a physicist in Israel's Weitzman Institute; a granddaughter had an early fight against cancer; two grandchildren divorced; one became a Kabbalist. The turning point for her was Zeyde Srulek's death in 1965. The passages about it in her *diario* are the ones where fear—*el miedo*—is felt most tangibly. But her family brought her back to life and kept her busy. Srulek's death, in fact, is the closest Bela comes to addressing pain—pain and tragedy. There is no reference in her narrative to her lost siblings, killed by the Nazis, or to the memory of her parents. Each time I reread it, I experience the same ambivalence toward her. While Bobe Bela is an enviably active person, she remains a Pole in Mexico, one who refused to speak a single word of Polish ever, ever again but only halfheartedly adopted the Spanish language—a hybrid, an in-between. The last pages of her narrative are dry, tense, and undescriptive. There is a feeling of uneasiness to them, as if the reader has been prepared for a monumental revelation in them, but the revelation, the denouement, is some-how evaded. Or is it? *"Mi último deseo,"* she writes, her last wish: to leave behind a financial legacy—real estate—in three equal shares, one for each of her children. No favoritism, she suggests. And, more importantly, she begs her heirs not to fight but to be in peace, with themselves and the others. She lists her properties: three lots and one apartment. "Be honest," she says. *Sean honestos. . . .*

Ilan, por favor, escríbele. . . . Quiere saber qué piensas de lo que te mandó. My father tells me again by phone to send a note to my grandmother. And what do I *really* think? *Sé honesto,* my father adds. What can I write to her? Any attempt at criticism would be misplaced, for Bela is my grandmother; objectivity is obviously not within reach. Besides, I have not been asked to critique her diary but to inherit it, to digest its memories and to make them mine, to be a link in the chain of generations, to pass along the torch. I should wholeheartedly applaud her effort. I should write to thank her, should I not?

I struggle to draft my first words of reply. Isn't there an element of comedy *and* tragedy in her? After all, she survived the xenophobia of her native Poland, emigrated to Mexico, and thrived; but she also helped build a community on the margins of history, one unconcerned with *lo mexicano,* things Mexican—an anachronistic enclave, disdainful of the rest of the world. Once again, I think of Yiddish, her portable ghetto. What am I going to say when I see her?

It strikes me, suddenly, that Bobe Bela's *diario* is a control mechanism specifically directed at me, that she is anxious to get my response, to hear—not from her Abremele, but from me directly—that I have read it conscientiously, processed it and have no qualms about its main story line. In the past year or so, I have been telling my family about my desire (or better, my "intention") to write a memoir about my own upbringing in Mexico and my emigration to America. How soon is it likely to happen, I do not say. The English-language readership that surrounds me is infatuated with autobiography as a literary form: to shape one's life into narrative has become a sport of sorts. My aim, although I dare not say it too loud, is to produce one in a few years where accuracy as such, objective truth, is questionable. For how much of what we are, what we know about ourselves is really *true*? We are merely a sum of viewpoints, and human memory is treacherous and inconsistent.

Life is experienced through language, isn't it? Gestures, voices, words. As I read and reread Bela's *diario*, time and again, the word *inauthentic* comes back to me. I try to imagine how Bela would have written to me in her *true* tongue: Yiddish. I conjure the warm, gentle sounds articulated in its sentences, the magic of recreating Nowe Brodno as it felt to her. By translating it for me, has she injected it with a dose of nostalgia? In seeking words absent from her childhood (simple forms: *se me declaró, un malparido, Puerco Judío*), has she amended her own past? I think of the challenge ahead of me. I'm aware that crafting my memoir in English will, in and of itself, be a form of treason. For shouldn't it be written in at least three if not four languages (Yiddish, Spanish, Hebrew, and English), the four tongues in which—and through which—I've experienced life? But no publisher in his right senses would endorse such an endeavor. It is perhaps an unrealistic dream, and ridiculous too. My aim, nonetheless, is to convey not my nationality but my *translationality*. To succeed, the original ought to read as if written already *in* translation—a translation without an original. I think of the segments in Englishized Yiddish in Henry Roth's *Call It Sleep* and those in "transliterated slang" in Richard Wright's *Native Son*; they appeal to me because they are bastardized forms of language, polluted, uncompromised. And an illegitimate language is exactly what I seek.

Bela, of course, has no clue about my thoughts. She simply knows I'm ready—or getting ready—to write a memoir: to reflect on the family's past and evaluate its present; to single out, as all autobiographers do, members of the family not only through a hierarchy of anecdotes but by means of what Martin Buber once called "comparative morality," the standing each member has *vis-à-vis* the rest of the group. And she knows—how can she not?—that she, Bela, is likely to share center stage with my father, *her* Abremele, as well as with my brother Darián, the Stavchansky trio whose influence on my *Weltanshauung* is most decisive. And so, before memory fails her, before it is too late, she makes up her mind: modestly yet decisively, she will write a memoir herself. Not a full-scale, multivolume one, like the one shaped by Sholem Aleichem, *In the Country Fair*, or the one by Israel Joshua Singer, *Iron and Steel*. No, Bela's will be a plain, simple narrative whose main objective is to set the record straight.

Straight? As I try to compose my reply to her *diario*, I realize she has produced it mainly for me—and through me, for the rest of the world—to get "the correct impression" of who she is. In all honesty, she is not the only one that has expressed concern. There is nothing to denounce in my life, no one to ridicule . . . except myself, of course. Still, the moment news went out that I was contemplating an autobiography, family members on both sides came to me with requests, people obsessed with their place in family history. But only Bobe Bela has gone out of her way to put down her version of the events and to send it to me through my father. She is concerned about the record. Or is she? Am I imagining secret motifs behind the innocent memories of a mature woman? Am I falsifying her message? Who cares if the story in her *diario* is a pack of lies, where Tío David, to name just one relative on whom Bela directed her merciless fist, is not even mentioned? Whose autobiography isn't far-fetched? Will I, when I'm finally courageous enough to speak my turn, be ready to face my own foibles, my own hypocrisies? Isn't the genre of autobiography about redefinition and redemption?

And so, I send her a quick note—in Spanish, how else?—via e-mail, to my father's address. I've done it before many times. Mexico's postal service is a disaster. Besides, Bela loves to be read messages by phone. Every Sunday, when she is brought to my parents' home in Colonia Cuicuilco, Insurgentes Sur, she asks to be connected to the Internet and without further delay writes to me. My mother usually types while she dictates. I've asked her numerous questions about Bialolenska Street in Nowe Brodno, about her arrival in Tampico on the *Sparndam*, about the Club Centro in Calle Tacuba No. 15. In fact, as she responds to me and my imagination is ignited, I feel the excruciating process of drafting my own memoir has begun.

"It's here, *suegra*," my mother tells her. "Ilan sent you a message."

"Really?" she smiles. Minutes later she sits in front of the screen. "The Internet. . . . We could not have imagined it in our *shtetl*."

"You were never in a *shtetl*, Mamá," my father replies.

Soon after, my mother reads out loud.

Querida Bobe:
Mil gracias por tu hermoso diario. I admire you. Your memories are mine already.

Te amo, I.S.

PERMISSIONS

Acknowledgment is made by the editor and publisher for permission to reprint the following material:

Marjorie Agosín: fragment of *Dear Anne Frank*. Translated by Richard Schaaf, Cola Franze, and Mónica Bruno. From *Dear Anne Frank*, by Marjorie Agosín. Hanover and London: Brandeis University Press, 1998. Used by permission of the author.

Alfonso X the Wise: fragment of *Las siete partidas*. Translated by Dwayne E. Carpenter. From *Alfonso X and the Jews: An Edition of and Commentary on* Siete partidas 7.24 *"De los judíos."* Berkeley: University of California Press, 1986. Used by permission of the author.

Homero Aridjis: "Sepharad, 1492." Translated by George McWhirter and Homero Aridjis. From *Eyes to See Otherwise/Ojos de otro mirar: Selected Poems*, by Homero Aridjis, edited by Betty Ferber and George McWhirter, translated by Lawrence Ferlinghetti, et al. New York: New Directions Publisher, 2002. Published by permission of the author.

Ruth Behar: "The Hebrew Cemetery of Guanabacoa." Copyright 1994 by Ruth Behar. First published in *Tikkun*. Used by permission of the author.

Gonzalo de Berceo: "The Jews of Toledo." Translated by David M. Gitlitz. From *Poetas castellanos anteriores al siglo XV*, edited by Tomás Antonio Sánchez. Madrid: M. Rivadeneyra, 1864. Used by permission of the translator.

Pinkhes Berniker: "Jesús." Translated by Alan Astro. First published in *Hopscotch: A Cultural Review*. Durham, NC: Duke University Press, 2000. Used by permission of the translator.

Jorge Luis Borges: "The Secret Miracle." Translated by Harriet de Onís. From *Labyrinths: Selected Stories and Other Writings*, by Jorge Luis Borges. Copyright 1962, 1964 by New Directions Publishing Corp. Reprinted by permission of New Directions Publishing Corp.

Luis de Carvajal the Younger: "The Autobiographical Essay of Luis de Carvajal the Younger." Translated by Martin Cohen. First published in *The Jewish Experience in Latin America*. Vol. I. Used by permission of Martin A. Cohen and the American Jewish Historical Saociety.

Américo Castro: fragment of *The Structure of Spanish History*. Translated by Edmund L. King. Princeton, NJ: Princeton University Press, 1954. Used by permission of the Estate of Anérico Castro.

Julio Cortázar: "Press Clippings." Translated by Gregory Rabassa. From *We Loved Glenda So Much and Other Stories*, by Julio Cortázar. Copyright 1983 by Alfred A. Knopf, a division of Random House, Inc. Used by permission of by Alfred A. Knopf, a division of Random House, Inc.

Rubén Darío: "Israel." Translated by Melanie Nicholson. From *Obras Poéticas Completas*, by Rubén Darío. Madrid: M. Aguilar, 1941. Translation copyright 2002 by Melanie Nicholson. Published by permission of the translator.

Ariel Dorfman: fragment of *Heading South, Looking North: A Bilingual Journey*. New York: Farrar, Straus, and Giroux, 1998. Copyright 1998 by Ariel Dorfman. Used by permission of the author.

Samuel Eichelbaum: "The Good Harvest." Translated by Rita Gardiol. From *The Silver Candelabra and Other Stories: A Century of Jewish Argentine Literature*, edited and translated by Rita Gardiol. Pittsburgh, PA: Latin American Literary Review Press, 1997. Used by permission of the publisher.

Moisés ben Ezra: "The Two Sons." Translated by T. Carmi. From *The Penguin Book of Hebrew Verse*, edited and translated by T. Carmi. Harmondsworth, UK: Penguin Books, 1981, 1985. Translation copyright 1981 by T. Carmi. Used by permission of the publisher.

Alicia Freilich: "Recollections of Criolla Zionist." Translated by Joan E. Friedman. From *King David's Harp: Autobiographical Essays by Jewish Latin American Authors*, edited by Stephen A. Sadow. Albuquerque: University of New Mexico Press, 1999. Used by permission of the publisher.

Solomon ben Gabirol: "Night Storm." Translated by T. Carmi. From *The Penguin Book of Hebrew Verse*, edited and translated by T. Carmi. Harmondsworth, UK: Penguin Books, 1981, 1985. Translation copyright 1981 by T. Carmi. Used by permission of the publisher.

Federico García Lorca: "The Jewish Cemetery." Translated by Steven F. White. From *Poet in New York*, by Federico García Lorca, translated by Greg Simon and Steven F. White, edited and with an introduction and notes by Christopher Maurer. New York: Ferrar, Straus and Giroux, 1988. Translation copyright 1988 by the Estate of Federico García Lorca, and Greg Simon and Steven F. White. Used by permission of Farrar, Straus, and Giroux, LLC.

Alberto Gerchunoff: "Autobiographical Essay." Translated by Stephen A. Sadow. From *King David's Harp: Autobiographical Essays by Jewish Latin American Authors*, edited by Stephen A. Sadow. Albuquerque: University of New Mexico Press, 1999. Used by permission of the publisher.

Isaac Goldemberg: "The Jew's Imprecise Sonnet." Translated by Stephen A. Sadow and Jim Kates. From *Self-Portraits and Masks: Thirty Jewish Poems and a Christian Song*, by Isaac Goldemberg. New York and Krakow: Cross-Cultural Communications, 2002. Used by permission of the author.

Yehuda Halevi: "My Heart Is in the East." Translated by T. Carmi. From *The Penguin Book of Hebrew Verse*, edited and translated by T. Carmi. Harmondsworth, UK: Penguin Books, 1981, 1985. Translation copyright 1981 by T. Carmi. Used by permission of the publisher.

Samuel Hanaguid: "Short Prayer in Time of Battle." Translated by T. Carmi. From *The Penguin Book of Hebrew Verse*, edited and translated by T. Carmi. Harmondsworth, UK: Penguin Books, 1981, 1985. Translation copyright 1981 by T. Carmi. Used by permission of the publisher.

Salomón Isacovici: fragment of *Man of Ashes* by Salomón Isacovici and Juan Manuel Rodríguez. Translated by Dick Gerdes. Lincoln: University of Nebraska Press, 1999. Used by permission of the heirs of Salomón Isacovici.

Kings Ferdinand and Isabella: "Edict of 1492." From *The Jews of Spain: A History of the Sephardic Experience*, by Jane S. Gerber. New York: The Free Press, 1992. Taken from Luis Suárez Fernández: *Documentos Acerca de la Expulsión de los Judíos*, Consejo Superior de Investigaciones Científicas, Patronato Menéndez Pelayo, Valladolid, 1964; quoted by David Raphael in *The Expulsion 1492 Chronicles*. N. Hollywood, CA: Carmi House Press, 1992. Used by permission of the Free Press.

Fray Luis de León: "Serene Night." Translated by Sir John Bowring. From *Poesía completa*, by Fray Luis de León, edited by José Manuel Blecua. Madrid: Gredos, 1990. Used by permission of the publisher.

Moisés de León: fragment from *The Zohar*. Texts edited and introduced by Nahum N. Glatzer. From *The Judaic Traditon*, by Nahum N. Glatzer. Boston: Beacon Press, 1969. Used by permission of the publisher.

Miguel Leví de Barrios: "One Well-Founded Faith." Translated by Timothy Oelman. From *Marrano Poets of the Seventeenth Century: An Anthology of the Poetry of João Pinto Delgado, Antonio Enríquez Gómez, and Miguel Leví de Barrios*, edited and translated by Timothy Oelman. Rutherford, NJ, and London: Fairleigh Dickinson University Press, 1982. Used by permission of the publisher.

Alcina Lubitch Domecq: "Résumé Raisonné." Translated by Ilan Stavans. From *King David's Harp: Autobiographical Essays by Jewish Latin American Authors*, edited by Stephen A. Sadow. Albuquerque: University of New Mexico Press, 1999. Translation copyright 1999 by Ilan Stavans. Used by permission of the publisher.

Maimonides: fragment of "Epistle to the Jews of Morocco." From *The Essential Maimonides*. Translated by Avraham Yaakov Finkel. Northvale, NJ, and London: Jason Aronson, Inc. 1996. Reprinted by permission of the publisher.

———: Fragment of *Guide of the Perplexed*, Chapter XV. Translated by M. Friedlander. New Yorker: Dover, 1936. 2nd edition, revised throughout. Used by permission of Rosa J. López, on behalf of the publisher.

Marshall T. Meyer: "Thoughts on Latin America." Published in *Proceedings of the Rabbinical Assembly: 1985*. Used by permission of the Seminario Rabínico Latinoamericano, the Rabbinical Assembly, and the University of Judaism.

Angelina Muníz-Huberman: fragment of *El mercader de Tudela*. Translated by Claudia Lucotti. Mexico: Fondo de Cultura Económica, 1998. Used by permission of the author.

Nahmanides: fragment of *The Disputation of Barcelona*. Texts edited and introduced by Nahum N. Glatzer. From *The Judiac Traditon*, by Nahum N. Glatzer. Boston: Beacon Press, 1969. Used by permission of the publisher.

Rosa Nissán: fragment of *Like a Bride*. Translated by Dick Gerdes. From *Like a Bride* and *Like a Mother*, by Rosa Nissán. Albuquerque: University of New Mexico Press, 2002. Used by permission of the publisher.

Francisco de Quevedo y Villegas: "To a Nose." Translated by David M. Gitlitz. From *Obra poética*, by Francisco de Quevedo y Villegas, edited by José Manuel Blecua. Madrid: Editorial Castalia, 1969–1981. Used by permission of the translator.

Ilan Stavans: fragment of "The Rise and Fall of Yiddish." From *On Borrowed Words: A Memoir of Language*. New York: Viking, 2001. Used by permission of the publisher.

Yehuda ben Tibbon: "On Books and on Writing." Texts edited and introduced by Nahum N. Glatzer. From *The Judaic Traditon*, by Nahum N. Glatzer. Boston: Beacon Press, 1969. Used by permission of the publisher.

Jacobo Timerman: fragment of *Prisoner without a Name, Cell without a Number*. Translated by Toby Talbot, introduction by Ilan Stavans. Madison: University of Wisconsin Press, 2002. Used by permission of the University of Wisconsin Press.

Benjamin de Tudela: "Jerusalem." Texts edited and introduced by Nahum N. Glatzer. From *The Judaic Traditon*, by Nahum N. Glatzer. Boston: Beacon Press, 1969. Used by permission of the publisher.

Mario Vargas Llosa: fragment of *The Storyteller*, by Mario Vargas Llosa. Translated by Helen Lane. Translation copyright 1989 by Farrar, Straus, and Giroux. Reprinted by permission of Farrar, Straus, and Giroux, LLC.

Miguel de Unamuno: "*Canción del sefardita*." Translated by Ilan Stavans. From *Obras Completas*, by Miguel de Unamuno, edited and with a prologue by Ricardo Senabre. Madrid: Turner, 1995. Translation copyright 2002 by Ilan Stavans. Used by permission of the translator.

Tino Villanueva: "At the U.S. Holocaust Museum, Washington D.C." First published in *Partisan Review*. Copyright 1997 by Tino Villanueva. Reprinted by permission of the author.

Portions of the introduction appeared in *The Forward*.

Despite every effort to trace and contact copyright holders of translations prior to publication, this has not been possible in every case. If notified, the publisher will be pleased to rectify any errors or omissions at the earliest opportunity.

INDEX BY THEME

Anti-Semitism
Berceo, Gonzalo de: "The Jews of Toledo"
Gerchunoff, Alberto: "A Jewish Gaucho"
Kings Ferdinand and Isabella: *Edict of 1492*
Nahmanides: Fragment of *Disputation of Barcelona*
Quevedo y Villegas, Francisco de: "To a Nose"

Faith and Religion
Alfonso X the Wise: "Concerning the Jews: *Las siete partidas*"
Barrios, Miguel Leví de: "One Well-Founded Faith"
Carvajal the Younger, Luis de: *Autobiographical Essay*
Ezra, Moisés ben: "The Two Sons"
Kings Ferdinand and Isabella: *Edict of 1492*
León, Fray Luis de: "Serene Night"
Maimonides: Fragment of *Epistle to the Jews of Morocco*
Nahmanides: Fragment of *Disputation of Barcelona*

Crypto-Jews and the Inquisition
Aridjis, Homero: 'Sepharad, 1492"
Barrios, Miguel Leví de: "One Well-Founded Faith"
Carvajal the Younger, Luis de: *Autobiographical Essay*
León, Fray Luis de: "Serene Night"

Transethnic Relations
Berniker, Pinkhes: "Jesús"
Castro, Américo: "The Spanish Jews"
Dorfman, Ariel: Fragment of *Heading South, Looking North*
Gerchunoff, Alberto: "A Jewish Gaucho"
Isacovici, Salomón: Fragment of *Man of Ashes*
Lubitch Domecq, Alcina: "Résumé Raisonné"
Muníz-Huberman, Angelina: Fragment of *The Merchant of Tudela*
Nissán, Rosa: Fragment of *Like a Bride*
Vargas Llosa, Mario: Fragment of *The Storyteller*

The Search for Roots